JAMES FITZJAMES STEPHEN

JAMES FITZJAMES STEPHEN

PORTRAIT OF A
VICTORIAN RATIONALIST

K. J. M. SMITH

Senior Lecturer in Law, Brunel University

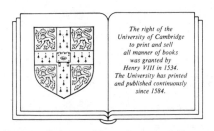

The right of the
University of Cambridge
to print and sell
all manner of books
was granted by
Henry VIII in 1534.
The University has printed
and published continuously
since 1584.

CAMBRIDGE UNIVERSITY PRESS
Cambridge
New York New Rochelle Melbourne Sydney

Published by the Press Syndicate of the University of Cambridge
The Pitt Building, Trumpington Street, Cambridge CB2 1RP
32 East 57th Street, New York, NY 10022, USA
10 Stamford Road, Oakleigh, Melbourne 3166, Australia

First published 1988

Printed in Great Britain by Redwood Burn Limited, Trowbridge, Wiltshire.

British Library cataloguing in publication data
Smith, K.J.M.
James Fitzjames Stephen: portrait of a
Victorian rationalist.
1. England. Law. Stephen. Sir James
Fitzjames
I. Title
344.2'0092'4

Library of Congress cataloguing in publication data
Smith, K.J.M.
James Fitzjames Stephen: portrait of a Victorian rationalist/
K.J.M. Smith.
    p.   cm.
Bibliography.
Includes index.
                    ISBN 0 521 34029 2
1. Stephen, James Fitzjames, Sir, 1829–1894. 2. Judges – Great
Britain – Biography. 3. Criminal law – Great Britain. I. Title.
KD631.S7S57   1988
347.41'014'0924 – dc19
[344.107140924]

                    ISBN 0 521 34029 2

To A.T.S. and A.A.S.

CONTENTS

viii CONTENTS

PREFACE

James Fitzjames Stephen was an outstanding, almost oversize, example of a variety of individual that Victorian England is sometimes credited with having made a symbol of the age: one who pursued an essentially conventional career alongside a broad vigorous intellectual absorption in the great social and political events England was then experiencing. The skeleton of Stephen's adult life was the law: mildly successful practice at the Bar between 1855 and 1869; service as Legal Member of the Viceroy's council in India from 1869 to 1872; and on returning to England, seven years of ultimately fruitless endeavour to codify the bulk of English criminal law, followed by twelve years on the High Court Bench from 1879 until retirement in 1891. They were years of legal practice complemented by the production of a collection of significant law texts, most importantly the *General View of the Criminal Law* (1863) and the *History of the Criminal Law* (1883), either of which would have been sufficient to establish Stephen as a criminal jurist of some distinction.

However, coexisting with Stephen the legal practitioner and theorist was Stephen the controversialist and polemicist, born of an avid, irrepressible sense of general inquiry coupled with an 'hereditary strain of Puritan energy . . . glowing alike through faults and virtues' (*Middlemarch*, ch. 1). It was a formidable energy turned in several directions largely through the medium of 'higher journalism'. In that expansive mid-nineteenth-century period of journals – when (particularly) the *Edinburgh Review* and *Quarterly Review* were joined by *Fraser's Magazine*, the *Saturday Review*, the *Fortnightly Review*, the *Contemporary Review* et al. – Stephen, with a host of other young, confident and ambitious intellectuals, was able to participate in opinion-forming debates and exchanges ranging over the large, sometimes momentous, questions of the day. Throughout his lifetime, political, social, artistic and religious issues, both singular and in combination, kept Stephen's intelligence and pen heavily, often angrily, engaged.

Although, beyond criminal jurisprudence, he was hardly a constructive theorist or creative thinker of the first rank when put alongside roughly contemporary figures such as John Stuart Mill, Matthew Arnold or Thomas Carlyle, Stephen's powerfully acute critical capacities – most convincingly demonstrated in *Liberty, Equality, Fraternity* (1873) – entitle him to a reputation as a notable influence and contributor to the intellectual climate of mid- and late Victorian England. Running across this wide span of Stephen's writings is a strong utilitarian attachment to formulating opinions, attitudes and actions on empirically established grounds; a core belief in the central guiding role of rigorous rationality and hostility to the subversively dangerous nature of intuitional thinking; a mode of thought unfairly regarded by some as a form of intellectual cynicism: always looking to the weight of evidence rather than its worth.

It is incumbent on any biographer to make out some sort of justification for offering a new study of a subject on whom two previous works have been published: Leslie Stephen's invaluable *Life of Sir James Fitzjames Stephen* (1895) and J.A. Colaiaco's *James Fitzjames Stephen and the Crisis of Victorian Thought* (1983). The earlier biography enjoys the inestimable advantages of the high skills of one of the last century's finest biographers, combined with insights into his brother's character normally only granted to intimates. Yet, close personal and temporal proximity to one's subject and his milieu also carries the 'wood for the trees' handicap – the inability to stand back and take in a wider historical sweep of events and ideas and the subject's place within them; to achieve something a little closer to that prized detached objectivity which the swarming minutiae of personal recollections inevitably render more difficult. Additionally, in his attempt to provide a complete record of his brother's life many areas receive less detailed and theoretical attention than might be considered justified, if not then, at least now. This is especially true of the treatment of legal issues which Leslie Stephen openly admits to in the biography's preface. On top of this, at many points, Leslie was restricted and reserved, by then current conventions or predilections, in his selection and release of the details of much source material. Too often the cutting edges of Fitzjames' privately expressed opinions are rounded off, sometimes losing their effect or producing misleading emphases. This literary technique, of nar-

ration with little direct quotation, also eliminated much of the zest
and tang of Fitzjames' character so often embodied in his writing; a
deficiency in Leslie's book noted by Charles Kegan Paul[1] and Julia
Wedgwood[2] in their contemporary reviews of the work.

By making use of a wider range of primary and secondary source
materials to supply a firm contextual setting, this new assessment of
Fitzjames Stephen attempts to provide a fuller and intellectually
more revealing account of the subject than has hitherto been offered.
The study is primarily thematic in its approach to examining the
principal areas of Stephen's intellectual output and involvement;
although, where possible, the natural chronology of events has been
followed to assist in promoting a sense of progressive development
of both intellect and opinions as they interact with the major social
and political concerns and figures of the times. Adopting this
scheme, chapter 1 briefly considers the early formative influences,
particularly of Sir James Stephen, and the lessons learnt by Fitzjames
at Eton and Cambridge. Chapter 2 examines the foundations of
Stephen's journalistic and polemical career, concentrating on
literary reviewing for the *Saturday Review* and his role in establishing
a social realist critique of imaginative literature. Stephen's work as
England's foremost nineteenth-century criminal jurist is analysed
over chapters 3 and 4, with the Indian element reserved for chapter
6, where the broader function of law in the growth of imperialistic
thinking and practice is considered. The nature and genesis of
Stephen's political and social philosophy – culminating in his fierce
attack on Mill in *Liberty, Equality, Fraternity* – form the substance of
chapters 5 and 7. Religious speculation (chapter 8) is the final area of
thought which greatly attracted and long exercised Stephen's
rationalist mind: a subject presenting the remorseless and earnest
pursuer of truth much the same problems of proof, evidence and
probability encountered by the criminal theorist; and, as demonstrated
in *Liberty, Equality, Fraternity*, constituting the third in a trio of
elements (with law and coercion) seen as the governing forces of a
modern state. The closing chapter, amounting to the epilogue of
Stephen's professional life, scrutinises the main features of his career
as a High Court judge.

Throughout, so far as possible, the text has been kept reasonably
free of technical detail with the intention of maintaining its
accessibility to anyone with a general knowledge of nineteenth-
century intellectual history. Desirable and important specialist discussion and information are set out in supporting notes.

In the course of writing this book I have become considerably in-debted to many individuals for help and advice so generously given: more particularly for the assistance of Mr S.J.D. Green, Dr Patrick Polden, Dr Barbara Goodwin, Dr David Sugarman, Mrs Diana Dilke, Dr Anne Polden, Professor W.C. Cornish, Professor John Burnett, Mr Mark Burnett, Ms D. Loudon, Mrs Sheila Sokolov-Grant, and Lord Halsbury. And for performing great feats in deciphering handwriting of legendary awfulness, my thanks are due to Mrs Donna Baston and Mrs Margaret Cook. I have also benefited extensively from the editorial skills of Mr Richard Fisher and Ms Pauline Marsh at Cambridge University Press.

I

EARLY IMPRESSIONS
SIR JAMES, ETON AND CAMBRIDGE

James Fitzjames Stephen was born on 3 March 1829[1] into the upper-middle classes of an England of which George IV was king, the Duke of Wellington Prime Minister with the Great Reform Act and the death of Jeremy Bentham still three years distant. The marriage, in 1818, of his father, James Stephen, to his mother, Jane Venn, represented a union of the Stephens, a recently established line of lawyers originating in Scotland, with the Venns, a clerical and scholastic dynasty stretching back to Tudor times. Both families brought to the partnership a pronounced evangelical work ethic coupled with a high regard for solid intellectual accomplishment. It was a marriage which also constituted a further connecting strand in a genealogical web of distinguished families that included (or would soon include) the Wilberforces, Macaulays, Diceys, Elliotts, Trevelyans, Stracheys, Thackerays and Arnolds.[2]

Unsurprisingly, the Stephen children,[3] particularly Fitzjames and his younger brother Leslie, were much influenced by Sir[4] James Stephen's complex character and temperament. Though he was principally known for his career in government service, it was not until 1825, after initially practising at the Chancery Bar, that Sir James Stephen took up a full-time post in the Colonial Office,[5] rising to Under Secretary in 1836. Even before reaching this level of seniority Sir James, through a combination of ability, appetite for work and unwillingness to delegate, 'virtually ruled the Colonial Empire'.[6] Such was Stephen's grip on his office and capacity to influence and shape policy that he earned the widely known unofficial titles of 'Mr. Over-Secretary' or 'Mr. Mother-Country' Stephen.[7] Absorption in his work and a punishing degree of conscientiousness on more than one occasion outstripped Stephen's mental endurance, resulting in a series of breakdowns during his professional life. It was a constant danger noted by Henry Taylor, a longstanding friend and colleague: when Stephen's brains 'run away with him he is likely to be thrown, as he has been three or four times with no little danger to life'.[8] Compounding the stressful demands of office was the handicap of a highly sensitive nature; of living life 'without a skin' and with a 'shyness that you could [not] imagine in anyone whose soul had not been pre-existent in a wild duck'.[9]

Sir James' temperament induced in the Stephen domestic 'atmosphere the faint smell of asceticism', with its members made to 'understand that somehow we were just a little different from other people'.[10] Plays, balls, or similar recreational frivolities were neither approved nor disapproved of; a theatre was as 'remote from us as an elephant'. However, any apparent austerity was not sensed by the inhabitants of the household, for the regime became the 'law of our natures, not a law imposed by external sanctions'.[11] But whatever the Stephen children may have missed in the way of lightweight entertainments or distractions, the extensive range of Sir James' acquaintances and friends ensured a steady exposure to the conversation and company of many of the great intellectual figures of the period, such as Nassau Senior,[12] John Austin, James Spedding, Aubrey de Vere, and Thomas Macaulay, with those on a less intimate footing including Carlyle[13] and J.S. Mill. Indeed at one time Sir James himself was tempted by the pull of a literary life, a fancy soon abandoned after modestly concluding that he was little more than a 'flash, splash, dash, blazing reviewer'.[14] Yet both Leslie and Fitzjames later offered the most ardent testimony as to their father's 'richness of mind and union of wisdom, good sense, keenness, ingenuity', of a degree that placed him on a level with Macaulay, Carlyle and Austin.[15]

Even if others might blink at such claims, there is no doubting the strength of admiration won by Sir James from his sons. Fitzjames, especially, developed a full and close relationship with his father, becoming an 'intimate friend and constant associate',[16] though the temperament of each party inhibited anything resembling an open demonstration of emotions. Consequently, in 1851, at the end of the period of convalescence in Paris spent with his wife and Fitzjames, Sir James felt hard pressed to compose an appropriate letter of thanks for his son's companionship:

I wish I knew how to write to [Fitzjames] to tell him how deep is the impression which his affectionate carefulness about me and which his pleasant talk with me . . . have left upon my mind. But . . . he is not much disposed to listen to the laudatory or the sentimental at any time.[17]

But the durability of this powerful filial affection and regard was evidenced many times over, on one occasion more than twenty years after Sir James' death by Fitzjames' reaction to the publication of Thomas Mozley's *Reminiscences*, which included 'depreciatory remarks' about Sir James' professional competence. To maintain his father's good name, Fitzjames solicited a 'line of vindication' from Gladstone (who had been a Colonial Office minister at the relevant time) which he followed up by a letter to *The Times* justifiably ridiculing the offending claims.[18]

Of his own early character, Fitzjames later admitted, 'I had a deal of the prig in me by nature, or rather liked to think myself as a highly intellectual little saint . . . on my way to make the best of both [spiritual and temporal] worlds.'[19] Yet even if the growing child's independent character and somewhat premature consciousness of his own dignity had deservedly earned him the household nicknames of 'Gruffian' and 'Little Preacher', to his parents 'young Fitzy' had always been a cause for much 'gratitude' and 'happiness'.[20] The 'Gruffian's' formal schooling began at the age of seven at the Reverend Guest's establishment in Brighton, chosen largely on the recommendation of its sound evangelical credentials by a relative from the Venn side of the family.[21] Overall, the six years spent at Brighton passed without major incident and left no painful memories.

The succeeding period at Eton (April 1842 to September 1845) provided experiences of a quite different nature. To enable Sir James to live with his family and commute to Whitehall each day, the whole Stephen family moved to Windsor in 1842. However, within this arrangement lay at least part of the cause of Fitzjames' considerable misery with life at Eton, for being an 'up-town boy' rather than a boarder carried a particular stigma. And despite Sir James being assured by the Provost of the absence of prejudice against non-boarders, the reality was patently otherwise.[22] Bullying at Eton was rife, but came in especially generous portions for the despised 'up-town boys'. Unlike Leslie, who chose where possible to evade bullying, Fitzjames met it with 'open defiance' – a 'difference between the willow and the oak'.[23] Although the occasions of conflict were virtually doubled in the elder brother's case through the strong protective sense felt for the younger's welfare, the most tangible victims of frequent conflict were Fitzjames' hats, the bills for which were reasonably believed to have 'amounted to a stiff figure'.[24]

Yet Stephen's 'up-town' status was a distinctly lesser source of friction than his aloof, even censorious, temperament. He sniffed at sport as 'childish', openly regarding school life in general as 'silly and frivolous'. It was an unconcealed disdain that bred resentment amongst others, and a state of affairs which Stephen later likened to a 'sensible grown-up woman among a crowd of rough boys'.[25] However, Stephen never totally lacked contemporaries, such as Charles Kegan Paul, well able to fathom the handsomer and truer side of his nature: 'no-one who ever penetrated [his] somewhat rugged exterior and real shyness, failed to like the man he found within'.[26] But at least the 'kicks, cuffs and hat smashing' served as an early lesson about the nature of life; 'that to be weak is to be wretched' and that a man could 'count on nothing in this world except what lies between his hat and his boots'.[27] On the academic side, Stephen put the inadequacies of Eton down to the limited ambition of parents for their children and the general low priority of scholastic achievement: parents wanted little more than for their children to become gentlemen, form friendships and enjoy themselves, 'and most of them had their wish'.[28] But despite rank unhappiness during the bulk of his Eton schooldays and frequent dissatisfaction with what he felt to be an indifferent academic ethos, Stephen performed well, though 'not brilliantly'.

Eventual parental discovery of Stephen's wretchedness at Eton led to the completion of his pre-university education at King's College, London. Such had been his dislike of Eton that he celebrated his departure (in September 1845) by ceremoniously tearing off his white tie and stamping on it, an act followed by a final visit to the College's ante-chapel to deliver a farewell scowl at the occupants.[29]

At King's,[30] amongst the more purposeful offspring of the professional and business middle classes, life was again 'most happy'. Both the independence of study and like-minded companionship conduced to Stephen achieving a good measure of academic success prior to going up to Trinity College, Cambridge in October 1847 to read Classics.

Stephen's Cambridge career was a blend of achievement and failure: success in a worldly sense by making a very definite mark with some of the intellectually most original of his peers who made up the 'Apostles'; failure in not achieving formal recognition of academic prowess through impressive examination performance. It was something Stephen himself in part accounted for by confessing to being one of the 'most unteachable of human beings', quite unable to digest anything second-hand, always needing to learn 'whatever I want to learn in a way of my own'.[31] This unhelpful combination of an acute, if inflexible, intellect, with wide interests and broad learning had tutors 'marvelling at and deploring the hopelessness of [their] tasks'. Certainly, it is quite impossible to imagine that Fitzjames ever experienced Leslie's conscious deference and feelings of inadequacy when in the company of a 'senior wrangler' – of being 'formed of inferior clay'.[32] And when faced with more single-minded and necessarily systematic contemporaries, it was not altogether surprising that Fitzjames twice failed to win a Trinity scholarship.[33]

However lacklustre his scholastic performance may have been, Stephen's character and abilities shone forth very brightly in the less academically refined rough and tumble of debate and dialectic. In the University Union, where more often than not his debating stance in matters of church and state was one of a moderate conservative, he became the 'terror' of the 'shallow and wordy', a 'merciless exposer of platitudes and shams': performances which won him the appellation 'British Lion'.[34] His entrée to the exclusive Apostles Society came through a chance meeting with Henry Maine at Filey in 1845 whilst both were staying with F.W. Gibbs, a long-established friend of the Stephen family then preparing for a Trinity fellowship. The 25-year old Maine, who had shown spectacular scholarship at Cambridge, was appointed to the Regius Chair of Civil Law two years later. Clearly Maine's early impressions of Stephen (doubtless confirmed by fellow Apostle Gibbs) between their Filey encounter and Stephen going up to Cambridge in 1847 were highly favourable. So much so, that Maine took the unusual step of proposing Stephen's Apostle membership at the end of October soon after the freshman's arrival at Cambridge.[35] It was an association which also marked the opening of a lifetime's friendship and two careers that would in many respects parallel each other.

The Society's aura of exclusivity – an active core of six or so – was enhanced by the semi-secret nature of its existence. Leslie Stephen quipped that one might infer an intimate friend's membership from his 'familiarity with certain celebrities and from discovering that upon Saturday evenings he was always mysteriously engaged'.[36] His brother was well set up with just those qualities so highly rated by the Apostles: intellectual independence and originality, and an energetic contempt for all varieties of humbug and wind-baggery. Such was the brotherhood's prestige that election to its ranks could be fairly regarded as a 'certificate from some of your cleverest contemporaries that they regarded you as likely to be in future an eminent man'.[37] Indications of Stephen's early intellectual attitudes may be gleaned from views expressed at Society meetings. However, the temptation in such bodies, particularly for budding controversialists, to adopt opinions and argue from standpoints foreign to their own purely as an academic exercise is not entirely discountable. This aside, at the time, Stephen 'felt a holy horror' of Benthamism,[38] yet traces of sympathy for utilitarian ethics appear in his agreeing that expediency was the proper basis for judging the propriety of action; although he was uncertain if altruistic activity could ever occur, and denied the claim that 'all general truths are founded on experience'. On theological matters, Stephen displayed a solid attachment to the notion that Christian faith both could and must coexist with rationalistic analysis. Unlike goings on at the other place, at Cambridge nothing resembling Tractarianism or Puseyism found its way into circles like the Apostles as a serious topic for discussion.[39]

Quite as much as testing intellect, Apostles' gatherings were occasions for racking a young man's nerve and self-confidence. This competitive and combative side of discussions was carried to a fine, almost legendary, level by Stephen and Vernon Harcourt,[40] a fellow Trinity man and future Liberal Party grandee. The pair were, according to Harcourt's biographer, 'born for mutual conflict, each equipped with a powerful understanding, vigorous expression and a boldness bordering on arrogance'.[41] A contemporary Apostle and informant of Leslie Stephen remembered the encounters as 'veritable battles of the Gods . . . with the most vivid recollection of the pleasure they caused'.[42]

After failing for the second time to gain a Trinity scholarship, Stephen saw the last real chances of an eventual fellowship and an academic life disappear over the horizon of possibility. His response was firmly to tackle the increasingly pressing question of what career he might be best suited to pursue after coming down from Cambridge. Rather than turn the matter over in his mind and consult others, he chose to reach a solution through a written profit and loss assessment of three professions: medicine, law and the church. His 'Choice of profession'[43] employed self-analytical findings of the subject's abilities and inadequacies in a series of tortuous syllogistic calculations. Looking back at this appallingly leaden exercise years after, Stephen asked 'Was any other human being ever constructed with such a clumsy, elaborate set of principles, setting his feelings going as if they were heavy machinery moved by big clock-weights?',[44] with one instance of this tendency provoking the painfully embarrassed author's simple marginal comment: 'Jesus wept.'[45] As to the substance and outcome of this 'Choice', medicine, whose presence was little more than tokenism to completeness, was soon discarded. Added to this is the doubtful genuineness of the whole performance, as, according to Leslie Stephen, consciously or otherwise, the true object of Fitzjames' 'Choice' was to reinforce prior inclinations to avoid a clerical career and go to the Bar.[46]

Stephen was called to the Bar in January 1854 after becoming a member of the Inner Temple and receiving the usual perfunctory legal education;[47] the great exception to this being Maine's jurisprudence lectures, in which he 'transfigured' Roman Law, one of the most tedious of disciplines, into 'all sorts of beautiful things' by setting it in its 'proper relation to other subjects' and in such a way that enabled him 'to sniff at Bentham's' ignorance of history.[48] Indeed, in the 1850s Maine's chambers became a meeting point for a cluster of talented young apprentices including Stephen, Harcourt, Grant Duff and Frederic Harrison, where, in preference to 'dry as dust' law, the worlds of 'general literature and politics' were the subjects most commonly discussed and set to rights.[49] To help remedy what he sensed to be the pitiful inadequacy of his legal training and knowledge, Stephen (unusually for the day) read for a law degree at London University and for the first time seriously encountered teaching in Benthamite philosophy: an event which set him well on course for conversion to the cause. For despite already being thoroughly familiar with Mill's *Logic*, Stephen had lacked much appreciation of utilitarianism's immediate relevance to legislation and law as expounded in Bentham's elaborate schemes.[50]

Once on circuit (the Midland), Stephen diligently applied himself to acquiring the advocate's skills and mastering the finicky procedures of his calling, though finding infinitely more absorbing at trials the pageant of representatives of hitherto unknown classes – 'as if they were dwellers in different zones or inhabitants of different planets'.[51] Neither did the 'high jinks' or 'buffoonery' of the circuit mess greatly appeal to Stephen, 'ponderous' reading and journalism proving a more attractive means of filling free time. His view of the profession, even if generally favourable, was not blind to the shortcomings of a good number of its members – 'callous insensitivity . . . brutal indifference . . . hardened vulgarity which can never rise above a sort of metallic bombast' – who 'degrade' themselves by being the 'foot stools of another person's malignity'.[52] It was, perhaps, a judgement somewhat jaundiced by a streak of naivety – or misplaced idealism – not unique amongst recent recruits to this or any other profession. But his singular lack of relish, even distaste, for the compromises and the rough and smooth of an advocate's life always remained.

These early professional years also coincided with Stephen's newly married state and fatherhood. Like Sir James, Fitzjames married into a clerical family, then headed by J.W. Cunningham, Vicar of Harrow, editor of the *Christian Observer* and friend of Sir James Stephen. He first met Mary Richenda Cunningham in the summer of 1850; they were eventually married in April 1855.[53] Little can or needs to be said of Stephen's marriage beyond his own simple claim, made on many occasions throughout his life, that he owed to his wife 'as much happiness as one human creature can owe to another'.[54]

2

A CONTROVERSIALIST IN THE MAKING: LITERARY CRITICISM AND LEADER-WRITING

Stephen once confessed that for him solitary confinement would have meant 'scratch[ing] newspaper articles on the wall with a nail'; indeed, if his brother is to be believed, it gave him the same pleasure 'that other men derive from dramdrinking'.[1] Much the same sentiment reveals itself in the claim that 'if my body ever had a call to anything by the voices of nature, I have a call to journalism'.[2] Running from early post-Cambridge days through to Stephen's last years, journalism was a continuous occupation paralleling the various phases of his legal career. A prodigious number of articles and reviews document an intellectual and personal development over, even by Victorian standards, an impressively wide range of interests taking in political science, history, law, philosophy, religion and literature; in Carlyle's estimate, someone 'with a huge heavy stroke of work in him'.[3] Journalism provided the first important public outings for a cast of mind greatly taken with empirically based rationalism – making reason the regulator of beliefs, actions and opinions, so much the hallmark of Benthamite utilitarianism. For Stephen the great practical significance of journalism, and, above all, of his association with the *Saturday Review* and *Pall Mall Gazette*, was the role it performed in establishing him as a coming man.

Of course Leslie Stephen was correct in suggesting that for Fitzjames 'the legal career always represented the substantive, and the literary career the adjective',[4] but the urge to commit his views to paper was an essential and irresistible element of Fitzjames' mentality. Whilst the law and a legal career made up the intellectual ballast in his life, a free-ranging intelligence and forceful personality made inevitable an active involvement in the wider intellectual and political community, a community whose opinions were to a considerable degree made and influenced by the 'higher journalism' of the mid-Victorian 'age of periodicals'. In Stephen's case, although his published views on law, religion and political theory spread themselves over more than half a lifetime and throughout most of the best-known and most prestigious journals of the day, the bulk of his activities as a literary critic lie concentrated within the relatively narrow channel of time between 1855 and 1865, appearing largely in the *Saturday Review*.

THE 'SATURDAY REVILER'

The year 1855 was exceedingly important for Stephen: during it he married Mary Cunningham and his career as a journalist and general controversialist began in earnest. Since leaving Cambridge he had written pieces for the Peelite *Morning Chronicle* and more obscure organs such as the *Christian Observer* and *Law Magazine*. The editor of the *Morning Chronicle* was 'particularly pleased . . . with my smashings and wit, but Alas and Alas [he] found me out and gradually ceased to put in my articles'; at £3 10s. a piece, a serious blow to Stephen's pocket.[5] However, it was not until 1855 that journalism became a firmly established and irrepressible element in his life. In 1855 the *Saturday Review of Politics, Literature, Science, and Art* was founded by Alexander Beresford Hope, a well-to-do Tory and later MP for the University of Cambridge.[6] As editor, Beresford Hope chose John Douglas Cook, former *Times* leader-writer and editor of the *Morning Chronicle*, who, although no scholar himself, 'was a lowbrow who knew how to pick the right highbrows'.[7] The new weekly's objective was to raise the intellectual level of journalism and set free 'thirty million people who are ruled despotically by *The Times*'. Its earnestness is well reflected in the *Review*'s manifesto set out in the first number published on 3 November. This lengthy and lofty declaration of intent committed the *Review* to

address[ing itself] to the educated mind of the country, and to serious, thoughtful men of all schools, classes and principles, not so much in the spirit of party as in the more philosophic attitudes of mutual counsel and friendly conflict of opinions . . . Its writers . . . have been thrown together by affinities naturally arising from common habits of thought, education, reflection and social views. Yet they all claim independence of judgment . . . In politics the SATURDAY REVIEW is independent both of individual statesmen and worn-out political sections; in literature, science and art its contributions are entirely free from the influence or dictation of pecuniary or any other connections with trade, party, clique, or section.

Translated into practice the *Review*, despite its owner's high Toryism, was inclined towards liberal Conservative attitudes. However,

Beresford Hope's political tolerance had its limits: certain of the more radical, less tractable, elements of the *Review*'s team were 'kept off' politics and Stephen was firmly on this list of proscribed authors. With backgrounds that hovered rather above the 'Philistines' and somewhat below the 'Barbarians' the *Review*'s contributors' collective ethos, in certain respects, anticipated Arnold's national cultural and spiritual manifesto released in *Culture and Anarchy* (1869), though in reality falling a great distance short, especially in its lack of 'disinterested endeavour';[8] yet Arnold did pay the *Review* the compliment of describing it as 'a kind of organ of reason'.[9] And in many respects the *Review*, as a classical example of nineteenth-century higher journalism, was practically an establishment 'organ of the mid-Victorian clerisy'[10] – scrutinising novelty, stirring up controversy, focusing debate and broadly generating the *right* intellectual, moral and political climate. It was a function which the Whig *Edinburgh Review* and Tory *Quarterly Review* began performing in the early part of the century, and which others such as the *Contemporary Review* and the *Fortnightly Review*[11] would soon join the *Saturday Review* in doing.

Recruited to the regular staff of the *Saturday Review* during its first year was a remarkable assembly of talent (many refugees from the *Morning Chronicle*) destined to shine in politics or scholarship, including Henry Maine, Vernon Harcourt, M.E. Grant Duff, Goldwin Smith, G.S. Venables and Fitzjames Stephen; with G.H. Lewes and Walter Bagehot among the less regular contributors. 'The prevailing complexion at the beginning was Cantabrigian',[12] Apostles holding a majority representation. For the most part its writers were 'young men with the proper confidence in their own infallibility' who with the *Saturday Review* succeeded in making as distinct an advance in literary journalism as had the *Edinburgh Review* nearly fifty years before.[13] During the 1850s and 1860s the *Saturday Review* was *the* great political and literary weekly. According to the historian F.H. Maitland, 'anyone who never wrote for the Saturday Review was no one'.[14] A fearsome and deserved reputation as a merciless reviewer of all forms of literature was rapidly gained; any form of cant or humbug being the most favoured target. However, critical zeal coupled with the need to build reputations meant that the cracking of nuts with sledgehammers and the breaking of butterflies on wheels were common events in the *Review*. Its popularity was established by a unique blend of cleverness, wicked irreverence towards popular heroes and institutions, and by an almost studied abrasiveness and determination to act as a vigorous dose of salts to the critical constitutions of its readers. For the novelist and critic Walter Besant, 'On Sunday the paper became part of the breakfast; it was read with savage joy.' Its character and reputation earned it a host of nicknames including 'Snarler', 'Scorpion', 'Slasher' and 'Saturday Reviler'; the last of which the *Review*'s contributors especially enjoyed and approvingly quoted. Characteristically, with rather greater subtlety Thackeray dubbed it the 'Superfine Review'.

Over the *Review*'s first decade Stephen contributed more than 300 articles,[15] ranging over literature, religion, law, ethics and history; enjoying graphic titles such as 'Bunkum', 'Groans of the Britons', 'British Enthusiasm' and 'Lying'. The circumstances of their composition was often dictated by the peripatetic lifestyle of a barrister on circuit. Distant hotel rooms in the early hours, chilly railway carriages, and even courtrooms were found sufficiently conducive to composition.[16] For T.H.S. Escott, later critic and editor, and himself a contributor to the *Review*,

As a journalist, Fitzjames Stephen did not only help make the *Saturday Review*. He *was* the *Saturday Review*. His views set forth in casual conversation, if they could have been correctly reported, would have run naturally into *Saturday Review* articles. The most characteristic effusions of Cook's best contributions on ethical or serious social themes were the echoes of Stephen's mind bodying themselves forth in articulate expression.[17]

Whilst literary reviewing was just one element of the *Saturday Review*, it was this more than anything else which established both the *Review*'s and Stephen's journalistic reputation. Looked upon with special suspicion was imaginative literature, and particularly the whole mushrooming literary industry geared up to producing novels at a rate and in sufficient quantity to satisfy the appetites of the growing mass-reading public. Along with this advancing commercialisation in the production of novels grew the fear that sound literary standards would be swamped. It was such a spectre of a general cultural tyranny by the under-educated masses that haunted the common psyche of the *Saturday Review* and motivated much of its critical savagery, with Stephen performing the role of leading 'Reviler'. For Stephen, as with others, literary reviewing often became little more than a peg on which to hang sizeable social and political notions. The moral and intellectual education of the masses was, of course, desirable, but Stephen and his fellow reviewers meant to ensure that this great enterprise was not allowed to subvert the nation's cultural heritage through literary mediocrities writing for and preaching to a reading population of mediocrities.

Although Stephen's published literary views are expressed most frequently in the columns of the *Review*, their first and lengthiest statement appeared in a contribution to the *Cambridge Essays* series (1855); an essay which probably played a sizeable role in convincing Cook that Stephen's talents might suit the *Review*.[18] In 'The Relation of Novels to Life' the 26-year-old fledgling barrister ambitiously sets about constructing a rationalistic account of the proper function of novels and how this is best achieved. Underpinning his reasoning was the commonly held belief in the enormous influence of imaginative literature: a power which had, at the same time, the potential to educate or corrupt. Years later in his obituary of Thackeray, Stephen ventured that novels had greater power over the morals and views of the public than the 'stage and pulpit put together'. And that 'novels and newspapers have a sort of analogy to Church and State. The one represents to innumerable readers the active and business life, the other the contemplative view of things.'[19] Consequently, novels were not only to be judged artistically but also assessed for their likely social influence. These two connected critical judgements, in one form or other, loom large in practically all the contemporary and later literary criticism. And because of such influence novels were required to be true to life, possessing something of a biographical quality. No great novelty attached to the notion of fictitious or 'mimic' biography, Carlyle, for one, having earlier explored it in *Sartor Resartus* and his essay 'Biography'.[20] Later Carlyle dismissed the novel form as practically worthless, suggesting to the committee investigating conditions at the British Museum that readers of novels (along with the insane) ought to be separated from serious readers[21] who sought truth in reality.

Stephen's essay is unremarkable in so far as it provides a fairly orthodox, albeit early, realist (and rationalist) approach to imaginative literature. It is inspired by speculation as to the generally disadvantageous obscuring effects of creative writing, a view typified in Macaulay's claim that 'We cannot unite the incompatible advantages of reality and deception, the clear discernment of truth and the exquisite enjoyment of fiction.'[22] What distinguishes the essay from most other realist critiques of the time is the ingenuity shown in blending support of the realist position with a utilitarian rationale. The backbone of Stephen's argument was that novels educate a reader's outlook on life, therefore the reader should be presented with a realistic view of the world at large; but the value to be put on such vicarious experience is limited by 'distorting' elements, inherent either in the 'rules of [the] art' or in the character of the writer. Major amongst these artistically distorting forces is the need to be interesting and consistent, a demand requiring an unreal condensing and sharpening of dramatic events and the representation of character 'as far more homogenous . . . than it ever really is'.

At least as influential as artistic demands are the internal 'distorting' forces of the writer's own character. Taking Thackeray's characterisation as an instance, 'the perfection of the observation, so far as it goes, is only equalled by the narrowness of its range. In the whole of Mr. Thackeray's books there is hardly a hint of such a thing as the serious business of life . . . There is not in all Mr. Thackeray's novels a character who is described by his great qualities; all are described by their small peculiarities.'[23] Equally subversive of novelistic realism was sentimentality, a frequent target of Stephen in subsequent years. Dickens is taken as the prime offender in using 'emotions of tenderness . . . as accessories for the purpose of heightening an artistic effect'. He is accused of continually bringing death 'upon stage [to show] his skill in arranging effective details so as to give them this horrible pungency'. Of this tendency Stephen caustically adds that 'A list of the killed, wounded and missing amongst Mr. Dickens's novels would read like an Extraordinary Gazette. An interesting child runs as much risk there as any of the troops who stormed the Redan.'[24]

The temptation to use novels for ventilating or propagandising social or political opinions is Stephen's final 'distorting' force. Although not considered inherently illegitimate, the dangers of 'partiality, or dishonesty, and hasty misconception' were extensive. Remorselessly following the logic of previously rehearsed arguments, Stephen concludes that on the basis of the dual standards of reality and social utility ' "Robinson Crusoe" is not only unsurpassed, but . . . almost unsurpassable.'

The most immediate impression created by the essay is of its author's singular lack of aesthetic appreciation; of a narrow rationalistic aridity bordering on Gradgrind's imperative: 'Stick to Facts, sir!'[25] This, as Stephen's later literary criticism reveals, is rather misleading. The chillingly logical and mechanical analytical style is substantially determined by the essay's central purpose (as its title suggests) of reconciling imaginative literature with personal and political inclinations. Viewed in this confining focus it represents one of the most sustained and elaborate attempts of the period to describe the function of novels within a general utilitarian framework detached from any evaluation of artistic worth.

As times of great critical volatility, during the 1850s and 1860s only the most primitive attempts were made to devise any coherent body of literary principles. Even recognition of novels as an art form in their own right was some way off, with the inability to separate fiction from history and biography still common. Acceptance of realism as the essential ingredient of imaginative literature was practically universal in England; although the relativistic nature of the concept was an immensely fertile source of endless wrangling. The most challenging critical peaks for conquest by the contemporary realist reviewer and social commentator included: just how exact a picture of life should be portrayed? Quite how was the imaginative faculty of the author to be exercised? Should novels be socially and politically didactic? If novels were to be 'real' then how were they to describe the immoral elements of life? In this formative period for literary criticism the *Saturday Review* and Stephen enjoyed a distinct and provocative presence.

THE ARTIST PROPAGANDIST AND THE SEARCH FOR REALISM

The political and social climate which fostered the emergence and growth of the realist school owed much to the twin forces of evangelicalism and utilitarianism; on first appearances they were worlds apart, but in practice the earnest temperament demanded by each frequently meant that 'the Sunday evangelist [was] the week-day utilitarian'.[26] Both persuasions in their strictest forms shared the belief that the undiscriminating consumption of imaginative literature was at best a time-wasting activity which, more seriously, might lead to spiritual or social corruption. To rigid Benthamites, literature could be a 'seducer' or 'harlot' completely enslaving the mind without 'regard for truth or utility [and which] seeks only to excite emotions';[27] and how could the 'universal pursuit of literature and poetry . . . conduce towards cotton-spinning'?[28] More than merely censorious, these extreme strains of evangelicalism and utilitarianism spawned a prolific number of societies whose primary aim was to channel reading energies in the right direction. Most famous of all in the utilitarian camp stood the 'Society for the Diffusion of Useful Knowledge' – Thomas Peacock's 'Steam Intellect Society' – whose narrow educative practices Carlyle characterised as the 'triumphant quackle-quackling . . . intent only on sine and cosine'.[29] Providing the evangelical counterpart was the 'Society for the Diffusion of Pure Literature', formed to ensure that only completely wholesome fare reached the family reading circle.

Despite a Claphamite and utilitarian inheritance, Stephen never displayed the slightest inclination towards heavy-handed attempts at imposing such restrictions on the availability or content of literature. He ridiculed the activities of the 'Society for the Diffusion of Pure Literature' aimed at requiring 'Not only . . . that you must not work [on Sunday but also] that you must have a set of Sunday feelings and habits quite different from those which are fit for weekdays. There must be not only Sunday clothes but "Sunday books." '[30] Consumption of the Society's specially refined reading products led to 'purity not of health, but of disease – the purity of distilled water or meat with all its flavour boiled away'. The relative deluge of novels with religious themes had Stephen pleading with authors to 'leave off writing novels about the origin of evil . . . As soon as anyone has gone through any religious experience which leaves any impression on his mind, he – or more frequently she – makes it into a novel, on the principle that it cannot be uninteresting to others to read about anything which it was so deeply interesting to feel.'[31]

More widely, the question of using novels as instruments of propaganda for social, political or moral teaching was something which, if not directly in issue, was never far off in most of his reviews. A particular bête noire was 'the political novelists with their . . . hasty generalisation and false conclusions [who] exercise a very wide and a very pernicious political and social influence',[32] failing to offer a balanced view between 'a blind admiration [and] a blind contempt of the institutions under which they live'. For instance, *Ruth* and *Mary Barton* were 'exquisite novels [yet] prove nothing at all, though we think their authoress intended that they should'.[33] But as the most widely read novelist of the time, amounting almost to an institution, Dickens was the natural and inevitable focus for most of Stephen's attention. Dickens was repeatedly identified as the leading offender of the class of novelists who in 'one way or other, hoists the flag and wears the uniform of the noble army of world betterers'. In 'Mr. Dickens as a Politician',[34] Dickens is lambasted as one who enjoyed considerable political influence yet showed little in the way of conviction or awareness of the realities of the political process; in short, a meddling political ignoramus who

would have the pace of legislation quickened by the abolition of vain debates – he would have justice freed from the shackles of law – he would have public affairs conducted by officers of vast powers unfettered by routine. He does not know his own meaning. He does not see the consequences of his own teaching; and yet he is unconsciously tending to a result logically connected with the whole of it. Freedom, law, established rules have their difficulties . . . No one can deny that

there are great abuses . . . Our law has enormous faults . . . Mr. Dickens's government looks pretty at a distance, but . . . it would result in the purist despotism.
There would be no debate . . . no laws to prevent judges going at once to the
merits of the case according to their own inclination.

Even though he was essentially correct in his assessment of
Dickens as a political being, there was much exaggerating and
overstating the novelist's political impact. Essentially a 'sentimental
radical', Dickens favoured public good works, generosity and
universal benevolence; with a political philosophy humanitarian in
its very clear concern with the general grey meanness of life for a
sizeable part of the nation. But how this concern could be translated
into political action was a question Dickens never seriously
attempted to answer. Not untypical of Dickens' political incoherency
(and a fair sample of the 'soft moisture of irrelevant sentiment')[35]
was his public claim in 1869 that 'my faith in the people governing is,
on the whole, infinitessimal; my faith in the People governed is, on
the whole, illimitable'.[36] Stephen's distinction was in being the first
persistent and most trenchant critic of Dickens the 'artist-
propagandist', to borrow Shaw's later characterisation.

Although the threatening European storms of 1848 had passed by,
unsurprisingly at home there lingered a clear nervousness over the
likely course and form of popular political expectations. For those,
like Stephen, out of sympathy with the wholesale democratic
radicalism of John Bright and the like, yet dissatisfied with the prevailing moral and social malaise, meeting the Dickens challenge presented an uncomfortable choice. True, the Poor Law in *Oliver Twist*,
imprisonment for debt in *Pickwick*, and the grinding procedural
slowness of the Court of Chancery which haunted *Bleak House* were
matters of concern to Stephen also; and while the causes in their time
may have been fair ones,[37] political agitation by stirring up popular
sentiments was seen as a decidedly hazardous and unacceptable
means of achieving desirable reforms.

Much of Stephen's criticism of the political content of Dickens'
novels resembles that levelled against Carlyle – although in Carlyle's
case the language is distinctly more respectful. But despite the difference of literary medium inhabited by each author, there was clear
common ground in their anger with administrative inefficiency, disillusionment with established forms of parliamentary procedure and
resistance to the interfering nature of increasingly centralised
government. Hostility to the Civil Service in Carlyle's *Latter-Day
Pamphlets* was matched by Dickens' *Little Dorrit* five years later.

Dickens' enormous esteem for Carlyle is well known: *Hard Times*[38] was dedicated to Carlyle as, in effect, was *A Tale of Two Cities*. Correspondence between the two suggests Carlyle to have been influential in Dickens' graduation to wider social criticism.[39] The similarities in Stephen's critical treatment of common themes in Carlyle and Dickens' works show not only a steady consistency of principle but an admirable objectivity and willingness to criticise with equal vigour two public figures, one of whom was a revered friend, and the other most certainly not.

Particularly in the case of the 'artist-propagandist', a natural expectation both of author and critic was that if novels were to be realistic they must be factually accurate in the events represented – or, at the very least, be internally consistent. On the question of authorial accuracy, two of Stephen's best-known skirmishes were with Charles Reade and Dickens. Both critical engagements originate in Stephen's *Edinburgh Review* article 'The Licence of Modern Novelists',[40] later spilling over into the *Saturday Review*'s literary columns.

Reade's particular forte was the exposé novel, partly fictionalising some current social or political outrage. And although realistic in the sense of basing his books on actual events, Reade unsparingly overlaid this realism with theatricality, melodramatic effects and sentimentality of the most lavish proportions. In *It is Never too late to Mend* the subject matter was the conditions and abuses of the prison system and particular occurrences at Birmingham Gaol in the early 1850s. During an inquest on the suicide of a young prisoner details of certain punishment practices came to light. The subsequent Commission of Inquiry reported on a regime of illegal and criminal punishments. As a consequence the prison governor was convicted and sentenced to three months' imprisonment. *It is Never too late* savages not only the prison system but complementary administrative and judicial institutions; the Home Office, magistracy, judiciary and legal professions are all indicted as co-conspirators in the affair.

Stephen methodically compared, fact by fact, the book with the Commission's report, concluding that Reade's work was riddled with exaggeration and distortion. Here was the 'chemistry of modern romance. The salts crystallize, the gases diffuse themselves, the metals agglomerate before our eyes. The process consists in twisting, perverting, misrepresenting, adding to or taking away from, every single truth which enters into the material basis.' Far from deserving its claimed quasi-historical status, it was little more than an 'hysterical effusion'.[41] A few weeks after the *Edinburgh Review* article appeared, Stephen returned to the attack, this time in the *Saturday Review*.[42] Adopting a slightly dishonest, tongue-in-cheek, pose, Stephen reviewed and generally endorsed the contents of his own views in the *Edinburgh Review*.[43] Reade himself was stung into responding by writing to the *Saturday Review*, 'You have brains of your own and good ones. Do not echo the bray of such a very small ass as the *Edinburgh Review*. Be more just to yourself and me.'[44] From the tenor of Reade's letter he seemed unaware of the common authorship of the two reviews. Those who did know were, no doubt, hugely entertained by it.

Running almost in tandem with this attempted dismemberment of *It is Never too late* was Stephen's determined effort to expose Dickens' factual inaccuracies. Petty as this now appears, it was then fair game for critics, as Dickens, like other authors of the time, frequently held himself out as never venturing beyond the realistic, and if elements of a novel had a recognisably factual basis then so much the better. From the prefaces of novels such as *Bleak House* and *Barnaby Rudge*, Dickens' anxiety to demonstrate verisimilitude in his works is painfully plain.

However, the main source of Stephen's agitation was *Little Dorrit*. During 1857 the book was to figure in no fewer than four *Saturday Review* pieces in addition to his *Edinburgh Review* references. Part at least of the motivation for this special concern with *Little Dorrit* is obvious; as Leslie Stephen confirms, Dickens' inspired satirical creation of the Circumlocution Office was 'especially offensive because "Barnacle Tite"[45] and the effete aristocrats . . . stood for Sir James Stephen and his best friends'.[46] A few years before Sir James had given public evidence to the Northcote-Trevelyan Commission on the Civil Service, adopting not so much a hostile attitude but rather a position of 'settled pessimism' towards possible reforms. However, Dickens, a founder member of the 'Administrative Reform Association',[47] saw Stephen as personifying conservative reaction and a worthy symbol of ineffective administration; and it was, therefore, with a special 'grim pleasure' that he awaited the likely effect of his attack[48] in *Little Dorrit*.

Fitzjames' criticism of *Little Dorrit* in the *Saturday Review* amounted to a charge against Dickens of ill-informed and misleading exaggeration; a charge amply demonstrated as well founded by C.P. Snow in 'Dickens and the Public Service'.[49] With his article in the July *Edinburgh Review* it had been Stephen's declared intention to make

Dickens 'howl',[50] but in the course of particularising his criticism and lauding the great quality of past holders of high public office with their receptiveness to innovation, Stephen fatally mentioned Rowland Hill of the Post Office. In reality Hill's attempts to introduce the penny post had been scandalously opposed and delayed at every turn by stagnant officialdom. Unfortunately for Stephen, Dickens knew this and with a lengthy and sarcastic rejoinder in *Household Words*[51] entitled 'Curious Misprint in the Edinburgh Review' he was able, on this count at least, to see Stephen off; although the view in some quarters was that Dickens had landed no more than a single and insignificant lucky blow. Snow, relying on an 'oral tradition which may not be reliable', suggests 'men such as G.M. Trevelyan, Desmond MacCarthy, [and] G.M. Hardy . . . used to talk of the general pleasure in Fitzjames Stephen's triumph'.[52]

Correspondence between Stephen and his father during 1857 shows that Sir James was naturally not displeased with his son's critical efforts.[53] However, following Dickens' response, Sir James delivered a warning that Fitzjames was playing a dangerous game.

About Rowland Hill he is not far wrong . . . He is evidently very angry as a man who has so long been buried in public applause must be at the first indication of failing popularity. I do not know that he has a right to be angry – but I should doubt the wisdom of exciting him any more. He is rather a formidable enemy to deal with, and you are best without enemies . . ., E.G. If the Govt. should offer you employment under the Attorney Genl's project Dickens would want neither the will nor the power to annoy you . . ., also if a man is to fight he ought not to be handicapped, and the ER has tied your hands so much as to prevent your planting some of the most effective blows which might have been struck.[54]

The reference to the *Edinburgh Review* ('ER') probably relates to the strong editorial control then exercised by Henry Reeve. Leslie Stephen suggests that Reeve himself may have been responsible for the insertion of the reference to Rowland Hill, for the *Edinburgh Review* regarded the offerings of young contributors in particular as 'raw material which might be rather arbitrarily altered by the editor'.[55] Set against Leslie's speculation, though, is Reeve's own opinion that Fitzjames was one of a group of *Edinburgh Review* contributors 'of the highest honour and the most consistent adherence to liberal principles'.[56] But, weighty as his father's advice always was with Fitzjames, there is no discernible change in the style or content of his subsequent handling of Dickens' works.

The interested hand of Sir James Stephen again appears in connection with the minor literary cause célèbre of Lady Scott's libel action brought against Mrs Gaskell. In her biography of Charlotte Brontë, Mrs Gaskell had implied, following current rumours, that Branwell Brontë had been involved in an adulterous liaison with Lady Scott, a friend of the Stephens. Between 21 May and 30 May 1857, the affair is referred to on three occasions by Sir James in correspondence with Fitzjames. On 30 May Sir James suggests that he 'should be glad if you could obtain a notice of the affair in the next Sat. R.'; adding, 'If Mrs G. had written for herself one penitential word I might perhaps be disposed to leave her alone. But as it is the enormity of her charges seem to me to call for some literary rebuke.' On the day the letter was written a formal public retraction was published in *The Times*. Presumably this had been seen by Sir James and accounts for his reference to Mrs Gaskell not having written 'for herself' any sort of apology. Shortly after, on 6 June, a hostile notice, 'Mrs. Gaskell's Recantation', appeared in the *Saturday Review*, probably of Fitzjames' authorship.[57] For good measure a few weeks later in the July number of the *Edinburgh Review*, Fitzjames,[58] in the concluding remarks of a review of Mrs Gaskell's offending biography, delivers a sharp rap to the author's literary knuckles for her 'hasty' use of such unverified material.

Calls for factual accuracy or the illusion of probability in novels frequently brought critics of the time around to considering the question of authorial experience. Henry James' overriding precept 'write from experience and experience only'[59] provides a typical late-nineteenth-century critical aphorism; he was, however, far from being its originator, authors long having been warned off territory foreign to their cultural and emotional experiences. In the particular case of women novelists Stephen credited them with special talents, even if they were somewhat prone to try and exceed these. 'Quick minute observation and reproduction of the ordinary affairs of life is their forte – the inculcation of broad principles is apt to be their foible.'[60] Neither the substance nor the unconscious patronising quality of such observations was in any way exceptional for the period, representing all but a very small number of progressives. Indeed, G.H. Lewes' views of women novelists at this time were surprisingly close to Stephen's.[61] Even George Eliot in 'Silly Novels by Lady Novelists'[62] found it necessary to offer a lengthy discourse on the juvenile nature of the bulk of the output of women writers: often of the 'mind and millinery species' or 'Most pitiable . . . the oracular species – novels intended to expand the writer's religious philosophical, or moral theories . . ., [Their] recipe for solving . . . the knottiest moral and speculative questions . . . is . . .: – Take a "woman's head stuff it with false notions of society bake hard, let it hang over a desk a few hours every day, and serve up hot in feeble English, when not required.'' '[63] Though, of course, Eliot, unlike Stephen and probably Lewes, was not suggesting that women in general were intellectually incapable of the full range of imaginative writing, but rather that too many without ability wrote from 'vanity . . . [and] busy idleness'.[64]

More generally, Stephen held the lack of the right sort of background to be a considerable limitation for any author, especially in their ability to comment on the 'various departments of social life'. In an illustrative comparison of Scott and Dickens, Stephen comments: 'Scott we all know was a lawyer and an antiquarian', but in Dickens' case 'his notions of law, which occupy so large a space in his books, are precisely those of an attorney's clerk'.[65] A later review of *A Tale of Two Cities*[66] shows Stephen in his most unflattering and snobbish form as a critic. Dickens' preface to the book refers to Carlyle's *French Revolution* as a 'wonderful book'. Stephen fixed on this reference, observing

The allusion to Mr. Carlyle confers the presumption which the book itself raises, that Mr. Dickens happened to have read the *History of the French Revolution* and being on the look-out for a subject, determined off-hand to write a novel about it. Whether he has any other knowledge of the subject than a single reading of Mr. Carlyle's work would supply does not appear, but certainly what he has written shows no more.

In fact Dickens in a letter to Carlyle in 1857 refers to reading 'that wonderful book for the 50th time',[67] and again to Carlyle in 1854 Dickens comments 'no man knows your book better than I'.[68] Making allowance for a little artistic hyperbole on Dickens' part, it seems unlikely that Stephen's superior jibe was remotely justified. Although this sort of sniping at Dickens was relatively rare at the time, it became increasingly less so in the 1860s. One similar early critical attack came from Bagehot,[69] whose views, very like Stephen's, were as much motivated by Dickens' political propagandising as by artistic defects. Lewes during this period and into the 1870s shifted his ground more than once,[70] but in 'Dickens in Relation to Criticism' (1872), his most thorough-going evaluation of Dickens,[71] on the issue of authorial background and education he offers largely the same opinion Stephen had expressed thirteen years before – albeit in a rather less directly offensive manner.

Stephen's reflections on authorial experience show him in a destructive and extreme mood. Much can simply be attributed to the vein of crude utilitarian literary appreciation, suspicious of imaginative creativity, which never wholly disappeared from his critical faculties. This, allied with a belief in the corrosive effect on the country's political and social institutions of the ill-informed meddlings of novelists, often generated a degree of ferocity that probably struck even contemporary spectators familiar with the every day knockabout of literary reviewing as wildly excessive. Certainly Sir William Robertson Nicholl, for one, had no doubt that Stephen had been 'The Arch-Enemy of Dickens'.[72]

IMMORALITY AND FRENCH REALISM

Although the virulence of Stephen's reviews was often exceptional, his preoccupation with factual correctness and authorial experience was not. This negative comparison of art to life was a dominant characteristic of most critical writing in the 1850s and 1860s,[73] with more effort poured into devising ways of classifying novels as 'unreal' than in formulating positive criteria by which good imaginative literature could be distinguished from bad. To the basic question 'what should novels seek to do?' there was certainly no discernible consensus. At one pole of opinion Trollope and others saw novels as, at best, refined entertainment which, perhaps, should be combined with some moral lesson: 'to make virtue alluring and vice ugly',[74] and, furthermore, 'novel reading like all amusements must not be indulged in too much'.[75] The opposing view, some considerable distance off, was well represented by George Eliot. For her, imaginative literature's greatest benefit was the extension of our sympathies: 'If Art does not enlarge men's sympathies, it does nothing morally.'[76] The weight of contemporary critical opinion lay closer to the Eliot position. To the obvious supplementary question 'how should novels attempt to instil good morality?', there was an even stronger degree of disunity and absence of critical agreement.

In the course of his journalistic career Stephen's views on such questions oscillated between the two poles of opinion. Early reviews place him close to Trollope, although often when speaking of Fielding, Scott and Thackeray he concedes the worth of imaginative literature in terms that propel him towards Eliot. But ironically for a professed patriot, it was French literature and especially the works of Balzac that opened and dazzled Stephen's critical eyes.

Unlike most other foreign literature, French works were quite well represented in the *Saturday Review* columns. Many of these novels were strong meat for English readers raised largely on home produce. The broad span of French novels unavoidably posed realists with embarrassingly awkward questions as to the function, permissible subject matter and moral content of fiction. In a half-dozen or so reviews published during 1857 and 1858 Stephen, in facing up to these issues, reveals literary attitudes not easily reconcilable with his views on English novels expressed both before and after.

His first and inconclusive critical encounter was with *Madame Bovary*, which, although not treated to a standard *Saturday Review* slashing, did provoke feelings of 'great disgust'.[77] Yet Stephen's initial relief that English novelists produce nothing that could not be read by a 'modest man . . . to a young lady' later softens to doubt as to whether we are right to 'plume ourselves' in the belief that 'purification of our light literature . . . prove[s] we are more moral than our neighbours'. Almost openly admitting second thoughts, he concludes as 'very questionable' the belief that the content of novels should be regulated by the 'shockability' of young women, as other branches of literature are not restricted in this manner: 'Theology, history, philosophy, morality, law . . . are all studied at the reader's peril.' On his return to the theme a few weeks later most of this equivocality has disappeared. In 'Light Literature in France'[78] he feels able to accept that immorality may justifiably be represented in novels. Provided the writer does not excessively dwell on the subject purely for dramatic effect he will be doing no more than portraying reality, for that 'large and important a part of actual life . . . occupied by illicit love cannot be overlooked'; literary immorality arose not in the subject matter but in its handling.[79]

It is in 'Light Literature in France' that Stephen volunteers some of his most perceptive and uninhibited observations on imaginative literature in general:

M. Masson is rather severe upon the principle of art pour l'art – of writing, that is, without any specific moral purpose. Surely, in so far as art is regulated by essential and eternal rules, it is its own justification. Art is but a version of life so contrived as to make a deep impression on the imagination. Unless therefore life is immoral, art can hardly be so . . . If, indeed the novelist represents the world as worse than it is, that is a fault of art; and it is more serious, because it may have bad moral consequences. We do not by any means deny that French writers of fiction have often erred in this matter; but they do seem to us to have kept in view a fact which some of our most popular English novelists appear altogether to forget – the fact that a work of imagination ought to be considered, not as a child's play-thing, but as a great and serious undertaking to be executed according to the rules of its own art, and not to be mutilated for the sake of pointing any moral which may strike the fancy of the writer.

When reviewing Prévost's *Manon Lescaut*, in the following year, he reaffirmed his hostility towards overt moralising, which, in any case was doubted to be 'very efficacious'. Overall, the work received thorough approval for treating immorality 'with fidelity, with frankness, without sermonizing, but with a largeness that looks to the whole life'. George Sand's *La Daniella* was found to be 'tedious, spiritless and flat', and lacking in the author's earlier freshness, although there were still glimpses of the 'master-hand' of this 'reflective and self-contemplative' writer. As for the book's appealing elements, he found Sand's treatment of the 'less obvious relations of the sexes – the treacherous delights of female friendship, and the rough differences of married lovers . . . its chief excellence'.[80]

Of all the imaginative literature publicly discussed by Stephen easily the deepest impressions on him were made by Balzac's novels.[81] He rated Balzac in his particular genre 'in some respects by far the greatest writer France has produced'.[82] The strongly admired Thackeray, Scott, Defoe and Fielding all seemed to be eclipsed (at least at the time of the review's composition) by the vivid hypnotic effect on Stephen of Balzac's work.[83] Balzac had a 'far higher conception of the objects and nature of his art'. For him novels were more than 'mere toys', being rather 'works of art, to be constructed according to rules of their own and to be valued for their inherent perfection, and not for any collateral purpose to which they might be made subservient'. As for the frequently vehement charges of immorality made against Balzac, Stephen conceded that Balzac 'had a love of stirring up dirty puddles',[84] but so long as he was a faithful observer and depicter of life he was 'entitled to the full weight of the defence . . . he made when charged with immorality. "J'écris pour les hommes, non pour les jeunes filles." ' The greater artistic freedom enjoyed by French novelists was put down by Stephen to a difference in temperament between the English and the French: novelists in France 'address the most plain-spoken, and in England the most reserved of modern nations'. Whether that was generally true or not, French professional critical opinion of Balzac's realism was, in the main, no higher than in England, with charges of immorality constantly levelled at his works for the greater part of the century.[85] Stephen was, though, rather coy as to whether he wished his own native writers to follow the lead of their French counterparts; the lingering impression is that Stephen himself was not really sure.

Less easily ignored is the distinct suspicion of inconsistency in Stephen's approach to the handling of morality in novels. Works of imagination were not to be 'mutilated' by the moral posturings of writers, yet, for example, Flaubert received a severe drubbing for showing greater dislike for the consequences of Madame Bovary's

lifestyle than he does for the inherent immorality of it. By impli-
cation, authors could (or must) show approval of the conventional
run of social mores but not be seen to have any truck with
immorality. A further connected area of apparent inconsistency is
best viewed as the consequence of jettisoning elements of utilitarian
orthodoxy which inhabited 'The Relation of Novels to Life'. If,
according to this essay, the worth of a novel is largely determined by
its didactic value – for what it tells the reader about the world and its
ways – then quite what is to be usefully gleaned from Balzac's works,
with their improbable plots, unbelievable overpopulation of 'virtuous fools and clever knaves' and frequently surreal view of
human nature?

Whether seen as inconsistency or simply the maturation of
literary appreciation, Stephen's enormous regard for Balzac was very
much out of step with the prevailing contemporary attitude. In addition to Stephen only a very small cluster of critics were well disposed towards Balzac during the 1850s and 1860s, such as Lewes and
H.S. Edwards, principal literary critic of *The Spectator*.[86] Until well
into the 1870s Balzac's English reputation hardly advanced beyond
the *Quarterly Review*'s 1836 condemnation that 'a baser filthier
scoundrel never polluted society than M. de Balzac's standard of
public morals'. Twenty-five years later even usually enlightened
progressives like Mill's disciple John Morley looked on Balzac's
works and French realism as 'only another name for a steady and
exclusive devotion to a study of all the meanest or nastiest elements
in character and conduct'.[87]

DICKENS' AND THACKERAY'S ARTISTRY

For Stephen, a good part of Balzac's appeal was his cynicism: his
'withering genius' provided a picture of 'reality' which chimed well
with Stephen's own unoptimistic assessment of the world. It was just
the opposite qualities in Dickens' novels that Stephen found so truly
indigestible. 'The goodness of his good men is always running over
their beards like Aaron's ointment.' Putting aside views on Dickens
the propagandist, Stephen's attitude towards Dickens' artistry was
divided. Never disguising his enthusiasm for the comic creations in
earlier works such as *Pickwick, The Old Curiosity Shop* and *Martin
Chuzzlewit*, he applauded Dickens as 'a great master of humour . . .,
Sam Weller, Dick Swiveller, and Sairy Gamp are his successes and
we thank him most heartily for them'.[88] Stephen was not to be
denied these pleasures by the snooty criticism of some reviewers

deploring the corruption of the English language by Dickens' linguistic caricaturing. Earnest and severe a critic Stephen often was; humourless and pompous he was not. Even in *Little Dorrit*, which Stephen concluded was so badly executed and poorly plotted that 'an Act of Parliament would fail to enforce the serious reading of [it]', he discerns 'the old cunning hand', anticipating that 'Mr. Dickens can, we believe recover himself.'

Stephen's most fulsome and measured praise of Dickens' humour is found in the *Saturday Review* of 8 May 1858. In 'Mr. Dickens' he attempts to provide some sort of historical account of the Dickens phenomenon:

We feel no doubt that one principal cause of his popularity is the spirit of revolt against all established rules which pervades every one of his books, and which is displayed most strongly and freshly in his earlier productions. Just as Scott owed so much of his success to the skill with which he gave shape and colour to the great Conservative reaction against the French Revolution, Mr. Dickens is indebted to the exquisite adaptation of his own turn of mind to the peculiar state of feeling which still prevails in some classes, and which twenty years ago prevailed far more widely, with respect to all the arrangements of society. So much cant had been in fashion about the wisdom of our ancestors, the glorious constitution, the wise balance of King, Lords, and Commons, and other such topics, that a large class of people were ready to hail with intense satisfaction the advent of a writer who naturally and without an effort bantered everything in the world, from elections and law courts down to Cockney sportsmen, the boots at an inn, cooks and chambermaids. Mr. Dickens had the additional advantage of doing this not only with exquisite skill, and with a sustained flow of spirit and drollery almost un-equalled by any other writer, but in a style which seemed expressly intended to bring into contempt all those canons of criticism which a large proportion of people were learning to look upon as mere pedantry and imposture. 'Pickwick' is throughout a sort of half-conscious parody of that style of writing which demanded balanced sentences, double-barrelled epithets, and a proper conception of the office and authority of semicolons. It is as if a saucy lad were to strut about the house in his father's court-dress, with the sleeves turned inside out and the coat-tails stuck under his arms. Whenever he can get an opportunity, Mr. Dickens rakes up the old-fashioned finery, twists it into every sort of grotesque shape, introduces it to all kinds of strange bedfellows, and contrives, with an art which is all the more ingenious because it was probably quite undesigned, to convey the impression that every one who tries to write, to think or to act by rule, is little more than a pompous jackass. It is impossible to describe the spirit of a writer of whose best books slang is the soul without speaking his own language. Mr. Dickens is the very Avatar of chaff, and bigwigs of every description are his game. The joviality, the animal spirits, and the freshness with which he acted this part in his earliest books are wonderful. We cannot mention any caricature so perfect and so ludicrous as the description of Messrs. Dobson and Fogg, and that of the trial of Bardell v. Pickwick. The mere skill of his workmanship would have unques-tionably secured the success of such a writer; but the harmony between his own temper and that of his audience must be appreciated before we can understand the way in which approbation grew into enthusiasm.

Repeatedly, throughout many reviews and in various guises, Stephen believed 'Mr. Dickens has a mission, but it is to make the world grin, not to recreate and rehabilitate society'; a conclusion much like Henry James' 1865 judgement that 'Mr. Dickens is a . . . great humourist, but he is nothing of a philosopher.'[89]

For Stephen, along with many contemporary critics, it was Dickens' serious and dramatic output that was spectacularly flawed, particularly by its saturation with sentimentality, a quality identified by the excessive use of or over-indulgence in 'tender emotions'.[90] On the death of Little Nell, Stephen accuses Dickens of 'gloat[ing] over the girl's death as if it delighted him, he looks at it from four or five points of view, touches, tastes, smells and handles as if it was some savoury dainty which could not be too fully appreciated'.[91] Characteristically, Wilde suggested that a person needed to have a heart of stone to read the death of Little Nell without laughing. Stephen may not have laughed, but he was certainly unmoved by it. Seven years later, R.H. Hutton complains '[he] gives us the sensation of absolute gluttony to enter into the appetizing spirit with which he spoons and stirs the subject of grief and death'.[92] Similarly, Henry James identifies Little Nell's pedigree as being 'the troop of hunchbacks, imbeciles and precocious children who have carried on the sentimental business in all Mr. Dickens's novels'.[93]

But even the great scourge of sentimentalism was occasionally laid low by Dickens' heady sentimental potions. In an amusing *Saturday Review* article published on Christmas Day 1858, entitled 'Sentimentalism', the theme was the general vulgar sentimentality of all the seasonal aspects of Christmas. Adopting a studied and self-conscious Scrooge-like posture, Stephen humbugs the whole idealised image of the festivities produced by the 'illustrated papers':

a crisp frost, and snow hanging from trees in picturesque wreaths. An ox is roasted whole and a plum-pudding the size of a high-priced globe [flaming in] a gallon of brandy . . . [The reality is that Christmas day is] nine years out of ten, a moist, mild day, when everything looks particularly green, sodden and sticky. People limit their beef by their reasonable appetites, and find that no illusion will persuade the digestion to work off more plum-pudding on Christmas-day than on other days.

Pursuing his theme of illusion and reality, Stephen generously (for him) concedes that although sentimentalism is a shallow emotion it can nevertheless be a genuine expression of feelings and 'it is better that men shall have shallow feelings rather than none'. True, the death of Paul Dombey is 'sentimental but its sentimentalism is of a decidedly high character'.

It was not only excessive sentimentality that flawed Dickens' artistry: his plotting and exaggerated characterisation were also regularly and savagely censured. Stephen along with Lewes, Bagehot, and most major critics of the day had no stomach for Dickens' unreal 'grand hyperbolic beings', unless they were vehicles for humour. To them the characters were failures because they lacked real emotions and feelings,[94] and did not lead to any expansion of human sympathies: they 'were wooden and ran on wheels'. Very few, such as David Masson, understood Dickens' caricatures as 'humanity caught . . . and kept in its highest and extremist mood'.[95] Reviewing *A Tale of Two Cities*, Stephen, with picturesque exaggeration rivalling Dickens' characterisation, accuses him of serving up 'puppy pie and stewed cat . . . [with] a bottle of sauce [that] has stood on the sideboard for a very long time'.[96] The level of invective apart, references to the mechanical use of the special effects of plotting and sentiment are echoed elsewhere even by Masson, who in the same year speaks of 'the recoil from [Dickens'] later writings among the cultivated and fastidious . . . who have caught . . . his mannerism or trick'.[97] Stephen's artistic evaluation of some of Dickens' later works finds endorsement in Henry James' 1865 review of *Our Mutual Friend*: 'For the last ten years it has seemed to us that Mr. Dickens has been unmistakably forcing himself. "Bleak House" was forced; "Little Dorrit" was laboured; the present work is dug out, as with a spade and pickaxe.' Indeed, of the book's few reviews the only journal to show any enthusiasm appears to have been the *Examiner* edited by John Forster, Dickens' close friend and later biographer.[98]

In his predictive powers Stephen failed as miserably as most of Dickens' critics, including Lewes, Trollope[99] and Meredith.[100] With them, Stephen was confident that the Dickens phenomenon was purely transitory. Shakespeare's wit endured because it was 'like spangles on rich velvet – the wit of Pickwick is like spangles on tinsel paper'. He did not see this as Balzac's fate; yet the resemblances of the two writers who played such major roles in his critical consciousness went (at least publicly) unperceived. Both occupied something like the middle ground between pure romanticism and realism; neither was a stranger to melodrama or 'exaggerated beings'. Perhaps it is rather a tall order to expect Stephen to have shown a Jamesian perception and seen the similarities in 'intensity of imaginative powers, the power of evoking visible objects and figures, seeing them themselves with the force of hallucination'[101] or kaleidoscopic multiplication. Underlying Stephen's general lack of appreciation for Dickens' non-humourous writing was probably his constitutional inability to separate the author and his works.

Like Arnold, Stephen saw literature not merely as a social force but also as a significant index of the nation's more general 'cultural' good health – or lack of it. For him Dickens was the leading literary and political representative of the swelling and increasingly influential philistinism of the (lower) middle classes; a class that sapped and deflected artistic and cultural energies, and one which Stephen regarded as totally incapable of performing the serious role of setting the course and nature of imaginative literature. To him theirs was a world of

smug little tradesmen of shallow and half-educated minds, with paltry ambitions, utter ignorance of history and philosophy shrinking instinctively from all strenuous thought and resenting every attack upon the placid optimism in which it delighted to wrap itself [with] no perception of the doubts and difficulties which beset loftier minds, or any consciousness of the great drama of history in which our generation is only playing its part for the passing hour.[102]

As a critic of Dickens, Stephen's views and public stance bear a clear resemblance to those of G.H. Lewes.[103] For both, Dickens was an entertainer, not an artist; his novels were unrealistic, failing to explore the inner lives of his characters, and bloated with gross sentimentality; as political and social critiques they were poorly informed and dangerously simplistic. Stephen and Lewes did, though, part company in two respects: whilst Stephen 'made a head-on attack with a cudgel, Lewes insinuates himself . . . the smylere with knyf under cloke';[104] to Stephen went the distinction of generally pre-dating Lewes in his criticism of Dickens.

Quite how much personal animus Stephen felt for Dickens himself is not easily gauged. Some small indication is provided by his reaction to Dickens' death. Writing to Anny Thackeray soon after the event, he was 'sad to hear of the death of a man of genius, which he certainly was, though his genius was by no means to my taste'.[105]

The relationship between Stephen and Thackeray, the other great literary celebrity of mid-Victorian England, could hardly have presented a greater contrast. Stephen's knowledge of Thackeray not only came through the latter's works but benefited from personal acquaintance. As first editor of the *Cornhill Magazine*, set up in January 1860, Thackeray knew Stephen as an early contributor, with 'very friendly relations' soon following both with Thackeray and his daughters.[106] After Thackeray's death a further link was formed through Leslie Stephen's marriage in June 1867 to his younger daughter Minny, who was to become a rather ingenuous but greatly appreciated correspondent of Fitzjames' during his Indian interlude.[107] It was through Fitzjames' existing friendship with the Thackeray sisters that Leslie first met his future wife, and with Thackeray's death his daughters came to rely upon Fitzjames as a general adviser on legal and business affairs.[108] Years later Fitzjames also played a role in facilitating Anny Thackeray's marriage to Richmond Ritchie by (in Leslie's words) bringing 'down his sledge-hammer upon poor Frank Cornish', Ritchie's brother-in-law, and until Fitzjames' intervention, a strong opponent of the marriage.[109]

Stephen's views of Thackeray's novels span a publishing period of nine years, from the 'Cambridge Essay' to a literary obituary appearing in *Fraser's Magazine* in April 1864. Additionally, during this period Thackeray figured in Stephen's *Saturday* reviews, both directly and incidentally along with other authors when literature in general was being picked over. Overall his high opinion[110] of Thackeray varies little. Thackeray was held up as a realist who created perfectly observed descriptions of life free of any tendency to select or manufacture facts to justify a particular stance or attitude which might please more simplistic readers. Unlike many, Stephen never viewed cynicism as too pervasive a characteristic of Thackeray's style; on the contrary, as with Balzac, it was seen as no more than astute social observation: Becky Sharp was a 'far more edifying representation than any number of saints'. Despite extensive use of the technique of the narrating and guiding author, Stephen thought Thackeray a model of self-effacement, neither approving nor disapproving of his characters and their actions. To Stephen, Thackeray's self-limitation to subjects and societies on which he was well informed was a source both of great approval and of regret: the narrowness of the range of lifestyles portrayed in most of Thackeray's novels excluded review of many large social and political realities. And some of those universally important matters which were dealt with were too often treated superficially. His handling of love is seen as rather anaemic in that 'he generally puts love in the light of an amiable weakness, which turns out happily, if at all, by chance rather than by design'. An observation which says as much about Stephen's attitude to the subject as it does about Thackeray's. References to these alleged failings and superficiality are scattered throughout a good number of other contemporary reviewers' assessments of Thackeray, with Stephen offering a substantially orthodox view.

Stephen's relative rating of Thackeray's novels was less conventional. At odds with the current consensus of reviewers (including other *Saturday* reviewers) he saw *Henry Esmond* and *The Virginians* as Thackeray's finest works. *Barry Lyndon*, however, was 'artistically' possibly the best, with its 'habitual freshness of Fielding', performing the difficult task of creating as a main character a scoundrel who believes 'himself one of the best and greatest of men', a characteristic that greatly appealed to Stephen, but which many contemporary critics found particularly hard to swallow. Elsewhere, the 'character of Becky Sharp alone was enough to make the reputation of any writer', but *The Virginians* and particularly *Henry Esmond* 'are in every respect superior to his other works except possibly "Barry Lyndon"'. For Stephen these 'historical novels' had the 'greatest weight and vigour'. However, to anticipate a vein of complaint opened up by later critics, *Vanity Fair* was ultimately not found to be an entirely satisfying meal, 'for although marvellously clever . . . when we view . . . as a whole, neither the tenderness which lies at the bottom, nor the satire which lies at the top, appear to have an adequate foundation; and both put together, leave all the great passions and strong emotions of life and vanity, unexplored and undescribed'.[111]

Good as general relations were between the *Saturday Review* and Thackeray, even he was sometimes the recipient of a public tap on the wrists in 'The Superfine's' columns. One of the best-documented occasions concerned Thackeray's excessively candid description of George IV, delivered during an American lecture tour devoted to the Georges, as 'not a man but an assemblage of stays, padding and silk stockings'. Henry Maine was roused into firing a lengthy *Review* leader at Thackeray, almost accusing him of lese-majesty, suggesting that 'it really seems as if there were no impulse too trivial, no prejudice too vulgar, no interest too sordid to overcome our sense of duty to the land which has nurtured us'.[112] Some sense of the strength of the feelings of disloyalty generated by the incident can be gauged from Stephen's own passing reference to the injudicious nature of Thackeray's remarks, made over 18 months later in a general article on 'Light Literature and the Saturday Review'. But occasionally the abrasive cocksureness of the *Review* provoked even the generally placid Thackeray. In 'Small Beer Chronicle'[113] Thackeray delivered a light but effective slap to 'The Superfine'.

It is a short while since a certain Reviewer announced that I gave myself pretensions as a philosopher. I a philosopher! I advance pretensions! My dear Saturday friend, And You? Don't you teach everything to everybody? and punish the naughty boys if they don't learn as you bid them? You teach politics to Lord John and Mr. Gladstone. You teach poets how to write; painters how to paint; gentlemen manners; and opera dancers how to pirouette . . .!

A particular recollection of Leslie Stephen provides an appropriate tailpiece to an account of Fitzjames' literary journalism and the Thackerays. Leslie recalls that in 1867, soon after his marriage to Minny Thackeray,

my excellent brother tried after his fashion (he was not very scrupulous about helping a friend in the press – or elsewhere) to do Anny a kindness by reviewing one of her stories . . . Fitzjames's article was very well meant, but he had not the light touch necessary for criticism of such delicate wares . . . I gave the article to Minny in the train as we were going to Anny's cottage at Henley . . . I remember her indignation. 'Fitzy', she exclaimed, 'does not see that Anny is a genius.'[114]

Beyond Dickens and Thackeray, two prominent authors of the time who, strangely, attracted no critical attention from Stephen were Trollope and George Eliot. Trollope was, in fact, briefly mentioned in passing, but Eliot, apparently, not at all.[115] Trollope's acres of realism received a consistently good rather than a wildly enthusiastic reception in the *Review*; Eliot was praised nowhere more highly, although this was fairly predictable for the work of a professed realist who substantially practised her critical creed. However, a private assessment of Eliot the novelist occurs in correspondence between Stephen and his sister-in-law, Emily Cunningham. Speaking of *Middlemarch* he much admires Eliot's powers of characterisation, with Dorothea's discovery of the worthlessness of Casaubon's studies singled out as of special merit.[116] Stephen and Eliot also knew each other, although not intimately. Her correspondence and papers contain a fair sprinkling of references to Stephen, revealing that their social paths crossed as common guests at dinner parties and similar occasions. He also appears to have been a very occasional tea-time visitor at the Eliot/Lewes Regent's Park residence; with an entry for May 1865 economically relating 'Kept up talk and tea from three – 7!'[117] Annoyingly, the conversational topics are not disclosed.

A later brief impression of Stephen's character by Eliot appears in a letter to Frederic Harrison in June 1873, with Eliot confessing 'a liking for him personally, and classifying men broadly as "bad and good", I should put him far within the borders of the good'. Eliot's opinion is given particular potency by its having been expressed in the context of a generally unflattering exchange of observations on Stephen's recently published *Liberty, Equality, Fraternity*; being well

disposed to Mill's philosophy, Eliot was naturally less than sympathetic to Stephen's fierce attack against *On Liberty*. Of Stephen's
opinion of Eliot little survies; although five years after her death, in a
lengthy, not to say prolix, letter to Lady Grant Duff, by then his most
regular confidante, he discusses Eliot's relationship with Lewes.
After a mixture of abstract and almost agonised moralising he
declares that for all its irregularity the liaison was a virtuous
one.[118]

As a literary critic Stephen is, perhaps, best characterised as a dilettante, yet, in many ways, a significant one. Inevitable comparison
with his brother's polished professionalism drives this home. With
the exception of his immature and narrowly conceived 'Cambridge
Essay', nowhere does Stephen make a concerted attempt to offer a
coherent body of critical principles capable of judging the artistic as
well as the social worth of novels. Such attempts were being made
particularly by the likes of Masson and Lewes from the 1850s and by
others, such as Leslie Stephen,[119] during the following decade
onwards. The 'Cambridge Essay' reveals awareness of this need, but
although collectively his reviews provide a substantial catalogue of
critical literary criteria they were never consciously shaped and
pulled together to form any unified and developed philosophy of
imaginative literature. This tendency to negativity was something
complained of by Goldwin Smith, who rather over-critically judged
both Leslie and Fitzjames to be 'hard men . . . Neither . . . set out to
construct anything, to prove anything, to establish anything.'[120]

Despite these considerable limitations Stephen merits recognition
as a prominent figure in 'higher journalism' on the mid-Victorian
literary scene, with a claim to historical significance resting principally on three grounds. As one of the earliest and most persistent
opponents of the cloying sentimentality which saturated a good deal
of the contemporary imaginative literature, he and other members
of the critical literati strenuously attempted to establish a literary
realism considered as more appropriate for the age. Stephen was also
in the vanguard of the assault on writers, and especially Dickens, for
their sometimes ill-digested and misinformed political and social
propaganda. Lastly, along with a very small cluster of other critics,
he played a noticeable part in advocating the artistic freedom of
novelists to portray in their works the whole range of human activity
including immorality, so that literature might truly educate and
enlarge human sympathies.[121]

THE HISTORICAL LITTÉRATEUR: CARLYLE, MACAULAY
AND FROUDE

At least in its opening years, the general stance of the *Saturday Review* towards literature is well demonstrated by the distinction often made between 'light literature' and 'literature'; the former being reserved for novels, the latter for purely intellectual works. In 'Literature and Society',[122] commenting on a public exchange between Thackeray and the *Westminster Review* as to the status of novelists, the *Saturday Review* acidly declared: 'We think that professional literary men do meet with quite as much recognition as they deserve, and we do not think that they enjoy a very high social position.' However, a class apart was that of the 'intellectual' writer, and high on the list of such writers were historians. For the nineteenth century was a golden age for historical writing and especially for the 'literary historian' who strove to present history as a vivid narrative drama. Macaulay, Carlyle and, to a lesser degree, J.A. Froude, as widely popular masters of this craft, all came under the close scrutiny of the *Saturday Review*, and all three were personally known to Stephen.

Stephen's friendship with Carlyle was originally through that of Sir James Stephen, who, according to Carlyle,[123] visited 'greatly often on an evening' after he was 'on ½ pay and a Cambridge Professor' (1849). Of Fitzjames' father, Carlyle, mischieviously alluding to Dickens' caricature of Sir James in *Little Dorrit*, notes 'we had a great deal of talk from him . . . always in that Colonial Office style, more or less. Colonial-Office *being* an Impotency . . . what *could* an earnest and honest kind of man do, but try and teach you How not to do it? Stephen seemed to me to be a master of that art.' According to Leslie Stephen,[124] on the occasion of Fitzjames' first visit alone to Cheyne Walk he was received by Jane Carlyle, 'who ordered him off the premises on suspicion of being an American celebrity hunter'. But the bewildered Stephen 'submitted so peacefully that she relented, called him back, and discovering his name, apologised for her wrath'.[125]

Friendship or no, Stephen's reviewing of Carlyle's works was some distance removed from any sort of fawning veneration.[126] In common with other *Saturday* reviewers, Stephen's tone was highly respectful to the great man; certainly nothing remotely resembling a standard literary lashing was ever handed out. However, as with Thackeray, there was no discernible reticence in offering direct and fundamental criticism when duty called. Stephen's carefully

measured and essentially fair assessment of Carlyle's works amounted
to one of enormous admiration for their literary and artistic power
coupled with the greatest reservations over their scientific and political
significance, both in terms of intrinsic value and influence:

Regarded as works of art we should put the best of Mr. Carlyle's writings at the
very head of contemporary literature . . . When we turn from the artistic to the
dogmatic point of view our admiration for Mr. Carlyle's is very greatly modified
indeed. . . A very large proportion of his most effective writing consists almost
entirely of the inculcation of duties and virtues which have always been
acknowledged as such . . . Mr. Carlyle is certainly entitled to the praise of having
preached on a very old subject in such a manner as to arrest the attention of his
congregation, but it does not follow that he has, as so many people seem to think,
made any wonderful discoveries in morality.[127]

More seriously, Stephen, in common with other contemporary
critics, charged Carlyle with distorting history through excessive use
of his great imaginative powers to such an extent that 'He appears to
us, on the whole, to be one of the greatest wits and poets, but the
most unreliable moralist and politician of our age and nation.'[128]

Six years later in 'A French View of Mr. Carlyle' (1864),[129]
Stephen, with cause, dismisses as futile an attempt by the French
philosopher and historian Hippolyte Taine to formulate a complete
and consistent theory of Carlyle's social and political philosophy.
Taine 'omits to notice . . . that the books which he criticises have
been published at intervals extending now over at least forty years,
during which the position, the views and even the style of their
author have undergone a great alteration'. Moreover, Taine had
completely misread the significance and impact of Carlyle in
England:

To take Mr. Carlyle as a great leader of English thought, to describe him as the
representative of a thing called English Idealism, is to misunderstand him
altogether. His thought . . . has had singularly little influence in the world . . . he
has exercised hardly any perceptible influence upon English philosophy . . .
[p]olitics, morals, theology, metaphysics, political economy [or] jurisprudence.

Carlyle was a great literary historian, but it was quite mistaken to
believe that he had 'materially influenced the main current of
thought in this country on important subjects'.

Stephen's most extended evaluation of Carlyle was published in
Fraser's during the following year. Of general literary interest are
Stephen's observations on Frederick the Great: 'When all is said and
done, it is difficult to care much about Frederick or his doings. . .
What the laws of eternal fact and nature and of everlasting justice
may be as to the power of the States of Bohemia over Erbver-

bruderungs appears to us a question as difficult as it is uninteresting',[130] a view largely sustained by other contemporary and
present-day judgements. Yet despite being unrelentingly antagonistic
towards a great deal of the substance of Carlyle's works, their marvellous packaging was hugely appreciated. For Stephen the description of 'pig-philosophy' in *Latter-Day Pamphlets* was 'Perhaps the best
and raciest explosion of this sort to be found in his works', '[P]ig-
philosophy' being Carlyle's favourite abusive term for utilitarianism.
And 'Even those unhappy persons who (like the present reviewer to
some extent) hold these pernicious doctrines, must enjoy the manner
in which they are handled.' However, the bulk of this very extensive
essay is used by Stephen to roam widely over Carlyle's political and
social theories – matters most appropriately considered when
Stephen's own views on such matters are more fully explored.

Even though Carlyle rarely bothered with reviews it is most
unlikely that he was not well aware of Stephen's public judgements
on his works; but this in no way prevented their friendship developing into one which closed with Carlyle's appointing Stephen his
executor so that 'there might be a "great Molossian dog" to watch
over his treasure'.[131] The nature of Carlyle's regard for Stephen
shows up in a codicil to his will[132] under which Carlyle gave him his
'Writing-table . . . as a distinguished mark of my esteem', adding
informally, 'He knows that I have written all my Books upon it
except "Schiller" and that for the fifty years and upwards that are
now past I have considered it among the most precious of my
possessions.'[133]

As with Carlyle, Macaulay was also first known to Stephen
through his father. Indeed Sir James owed his appointment to the
Regius Professorship of Modern History at Cambridge largely to
Macaulay's recommendation of him to Palmerston. Furthermore,
Leslie Stephen suggests that Sir James had initially been offered the
new post of Legal Member of the India Council, which, despite
Macaulay's strong counsel, he eventually declined.[134] Not long
after, Macaulay himself took up the post – one which years later was
to be occupied by Fitzjames Stephen.

In many ways Stephen's critical treatment of Macaulay keenly
resembles his approach to Carlyle: the literary power of both receiving sincere and profuse praise while the substance of their works is
regarded as suspect. Stephen's *Saturday Review* obituary of Macaulay
in January 1860 speaks of his *History* as 'that massive and wonderful
fragment glowing with enthusiastic ardour, and testifying, in its very
defects to the rush and riot of genius by which it was moulded'.

However, six years of reflection led Stephen to the more severe but not uncommon contemporary assessment that 'his silence on [morals, politics and theology] is the great weak point of his literary character, just as the extraordinary vigour and massive thought which he delighted to lavish on matters of far less importance – the scum of events – was its strong point'.[135]

The third member of this trio of literary historians was J.A. Froude. One-time editor of *Fraser's Magazine*, and Carlyle's close friend and biographer, he also formed a lasting friendship with Stephen. Froude's unhappy connection with the *Saturday Review* was through his controversial *History of England from the Fall of Wolsey to the Death of Elizabeth*. The reviewing of successive volumes of the work in the *Saturday* was marked by a steadily increasing level of abusive criticism. From 1860 onwards, such was the intensity of these attacks that the term 'Froude-slaughtering' was coined to indicate the scale of critical savagery involved.[136] Froude's persecutor was the historian E.A. Freeman, unflatteringly described by Leslie Stephen as 'a bit of a pedant... [with] a rough and uncouth surface'.[137] Naturally Fitzjames Stephen had no hand in this sport, and much later in the celebrated row over the accuracy and propriety of Froude's biography of Carlyle, Stephen was to line up alongside Ruskin and others in support of Froude's[138] 'unroofing' of Carlyle's home and the 'unveiling of his hearth'.[139]

THE *PALL MALL GAZETTE*

Between February 1861 and February 1863 Stephen's close association with the *Saturday Review* was interrupted by some form of dispute. Leslie Stephen speculated that this 'secession' was brought on by restrictions that Cook, its editor, wished to put on contributors to prevent them writing for other periodicals. With a distinct hint of sour grapes, a more colourful version of events was recorded by the *Review*'s owner, Alexander Beresford Hope:

Stephen and Maine enticed over to the Cornhill by Thackeray like a jobber as he is. Stephen who is very avid of money,[140] agreed without Cook's knowledge to write a continuous series for the Cornhill, which is obviously treason, and he got his dismissal accordingly. I think his departure will improve the religious tone of the paper for with all his ability and often rightness of view there was a self-will and frequent slyness in him which made him a very dangerous horse and a disturbing element.[141]

Consistent with Hope's references to the 'religious tone of the paper' was the claim that had it not been for his own firm control the *Review* would have 'been given to radicalism and unchurch': a comment that receives corroboration, of sorts, from Charles Pearson, a *Review* contributor and friend of Stephen. Pearson recalled that Stephen was outraged by Hope's insistence that the *Review* should give no support or endorsement to *Essays and Reviews*, the recently published controversial religious tract edited by Benjamin Jowett and Rowland Williams. To Stephen, Hope's restrictions amounted to a 'treason to free thought', making impossible his continued relationship with the *Review*.[142] It was no surprise, then, when Stephen was sought out to act as defence counsel at Rowland Williams' trial in the following December[143] for the heresy of denying the doctrine of eternal punishment. But after two years feelings had subsided sufficiently for the rift between the *Review* and Stephen to be closed.

Up to the launching of the *Pall Mall Gazette* in February 1865, he steamed along contributing mainly to the *Cornhill* and *Fraser's* in addition to the *Saturday Review*. Outside literature Stephen's most prominent journalistic topics were law, political science and religion. Beyond these, his eclecticism was indulged with a fair crop of topics ranging from 'Sceptical humility', 'Superstitution and education', and 'Luxury' to 'Keeping up appearances', 'Dignity', 'Money and money's worth' and 'Anti-respectability'.

Stephen's good fortune in being in at the founding of the *Saturday Review* was to be repeated with the *Pall Mall Gazette*. George Smith, publishing entrepreneur, founder of the *Dictionary of National Biography* and proprietor of the *Cornhill*, began publication of the new daily paper on 7 February 1865. Like its namesake in *Pendennis*, the *Pall Mall Gazette* was written by Gentlemen for Gentlemen. The friendliest of relations existed between Stephen, Smith and the editor, Frederick Greenwood, who previously had succeeded Thackeray to the editorship of the *Cornhill*. The *Gazette*'s initial team of regular writers was as formidable as that first assembled for the *Saturday Review*. In addition to Stephen, the 'heavy guns' were Henry Maine, the distinguished critics R.H. Hutton, Frederic Harrison, G.H. Lewes, and the renowned Matthew Higgins, former columnist of *The Times*. Occasional contributors included Eliot, Kingsley, Trollope, Leslie Stephen, Froude and Matthew Arnold. In the *Gazette* Stephen was for the first time regularly 'able to speak out with perfect freedom upon all the graver topics of the day'.[144]

According to Greenwood 'With the second number Fitzjames Stephen began the long fast-following series of articles which were a delight to him to write and to us no small credit to print. No journalist that I have known took so much pleasure in his work or brought more conscience to it or more eagerness and endeavour.'[145]

During the five years leading up to his departure to India, Stephen maintained a phenomenally high journalistic output. In addition to his Bar practice, legal publications and other occasional contributions to magazines and journals, Stephen produced over 800 leading articles and nearly 200 'notes' for the *Gazette*.[146] When in London, Stephen's routine was to start the day with a pre-breakfast writing session, then call at the *Gazette*'s office in Northumberland Street, just off the Strand, en route to his chambers at 4 Paper Buildings in the Inner Temple. At Northumberland Street he would either deliver his completed leader to Greenwood or write one there and then. Leslie Stephen relates that on circuit he 'kept up a steady supply of matter. I find him remarking, on one occasion, that he had written four or six leaders for the week, besides two *Saturday Review* articles. Fitzjames seemed perfectly insensible to labour; articles came from him as easily as ordinary talk; the fountain seemed to be always full and had only to be turned on to the desired end.'[147] Over the first five years of the paper's life, on average, he contributed more than half the leading articles. Small wonder that with striking similarity to T.H.S. Escott's comment that Stephen '*was* the "Saturday Review" ', Sir Courtenay Ilbert in his obituary notice observed that Stephen '*was* the "Pall Mall Gazette" in its days of vigorous youth'.[148]

The sensation of Stephen's personality so distinctively expressing itself in the *Gazette*'s columns was something which Leslie Stephen was much struck by. In the same way as he found a peculiar flavour and distinction in his brother's contributions to the *Saturday Review*, again with the *Gazette* he reflected with unconcealed admiration on Fitzjames' powerful presence as a writer. Fitzjames was immune to the embrace and anonymity of a paper's house style, and on looking back

I recognised his words just as plainly as if I had heard his voice. And although the general public had not the same means of knowledge, it was equally able to perceive that a large part of the 'Pall Mall Gazette' represented the individual convictions of a definite human being . . . Fitzjames . . . was not of the malleable variety; he did not fit easily into moulds provided by others; but now that his masterful intellect had full play and was allowed to pour out his genuine thought, it gave the impress of individual character to the paper in a degree altogether unusual.[149]

His brother's words would probably have given considerable satisfaction to Fitzjames in that he regarded leading articles as the conversation of educated men 'methodized and thrown into a sustained and literary shape'.

The lighter side of Stephen is revealed by George Smith in his recollection of one of the libel suits brought against the *Gazette*. Smith recalls the case of Dr Hunter, who sued the paper for having more or less accused Hunter of quackery over his claims for having a cure for 'consumption'. Even before the offending piece had been published Stephen had warned Smith 'if you are going to print *that* article you will hear of it!' At the action's hearing in the autumn of 1866, when it had become apparent from Lord Chief Justice Cockburn's summing up that the case was going their way, Stephen, one of the *Gazette*'s counsel, 'fairly beamed. He wrote on a piece of paper and passed to me the nursery rhyme

"Take him by the right leg
Take him by the left leg
Take him by both legs
And fling him downstairs." '[150]

Politically the *Gazette* was professedly unaligned, although insofar as it was anything, in its early years it was 'Liberal in the Palmerstonian sense', with a steady drift in the 1870s to an openly anti-Gladstonian stance;[151] a process terminated by a transfer of ownership and change of editor in 1880.[152] To Stephen a 'free press is one of the greatest safeguards of peace and order', although he frankly conceded that even the 'ablest' newspapers will 'err on the side of making too much of the interests of . . . the comfortable part of society [rather] than on that of neglecting them'.[153] Leading articles were seen as highly influential because the greatly restricted time and hectic lifestyle of most people forced them 'to live upon intellectual mince-meat [which] must be prepared so as at once to tempt the appetite and assist the digestion'.[154] But in leader-writing party political issues were considered of distinctly subordinate importance; a journalist should not attach himself to 'a particular party or cry' – party squabbling and infighting most of all discredited or devalued the standing of the participants.[155] Stephen is reported by his brother as having 'scandalised' a mutual friend 'by his attitude of detachment in regard to the party questions of the day'[156] Rather, Bentham and Mill make frequent appearances in Stephen's often densely reasoned columns; and, no doubt, this strong tendency to construct leaders from general political principles in place of the more immediately digestible invective of personalised and party knockabout did not always appeal to every type of reader. Distaste for the common realities of political life even showed through in his reactions to acting as counsel in a number of election petitions, following the 1868 general election. Such work, he wrote, would be 'thoroughly repulsive and disgusting [and] wearisome . . . even if one were paid £100 a day'.[157]

The *Gazette*'s earliest days witnessed the playing out of the final acts of the American Civil War. Contrary to the general weight of established opinion, Stephen and the *Gazette* sided with the 'justice' of the Federal cause. True to his Claphamite inheritance, the Confederates were irredeemably tarnished with the 'great sin and curse' of slavery. Predictably Lincoln was fulsomely praised not merely for his patent honesty and rectitude, but for his 'stateliness' and freedom from any tendency to 'grovel before the people who elected him'.[158] Lincoln's Vice-President, Andrew Johnson, on the other hand, was held up as an ignorant and vulgar product of American political populism. Of course the real target for such attacks was the long-running domestic debate on franchise reforms. In the politically faltering and hiccuping two years that led up to the Second Reform Act, Stephen and the *Gazette*, if not openly opposing a wider franchise, gave it little more than the most luke-warm support. Seeing it as inevitable, the *Gazette* campaigned for an end to party manoeuvring and the government's prolonged equivocations; with its positive contributions being confined to the manner and mode of changes rather than the issue of their overall desirability.[159] And although the 1867 Act was viewed as a measure of questionable wisdom, Stephen at that time did not remotely attach to it the scale of risks conjured up by Carlyle in his doomful 'Shooting Niagara'.

Stephen's association with the *Gazette* was interrupted between November 1869 and May 1872 by his appointment as Legal Member of the India Council. Characteristically, and as for Macaulay, sub-stantial parts of the outward and return journeys were filled with journalistic enterprises. Writing to his Apostle friend, and *Saturday* reviewer, G.S. Venables, he reports that between leaving england and arriving in Bombay he has written twenty articles for the *Gazette*.[160] On the final leg of his return journey, between Paris and London, he penned an article which appeared in the following day's *Gazette*. Earlier, homeward bound, Stephen amused himself with what was to form the basis of a series of articles first published in the *Gazette* during November and December 1872 and January 1873; later published together as *Liberty, Equality, Fraternity*.[161] Publication in a newspaper of articles of the nature of Stephen's great assault against Mill's *On Liberty* was quite remarkable: as Frederick Greenwood commented, 'no such work was ever seen in a daily or weekly paper'. It well demonstrates both the imaginative quality of Greenwood's editorial judgement and his great regard for Stephen's work. Moreover, the political and philosophical themes that figure so prominently in *Liberty, Equality, Fraternity* were no strangers to the *Gazette*'s leader columns. During 1872, both before and after the serialisation of *Liberty, Equality, Fraternity*, Stephen can be found leading with lively but demanding discussions on matters such as the possible incompatibility of freedom and wider suffrage or the uneasy relationship of freedom and public order.[162]

With a steady expansion of interest and effort in other directions, Stephen gradually wound down his commitment to the *Gazette* from over 100 leading articles in 1872 to a mere nine two years after. Effectively, the career in higher journalism dropped away as his enthusiasm for codification schemes gathered momentum. Even someone as appallingly industrious as Stephen could not comfortably take on this new burden alongside existing ones. And besides, the sort of prominence that came with journalistic polemics might possibly compromise the chances of successful legal and legislative ventures. Writing to Emily Cunningham, in April 1874,[163] he recognised that the 'Pall Mall Gazette is leaving me and I am leaving it'. And apart from a single article in 1878, Stephen's final contributions appeared in 1875.

3

A SCIENCE OF CRIMINAL LAW

THE PRACTICAL EXPOSITOR

Stephen, in the course of a letter to his longstanding friend and confidante Lady Grant Duff, described himself as possessing 'A good useful cut and come again intellect, which makes itself happy with quantities of cold meats and potatoes and table beer in the shape of law, and is greedily fond of pastry in the form of novels and the like'.[1] Although here he distinctly understates his mental powers, there was some truth in this moment of half-serious insight, for Stephen's instinct was very much to keep his intellectual centre of gravity close to the ground. In him philosophical speculation tended to be guided by and inclined towards practical relevance, a turn of mind that not only found vent in journalism but also very much characterised his writing on general jurisprudential questions and his particular interest in the criminal law. The intellectual temperament with which Stephen approached legal theory was, in part, Benthamite, in the sense that he was 'absolutely resolved that whatever paths he took should lead to realities, and traverse solid ground instead of following some will-o'-the-wisp through metaphysical quagmires'.[2] Benthamism's fundamental attraction was its 'reverence for facts' – its belief that the source of knowledge was observation and the systematic appeal to experience. According to Leslie Stephen, his brother's Benthamism 'was less a case of influence, however, than of "elective affinity" of intellect'.

While Benthamite thinking underpinned the general tone of Stephen's empirical scepticism, it was principally John Stuart Mill who provided him with the methodological apparatus for analysing and describing the phenomena of social behaviour and institutions.

Along with Bentham, Mill took bad institutions to be the product of bad philosophy; without the proper means of separating truth from fiction – knowledge from unsupported conjecture – reform and advance would necessarily be all the more haphazard and ill directed. In book VI of *A System of Logic* (1843), 'On the Logic of the Moral Sciences', Mill sought to devise a system of investigation[3] that could identify the regular laws which would account for the establishment, existence and changes in any society: his 'logic of the moral sciences'. The 'moral sciences', broadly Mill's term for the 'social sciences', were psychology, political science, sociology, economics and history, but not jurisprudence. Yet, although jurisprudence was not included in his *Logic*, Mill appeared, from his 1863 review 'Austin on Jurisprudence', quite clearly to regard it as in need of and susceptible to such scientific analysis.[4]

Indeed, as David Masson claimed in his 1865 Royal Institute lectures, Mill enjoyed, and had enjoyed for nearly two decades, a wide, unmatched popularity in philosophical matters: 'It is Mill that our young thinkers at the Universities, our young legislators in Parliament, our young critics in journals and our young shepherds on the mountains, consult, and quote and swear by.'[5] Like the bulk of his generation, Stephen was especially influenced by Mill's *Logic*, adopting the basic empiricist stance that to believe 'truths may be known by intuition independently of observation and experience is the great intellectual support of fake doctrines and bad institutions'. At Cambridge, Mill's work was hugely admired as the repository of 'good downright hard logic, with a minimum of sentimentalism'; so much so, that the 'stock summary answer to all hesitating proselytes was "read Mill" '.[6] Stephen's contribution to this emerging social scientific movement was *A General View of the Criminal Law of England*.[7] Published in 1863, it constituted a measured attempt, of no mean originality,[8] to place the study of criminal law amongst the empirically based social sciences and reveal its general relevance to any interested observer of society's workings; and to turn the study of criminal law into an 'art founded on science, the art of making wise laws, the science of understanding and correctly classifying large departments of human conduct'.[9] His prefatory remarks to the *General View* ensured that no reader would be left in any doubt as to the author's belief in the importance of the book's subject matter and range:

Its object is to give an account of the general scope, tendency and design of an important part of our institutions, of which surely none can have a greater moral significance, or be more closely connected with broad principles of morality and politics, than those by which men rightfully, deliberately, and in cold blood, kill, enslave, and otherwise torment their fellow creatures.

Stephen's attitude towards the growth of social scientific knowledge and its potential applications was enthusiastic but realistic. Unlike many of his contemporaries he had firmly grasped the vital distinctions between predictive and prescriptive rules. With the growth of the social sciences in the 1850s and 1860s a widespread failure to appreciate the predictive nature of social scientific knowledge fostered misunderstandings as to its implications for notions of free will, morality and law. Through a series of articles in the *Cornhill Magazine* and the *Edinburgh Review*, Stephen played a significant role (acknowledged by Mill) in demonstrating the true nature of the social sciences. In a telling graphic denial of the deterministic or prescriptive nature of social scientific knowledge, Stephen claimed that social science stood 'to its subject-matter exactly in the relation in which a map stands to the country which it represents, and that it has no more tendency to govern . . . the conduct to which it refers than the Nautical Almanack has to govern the tides'. Moreover, contrary to then current claims (particularly by Thomas Buckle) of the predominance of great impersonal forces in shaping national destiny, Stephen (along with Mill) insisted on the major role attributable to individual endeavour and ideas in producing social and political changes.[10]

Within these wider social scientific developments but at a more localised level, Stephen the jurist was, in the main, a follower of Bentham's disciple, John Austin. His broad adherence to Austinian jurisprudence reveals itself both expressly and implicitly throughout the *General View*. However, his most direct discussion of general jurisprudential questions occurs in his comparative review of Austin's *Province of Jurisprudence Determined* and Henry Maine's historic (in all senses) *Ancient Law*, both published in 1861.[11]

Although originally appearing nearly thirty years before, Austin's *Province* was not widely known at the time of its second edition. Yet despite this the analytical or 'positivist' school of jurisprudence, primarily as a result of Bentham's earlier influence, already dominated techniques of legal analysis during Stephen's formative years. The basic tenet of this legal positivism was (and is) the separation of analytical from evaluative issues; distinguishing the actuality of law from speculative or contentious questions as to its ideal or desirable state. Law and morality are distinct, although it is accepted that the latter influences the content of the former: in short, an adapted employment of Hume's[12] suggested analytical cleavage between law as it *is* and law as it *ought* to be. For the new order Bentham supplied a principle of utility that identified the nature and extent of desirable political, social and legal reforms; Austin sought to supply the system's jurisprudential structure. In the *Province* Austin attempted to settle the substance and boundaries of law by constructing a permanent and universally valid definition of 'law' and its component parts, such as 'duty', 'right' and 'obligation'; with the central definition of law being embodied in what came to be known as his 'command theory': law as a command from a political sovereign to a political subject issued under a threat of a sanction.

Overall, Stephen felt the *Province* succeeded in establishing jurisprudence as a moral science with 'as much importance as the [a priori] propositions of Adam Smith and Ricardo on rent profits and value'.[13] As a recent biographer of Austin's rightly maintains, Stephen's assessment of the general objectives of the *Province* stood alone at the time in showing 'a clear understanding of what Austin was about'.[14]   Probably closest to this early recognition of the importance of the *Province* was Mill in his 1863 *Edinburgh Review* article, part of which he devoted to discussion of a wider science of jurisprudence; although soon after the appearance of Stephen's review Mill commented that it suggested the 'writer does not seem to know much of the subject beyond what he has learnt from the two books he is reviewing'.[15] For Stephen not the least valuable feature of Austin's analytical precision was its great capacity to expose the confusing and mischievous use of the term 'law'. The scientific authority of Austin's techniques was seen as providing an investigative path free from the obscuring debris of metaphysical and natural law speculation.

We hear in every direction of laws of . . . health, the laws of progress, the laws of physiology, the laws of sociology, the laws which regulate the increase of the species, and all kinds of other laws are declaimed about as if a parliament of abstraction exercised an iron despotism over the human race.[16]

Of course, everyday common usage was neither here nor there: what was of central importance was that Austin's definitions and classifications provided the means of preventing or clearing up the analytical muddle

which is continually arising between an actual and ideal state of things; between the rights or powers protected by laws which do exist, and those which upon some principle or other ought to exist, and this confusion has given the tone to almost all the controversies upon such subjects which have agitated and still continue to agitate mankind.[17]

The publication alongside Austin's *Province* of Maine's *Ancient Law* was a landmark of a different sort, arguably doing for social science what Darwin had recently done for natural science. *Ancient Law* launched the English historical and comparative school of jurisprudence and held sway over it for a good part of the remainder of the nineteenth century. Employing investigative techniques partly borrowed from the German juristic tradition (particularly of Savigny and Jhering),[18] Maine had the objective of dislodging the dominating influence of narrow positivistic analysis and achieving a fuller understanding of legal institutions by demonstrating how they became established and grew into their present form – a study of 'social dynamics'. This was unlike the Austinian conception of 'law', which entailed identification of actual laws, their classification and simplification – a matter of 'social statics'. Law, according to Maine, originated not directly from the state but rather from basic sociative instincts in human nature, evolving along with changes in environmental influences, and to a considerable degree reflecting movements in the intellectual climate of successive societies.[19] Warmly applauding the work of his friend Maine, Stephen held that although historical and analytic methods had often been regarded as independent or even conflicting approaches, in truth they were complementary rather than inimical, for 'History without analysis is at best a mere curiosity; and analysis without history is blind, though it may not be barren.' It was a view widely subscribed to in succeeding decades by other prominent English jurists such as Sheldon Amos and Frederick Pollock.[20] Additionally, Stephen, and later Mill,[21] saw that a particular virtue of historical investigation was its practical lesson that institutions which, in modified form, still existed, originated from ideas often long since discredited. At least in this respect they were at one with Savigny, the great historical jurist of the age, who earlier had justified historical jurisprudence as the process 'whereby that which still has life may be separated from that which is lifeless and belongs only to history'.[22]

Generously Stephen saw Austin, by his extensive references to Roman law, as having to some extent anticipated Maine's historical techniques.[23] Moreover, he thought that Maine had failed adequately to acknowledge the complementary role of analytical studies in historical investigations. The conceptual definitions provided by Austin and Bentham had 'supplied a starting point for all [of Maine's] inquiries, and in fact rendered them possible'. Furthermore, Maine, he suggested, seemed to imply that charting the chronology of juristic ideas was equivalent to assessing their value, whereas carrying out such evaluations and inquiries necessitated use of the a priori analytic methods of Austin and Bentham. It was just these methods that had given direction and coherence to Maine's historical research.[24] This compatibility of the methodological approaches of Austin and Maine was optimistically seen by Stephen as opening up the way 'for a vast amount of historical investigation . . . into the modes of thought and feelings of past ages; [and by] compressing masses of detail into broad and connected statements . . . jurisprudence and morals may be studied . . . with a scientific and practical completeness unknown elsewhere'.[25]

By 'practical completeness' Stephen had in mind the utility such studies might have in establishing some sort of 'ethical teleology' or scheme of legislative objectives to be pursued as a means of achieving general human happiness. For him the respective roles of jurist and legislator were distinct and relatively clear cut. The province and task of jurists and the science of jurisprudence were to draw attention to the legal character of social problems and the limitations which the nature of human affairs places on their legislative solution: essentially an ethically neutral role. Austinian jurisprudence provided the analytical method for exposing the nature and structure of law. It did not prescribe what its content should be:

In this way jurisprudence . . . is not, strictly speaking, the science of law but the science which classifies and describes the relations with which law has to deal. Thus the first service rendered by the jurist to the legislator is to submit to him the series of alternatives placed at his disposal by the state of human affairs. [For example,] he can say you may regard a crime either as a sin against God; an injury to the abstraction called the state; an injury to the sovereign; or an injury to a private person . . . which of these views shall be taken, is a question for the legislator not for the jurist.[26]

It is a functional division bearing an obvious resemblance to Bentham's separation of the sciences of law and legislation.[27] However, at odds with these generally mainstream Benthamite sentiments was Stephen's attitude to 'subordinate legislation'. Here jurists in the form of judges had a creative legislative role to play; quite how extensive a role was envisaged is obscure, probably because Stephen was himself then uncertain. A necessary first step was to throw aside the ancient fiction that judges merely declared existing common law, something Bentham pilloried as a 'mischievous delusion'.[28] Indeed for Bentham all legal fictions, in one way or another, were the means of stealing away legislative power; fiction

played the same role in law as swindling did in trade.[29] But Stephen
proposed giving explicit recognition to the reality of judicial creative
functions. The effect of the fiction of declaratory law was 'that the
judges legislate with their hands tied, and are obliged to perpetuate
many rules which to their knowledge are absurd and mischievous'.[30] Furthermore the necessarily ex post facto nature of judicial
law-making, whereby the need to accommodate the particular case
in immediate issue dictated the form and content of a legal pro-
nouncement, severely handicapped the construction of consistent
and coherent law. The remedy for these 'evils' was to bring judicial
law-making powers 'into harmony with the legislative power of
parliament'. Such harmony could be achieved by a 'Department of
Legislation and Justice, or . . . Ministry of Justice' whose primary
functions would be to oversee legislative drafting and provide
accompanying explanatory reports; to administer an effective system
of law reporting; and, when necessary, to call for judicial declarations of the state of the law in difficult and complex areas.[31]
Suggestions of this nature appear in the 1863 edition of the *General
View*, but later extensive activities in the direction of codification
and the views expressed in that context strongly indicate that the
appeal of judicial legislation faded as his familiarity with the system
grew.

    As for a general legislative strategy and the particular content of
laws, Stephen was broadly but by no means invariably Benthamite.
Basic allegiance to Benthamite utilitarianism is expressed in his
article 'Bentham's "Theory of Legislation" ',[32] where it is agreed
that 'Bentham was perfectly justified in saying that . . . two things
only remain positive rules – the will of . . . a legislator, and the
principle of general utility . . . The object of the legislator [being]
to produce the happiness of society.' At the same time he was, of
course, alive to the endless difficulties of particularity and application in law-making that inhabited this central doctrine of utilitarianism: 'What that general happiness is which it is the object of
legislation and morals to produce [is] one immense question . . .
and is the least satisfactory part of [Bentham's] principles of morals
and legislation.'[33] But he could see no serious alternative legislative
philosophy; for him utilitarianism's fundamental recommendation
was that it gave 'one great pledge of truth . . . [it] solved real problems'.

    Lack of practical utility was just one of an assortment of reasons
that coloured Stephen's attitude towards theories of natural law:
'natural law' in the wide sense of unchanging universal standards of

justice and morality which underlie, guide and validate the content and enforceability of all laws. At one level, taking an Austinian account of 'law', notions of natural law were for him quite meaningless. Uncritically adopting Austin's definitions,[34] he accepted that the terms 'liberty' and 'justice' carried particular meanings dictated by the general theory of sovereignty rather than by nebulous and imprecise ideals reflecting common sentiments. Thus 'justice' meant in accordance with and obedience of laws, whether good or bad; 'just' meant 'generally beneficial'; and 'liberty' meant no more than the absence of restraint which a sovereign leaves to its subjects.[35] Yet, in one sense at least, 'natural law' had some meaning, and one that was of considerable relevance to the legislative process in that

the relations of men to each other are antecedent to, and to a great extent, independent of law. The aggregate of them for the time being constitute human nature for the time being; and laws which are framed on a true view of human nature may properly be called 'natural' laws. The phrase 'a natural law', is, therefore, analogous to the phrase 'a natural manner'. They mean respectively laws or manners agreeable to the nature or state of things existing at the time.

Moreover, when this account of natural law is coupled with Stephen's frequent assertions as to the actual and desirable connections between the criminal law, morality and politics, the resemblance to Bentham's views on the legislative utility of enacting popular laws becomes apparent.[36] In the *Theory of Legislation*[37] Bentham (following Hobbes) reasoned that sovereign laws from their nature must always be applications of force; where there is no force, there can be no sanction; where there is no sanction there can be no law; the use of force, as an evil, requires justification and one important factor affecting the frequency of its use was the extent to which laws conformed to natural expectations. The wider implications for political theory of alleged natural laws, such as those relating to the 'equality of men' raised by Maine in *Ancient Law*, were, as will be seen, addressed at length by Stephen in *Liberty, Equality, Fraternity*.

Stephen's attraction to Austin and Bentham was less one of a detailed and formal theoretical acceptance than of a commonality of general attitudes and perceptions. Nowhere, for instance, does Stephen appear to have expressed unease with the uncompromising rigidity of Austin's command theory as highlighted by Maine's discussions of custom law in *Ancient Law* and *Village Communities in the East and West* (1871);[38] weaknesses which had certainly not escaped commentators like Frederic Harrison[39] and Frederick Pollock.[40]

Yet crucially, Stephen did appreciate the great limitation of Austinian analysis: that, unlike serious historical studies, it could not provide a causal account of a legal system; and that legal phenomena were the product of political and social forces, only the complementary examination of which could adequately explain the creation, perpetuation and decline of legal institutions. It is an awareness that is apparent in the *General View*, and one which manifests itself even more strongly twenty years later in his *History of the Criminal Law*, and enables Stephen to manage the initially tricky feat of simultaneously straddling the competing, if not diverging, horses of the historical and analytical schools.

Stephen's contribution to general jurisprudential theory was largely limited to ably preaching the gospel of Austin and Maine; paradoxically, nothing he wrote in the broad field of jurisprudence seriously competes with the sustained power, originality and internal coherence of *Liberty, Equality, Fraternity*. His deserved reputation as *the* great English criminal lawyer of the nineteenth century rests on a combination of an untiring crusade to expound and reshape the nature, form and content of the criminal law, and a range of texts written over two decades or so. These works provide insights into all features of the criminal law: its history, the substantive law, procedure, evidence and punishment. Collectively they are a remarkable achievement, not only by virtue of intrinsic merit but also in the light of the conditions under which they were produced: all were written as part-time projects or as subsidiary enterprises to Stephen's main occupations as jobbing barrister (cum journalist), colonial legislator and, eventually, judge.

In one way or another, each book was innovatory. So much so, that in Pollock's final estimation, 'Maine, Fitzjames Stephen and Maitland renovated (if it is too much to say created) the scientific and historical study of the law of England, each in his thoroughly individual manner.'[41] The *General View* was a true pioneering attempt to bring to legal analysis an approach which revealed not merely the nature and relationship of the subject's principal theoretical elements but, additionally, succeeded in no small measure in showing the wider social scientific setting in which law might be advantageously studied. Not until thirteen years later with the appearance of Pollock's *Principles of Contract* [42] was any legal text published which sought to treat an area of law in anything like this fashion. And only after nearly forty years, with Courtney Stanhope Kenny's *Outline of Criminal Law* (1902), was a theoretical text on the subject finally published that was remotely comparable to the *General View*.[43]

Primarily written as a step towards codification of the subjects, each of the three *Digests*, on Evidence (1876), Criminal Law (1877) and Criminal Procedure (1883), was extensively applauded as a considerable feat in the art of 'boiling down' (almost Stephen's professional leitmotiv) vast quantities of diverse case and statute law to produce succinct principles of impressive accuracy and clarity. Far from a labour of love, Stephen complained their production demanded substantial reserves of endurance and the ability to cope with the 'killing' tedium of sifting and unravelling confusing source materials. It was a lead which others followed, with further digests in similar form appearing in many areas of law, Pollock's *Digest of the Law of Partnership* (1877, being the first.

A History of the Criminal Law of England[44] was the last and possibly most impressive of all his works on criminal law. As the legal historian Cecil Fifoot perceptively suggested, it is a revelation not only of the growth of law but also of the author's own 'elemental character, a self-portrait of unconscious fidelity, warts and all'.[45] Indeed, Stephen confessed to friends during its writing that the *History* had 'become more or less the plague, and also one of the great pleasures of my life', and that later on its completion he had experienced a sense of loss bordering on bereavement.[46] The three volumes, completed in 1882 and published the following year, range over the origins, growth and development of the substantive criminal law, the structure of the courts, punishment, procedure and aspects of evidence.

Its obvious originality and great advance over anything of a similar nature previously produced in the field of English criminal law ensured early and lasting recognition of the work's considerable merits, something firmly driven home by a cursory comparison with L.O. Pike's roughly contemporary *History of Crime in England* 1873–6).[47] Its shortcomings are partly a consequence of an unrealistic optimism that such a vast subject might be adequatley dealt with in the compass of even 1,500 pages or so. This misjudgement was aggravated by Stephen's, perhaps inevitable, tendency to dwell on his own interests, which resulted in an occasional lack of proportion in the treatment of certain topics. 'Offences against religion' occupy more than one hundred pages, yet the far more substantial and important subjects of theft, accomplices, conspiracy and attempt are all dismissed in a total of fewer than eighty pages. Even Stephen admitted that the organisation and mode of handling the whole subject was 'something of a jumble'.[48] The extensive comparative use of references to French and German law was certainly novel, but their rather compartmentalised insertion and the failure to absorb them into the general body of the work meant that the benefits of the technique were not fully realised. Furthermore, comparative references to other important scholarly views and opinions occur less often than might reasonably be anticipated. An instance of this practice is Stephen's preliminary reference to the 'Right to Punish'. With a touch of unscholarly arrogance he observes

Much discussion has taken place on subjects connected, or supposed to be connected, with criminal law, which I leave on one side, because it seems to be at once idle and interminable. The subject in question is usually called the Right to Punish. On what ground, it is asked and under what limitations, has society a right to punish individuals? These questions appear to me to be almost entirely unnecessary and quite unimportant.[49]

Judged by present-day historical techniques, the most restricting fault of the *History* is its general adherence to what has been described as the 'serial presentation of the shape and contents of legal concepts in order of appearance';[50] the failing of this once common approach being the inadequate emphasis given to the interrelationships of contemporary beliefs and institutions that were responsible for the law's development. Nevertheless, despite this catalogue of limitations, the *History* has been rightly judged by historians from Maitland to Radzinowicz as a 'unique work' meriting the greatest admiration, and one which is still a first book of reference and source of 'endless borrowings'.[51]

Turning to Stephen's general criminal theorising, three related areas demand particular attention for their importance as indicators of Stephen's place in the evolution of nineteenth-century criminal jurisprudence: the function of punishment and the fundamental subjective and objective conditions of criminal responsibility.

PUNISHMENT AND DENUNCIATION

Both the *General View* and the *History* were professedly written not only for the edification of lawyers but for all who were absorbed by the social and political workings of the society they inhabited. And it is likely that those elements dealing with the relationship of punishment and morality drew – as they continue to draw – a degree of attention quite disproportionate to the space devoted to them. Stephen held the unremarkable standard utilitarian view that the law, and particularly criminal law, was 'an exclusively practical system invented and maintained for the purpose of an actually existing state of society'.[52] But although, for him, the law had nothing to do with notions of absolute truths, the relationship and interaction between the criminal law and morality was still of extensive importance. Here the relevant morality was the contemporary or 'positive morality of our time and country, that which as a fact, is generally regarded as right or wrong by people of average education and sensibility'.[53] The relation of law and collective morality was of significance both to the very substance of criminality as delineated in individual offences, and for the whole institutionalised system of punishment.

Obviously the criminal law and morals were not, could not, and should not be co-extensive or completely harmonious, otherwise 'all mankind would be criminals, and most of their lives would be passed in trying and punishing each other for offences which could never be proved'.[54] Rather, he maintained, the scope of the criminal law should be limited to provable overt acts or omissions that inflict 'definite evils, either on specific persons or on the community at large'.[55] Stephen's views on the wider political implications of less 'definite evils' that the community might suffer through immoral behaviour, and whether a realm of private morality existed that was no concern of the law, are, as will be seen, forcefully ventilated in *Liberty, Equality, Fraternity*.

The coincidence between existing law and morality he saw as turning on the particular class or nature of offence: some harmonised with and closely reflected universal moral values, while others – like regulatory or trading offences under the pawnbroking or licensing laws – were remote from if not independent of morality. Furthermore, with some crimes law and morals might conflict, as in political and religious offences. The morality of punishing individual instances of political offences, such as treason or sedition, hung very much on the particular surrounding circumstances, which might be such as to make the actions either at variance or in accord with the prevailing common morality: treasonable actions against a despotic government were still treason although generally approved of by the populace, and vice versa.

Only with the category of 'gross offences which consist of instances of turbulence force or fraud' was there a vital coincidence of law and morality; although even here the legal definition of an offence could not usually completely embody common moral sentiments because of the necessity for reasonable precision capable of practical application. For Stephen, the criminal justice system was largely founded on and sustained by the commonality of moral attitudes towards these 'gross' offences. Here 'law and morals powerfully support and greatly intensify each other . . . ; the reflection of punishment by law gives definite expression and a solemn ratification and justification to the hatred which is excited by the commission of the offence'.[56] In effect, law and morality reinforce each other; even the process of making an immoral act a crime will in itself elevate or intensify the level of moral opprobrium with which the act is regarded.[57] Although pungently turned out, this particular belief was by no means original, with a pedigree stretching back at least to Hobbes, and on through to modern times via jurists contemporary with Stephen, such as Sheldon Amos[58] and Frederick Pollock.[59]

The coincidence of common morality and 'gross' criminality also meant that the law served as a conduit for the controlled use of general community hatred of highly immoral behaviour. Failure by the law to deal with serious violations of current morality generated a distinct risk of direct community reaction leading to an erosion of the law's general standing. Moreover, far from seeing anything inherently wrong with it, Stephen believed it was highly desirable that criminals should be 'hated, that the punishments inflicted upon them should be so contrived as to give expression to that hatred, and to justify it so far as the public provision of means for expressing and gratifying a healthy natural sentiment can justify and encourage it'.[60] Such feelings were

deeply rooted in human nature. No doubt they are peculiarly liable to abuse . . . but unqualified denunciations of them are as ill-judged as unqualified denunciations of sexual passion. The forms in which deliberate anger and righteous disapprobation are expressed, and the execution of criminal justice is the most emphatic of such forms, stand to the one set of passions in the same relation in which marriage stands to the other.[61]

Where or how, then, does Stephen fit into the nineteenth- and twentieth- century philosophical divide on the function of punishment? It is a fundamental tenet of utilitarian theories of punishment that crime is to be prevented with the minimum amount of suffering on the offender's part; for punishment in itself is an evil and must, therefore, be used as economically as possible. The infliction, or threat, of punishment prevents crime either by incapacitation, reform or deterrence. Contrastingly, retributive theories of punishment look to ensuring that the offender receives his just deserts; he should in some way 'pay' for his actions; his guilt must be purged or cancelled out by a proportionate or appropriate measure of punishment. In Kantian logic, punishment is intrinsically right for a breach of the law – it is an end in itself. It was a philosophy the essence of which Carlyle vigorously voiced in 'Model Prisons' (1850), taking the opportunity to flay all advocates obsessed with deterrence and reform – that 'mournfullest twaddle' of those 'preaching and perorating from the teeth outward!'[62]

The nineteenth century, and especially its latter half, saw the general issue of the justification for the nature and practice of judicial punishment fuel frequent public debates. A year after the publication of the *General View*, for Henry Maine 'All theories on the subject of Punishment have more or less broken down; and we are at sea as to first principles.'[63] At the time that Stephen was preaching his denunciatory theory, Bentham and Austin's utilitarian accounts of punishment (as considerably refined by Mill in *Utilitarianism* (1863)[64]) were under seige from the 'British Idealists', an influential school of 'neo-Hegelian'[65] retributivists of which F. H. Bradley and T. H. Green were early and leading figures. Both Bradley in *Ethical Studies* (1876)[66] and Green in *Lectures on the Principles of Political Obligations* (1881) provided differing but basically retributivist justifications of punishment. For Bradley the vital characteristic of punishment was its power to 'cancel' or 'annul' guilt, whereas Green, rather than fully adopting the Hegelian notion of annulment of guilt, instead saw punishment in terms of payment for the wrongdoer's violation of another's rights.

Although Stephen quite explicitly believed in the importance of the 'direct' prevention of crime by 'fear, or by deterring' the offender,[67] less clear was whether he saw the denunciatory element in punishment as preventive or retributive in complexion. Was Stephen arguing in some corrupted Kantian fashion that the gratification of vengeance was a proper end in itself? Or did he believe its legitimacy lay in its ability to strengthen the system of criminal justice through the reinforcement of moral attitudes or enhancement of respect for the system, both of which would amount to a utilitarian justification?

Pinning down his position requires a careful exercise in separating the substance of an argument from its often highly robust packaging. George Eliot perfectly captured the nature of this obscuring polemical characteristic of Stephen by describing it as a ' "rimbombo" of rhetoric (like the singing into big jars to make demon-music in an opera) which is the disease of Carlyle's later writing'.[68] Shorn of this rhetoric many elements of his discussions suggest an essentially utilitarian stance.[69] His dissent from the opinion that individual offenders should not be punished any more than necessary to deter others likely to commit crimes is based on such an argument's failure to take account of the 'efficiency' of punishment in supporting or reinforcing 'the general detestation of crime'.[70] This is distinct from the mechanism of conscious deterrence by the fear of a penal sanction, being rather the notion that subconsciously generated inhibitions are built up by the universal practice of punishment, for 'whatever effect the administration of criminal justice has in preventing the commission of crimes is due as much to [the detestation of crime] as to any definite fear entertained by offenders of undergoing specific punishment'.[71]

Even in passages where Stephen urges that greater severity of punishment is desirable in some areas, his accompanying references to Bentham and the need to avoid excessive and indiscriminate severity so as to be 'effective' and not self-defeating all tend to look towards utilitarian justification.[72] Indeed the morally educative function and force of punishment received some recognition from Bentham, although he saw its relevance being limited to the case of 'exemplary' and 'popular' punishments.[73] Consistent with and illustrative of Stephen's general views on the severity of punishment was his attitude to the use of the death penalty. The unique quality of capital punishment, he believed, was not so much its power to deter directly as its ability to provide the ultimate expression of society's detestation of the serious criminal conduct involved, which 'is the greatest safeguard against crime'.[74] And although broadly supporting a more discriminating use of capital punishment, he strongly opposed abolitionist campaigns of the 1860s, claiming there to be as 'much moral cowardice in shrinking from the execution of a murderer as in hesitating to blow out the brains of a foreign invader'.[75]

In sum, for Stephen a vital element in suppressing crime was general social attitudes both to criminal behaviour and the whole institution of the criminal law; failure to reflect natural human feelings, including those of vengeance and hatred, in the substance and practice of punishment would undermine the system's necessary popularity whilst dangerously diminishing hostility towards criminality. The ultimate result of such a weakening of this vital relationship of law and common morality would be a potentially catastrophic loss in the general cohesiveness of society.[76]

One of Stephen's earliest fellow travellers, if not followers, was

Sheldon Amos. In the *Science of Law* (1874),[77] Amos accepted that one function of punishment was the re-establishment of 'the violated order. It asserts in emphatic terms outraged authority', and although Amos makes no reference to Stephen's *General View*, it is inconceivable that he was unfamiliar with what was by then a widely known work. However, unlike Stephen, he did not advance the argument so far as to suggest that social solidarity is also reinforced by punishment. One who did, and rather more important and closer to Stephen, was the French sociologist Emile Durkheim, who similarly believed that the maintenance of 'social cohesion' was punishment's 'true function'. In his *Division of Labour in Society* (1893), he argued 'It is necessary then that [the criminal law] be affirmed forcibly at the very moment when it is contradicted, and the only means of affirming it is to express the unanimous aversion which the crime continues to inspire by an authentic act which can consist only in suffering inflicted upon the agent';[78] law symbolises social solidarity and punishment is an expression that the sentiments of this collectivity have not changed. Although he had clearly read Maine,[79] quite whether Durkheim was aware of Stephen's theory is impossible to say. But Stephen's high standing as a jurist in France, as evidenced by his 1888 election to the Institut de France, makes the possibility of such awareness less than fanciful.

Stephen's denunciatory theory has survived through to present times. The philosopher A. C. Ewing in *The Morality of Punishment*(1929), after discarding retributivistic and more orthodox utilitarian justifications, puts forward a broadly denunciatory account of punishment, although, unlike Stephen, he suggests that the emphatic condemnatory nature of punishment not only produces a long-term educative effect but also acts directly as a deterrent force. Beter known is the evidence offered to the Royal Commission on Capital Punishment by Lord Denning, former Master of the Rolls.[80] For Lord Denning, punishment 'for grave crimes should adequately reflect the revulsion felt by the great majority of citizens [and the] ultimate justification of any punishment is not that it is a deterrent but that it is the emphatic denunciation by the community of crime'. Lord Denning may have out-Stephened Stephen, for in referring to the 'ultimate justification' he comes close to expressing a purely retributivistic attitude. Moreover, unlike Stephen, Lord Denning implies that, for serious offences at least, deterrence is subordinate in importance to denunciation. But by far the most substantial and recent advocacy of what bears a strong resemblance to Stephen's theory comes from the American jurist Hyman Gross.

In *A Theory of Criminal Justice* (1979), relating to what he sees as a 'deterrence theory', Gross maintains that

> punishment for violating the rules of conduct laid down by the law is necessary if the law is to retain a sufficiently strong influence to keep the community on the whole law abiding and so to make possible a peaceable society . . . there is punishment for violation of these rules in order to prevent the dissipation of their power that would result if they were violated with impunity.[81]

Stephen's denunciatory theory undoubtedly carries strong 'intuitive plausibility', and, as the frequency with which variants appear in judicial statements suggests, it enjoys widespread contemporary credibility with the judiciary as well as with some academics. It is, though, a credibility which must partly rest on the difficulty of disproving its claims concerning long-term social or moral education; and, at the same time, it is this lack of the practical means of verification that has always been the theory's most suspect and vulnerable feature.

THE CULPABLE MIND

With the *General View* and the *History* Stephen provided an analysis of the specific subjective and objective elements basic to all criminal responsibility which amounted to the most coherent and systematic account of the theory of responsibility to emerge from any common law country during the nineteenth century; and a theory which, with varying degrees of success, incorporated or reflected much of the period's social, scientific and philosophic concern with tying responsibility to the behaviour of free-thinking and free-acting agents. His treatment of the subject falls into two broad parts: the mental and the external elements of liability, commonly labelled *means rea* and *actus reus* respectively.

Stephen's approach to the issue of *mens rea*, or mental culpability, reveals an interesting (though not inconsistent) contrast with his highly moralistic account of the criminal justice system and the nature of punishment. Rather than claim, as was frequently done at the time, that the imposition of liability was subject to a principle requiring personal moral culpability of some sort, Stephen recognised its desirability but made no attempt to give such an expectation the status of a presumptive principle. At the heart of the belief, widespread amongst nineteenth-century commentators and judges, that criminal responsibility always required some kind of individual moral culpability, was the great legal maxim *Actus non facit reum nisi mens sit rea* – taken to mean an act was not criminal unless accompanied by a guilty mind. Stephen dismissed the maxim as highly misleading in that it implied 'laudable motives' prevented an act from being criminal; or that immorality was essential to liability. With a touch of irreverence doubtless calculated to catch the eye, he suggested that

legal maxims in general are little more than pert headings of chapters. They are rather minims than maxims, for they give not a particularly great but a particularly small amount of information. [The truth of the matter was that the maxim meant] no more than that the definition of all or nearly all crimes cointains not only an outward visible element but a mental element, varying according to the different nature of different crimes . . . [and] the only means of arriving at a full comprehension of the expression 'mens rea' is by a detailed examination of the definitions of particular crimes, and therefore the expression itself is unmeaning.[83]

The dispute over the existence or otherwise of a general principle of *mens rea* was of considerable practical significance in the latter half of the nineteenth century, for regulating the period's great industrial, commercial and municipal development was an enormous volume of social legislation, including that touching public health and safety in industrial activity. Through legislative neglect rather than calculation, the offences created to enforce observance of these regulated practices were, more often than not, lacking any clear definition of the offender's mental culpability – whether or not, for example, a defendant needed to have intended the prescribed harm or have had knowledge of certain facts, or even whether any fault element at all was essential to liability. In the approach to this expanding problem of statutory interpretation the notion of a general principle of *mens rea* was of distinct importance and frequently enlisted by the judiciary when construing individual offences. According to Lord Chief Justice Cockburn (in 1861),[84] the principle of *mens rea* was the 'foundation of all criminal justice'; a sentiment liberally distributed through an abundance of other nineteenth-century judicial pronouncements. However by the mid 1870s, even with non-regulatory offences,[85] the judiciary were coming to accept that there was no automatic importing of *mens rea* into statutory offences where no reference to it existed, but that the broad policy objectives of such legislation ought to enter into the process of statutory interpretation.

Stephen's guarded attitude towards endorsing any general principle or presumption of *mens rea* was the likely product of tension between two beliefs: one was that the criminal law was and should generally be underpinned by moral disapproval; and the other, that the exact content or form of this relationship could only be deter-

mined on the basis of individual offences, and that settling
definitional requirements of particular crimes could not usefully be
aided by the judicial invocation of any general principle of *mens rea*.
His long-standing hostility to the notoriously widely operating
'felony-murder' rule is an outstanding illustration of this opposition
to the use of imprecise generalised notions of mental culpability.

Under the 'felony-murder' rule killing in the course of a felony
was murder even though the fatal injury might have been inflicted
without intention to cause serious harm or even accidently.
Stephen attacked the rule as a 'monstrous doctrine'[86] and 'open to
great objection',[87] making murder more a matter of chance than
culpable calculation. His Homicide Bill of 1872–4 and Draft Criminal
Code of 1878 represented enlightened attempts to eliminate this
form of constructive culpability and restrict murder to cases where
the accused had at least foreseen the likelihood of serious harm
resulting from his actions.[88] Stephen's degree of commitment to the
reforms in the 1872–4 bill vividly stands out on every page of the
bill's Select Committee Report[89] covering his oral evidence. The
Committee, whose principal witnesses included Baron Bramwell
and Mr Justice Blackburn, two of the period's most acute and
distinguished judicial minds, must have been aghast at Stephen's
performance:

'Amazing' is the only proper epithet to apply to the vigour and tone of Stephen's
reply to the criticisms of the Bill made by [Bramwell and Blackburn]. Seldom in
the history of English Law can a member of the Bar have dared to shake occupants of the Bench so thoroughly as he did on this occasion. He was not satisfied
with trouncing them separately; with a devastating show of logic, he truculently
and sarcastically used the one to knock the other down.[90]

Stephen's analysis of the mental element in criminal responsibility
in many ways represented a theoretical *via media* between the
more moralistic interpretation of the doctrine of *mens rea* on one
side, and, on the other, the objective theory of criminal liability, of
which the weightiest advocate was the American jurist and later
Supreme Court judge Oliver Wendell Holmes. Holmes, a friend
of Frederick Pollock and Leslie Stephen, published his *Lectures on
the Common Law* in 1881, eighteen years after Stephen's *General
View* and two years before the *History*. Holmes and Fitzjames
Stephen met in June 1866, the first time whilst dining at London's
Political Economy Club, when the 37- year-old Stephen 'went to
sleep at the table', although later they walked the streets and
enjoyed a 'good talk'.[91] Subsequent meetings occurred in the summer
of 1874 during Holmes' second European visit.[92] They had much in

common: both wished to see a scientific reorganisation of the law; both were staunch empiricists implacably opposed to the natural law theories offered by Kant and Hegel.[93] Yet despite this no friendship ever developed.

With his *Lectures*[94] Holmes implicitly challenged Stephen's orthodoxy by arguing that the criminal law had repudiated the former primitive rationale of personal fault and, as a matter of reality and desirability, the criminal law did not and need not consider the mental state of the defendant. Instead, the law was on the 'high-road to an external standard' where liability was founded on the objective non-individualistic moral norm of the 'average man, the man of ordinary intelligence and prudence'. According to Holmes,

Acts should be judged by their tendency under known circumstances not by the actual intent which accompanies them . . . the *mens rea*, or actual wickedness of the party is wholly unnecessary, and all reference to the state of his conscious-ness is misleading if it means anything more than that the circumstances in con-nection with which the tendency of his act is judged are the circumstances known to him.

The primary basis of his attitude was neither the practical dif-ficulty of establishing mental states, nor any adherence to be-haviourist views, but rather one of social theory. Holmes was, in this respect at least, an unrelieved utilitarian;[95] the criminal justice system was overwhelmingly preventive in nature, and even if 'fitness of making [a person] smart' was an element, it was very much a subsidiary one. However (unlike with Bentham, Austin and Stephen), the notion of deterrence does not easily fit within his sys-tem, where personal calculation or deliberation have little to do with liability; for if a defendant does not need either to foresee or intend an action or a consequence, how effectively can he be deterred from causing the criminal harm? Holmes contended that there could be no reason why the law should concern itself with the mental state of the defendant because it was the outward conformity to criminal law standards that counted: that was the evil which the criminal law sought to avoid. 'Blameworthiness' was the foun-dation of liability, but the external rather than its mental dimen-sion.[96] Whilst not denying that the law should correspond as far as possible with the 'actual feelings and demands of the community, whether right or wrong . . . if only to avoid the greater evil of private retribution', he maintained that the law should not reflect this collective morality by requiring particular mental states. Instead the most effective and 'perfectly proper' way of increasing general welfare by preventing criminal harm was through the imposition of external standards of behaviour, even though, accepting the full rigours of social utility, it meant individuals being sacrificed for the common good.[97]

Without expressly referring to him, it is very likely that Stephen had Holmes' theory of objective liability in mind when discussing in the *History*[98] 'modern writers of eminence [who] have been in the habit of regarding criminal law as being entirely independent of morality'. Although making no direct and systematic attempt to evaluate Holmes' arguments, Stephen provides the ammunition which destroys much of the credibility of the general theory of objective liability. For instance, it was true in 1881, in both England and America, that objective liability existed, but only on a restricted scale in crimes such as manslaughter and regulatory or strict liability offences; with additional manifestations of objective liability being the defences of provocation and self-defence. But, as Stephen easily demonstrated, the Anglo-American system did, as it still does, in theory and practice require specific forms of mental culpability for most serious offences. Moreover it is a scale of personal culpability that is also very much reflected in the nature and severity of individual penalties. Holmes' central error was to assume that taking account of personal mental culpability was necessarily incompatible with the utilitarian aim of reducing criminal harm; and that to require some form of mental culpability inevitably assigned a retributive function to punishment. Bentham had indeed maintained that the mischief of an act is measured by its consequences, but an actor's mental state was also germane to both the deterrent effect of the threat of punishment[99] and the question of 'secondary harm' caused – for example, the extent of alarm generated by the act. Therefore because of its relevance to the utility of punishment, the subjective nature of an act ought to be taken account of in determining an actor's degree of criminality.[100] Such claims aside, more convincingly, subsequent jurists[101] have argued that Holmes presented a false antithesis, for it is quite possible to justify a requirement of subjective culpability on the independent grounds of justice and fairness, while at the same time effectively supporting the general objective of reducing criminal activity.

Curiously Holmes offered no express response to Stephen's opposing account of criminal responsibility, although he did venture a general observation on the *History* in a letter of 1883 to Frederick Pollock, noting that 'My opinion of him as a law writer does not grow higher as I read this or his former books. He knows nothing, it seems to me, of the scientific aspects of the history of law, and he is to my mind rather a model of a fine old 18th century controversialist rather than a philosopher.'[102] Holmes' view of Stephen, as revealed in his correspondence with both Pollock and later Laski, is at best neutral with a slight tilt towards the hostile. Stephen's gratuitously provocative description, in *Liberty, Equality, Fraternity*, of America as the home of 'self-satisfied, and essentially slight people'[103] could well have taxed Holmes' powers of objectivity. Surprisingly, nowhere does he concede in the slightest the intellectual debt undoubtedly owed to Stephen. And, bearing in mind Holmes' early extensive use of and borrowings[104] from the *General View*, his remarks on the *History*, together with the implicit assessment of earlier works, are distinctly less than generous. Whether or not Holmes was in any way justified in placing Stephen's talents in the eighteenth century, and notwithstanding the later proliferation of strict liability offences, Holmes certainly lost the debate over *mens rea* to Stephen.

THE VOLUNTARY AGENT

The other broad area of Stephen's account of the general conditions of criminal responsibility largely relates to problems of voluntariness of action, and the effects of 'compulsion' or insanity on liability. Stephen recognised that attempts to construct a juristic definition of voluntary action arose from the need to provide a unifying rationale for the exceptions to the general rule that people were accountable for their criminal actions. Why, for instance, were reflex actions or automatic behaviour, such as those of an epileptic or a sleepwalker, excused not simply on the basis of the absence of the necessary mental element but rather on the grounds of there being no voluntary act?

In common with most criminal theorists, his treatment of the question owes much to Austin, who in turn was indebted to the theory of human action propounded by the Edinburgh philosopher Thomas Brown in his *Enquiry into the Relation of Cause and Effect* (1818). Brown and Austin[105] characterised a human act as no more than a muscular contraction caused by a 'volition' or act of will. It is this antecedent element of 'will' or 'volition' that was the kernel of voluntariness. Without it muscular contractions or motions were involuntary – indeed, strictly, they were not even acts. 'Will' was the basic essential link between mind and body required for all criminal responsibility. Only human 'will' could respond to the threat of punishment; only 'willed actions' could be morally culpable. However, Stephen, in company with other adherents of Austinian notions, failed to address the theory's inability to account convincingly for omissions and everyday actions such as writing and talking, deficiencies which have led to the more persuasive argument that the ability to control and produce desired bodily actions is a superior criterion for determining voluntariness.[106]

In Anglo-American jurisprudence of the nineteenth and first half of the twentieth century differences that arose in respect of theories of action and voluntariness were generally not directed towards challenging the essential validity of the Austinian analysis of them. Holmes' definition of an act is as narrow as Austin's – an act is no more than a willed muscular contraction.[107] For both the expression 'voluntary act' was tautological as without will or voluntariness there was no legally recognised act, just an occurrence. Although for Stephen the basis of voluntariness was also the presence of 'will', the additional element of 'intention' was engrafted on by him as a precondition of all liability. [108] Thus a sleepwalker's actions are willed and voluntary but are not 'intentional'. This puzzlingly suggests that 'will' to Stephen was something which could be exercised unconsciously. The element of 'intention' appears to relate to the co-ordination or directing of muscular action towards the occurrence of bodily conduct; it is the directional aspect of 'will'. This attempt at a more complete and sophisticated model of voluntary action added nothing useful to Austin's original version; and, indeed, by introducing the notion of a willed but unintended action, Stephen further muddied the waters.

A different aspect of his examination of voluntariness involved the legal relevance of certain forms of 'compulsion'. Compulsion in the sense of forced physical manipulation by one person of another of course precluded voluntariness. But could action compelled by a threat of physical harm be similarly regarded? Stephen believed it would not and should not be, because even in extremis, when acting under the threat of death, an individual is still exercising the ability to choose whether to act in a particular way. In graphic terms, typical of Stephen: 'A criminal walking to execution is under compulsion . . . but his motions are just as much voluntary actions as if he was going to leave his place of confinement and regain his liberty.' For compulsion in this sense meant no more than being faced with 'a choice of evils' and 'to escape what he dislikes most he must do something which he dislikes less'.[109] His conclusion that the nature of any possible defence of what is now termed 'duress' was not based on the notion of involuntariness is consistent with the current English view that the true basis of the defence is one of the law making 'a concession to human frailty' that excuses liability.[110]

In the nineteenth century the law, although unclear, did concede the existence of a defence of duress; Stephen, however, was firmly opposed to any such defence 'on the grounds of expediency'. Invoking Hobbes' initial premises but parting company with his conclusions, he argued that the whole criminal justice system was

a system of compulsion on the widest scale. It is a collection of threats of injury to life, liberty and property if people commit crimes. Are such threats to be withdrawn as soon as they are encountered by opposing threats? . . . Surely it is at [this] moment when temptation to crime is stronger that the law should speak most clearly and emphatically to the contrary . . . If impunity could be so secured a wide door would be opened to collusion, and encouragement would be given to associations of malefactors.[111]

To avoid this supposed serious risk of abuse of any defence of duress he believed the most appropriate way of reflecting the obviously diminished moral culpability of such an actor was in mitigation of punishment.[112]

As for 'compulsion by necessity', Stephen was similarly out of sympathy with both the law and general legal opinion of the time. In contrast with duress, here the law did not recognise a general defence, but Stephen thought it should. Taking the classic illustration of shipwrecked sailors in a boat unable to carry them all, he maintained that should any murder charge follow from a struggle for survival 'it is impossible to suppose that the survivors would be subjected to legal punishment', for although 'self-sacrifice may or may not be a moral duty, . . . it seems hard to make it a legal duty'. As a solution to the formidable difficulties of settling in advance the appropriate cases where a defence of necessity should exist, Stephen somewhat lamely proposed that they be 'adjudicated upon by a jury afterwards'. Surprisingly he failed to explain what it was in the nature of the defences of duress and necessity that required a different treatment for each; why it was more 'expedient' to recognise a defence of necessity than one of duress; or why there was a significant moral distinction between action under the threat of death where the source is human rather than where it was not.

Considering the attendant difficulties, Stephen's advocacy of a defence of necessity was decidedly dogged; it appears in clause 23 of his own 1878 Draft Criminal Code Bill, but is absent from the 1879 Draft Code produced by Stephen in collaboration with his fellow Code Commissioners.[113] Reaffirmation of support for the defence in the *History*[114] demonstrates he had undergone no permanent conversion in 1879. Ironically, in 1884 what has remained probably the leading English authority on a possible defence of necessity was heard. In *Dudley and Stephens* the classical shipwreck example became reality with the defendants being charged with murdering a cabin-boy so that his body could provide the means for their survival. At their trial the jury, rather as Stephen had predicted, felt unable to deliver a normal verdict, and, unusually, referred the issue back to the judge. Headed by Lord Chief Justice Coleridge, a bench of five judges eventually (effectively) rejected the principle of a necessity defence as being 'dangerous, immoral and opposed to all legal principle', though the decision is, as Stephen acknowledged, pregnant with ambiguity.[115]

Considerably more substantial and significant in Stephen's examination of the 'conditions of responsibility' is his analysis of the 'Relationship of Madness to Crime' in the *History*.[116] This lengthy discussion, headed by its impressive bibliography of medical works, reveals both a strong and, for a lawyer, unusually well-informed interest in the subject; although this was hardly surprising, for the subject represented a rare example of the intersection of legal, moral, social and scientific questions with clear practical as well as theoretical implications. At the time, his treatment of this issue was juristically unrivalled and, even if clearly dated in parts, still offers many valid insights.

Since 1843 the main basis of Anglo-American law relating to insanity and criminal responsibility has been the M'Naughten Rules. Formulated by a special gathering of fourteen judges, the rules were a response to a request by the House of Lords for a definitive statement of law; the request had been prompted by Daniel M'Naughten's acquittal on a charge of murdering Sir Robert Peel's secretary whilst suffering from the paranoid belief that he was being persecuted by the Tories. In substance, the rules establish a defence of insanity if an accused's reasoning was (at the time of the alleged offence) so impaired by 'disease of mind' as to prevent him from knowing 'the nature and quality of the act he was doing, or if he did know . . . , that he "did not know he was doing what was wrong" '.

Dissatisfaction with the rules grew in proportion to the nineteenth-century expansion of scientific knowledge of human psychology and psychiatry. Predictably it was between the medical and legal profession (including the judiciary) that the division of opinion was deepest and most hostile; the extent of such hostility being evidenced by Mr Justice Stephen's candid admission of concern over the possible effect on his objectivity of 'the harsh and rude' attacks 'upon a small body of which he is himself a member'. The nub of this dispute he saw as involving confusion over what were legal and what were medical issues, with doctors claiming that the question of legal responsibility in cases of insanity was a scientific one which judges and lawyers perversely determined by employing narrow and antiquated notions of cognition. Set against this was the legal profession's counter-claim that doctors were attempting to dictate what mental maladies ought to excuse an accused, which was not a question of medicine but of law. True as he believed this to be, Stephen strenuously objected to the treatment of 'medical writers'

in courts of justice, even by judges, in a manner which, I think, they are entitled to resent. Sarcasm and ridicule are out of place on the bench . . . particularly when they are directed against . . . a man of science who, under circumstances which in themselves are often found trying to the coolest nerves, is attempting to state unfamiliar and in many cases unwelcome doctrines, to which he attaches high importance.[117]

Earlier in the first edition of the *General View* Stephen's treatment of the M'Naughten Rules had been largely uncritical, although he did briefly touch upon the question of 'irresistible impulse' or 'impulsive insanity', noting that if an act were to be 'irresistible' the accused should be acquitted because the act would not be voluntary: an a priori argument and part of the general question of what constitutes voluntariness rather than a supposed derivative of the M'Naughten Rules. The effect of twenty years' reflection was his vastly different handling of the subject in the *History*. Here Stephen, after a demanding (for reader and writer) excursion through the current theories[118] of clinical mental abnormality, offers a full and technically sophisticated account of the relationship between cognitive and volitional incapacity. Opposing the common interpretations of the M'Naughten Rules, Stephen argues that they could (or at least should) be construed as extending beyond cognitive incapacity to include volitional malady so as to cover 'impulsive insanity' or 'irresistible impulse'. This conclusion he based on a theory of the integrated personality: that serious mental disease necessarily impaired all principal aspects of the personality; and that serious impairment of the ability to understand and reason inevitably affected the power of self-control – and vice versa. In all essential respects, it is rationale of 'irresistible impulse' that enjoys widespread current credibility amongst both psychiatrists and jurists.[119] In Stephen's words:

I understand by the power of self-control the power of attending to general principles of conduct and distant motives and of comparing them calmly and steadily with immediate motives and with the special pleasure or other advantage of particular proposed actions . . . [T]he absence of the power of self-control would involve an incapacity of knowing right from wrong [because] [k]nowledge and power are the constituent elements of all voluntary action and if either is seriously impaired the other is disabled. It is as true that a man who cannot control himself does not know the nature of his acts as that a man who does not know the nature of his acts is incapable of self-control.[120]

Stephen's advocacy of a more enlightened approach to insanity failed to produce a dividend for many years. His attempts to widen the scope of the M'Naughten Rules through judicial reinterpretation[121] were almost totally ignored by the English courts. Nor was he any more successful in persuading fellow Code Commissioners to incorporate the reforming provisions of his 1874 Homicide Bill or 1878 bill in the 1879 Draft Code.[122] Although already established in the French and German Penal Codes, the general climate of English legal opinion was unreceptive to such a widening of the conditions under which mental incapacity might excuse criminal liability. Not until the enactment of the first Infanticide Act of 1922 and the Homicide Act of 1957 did English law accept two forms of a defence roughly based on the diminished powers (as distinct from the absence) of self-control. Even here, though, they are confined to cases of what would otherwise be murder, and reduce liability to manslaughter, being equivalent to what Stephen recognised as situations where the 'power of self-control was diminished by insanity' in such a way as to make it appropriate to convict yet punish less severely. But nothing in the modern law approaches recognition of Stephen's far-reaching conception of 'irresistible impulse' which, like the M'Naughten Rules, was potentially relevant to any offence and completely excluded criminal liability. Only in the last decade or so has anything resembling such extensive reforms found favour with any officially appointed body in England.[123]

Overall, Stephen's impact on the development of common law criminal jurisprudence was considerable: he was probably the single most formative influence of the nineteenth century. Few of the fundamental elements of general criminal theory were not enhanced by exposure to his penetrating scrutiny and remarkable expositional skills. His stance was markedly progressive and, occasionally, far-sightedly radical. Yet for all this certain features of Stephen's theoretical discourses are uncomfortably murky, and in some cases there may be more than simple want of clarity or even completeness – more seriously, there may be irreconcilability or inconsistency of argument.

One such issue is his attitude towards general notions of justice. His response to Austin's clinical definition of 'justice' has all the appearance of not going beyond the level of analytical acceptance. What cannot be hazarded with any confidence is whether Stephen's utilitarianism was full-blooded enough to overcome any instinctive scruples that might be involved in sacrificing individuals for the general good. His belief in the importance of criminality reflecting immorality, and the criminal justice system acting humanely is capable of two constructions: either belief in justice for, so to speak, justice's sake; or, out of utilitarian calculation, that a system must enjoy general approval to be credible and most effective. In *Liberty, Equality, Fraternity*[124] Stephen concludes that 'the justice and expediency of a law are simply two names for one and the same thing'. Of course, exactly what is 'expedient' turns on what is meant by 'utility'. As will be seen, in Stephen's case defining this is no simple thing. Certainly in his general and evaluative account of the conditions of criminal responsibility the explicit justification of utility is not offered as the underlying reason for the existence of these conditions. Similarly, his assessment of the whole system of criminal procedure is well leavened with expressions, such as 'dignified tenderness' and 'compassion', all of which tend to promote the impression that their author has in mind something beyond pure utility.

A further and even more telling area of ambivalence relates to Stephen's views on the interaction of law, public opinion and collective morality. Exactly whose opinions are being invoked in the frequent references to public sentiments? When his cousin Albert Dicey later spoke in *Law and Public Opinion*[125] of law being the expression of public opinion, he had in mind the opinion of 'those citizens who . . . have taken an effective part in public life'. For Walter Bagehot it was the much less exclusive views of the 'ignorant multitude'.[126] For Stephen the 'positive morality of our time and country' was that which was 'generally regarded as right or wrong by people of average education and sensibility'.[127] Quite which social groups or classes came within this description is obscure; whether they were restricted to the professional classes or extended to the lower middle classes of clerks and traders, or even artisans, Stephen fails to specify. Most awkward of all, did this representative section of society include the same group of people whose literary taste and general outlook he so scathingly dismissed as that world of 'smug little tradesmen of shallow half-educated minds, with paltry ambitions, utter ignorance of history and philosophy, [and] shrinking instantly from all strenuous thought'?[128] To exclude the working classes and the bulk of the middle classes would be to rest an institution on its acceptance by and credibility to little more than an elite; a conclusion which hardly chimes well with the general vox populi emphasis in Stephen's account of the criminal justice system. Consistency, if not complete coherence, seems to require that 'people of average education' included the wider elements of the population equipped with 'half-educated minds'.

Yet anyone with only a fragment of Stephen's reforming inclinations would not, it might be assumed, wish to rely upon the narrow and unimaginative prejudices of such people; what then is the law's potential as a morally (and politically) educative force or agent? How far might it be used to lead and mould opinion rather than follow it? Stephen acknowledges that 'Law may be intended to supplant or to correct morality'[129] and that 'Even indifferent or virtuous acts will come to be condemned by moral sentiment . . . if the law condemns them.'[130] But what determines when popular opinion should be overriden? Presumably adherence to the general principle of utility would suggest that the law might often be compelled to flout current general opinion as the price of achieving wider or longer-term, and ultimately popular, objectives. It is through such ambivalence that Stephen constantly eludes confident classification as either a utilitarian, believing that moral soundness is determined by what conduces to the general welfare, or a social relativist, who looks to the broad consensus to reveal sound morality.

4

'LAW LIVING AND ARMED' [1]
THE MECHANISM OF ENFORCEMENT

The English criminal justice system was seen by Stephen as 'generous, humane, and high minded . . . , a great practical school of truth, morality, and compassion . . . , eminently favourable to individuals'.[2] Institutional jingoism of this order greets the reader throughout Stephen's writings on the system, appearing quite as often in his earlier as in his maturer works. But this almost emotional enthusiasm was reserved for matters of general theory and principle; the substantially uncritical devotion certainly did not extend to the functioning realities of the institution. Rather, he was a persistent and trenchant critic of its many inadequacies for the greater part of his adult life. It was a dissatisfaction largely inspired by the ramshackle and diverse obscurity of the sources of law; by the antiquated and unscientific approach of the rules of evidence – the life blood of the trial process; and by the casual laissez-fairism surrounding the prosecutorial process. In Stephen's lengthy career as the system's self-appointed professional critic and reformer, these areas of concern manifested themselves most distinctly in his attempts at codification; in his reformulation of the general theory of evidence; and in his efforts to formalise the responsibility for prosecutions and to regularise the provision of legal representation of prisoners. Yet for such a heavy and sustained drain on his time and resources the immediate and concrete return was pitifully small. Of the many ventures in Stephen's life those aimed at eliminating some of the worst quirks and downright injustices of the criminal justice system must stand high amongst his small crop of failures and disappointments.

CHAOS AND CODIFICATION

A prominent and constantly recurring theme in Stephen's writing on English law was its appallingly disordered state, even after the improvements effected earlier in the century. It was a state of affairs produced over the ages by the irregular, unsystematic accretion of statute and case law, characterised by Mill as involving 'the deposit of each successive period, not substituted, but superimposed on those of the preceding'.[3] Stephen's Indian experience heightened a longstanding devotion to bringing about changes in the content and particularly the form of the criminal law. For him, in common with Bentham and Austin, recasting the law into a clear form was an essential first stage in a general and continuing process of scrutiny and, where necessary, reform. Addressing the Social Science Association in November 1872,[4] following his return from India, he confessed that for him 'to compare the Indian Penal Code with English criminal law is like comparing cosmos with chaos'.[5] And for the remainder of the decade no small part of Stephen's considerable energies was engaged in the ultimately abortive struggle to purge the criminal law of a vast quantity of its superfluities and bring order into this chaos. Events which in this particular period of the history of law reform – or non-reform – present a depressing story of failure through a fatal combination of political equivocation and indifference, pure chance and judicial opposition: a formula which had successfully sunk many earlier reforming movements.

The antecedents of both Stephen's hopes and the forces which would prevent their fulfilment stretched back through various nineteenth-century reformist phases to Bentham. A foundation assumption in Bentham's utilitarian calculation was that the law, and especially the criminal law, could only regulate each individual's behaviour if it were readily comprehensible to all. As Austin put it, 'the law had to be knowable'.[6] The reality was that the organically developed comon law mixed with piecemeal legislation had produced a body of law the mysteries of which could hardly be penetrated even by lawyers, who found it 'less fatiguing to be proud of their past than to know it'.[7] With forgivable exaggeration, Bentham likened judicial law-making to training a dog: 'When your dog does anything you want to break him of you wait till he does it and then beat him.'[8] A wholesale remodelling of the law was, therefore, seen, at least by utilitarian radicals, as a pressing necessity. Bentham's codification programme involved no half-measures; both substantive and procedural law were to be formulated on the twin bases of utility and logic. Complexity was the 'nursery of fraud', simplicity the 'handmaiden of beauty, widsdom, virtue – of everything that is excellent'.[9] Nothing outside the codes was to be law. The creative judicial role was seen as a prime example of arbitrary power and, necessarily ex post facto law.[10] Ambiguities and deficiencies in the new codes were to be remedied by the legislature, never through the 'chance medley of litigation' and judicial discretion.[11] Such were the essential premises of Benthamite codification. Bentham, though, operated in a rarefied and detached environment; as the penal reformer Sir John Romilly wrote to Etienne Dumont,[12] 'Bentham leads the same kind of life as usual in Hendon, – seeing nobody, reading nothing, and writing books which nobody reads.' Awkwardness of style and arrangement of much of Bentham's output provoked Hazlitt's suggestion that 'His works have been translated into French – they ought [also] to be translated into English.'[13] There was also a grain of truth in Hazlitt's jibe that Bentham's name was 'better known in Europe' but 'best of all in the plains of Chile and mines of Mexico'.[14] But however politically and practically unrealistic many of his schemes were, their enormous contribution towards creating an intellectual climate sympathetic to detailed scrutiny and reform is hardly disputable.[15]

One of Bentham's most important standard-bearers was the great Whig, Lord Brougham: a major political force in the passing of the first Reform Act, a fierce anti-slavery campaigner and a co-founder of the *Edinburgh Review*.[16] In 1833 Brougham, as Lord Chancellor, was instrumental in the appointment of five 'learned, industrious and well paid' commissioners of Benthamite hue (one of whom was John Austin) eventually charged with the task of a complete principled examination of the criminal law.[17] With fresh commissioners appointed in 1837 and 1845, a total of thirteen reports and draft legislation covering all indictable offences and procedure had been produced by 1849.[18] After a succession of failed bills, in 1853 the Criminal Law Amendment Bill (No. 1), dealing with offences against the person and based on commission reports, encouragingly received a second reading in the House of Lords and was then referred to a select committee. At this stage the view of the judiciary was sought, with their solidly hostile response to what they saw as the undesirable inflexibility of the proposed measures being published in February 1854.[19] An accurate contemporary measure of the quality and nature of this rejection is provided by an unattributed comment in the *Edinburgh Review*,[20] since identified as being of Brougham's authorship.[21] Scathing in his criticism of the judiciary, Brougham accused them of putting their own convenience and self-interest (in not having to master new laws) before the public benefit that the introduction of such reforms would bring. As for the quality of their answers: 'Satire, sarcasm, irony and something akin to petulance, each play their several parts; and almost the only weapons that are sparingly used are accurate facts and logical reasoning.' Furthermore, it was clear that many judges had not bothered to read carefully the code provisions but 'have pronounced an unhesitating judgment on many portions of [it] and have thus . . . fallen into errors quite as glaring as those they hastily imputed to the work on the merits of which they were deciding'.[22] The bill was not reintroduced.[23]

Early evidence of Stephen's reforming inclinations shows up in his *Saturday Review* articles of February and October 1856,[24] written in an atmosphere principally coloured and informed by the failure of the 1853 bill. Stephen likened the piecemeal reforming legislation in England to cutting holes in shoes wherever they pinched. With only slight exaggeration he characterised the declaratory theory of judicial law-making as being decided 'not with reference to what would be most expedient now, but by . . . conjecturing what it ought to have been under the Plantagenets'. The unpredictability and obscurity of much of the law and legal procedure were comparable to 'a huge heap of building materials', the safe traversing of which was largely determined by chance:

By signal good luck you may avoid holes, and pick your way in safety over the heterogeneous mass; but if you are not very careful of your steps some treacherous clause will give way, and you may disappear into all sorts of pitfalls and caverns – you may fall from statute to statute, all touching, but none meeting your case – till your descent is arrested by some antiquated monument of mediaeval legislation or by the unfathomable mysteries of the common law.[25]

As for the frequently vaunted virtues of the common law, they were in truth not so much 'principles' but 'the source of some of the most arbitrary and irrational of all our legal rules'; moreover, 'an unwritten law may be an instrument of oppression, not because of its inherent treachery, but simply because it is not written'.[26]

His direct participation in English law reform and codification began [27] with a request by the Attorney-General, Sir John Coleridge, in the autumn of 1872 for Stephen to draft an Evidence Code on the lines of his recently enacted Indian Evidence Act. But, according to Stephen, the bill, because of pressure on parliamentary time, could not be introduced until the end of that particular session in August 1873; and the absence of clear practical and political need ensured that it was not revived in the following session. The career of the Homicide Bill of 1872 was rather longer lived. Following his membership of the Royal Commission on Capital Punishment, which reported in 1866, the radical John Bright approached Russell Gurney, a Member of Parliament and Recorder of London, with the object of drafting a bill that would, amongst other things, substantially restrict the scope of the offence of murder. Gurney in turn recruited his cousin, Stephen, to assist in preparing the bill, the drafting of which was completed in August 1872.[28]

The bill was first introduced in 1872, and then reintroduced in 1874. Though not pessimistic, from the outset Stephen was only too keenly aware that the odds were against success. Not long after his return from India, in June 1872, English government appeared to him, compared with the relative political simplicity of India, to be a 'centre of indifference . . . [and] the queerest conceivable hubble-bubble, half energy and half impotence, and all scepticism in a great variety of forms'.[29] On its reintroduction, the bill predictably went before a Select Committee (chaired by Robert Lowe) that eventually declared the project unsatisfactory, feeling that the enactment of a penal code should commence with principles of more general relevance and applicability and, furthermore, that the changes in the law incorporated in the bill ought to be referred to the House, not a Select Committee.[30] Failure of yet one more reforming exercise on such grounds openly annoyed many, with the *Law Times* declaring the reasons as 'ingenious but cowardly'.[31]

As in 1853, the views of the judges had been canvassed, and again the response had been unfavourable to change. In the vanguard of judicial opposition was Lord Chief Justice Cockburn, whose main objection was that partial codification required the unsatisfactory practice of incorporation of references to non-code sources of law; an argument fielded by Cockburn as Attorney-General to undermine the chances of the wider reforms of the 1850s. But as Stephen was later to point out, the suggested dilemma of codification en bloc or no codification was a false one; a staged transition during which common law concepts could be phased out was quite feasible. Yet the centrepiece of explicit judicial antagonism, as before, was the expectation that codification would remove the valuable flexibility of the common law to meet both the exigencies of social change and novel situations. Additionally, it would not be unfair to suggest, as Stephen expressly did, that fears for the general standing of the judiciary were probably just as potent a motivating force in creating opposition. Giving evidence before the Select Committee over two days Stephen pulled no punches, insisting it was quite natural that judges should feel an 'irresistible temptation' to work with a familiar system of unwritten rules rather than accept the upset and restrictions of change. However, 'this quasi-legislative authority should not be left in the hands of the Judges' in its present form.[32] Quite what degree of judicial discretion Stephen did favour became more apparent later in his final and most extensive codifying efforts of 1879.

Stephen's experiences with the Evidence and Homicide Bills convinced him – as Bentham and Austin[33] before him believed – that private enterprise could provide some of the initial impetus for reforms. This was at least part of the motivation behind the production of his *Digests* on evidence (1876) and criminal law (1877); the hope that they could serve as the basis of codifying measures as well as enhancing his reputation as a skilled legal draughtsman and expositor. Working on the *Digest* of criminal law Stephen describes the confusing unsystematic layout and arrangement of the standard text, *Russell on Crime*, as 'enough to make one go crazy'. Of this authoritative three-volume, almost 2,700-page work, Stephen acidly notes later in his *Digest*, 'The cases as they stand in Russell are like the stores at Balaclava in the winter of 1854–1855. Everything is there, nothing is in its place, and the few feeble attempts at arrangement which have been made serve only to bring the mass of confusion to light.'[34] Equally unflatteringly frank was his assessment of *Archbold*, the advocate's bible: 'to try to read it is like trying to read a Directory arranged partly on geographical and partly on biographical principles'.[35]

Early in 1877[36] Stephen wrote to the Attorney-General, Sir John Holker, proposing the preparation of a draft code for the greater part of the substantive and procedural criminal law, of which his *Digest* would serve as the basis. Holker was taken with the idea and by August[37] Stephen had received instructions from Lord Chancellor Cairns to draft bills for a penal code – followed by instructions for a procedural code. The following May the Criminal Code (Indictable Offences) Bill was introduced into the Commons by the Attorney-General. More than codification, the bill contained many distinct reforming elements, including changes in the law of homicide, larceny and evidence and the establishment of a Court of Criminal Appeal.[38] After its second reading the bill became the subject of a Royal Commission composed of Lord Blackburn, Mr Justice Barry, Lord Justice Lush and Stephen.[39] The Commission sat from November 1878 to May 1879 'daily during nearly the whole of that time, and discussed every line and nearly every word of every section'.[40] But parliamentary time ran out because, according to the

Attorney-General, of the more pressing 'condition of public business',[41] and the bill received no third reading. The bill was
reintroduced in February 1880; however, its remaining momentum
was effectively dissipated with a change of government in April.
Criminal law reform being a frail craft at the most favourable of
times, the bill was predictably 'wrecked in an Irish storm in the
Grand Committee of the Commons'.[42] And although in the following year Gladstone himself indicated to the House his willingness to take up the code, it was not salvaged.[43]

The fate of Stephen's great codification effort was chiefly settled
by the conjunction of two factors: latterly the Irish question's domi-
nation of parliamentary time and initially the carefully timed opposition of the Lord Chief Justice. On the same day as the Commons'
Report was published and, it seems, without having sight of it, Lord
Chief Justice Cockburn wrote to Sir John Holker a letter containing 'Comments and Suggestions in relation to the Criminal Code
(Indictable Offences) Bill'. As in the 1850s and in 1874, Cockburn
oozed sympathy for the general notion of codification whilst feeling compelled to express opposition to what he regarded as the
undesirable practice of partial codification. But both Holker and
Stephen were going to have none of it, revealing in private correspondence a clear and firm resolve not to be thwarted. Writing on
8 July 1879, Holker tells Stephen 'I think nothing of Cockburn's
criticisms and I do sincerely hope you may be able to hold him up
to ridicule', at the same time promising to make a strong effort to
pass the bill in the next session. Stephen's feelings spill out in a letter
to his friend Lady Grant Duff.[44] Discussing his forthcoming public
response to Lord Cockburn, Stephen confides:

I have tried to make it profoundly respectful, and even flattering to his vanity,
but I have had to struggle with what in sermons is called the Old Man – . . . this
monster of vanity, and of pure pique at not being made a member of the Criminal
Code Commission,[45] has written what he probably regards as an effective attack
on the Code. He has succeeded in proving nothing, except that wounded vanity
will induce him to take a great deal of trouble and that he has really never given
any serious thought to this subject or attempted in any way to understand its
difficulties. I hope however I have been able to keep this old man in the sense of
corrupt human nature, pretty quiet – and to heap the Old Man Cockburn (he is
in his 88th year I believe) with all the respect which certainly is due to him, both
as the High Priest for the time being, and as one of the very cleverest fellows
(with all his faults) in all England.

Stephen's detailed and measured reply to Cockburn was published
a few weeks later in the *Nineteenth Century* of January 1880. His

appointment as a High Court judge a year before provided the public with the rare spectacle of an open clash of judicial opinion on principles of legislation and the role of the judiciary.

Cockburn's prefatory suggestion that the report and bill showed 'signs of haste' stung Stephen into brusquely pointing out that the bill represented 'not the labours of a Commission of four members which sat for five months but the judgment formed by such a Commission on a work adopted by the Attorney-General after most careful study, and on which I had expended a considerable part of the work of twenty-five years'. However, the gravamen of Cockburn's criticism was of a substantive nature, succinctly summarised by Stephen:

The Bill laid before Parliament is neither complete nor perfect. It is not perfect because it is open to many objections in detail. It is not complete because it does not express the whole of the criminal law, but leaves still existing many statutes which create offences, and some parts of the common law relating to matters of excuse and justification. If, therefore, the Code should become law, it would not contain the whole of the criminal law. There would still be statutory offences in other Acts of Parliament unrepresented by it and there would still be a certain quantity of common law which would be contained in no authoritative written document. The result is that the so-called Code is not properly entitled to that designation, which ought to be reserved for Acts reducing to writing the whole of the body of law to which they apply.[46]

As for the charge of imperfections of detail, Stephen saw this as 'a reason not for rejecting but for amending [the bill]', adding with a touch of unconcealed anger that

Parliament in enacting a Code must, from the nature of the case, place much confidence in someone. They were asked in this instance to place that confidence in a bill introduced by an Attorney-General who had had exceptionally wide experience in criminal cases, and approved by the Lord Chancellor; a bill representing the labour of many of the best years of my life; a bill which had been revised and settled by three eminent judges. I think something more than imperfection ought to be proved against such a work before it is rejected on that ground. It ought to be shown to be a failure, to be so faulty that no confidence can be placed in it or so incomplete as not to deserve the title which it claims.[47]

Cockburn's weightiest objection was that the Code was not autonomous and independent of all common law principles and was, therefore, untenable as a comprehensive code. Stephen admitted the fact but denied the conclusion, arguing that it was not inconsistent to remove ill-defined common law offences whilst retaining common law defensive principles of justification and excuse. Essentially, he thought that the flexibility to deal with occasional unpredictable instances of injustice should be retained but that the common law's potential for arbitrary and oppressive use should be removed:

The only result which can follow from preserving the common law as to justification and excuse is, that a man morally innocent, not otherwise protected, may avoid punishment. The worst result that could arise from the abolition of the common law offences would be the occasional escape of a person morally guilty.

In contrast,

The continued existence of the undefined common law offences is not only dangerous to individuals, but may be dangerous to the administration of justice itself. By allowing them to remain, we run the risk of tempting the judges to express their disapproval of conduct which upon political, moral, or social grounds, they consider deserving of punishment by deciding upon slender authority that it constitutes an offence at common law; nothing, I think could place the bench in a more invidious position, or go further to shake its authority.[48]

The House of Lords' exhumation of the offences of conspiracy to corrupt public morals in 1961[49] and conspiracy to outrage public decency in 1972[50] are particulary prominent examples of the sort of judicial activity Stephen had in mind.

The Code Bill's failure marked a miserable end of the greatest single criminal law codifying effort attempted before or since in England.[51] In addition to the more tangible and specific causes of the bill's failure, other less easily definable forces also played their part. Certainly, many influential officials from the Lord Chancellor's department and Home Office regarded Stephen as something of a self-seeking interloper, attempting to interfere with the existing gradual and staged pace of change. Such feelings were a likely consequence of Stephen's own private initiatives having upstaged high officialdom's collaboration in the work of the Statute Law Committee, which, since its establishment in 1868, had been steadily inching towards the possibility of codifying reforms. Moreover, the Committee had, prior to Stephen being asked to draft his Code, commissioned its own report and for this job, rather than Stephen, had chosen the lesser-known barrister Robert Samuel Wright.[52] Although owing much to personal connections,[53] the choice was also prompted by reservations over the quality of Stephen's draughtsmanship and his general tractability. Doubtless the Committee's failure[54] to turn the Lord Chancellor against Stephen's enterprise ensured a degree of official coolness that is unlikely to have enhanced the Code's chances of enactment.

Beyond such matters the whole legal profession was just beginning to settle down to the radical new procedures introduced by the recently enacted Judicature Acts, and the prospect of further innovation on the scale of a new penal code must have proved singularly resistible to most.[55] More seriously, unease existed amongst the judiciary and legal profession over this particular current of change, perceived by many as threatening the judiciary's established role. Fears of this order were at two levels. At a practical level it was suggested that the elasticity of the common law enabled the courts to respond to demonstrable social needs, case by case; that the floating principles of the unwritten common law represented the accumulated judicial wisdom of centuries honed on practicalities. More abstractly, it was felt by some that the transition from organically developed law, like the common law of England, to a codified state of law 'implies a mental and almost moral metamorphosis of the whole legal intellect of the country'.[56] It was a theory of identification of national spirituality and culture with the form of its law borrowed from the German philosopher and jurist Savigny, later described by Maitland as the 'man who is nervously afraid lest a code should impede the beautiful processes of natural growth'.[57] For Savigny law was to be found, not made; most reform could evolve by the silent internal forces of a country's national consciousness being exercised through its legal profession;[58] a substitution of 'organism for mechanism'.

Stephen's sound response to grand national metaphysics of this order was that codification did not arrest the law's development and that, in general, reform more properly lay with Parliament; furthermore, that the 'elasticity' of the common law is 'a form of expression which conceals a power vested in human beings by describing it as a quality inherent in a collection of words';[59] and lastly, that in any case much of the so-called 'elasticity' was far from elastic in nature and bound the judiciary quite as tightly as any statute. Pollock, whose deep common law instincts were not the most natural allies of codification, found Stephen's position the most convincing. Pollock saw in the common law great benefits of ethical refinement and adaptability[60] but, as he admitted in a letter to Oliver Wendell Holmes,[61] 'Stephen met the supposed scientific objection with (as I think) the right answer: that laws exist not for the scientific satisfaction of the legal mind, but for the convenience of the lay people who sue and are sued.' At the time Holmes himself was lukewarm towards ideas of such codification.[62]

The 1879 Code Bill had proposed to restrict any judicial power to create or extend liability whilst leaving untouched the ability to prevent the imposition of liability, whether through unexpressed notions – such as a possible defence of necessity – or general principles (maxims) 'too indefinite to be stated in the form of categorical propositions, but which are useful guides [for example] in the interpretation of statutes'. Fears that the nature of English law along with the standing and function of the judiciary would be substantially transformed were misconceived. The removal of the limited potential to develop existing offences by sharpening and converting their definitions into statutory form was no more than a progressive and formal regularisation of the *de facto* judicial role of the late nineteenth century. However, that said, there must remain a lingering doubt over Stephen's long-term expectations, for in places he appears to countenance the further erosion of the creative element in the judicial function as codes became better established and legislatively refined: 'The nearer we are able to approach a complete codification . . . the less frequently will there be occasion to resort to the use of such maxims.'[63] Taken at face value such an attitude was hardly sympathetic to the indefinite continuation of a significantly creative judicial role or to the existence of common law principles, and no great distance from that much favoured by Bentham. Yet, though seeing a limited role for judicial creativity, Stephen was no adherent of the 'formalism' which took law to be essentially a 'deductive science of principles',[64] for as much as anyone he was alive to the inseparable relevance of political and social factors in law-making.

On a broader plane, what might be called 'national forces' of the kind which propelled countries such as France and Germany towards codification in the nineteenth century were absent from the English political consciousness. In these countries codification was more than a means of achieving national unity: it also had clear symbolic significance.[65] It was a dimension of codification that had not escaped Stephen, but for him it was moral as much as political. In an age of rising scientific knowledge and correspondingly increasing religious scepticism he believed a criminal code could constitute a powerful collective moral statement able to reinforce common feelings against criminality; something that

would represent nothing less than the deliberate measured judgment of the English nation on the definition of crimes and on [their] punishments . . . that judgment representing the accumulated experience of between six and seven centuries . . . The criminal law may then be regarded as a detailed exposition of the different ways in which men may so violate their duty to their neighbour as to incur the indignation of society . . . I think that there never was more urgent necessity than there is now for the preaching of such a sermon in the most emphatic tones. At many times and in many places crime has been far more active and mischievous than it is at present, but there has never been an age . . . in which so much genuine doubt was felt as to the other sanctions on which morality rests.[66]

EVIDENCE AND THE LOGIC OF RELEVANCE

In December 1875, Stephen as Professor of Common Law at the Inns of Court, chose the law of evidence as the subject of his first course of lectures. Admittedly[67] it was a choice partly determined by the hope of capitalising on the considerable efforts expended in preparing the draft of the abortive 1873 Evidence Bill, but, practicalities aside, evidence was something that Stephen clearly found of intrinsic interest. His principal contributions to the subject are found in the *General View*, the *Introduction to the Indian Evidence Act* (1872) and the *Digest of the Law of Evidence* (1876), with most theoretical speculations being confined to the first two works. The *Digest*, written primarily to provide a concise account of the law for students, practitioners and possible code purposes, is a remarkable product of compression and clarity, demonstrating considerable novelty in the arrangement and classification of a vast and sprawling subject. As Stephen candidly complains in the *Digest*'s introduction, 'The labour bestowed upon it has, I may say, been in an inverse ratio to its size.'[68]

All of these works display a high level of understanding of the intricacies of the law coupled with a sharp awareness of the many latent theoretical difficulties lurking within it. Stephen's thinking was inevitably strongly conditioned by Bentham's mammoth efforts in this area, particularly his five-volume *Rationale of Judicial Evidence*[69] (edited by J. S. Mill in 1827) and Dumont's translation of the *Treatise on Judicial Evidence* (1825). Stephen compared the effect of the *Rationale* to 'a shell bursting in the powder-magazine of a fortress, the fragments of the shell being lost in the ruins which it has made'; the main objective of the attack being to show that 'rules tending to the exclusion of evidence must be pernicious – something which, subject to exceptions, Bentham proved with immense advantage to the cause of truth and justice'.[70] Equally influential, in a reactive sense, was the unwieldy bulk of the *corpus* of the rules of evidence, with overwhelming standard works of reference that consisted of 'thousands of pages and refer to many thousand cases', rendering the law highly inaccessible, not to say virtually impenetrable, to any student of the subject. As with substantive criminal law, Stephen's concern was not simply to achieve a concise and evaluative exposition of law and principle, but also to expose and reformulate the subject's elusive and disputed theoretical basis.

Yet despite great dissatisfaction with its unsystematic form and theory, unlike Bentham, Stephen was, with certain strong exceptions, broadly content with the substance of the law of evidence. For Stephen the substantive law was 'full of the most vigorous sense, . . . the result of great sagacity applied to vast and varied experience'.[71] Partly through his deep distrust of what he saw as a self-aggrandising judiciary and legal profession – 'Judge and Co' – Bentham's revolutionary proposals entailed eliminating practically all rules of evidence and substituting a principle of universal admissibility; although legislative guiding 'instructions' or 'rules' were to be given.[72] Technicality in the law, as well as suiting professional self-interest, indiscriminately excluded much valuable evidence, so diminishing the chances of conviction. Indeed Bentham, in contrast with Stephen, did not in any real sense provide a code, but rather a great wealth of arguments, propositions and principles upon which a working code might be constructed. And although Stephen frequently acknowledged the reforming impetus set off by Bentham which brought an 'immense advantage to the cause of truth and justice',[73] at the same time, he judged him 'too keen and bitter a critic to recognise the substantial merits of the system he attacked'. For him, Bentham failed to take adequate account of the vital function performed by the law of evidence in trying 'to prevent fraud and oppression in their worst form, to keep out prejudices which would be fatal to the administration of justice'.[74] Moreover, abandoning the system of exclusory rules would see courts overwhelmed by 'floods of irrelevant gossip and collateral questions'.[75] Bentham lacked realism because 'he had not the mastery of the law itself which is unattainable by mere theoretical study, even if the student is, as Bentham certainly was, a man of talent, approaching closely to genius'.[76] Put crudely, Bentham was the conceptual radical while Stephen was the practical innovator.

Turning to the process of reasoning underpinning judicial evidence,[77] Stephen was much taken by the analytical and expositional usefulness of logic (particularly of J. S. Mill's system) in revealing the inferential nature of evidence. In the *General View* he demonstrated this syllogistic basis of evidential reasoning:

Men found in possession of stolen goods soon after thefts
are generally the thieves [major premise]
B was found in possession of a stolen watch soon after the

theft [minor premise]
Therefore B has on him a mark frequently found in
thieves.[78] [conclusion]

Of course, as Stephen recognised, crucial in all syllogistic reasoning is the accuracy and precision of the major premise, because
'The probative force, or weight of evidence depends to a great extent upon the degree of confidence with which [a judge of fact] is
prepared to affirm the truth of the general rule and the clearness
and fullness with which it is expressed.'[79] And he was under no illusion either that logic could determine whether individual items
of evidence were true or were to be believed, or as to whether the
degree of probablity of guilt established against a defendant was
beyond all reasonable doubt. These were questions for subjective
assessment – of 'prudence . . . not . . . of calculation . . . The only
way of measuring the weight of evidence is by seeing what effect it
produces', that is whether 'it induces 12 men . . . to say [they] are
satisfied of the truth of the proposition to which [the evidence]
affirms'.[80]

In the *General View* logic is used purely as an explanatory or
descriptive account of the process of evidential analysis. Earlier
works of evidence, beginning with Sir Geoffrey Gilbert's *Law of
Evidence*, published in the mid eighteenth century, had employed
Locke's probability theory to produce a formula for the weighting
of evidence; Stephen, like Bentham, thought such theories defective.[81] However, Stephen's views on evidential theory developed
significantly between publication of the *General View* and the *Introduction to the Indian Evidence Act*; and with this development logic
assumed a more prescriptive emphasis. The Indian Evidence Act[82]
introduced his theory of relevance, the roots of which are firmly
planted in inductive/deductive reasoning: what is a relevant fact is
determined inductively from general experience particularised and
tested by syllogistic means. According to Stephen's 'classic'[83] definition of relevance:

The word 'relevant' means that any two facts to which it is applied are so related
to each other that according to the common course of events one either taken by
itself or in connection with other facts proves or renders probable the past,
present or future existence or non-existence of the other.[84]

The doctrine of relevancy was the means by which Stephen
sought to produce a central articulated 'scientific' rationale for the
admissibility of evidence. Before this, the only acknowledged general principle of admissibility was the 'best evidence rule' ('the best
that the nature of the case will allow'),[85] the clearest early develop-

ment of which is found in Gilbert's treatise. Despite the intervening and antagonistic (to Gilbert's theory) presence of Bentham, the theory's strong influence permeates standard works of Stephen's time, such as those of John Pitt Taylor and even William Best's Benthamite-inclined *Principles of Evidence*. For more than a century the best evidence rule had generated little light but rather extensive confusion and misunderstanding.[86] With the objective of releasing evidence's theoretical basis from the stranglehold of the best evidence rule, Stephen advanced his principle of relevancy as being the true general foundation of admissibility:

The great bulk of the law of evidence consists of negative rules declaring what, as the expression runs, is not evidence. The doctrine that all the facts in issue and relevant to the issue, and no others may be proved, is the unexpressed principle which forms the centre of and gives unity to all these express negative rules. [To say something is or is not evidence] . . . means that one fact either is or is not considered to furnish a premise or part of a premise from which the existence of the other is a necessary or probable influence – in other words, that one fact is or is not relevant to the other. When the inquiry is pushed further and the nature of relevancy has to be considered in itself, and apart from legal rules about it, we are led to inductive logic, which shows that judicial evidence is only one case of the general problem of science – namely, inferring the unknown from the known . . . The logical theory [of which] was cleared up by Mr. Mill.[87]

The contemporary reception of Stephen's theory was initially favourable. Maine, in his *Fortnightly Review* article 'Mr Fitzjames Stephen's Introduction to the Indian Evidence Act',[88] enthusiastically endorsed Stephen's conclusions on the central function of relevancy: 'a theory of judicial evidence which seems to me more nearly correct than any hitherto given to the world by a lawyer'. It was left to James Bradley Thayer of Harvard to expose the shortcomings of relevance as a comprehensive explanatory and unifying theory.[89] Thayer, an almost exact contemporary of Stephen, adopted in his highly regarded historical study, *A Preliminary Treatise on Evidence* (1898) the, more or less, modern view that logical relevance is *a* fundamental basis of admissibility, but not the sole one: 'Admissibility is determined, first, by relevancy – an affair of logic and experience . . . , second, but only indirectly by the law of evidence, which declares whether any given matter which is logically probative is excluded [on additional policy grounds].'[90] In other words, Stephen failed to make explicit the distinction between logical and legal relevancy; that logic alone does not (and cannot) determine what evidence should be regarded as both material and admissible; and that relevance in itself cannot supply an adequate explanation for the range of key exclusionary rules, such as that against hearsay or character evidence.[91] For Thayer, Stephen's great enterprise was 'a tour de force' yet flawed,[92] showing that even for Stephen 'it is impossible to take the kingdom of heaven by force'. Stephen had been mistaken, but it was, as Pollock would have it, 'a splendid mistake'.[93]

Beyond such grand theorising two particular features of the rules of evidence that attracted Stephen's consistent criticism concerned the admissibility of confessions and the competency of witnesses.

In much the same way as is presently true, the law in Stephen's time provided for the exclusion of confession evidence obtained in certain discreditable circumstances. An important distinction, though, was that the use of trickery or deception to extract a confession in no way affected admissibility. Stephen was an early advocate of extending the mandatory exclusion rule to include 'confessions extorted by spiritual terrors, or obtained by fraud'.[94] Significant, but not surprising, is Stephen's expressed justification for the change. His concern was not simply (as was the standard justification)[95] that such confessions might be untrue but for the general standing and reputation of the criminal justice system:

It must never be forgotten that the poor and ignorant are the persons most affected by the administration of criminal justice; and the ministers of justice, with whom they have most to do, the police, have just that amount of intellectual and social superiority to day-labourers, and the lower class of mechanics which makes them the objects of peculiar jealousy, and renders it desirable to take special precautions against abuses of their power. Their rough and ignorant zeal would frequently lead them into acts of real oppression, if the law of evidence [made] . . . such oppression useful.[96]

As in the case of substantive law and punishment, Stephen saw as of prime importance the promotion of public confidence in the system.[97]

In 1863, when the General View was first published, atheists were not considered competent to act as witnesses in a trial. One practical consequence of this disqualification was that offences committed against them or in their presence could not be prosecuted unless adequate alternative evidence was available. Taking up where Bentham had left off,[98] Stephen effectively skewered the absurdity of the rule. Even accepting religious beliefs at their strongest, he suggested the dread of damnation that might dissuade some from lying under oath was only one of many possible reasons why a person might tell the truth; and in any case those with religious beliefs were also lead to believe future supernatural sanctions could be avoided by repentance. Moreover, 'A man who has the courage and honesty to avow himself an atheist in a public court gives, in fact, the strongest possible pledge of his sincerity, yet he is incompetent as a witness, though the vilest and most dishonest criminal . . . is competent.'[99] Getting to the heart of the matter, Stephen, with some justification, identified

The reason why the rule is maintained is a vague impression that it is a legal protest against atheism and sets a stigma on that way of thinking, and that its removal would indicate something like a relenting on the part of the nation at large towards atheists [but] . . . it may be well to observe that the barren satisfaction of protesting . . . is dearly purchased at the expense of the reproach that the law of England practically extends impunity to the most atrocious crimes committed against atheists or in their presence.[100]

Removal of this general absurdity eventually came with the Oaths Act 1888.

A further anomalous aspect of competency was the disqualification of defendants from testifying under oath. Until 1885,[101] with very limited and unimportant exceptions, the accused, although permitted to make an unsworn statement from the dock, was not competent to give evidence under oath. Stephen's stance went beyond simply making the accused competent and involved the accused at the end of the case against him being invited to comment on the evidence. Additionally he proposed making clarificatory judicial questioning the norm rather than the exception. Stephen believed such measures would work towards greater fairness to the accused:

a poor wretch who, whatever his crimes may be, is fighting for his life – sometimes literally – against terrible odds. Judges or counsel who are harsh to prisoners, however vile . . . are as much in the wrong as a strong man who strikes a child or a sick woman . . . None but those who constantly see it can appreciate the gross stupidity of prisoners, or the state of abject helplessness to which terror and the apparatus of courts of justice reduce them.[102]

Not until the Evidence Act 1898, supported by the generally anti-reformist Lord Chancellor Halsbury,[103] did defendants become competent witnesses, in all cases; although Stephen records in 1882 that, as a matter of practice, he and a few other judges regularly permitted all prisoners to make unsworn statements from the dock.[104]   By 1898 the procedure had become commonplace and was preserved by the Act. Stephen's proposals for judicial interrogation at committal proceedings and at trial were embodied in his Indian Code of Criminal Procedure of 1872.[105] Although never enacted domestically, the general ethos and some central features of

Stephen's approach surfaced a century later in the controversial
proposals of the Criminal Law Revision Committee's Report on
Evidence, published in 1972.[106] Judging by the Report's generally
hostile reception, the intervening years between the Indian Code
and the publication of the Report did little to enhance the appeal of
attempts to introduce greater rationality into the law. Perhaps the
most surprising feature of Stephen's attitude in this area is that
rather than moving away from the radical Benthamite position in
later life, the temporising of youthful idealism by experience
gained at the Bar and on the Bench had the reverse effect of pro-
pelling him closer to Bentham's injunction to 'Hear everybody who
is likely to know anything about the matter, hear everybody but most
attentively of all, and first of all, those who are most likely to know
most about it – that is the parties.'[107]

Stephen and Bentham's great common concern in the law of
evidence was its 'demystification'; to bring about its principled
articulation and reduction into direct and accessible language: in
Bentham's words, 'to draw aside that curtain of mystery which fiction and formality have spread so extensively over the law'.[108]
They shared the basic presumptive premises which have supported
and inhabited Anglo-American theories of judicial evidence since
the beginning of the nineteenth century: a 'rationalist tradition'
founded on the interlinked assumptions of the independent existence of facts and objective truth which, because of our usually
incomplete knowledge of relevant past events, may normally only
be established to varying levels of probability.[109]
    Also common to both was the enormously valuable facility of 'a
fly's eye for data, with an eagle's eye for illuminating generalisations';[110] although Stephen generally displayed a stronger vein of
scepticism and practicality in his beliefs as to what the rules of evidence might achieve. Besides the irremovable limitations of human
psychology, he also recognised the financial reality that justice
came at a price: 'goodness and cheapness . . . are diametrically opposed . . . either object may be attained, but not both'. Looking
down from the bench in the mid 1880s Stephen found it quite
unacceptable that 'A certain number of criminal trials are still dealt
with . . . without that degree of care to find out the truth which
ought to be employed in every case in which liberty and character
. . . may be at stake . . . ' The proper degree of care might well
lengthen and increase the cost of trials, but it was a price that had to
be met.[111]

Overall, Stephen's works on evidence are notable for their recognisably modern assessment of the role and form of judicial evidence. They differed from contemporary works in their novel evaluative approach and strenuously simple style of exposition of principle. Stephen's most impressive and lasting contribution to the law of evidence was the way in which he 'washed, trimmed, shaved and forced into clean linen'[112] the vast bulk of the common law, employing on the way much potent but neglected Benthamite wisdom on the subject.

PROCEDURAL BACKWATERS

The substantive content and general principles of a good proportion of the criminal law in the second half of the nineteenth century have changed little over the last 100 years. In its primary theoretical conceptions of responsibility the substantive criminal law of Stephen's time is recognisably that of the present day. However, any similar exercise comparing modern and nineteenth-century procedural practices reveals a vastly different state of affairs. During the second half of the last century the pace of reform in many areas of procedural law was so slow as to be almost undetectable. Those developing perceptions of the state's responsibility to regulate properly public health and commercial practices which had encouraged widespread legislative intervention in the field of social policy largely failed to touch the creaking body of eighteenth-century procedure inherited by the nineteenth-century criminal justice system. The political irresistibility of much public welfare legislation and the economic pressures exerted by commercial convenience ensured steady, if not spectacular, reforms in these areas. But in matters of criminal justice equivalent forces and interests of sufficient strength were scarce.

Stephen well understood that however generally satisfactory the substantive law might be it counted for little unless the apparatus for regulating its enforcement was effective: effective not merely in the sense of ensuring that offenders were convicted and received their deserts but, at least as important, that this was done in a manner which generated popular assent and respect. For him the whole system had to be efficient and demonstrably just because

The administration of criminal justice is the commonest, the most striking and the most interesting shape in which the sovereign power of the state manifests itself to the great bulk of its subjects . . . No spectacle can be better fitted to satisfy the bulk of the population, to teach them to regard the Government as their friend and to read them lessons of truth, gentleness, moderation, and respect for the rights of others, especially for the rights of the weak and the wicked, than the manner in which criminal justice is generally administered.[113]

Of course, against a political backdrop of rumbling agitation for franchise reforms it would be naive to expect Stephen to have conceded also that that section of society which possesses most has most to lose from ineffective and ill-respected law enforcement, an economic reality voiced by Adam Smith a century before.[114] This strong concern for the system's fairness and political credibility shows through particularly in his attitudes towards questions of the responsibility for initiating prosecutions, the accused's rights at trial, the system of appeals and the value of juries.

With considerable justification Stephen, writing in 1863, saw as a 'great evil' the absence of any standardised system for the detection and prosecution of offenders.[115] Everyone had the right to prosecute but no one was fixed the duty to do so. At the time, police forces were still in an early and immature state, lacking professionalism, education, competence and, sometimes, honesty. More often than not, prosecutions were, of necessity, brought by the injured party or his representatives; an exercise demanding time, tenacity and money. As *The Times* fairly observed:[116] 'None but a fool or a rogue . . . will prosecute in an English court of justice; and it is notorious that those who have done so rarely repeat their example of public spirit.' This astonishingly haphazard state of affairs had hardly rumbled along unnoticed, with a formalised system of public prosecutions being advocated from the beginning of the century by Bentham, and later followed by others such as Sir Samuel Romilly and Lord Brougham. Yet a succession of parliamentary attempts between 1854 and 1878 brought forth nothing except the establishment of the office of Director of Public Prosecutions, which had no more than a negligible effect on the general system of prosecutions until well into the twentieth century.

Stephen approached the whole issue first through a comparative study of the French and English methods of prosecution, identifying the underlying and far-reaching distinction between the two as turning on the 'inquisitorial' nature of French procedure and the 'litigious' nature of the English. Under the highly formalised French system supervision of the investigation of the offence and the decision to prosecute were (and are) undertaken by a magistrate equipped with wide-ranging investigative and interrogatory powers. All this offended Stephen's Whig/Liberal sensitivities on the proper purview of government and its instrumental institutions. However effective it might be, he regarded it as unacceptably intrusive: the investigation treated 'the comfort, the privacy, even the personal liberty of any number of innocent persons, as unimportant in comparison with the possibility of detecting a crime. Such a system would never be endured in this country, and if established, would cover the whole administration of justice with odium.'[117] It was a hostility to the French system that was founded on more than just chauvinism and a distaste for what he saw as an excessively zealous pursuit of the truth. For him even greater significance attached to the absence of a clean separation of prosecutorial and judicial roles. The French system of an investigating magistrate followed by trial under a much more active and interrogatory trial judge than was the practice in England dangerously blurred this greatly cherished political and constitutional distinction.

But, of course, as Stephen knew, the introduction of an organised body of officials into the English system did not necessarily involve a slavish duplication of French quasi-judicial investigative functions. However, rather than establishing a new class of public officials to supervise the bringing of prosecutions, he favoured this role being performed by chief constables armed with adequate public funds to enable the effective instruction of solicitors and counsel; a solution which avoided 'the great amount of patronage'[118] produced by a system of public prosecutors supported by full-time lawyers. Just how different the patronage placed at the disposal of chief constables was from that entailed in employing public prosecutors is not startlingly obvious; possibly he felt that diffused patronage was preferable to a concentrated centralised exercise of it. Certainly Stephen's preference on this occasion was hardly based on the weightiest of considerations, although his choice was historically validated.

Complementary to such criticisms of the hopelessly inadequate prosecutorial system was his concern for the widespread inability of defendants to conduct their cases properly. The cost of legal representation and the attendance of relevant witnesses was beyond the means of the majority of defendants. This single economic fact sapped the credibility of any general claim of equality before the law, frequently showing it up to be little more than a pious platitude. True, it was a condition alleviated to a limited degree by the practice of 'dock briefs', under which any barrister present in court was obliged to accept the presentation of an undefended prisoner's case for a fixed fee of one guinea. But a guinea was still beyond the pockets of many prisoners; and, even for those who could pay, their defence was usually little more than a hastily presented pro forma plea in mitigation, or, according to Stephen,[119] whatever 'occurs at the moment to the solicitor and counsel [rather] than of what the man himself would say if he knew how to say it'. In the *General View* Stephen vividly presented an accurate and telling picture of affairs in 1863:

Our system not only cripples the efficiency of prosecutions and favours the escape of criminals, but it inflicts cruel hardship on innocent persons who have the misfortune to be accused. A day-labourer or mechanic is accused of an offence, and committed to trial at the assizes. If he is unable to procure bail, or the magistrates are unwilling to take it, he must remain in prison for several months, during which he has no means of supporting his family. In order to raise a few pounds for legal assistance he has to sell his furniture, and even if he is acquitted he leaves prison a beggar. There is, however, great risk that he will not be acquitted if he has to call witnesses for his defence. To obtain and arrange their evidence; to bring them to the assize-town, and to keep them there till the case comes on, is so expensive, that to almost every labouring man it is simply impossible. If the public inquired into the whole question whether the accused man was innocent or guilty, witnesses, whose evidence might prove his innocence, would be sought out and brought forward at the public expense as much as witnesses whose evidence would prove his guilt; but the notion that the trial is a litigation, in which the public at large is the plaintiff, throws a burden on the defendant, which his ignorance and poverty generally render him unfit to support. When money is no object on either side, the English system of instruction is almost perfect. Everything that can possibly be said on either side of the question is collected, arranged, and brought forward at the trial by men of the highest professional skill. The jury have before them all the materials for forming an opinion which the rules of evidence will allow them to use; and they may properly infer that, if a witness is not called or a question is not asked on either side, the course taken is significant, and suggests an inference that the evidence which would be so obtained would make against the side which passes it over. In the common run of cases it is far otherwise. The prosecutor is often careless, the prisoner generally poor and ignorant; and the consequence is, that the case goes to the jury in an imperfect and unsatisfactory form.[120]

It is obvious from Stephen's later treatment of these issues in the *History* that nothing had occurred during the intervening twenty years, three of which he had spent on the Bench, to lessen the intensity of his dissatisfaction.

As a means of easing the plight of poor prisoners he urged abandoning the dock brief and substituting a system of 'standing counsel' drawn from junior barristers commonly present at assizes or quarter sessions. In retrospect, Stephen's proposals appear anaemic and unimaginative. Yet belief in what amounted to an entitlement to reasonable legal representation (at least for trial on indictment) was distinctly radical and rarely publicly advocated until the late nineteenth century. Opposed to any such developments was the substantial residue of judicial and parliamentary opinion previously hostile to the 1836 reforms that had given all defendants at least the theoretical right to representation. Lingering on from those times was the conviction that defence representation was a superfluous adornment to the trial process and that judges could be depended upon to act as 'counsel for the prisoner'.[121] No serious attempts were made to tackle the problem of representation until the Poor Prisoners Defence Act 1903; and even this measure was of very restricted scope.

The patent inadequacies in the provision of defence lawyers no doubt considerably influenced Stephen's attitude towards the system of appeals, for incompetency in either prosecution or defence diminished the likelihood of a fair and true verdict. In 1863 the position appeared 'strange and unsatisfactory in the extreme';[122] twenty years on, he still regarded matters of appeal as 'one of the greatest defects in our whole system of criminal procedure'.[123] The grounds for judicial review of criminal verdicts were narrow and offered no effective means for appeals on questions of fact. Instead this function was exercised by the Home Secretary without clear rules in respect either of the right to petition or of how petitions were to be settled. Efforts at reform revealed a general consensus in the legal profession and amongst the judiciary on the need to revise the method of appeals on matters of law; but on the practically far more important issue of appeals on questions of fact there existed a sharp division of opinion, with a strong preponderance of views hostile to change. Where new evidence came to light after conviction, normally the only procedure available was to petition the Home Secretary to advise the sovereign to grant a pardon.

The evidence of witnesses appearing before the Select Committee of the House cf Lords in 1848, established to consider the question, reveals judicial opinion as almost totally united behind the Lord Chief Justice in his opposition to the setting up of a Court of Criminal Appeal to hear appeals on issues of fact. Charles Greaves, one of the leading English criminal lawyers of the nineteenth century and editor of *Russell on Crime*, the famous practitioner's manual (much cursed by Stephen), spoke strongly in favour of an unrestricted right of appeal upon fact or law, arguing that one considerable indirect benefit of such a right would be greater care being exercised by the prosecution and judge at the trial stage. Greaves was, however, in a very small minority and his proposals stood not the slightest chance of adoption.[124] The Report of the Capital Punishment Commission in 1866[125] showed that the broad climate of legal opinion, as represented by expert testimony, had changed little since 1848. One of the weightiest objections was that the risk of the increased burden of costs to be borne by the prosecution on any appeal would act as a further powerful disincentive to prosecute. Bearing in mind the still largely private nature of prosecutions this was an unfortunate double-bind: an effective appeals system was made pressing by the inadequacy of defence representation, but improving the appeals system might further weaken an already fragile system of prosecution.

The general issue of appeals was a rare instance where Stephen changed his view on an aspect of criminal law; in the case of appeals he not only changed his mind, but he changed it three times. It seemed to be a matter where Stephen's utilitarian nerve failed him, and where for a time he was visited by a lingering emotional commitment to legal traditionalism. Originally, in 1863 he had advocated the setting up of a Court of Criminal Appeal 'charged with the duty of doing openly and judicially what the Home Secretary at present does in secret',[126] able to hear appeals based on new evidence or where the trial judge was dissatisfied with the verdict. Fourteen years later, after 'Further experience and reflection' he openly expressed a change of heart now favouring retrials as being 'more in accordance with all our habits to let the final decision of all questions in fact rest with a jury than to send them before a small number of specially selected judges'.[127] As for the likely objection of the inadequacy of judicial time and facilities needed to cope with this additional burden, Stephen urged the appointment of more judges rather than toleration of the alternative of 'a criminal and flagrant denial of justice'. However, less than two years later in the Report and Draft Code Bill of the Royal Commission on Indictable Offences, of which Stephen was a member, the establishment of a Court of Criminal Appeal was recommended.[128] Subsequently in his treatment of the topic in the *History*, he in no way dissented from the Report and Code proposals, offering no explanation for his further change of mind.[129] Yet in the second edition of the *General View* (1890) Stephen, though favouring modifications, once more moved back to the orthodoxy of opposing the establishment of a Court of Criminal Appeal. For although he 'concurred' in the 1879 Code, 'subsequent experience' had demonstrated objections to be stronger than advantages.[130] It took the public notoriety of the Adolf Beck mistaken identity scandal and Beck Commission Report[131] finally to generate sufficient political interest to take up the 1879 proposals and establish a Court of Criminal Appeal in 1907.

Perhaps the most prominent distinguishing feature of English criminal procedure to come under Stephen's scrutiny was jury trials. Despite the nineteenth-century growth of summary proceedings, jury trials still continued to be very much the focal point of the system. In 1883 Stephen realistically alleged that it was 'perhaps the most popular of all our institutions and has certainly been made the subject of a kind and degree of eulogy which no institution can possibly deserve'.[132] Not being overimpressed by general democratic claims, for him the limitations of juries were brutally obvious: their members were individually unknown quantities; unlike judges they were not public figures open to criticism; and most seriously

the great bulk of the working classes are altogether unfit to discharge judicial duties, nor do I believe that, rare exceptions excepted, a man who has to work hard all day long at a mechanical trade will ever have either the memory, or the mental power or the habits of thought, necessary to retain, analyse, and arrange in his mind the evidence of, say, twenty witnesses to a number of minute facts given perhaps on two different days.[133]

Certainly with compulsory elementary education not being nationally established until the late 1870s many jury members were inevitably lacking in scholastic skills, although the existence of a standard property qualification meant that most of the poorest elements of society were in any case ineligible for service. As a compromise remedy, greater use of special juries selected from the educationally well qualified for complex cases or those 'of importance' was proposed. Stephen was far from alone in such veiws,[134] but in a political climate generally inclined towards wider franchise reforms anything other than a steady decline in the use of special juries would have been surprising.

For Stephen, however, the self-evident drawbacks of juries should be overlooked; some effectiveness in arriving at the truth in criminal trials had to be sacrificed to the overall political gain secured by the use of juries:

Though the judges are, and are known to be, independent of the executive Government, it is naturally felt that their sympathies are likely to be on the side of authority. The public at large feel more sympathy with jurymen than they do with judges, and accept their verdicts with much less hesitation and distrust.[135]

Moreover, jury trials actually directly engaged citizens in the administration of justice:

It is difficult to over-estimate the importance of this. It gives a degree of power and popularity to the administration of justice which could hardly be derived from any other source . . . In short, if trial by jury is looked at from the political and moral point of view, everything is to be said in its favour, and nothing can be said against it.[136]

The notion of the political potency of juries has been used since by others to justify their continued use; one of the earliest to follow Stephen was the nineteenth-century political scientist Henry Sidgwick in his *Elements of Politics*.[137] It is, though, a theory that has to be distinguished from a quite separate argument,[138] propounded in various formulations by judges and jurists from Sir William Blackstone[139] to Lord Devlin,[140] that jury trial is a valuable defence against executive repression through the courts; that it is a true 'bulwark of liberty'. To Stephen the main political value of the jury lay not so much in the direct effect of its participation but rather in its symbolic power.

The twenty-year span between the appearance of the *General View* and the *History* was a highly eventful time for Stephen, encompassing his association with the *Pall Mall Gazette* from the mid sixties to the mid seventies; his period with the Indian Council; the lengthy frustrating encounters with the unwieldiness of the parliamentary process during his fruitless codification efforts; and ending with his appointment as a High Court judge in January 1879. More widely, legal scholarship, and particularly the influence of the historical school, had experienced a strong surge in popularity; the so-called[141] economic and social 'collectivist' tendencies of state activities had begun to accelerate; and all this along with the vast enfranchisement changes which had or were about to take place under the 1867 and 1884 Reform Acts. Was Fitzjames Stephen the lawyer of 1883 recognisably the lawyer of 1863? In all essential respects he was. His observations on the legal system had grown no less weighty in content or robust in style. Some earlier half-digested ideas were abandoned and others were more fully developed, but changes of substance were few. His much-prized elevation to the Bench neither dimmed his eye nor moderated his tone towards the many appalling deficiencies that were still commonplace in the administration of criminal justice in England.

Any natural leanings he had towards the social and economic gospel of Samuel Smiles were quite absent from his perceptions of the proper nature and function of the system of law enforcement; the poor and the ignorant were not to be expected to take their chance and cope unaided with the rigours of a criminal trial. If Stephen understood anything, it was the political dimension to the substance and enforcement of the criminal law.[142] The criminal law was 'by far the most powerful and by far the roughest engine which society can use for any purpose'.[143] Trials were occasions where the state was also on show alongside the defendant; fairness and thoroughness in its treatment of citizens in the dock were not only sound political investments but also a statement of the country's ethical standards.

Stephen was never tempted by anything resembling Bentham's broad iconoclastic approach to reforms. To borrow from Horace Walpole, the difference between them was the 'wide difference between correcting abuses and removing landmarks'.[144] High as his contemporary standing as a jurist was, as a force in the development of English law Stephen's immediate and direct influence was negligible. The effects of his longstanding campaign to push the grimy and grim reality of much of the administration of criminal justice closer to its lofty ideals were a good time in maturing and producing even a meagre crop of successes. Rather like Sydney Smith's 'gigantic' Brougham, who could not quite convert law-reforming zeal into parliamentary action either, Stephen should be seen, if not as a great reformer, at least as a great educator, usually running ahead of contemporary opinion although occasionally assuming a reactionary guise.

5

THE THREAT OF 'HOOFS AND HOBNAILS'

Liberty, Equality, Fraternity, the great flowering of Stephen's political and moral philosophy, was produced during and soon after his return from India, marking a sort of midway point between the *General View* and the *History*. In it Stephen attempted to expose, almost in a 'stream of consciousness', the principal political life forces and moral currents responsible for the modern state. India was more the catalyst than the cause of *Liberty, Equality, Fraternity*; rather its origins lay in the decade surrounding the 1867 franchise reforms, events that compelled Stephen, along with many of his social and intellectual contemporaries, to examine closely and weigh his own beliefs on the proper direction and nature of parliamentary and popular democracy in England. It was a process of reassessment demanding deep excavations through several layers of social and political existence, involving Stephen rubbing shoulders with the most active and prominent figures of the day, all at least as concerned as he was with the nation's moral, cultural, and political destiny.

BENTHAMITE CHICKENS RETURNING TO ROOST

The crusading role of Benthamite utilitarianism as a force in generating the intellectual momentum leading to the 1832 Reform Act, along with subsequent legal and social developments, is common knowledge. The creed's strong attraction lay in its ability to slice through the confusions of tradition and prejudice congesting every facet of life: ethics, law and politics were all susceptible to utilitarianism's engagingly simple 'greatest happiness' formula. However, the Whig and, later, Liberal strain of utilitarianism harboured doctrinal tensions, eventually contributing to open and deep party divisions.

The dual elements of this source of conflict were Bentham's and James Mill's views on popular government and the proper level of governmental activity. To Bentham and Mill senior a universal franchise was the cornerstone of efficient government, the 'best security for good legislation'. Supremacy of enlightened self-interest as a motivating force meant that effective government must be self-government: a claim fervently opposed by many Whig liberals, and one provoking Macaulay's strenuous denial in 'Mr Mill's Utopian democracy' that it was 'utterly impossible to deduce the Science of Government from the principles of human nature'.[1]

For Bentham, like Hobbes, 'All government' was 'one vast evil', but, obviously, the evil of governmental coercion was a lesser evil than the alternative of insecurity and disorder. How far, though, might a government pursue the cause of general utility? How interventionist should it be, for example, in matters of economics or in proscribing individual freedoms? Whilst Bentham was aware of these potentially competing interests, the difficulty was not seriously addressed by utilitarians until the mid nineteenth century, and then by John Stuart Mill. By this time the general political ramifications of basic Benthamite[2] philosophy were beginning to unnerve those otherwise well disposed to a broad reformist outlook and who, like Macaulay, favoured abating the 'vile abuses' of the constitution 'without defacing the shrine'.[3] It was the ever-present question of franchise reforms that was the most visible and at the same time the primary cause of this political discomfort: a steadily darkening and expanding cloud which had hung over a succession of ministries for fifteen or so years prior to 1867, with six Reform Bills coming to nothing. During this period as the likelihood of an ultimately successful Reform Bill grew, so also did doubts over its wisdom; and 'as the incidental drawbacks of the creed came into view a Tory instinct . . . revolted . . . against theories of liberty, equality and fraternity'.[4] This observation on the *Pall Mall Gazette*'s editor Frederick Greenwood by the radical Liberal John Morley well caught the mood amongst the more cautious so-called 'classical' Liberals.

The Liberal revolt led by Robert Lowe against Gladstone's 1866 Franchise Bill was the manifestation of deep philosophical fissures in the party between (simplistically) the new progressive – or populist – elements, seen as only too willing to compromise and kow-tow to popular clamour and the unprincipled politics of the hour, and the old-style classical liberalism represented by those such as Robert Lowe within Parliament and Fitzjames Stephen outside. For these Liberal utilitarians politics was a matter of effective and efficient government coupled with an individualism intended to allow full rein to ability and enterprise. Stephen's 1862[5] account of his own understanding of liberalism embodies the essential lofty qualities of this classical liberalism: 'generous and high-minded sentiments upon political subjects guided by a highly instructed, large-minded and impartial intellect . . . the opposite of surliness, vulgarity and bigotry, [and which aimed at] raising . . . the general tone of life . . . causing it to be pervaded by a higher conception of the objects of national existence'. It is a declaration of political faith almost but not quite toppling into pomposity, and illustrative of a tendency within the Liberal party characterised by G. M. Trevelyan as 'a tail of young men of fashion, the scions of great Whig houses who might just as well have been the scions of great Tory houses so far as their opinions were concerned',[6] contributing to a political 'deep-seated folding, straining and faulting: old strata and new shifting against each other into fantastic and precarious poises'.[7]

With the First Reform Act had come the ownership of property as the single test of voting eligibility – a standard that produced an electoral body seen by opponents of a wider franchise as providing a tolerably fair barometer of the national mood from those quarters that mattered; a body and a system which, for its defenders, was the embodiment of Bagehot's attractive maxim that Parliament should represent 'interests', not 'numbers'; and a body sufficiently far above the working classes not to be oversensitive or vulnerable to the volatility of populist forces, taken by many as the prime source of the chronic governmental instability experienced in France. Indeed it was argued that the very survival of the great institutions and higher culture of society depended on a selective franchise. The formidable Lowe, who dazzled, uplifted and entertained fellow Parliamentarians during the Second Reform Act debates, had few doubts what the choice was: 'If you want venality, if you want ignorance, if you want drunkenness, and facility for being intimidated, impulsive, unreflecting and violent people . . . Do you go to the top or to the bottom?' Lowe, like Macaulay and other great liberals before, understood social inequality as the natural and inevitable order, something to be reflected in the composition of political institutions: it was the 'order of Providence that men should be unequal and . . . the wisdom of the State to make its institutions conform to the order'.[8]

Outside the active central arena of politics, unease at the seemingly inexorable and accelerating movement towards a wider

democracy insinuated itself into the many shades of political mentality making up the intellectual establishment; from Carlyle and
Ruskin across to Bagehot, Lecky, Maine, Matthew Arnold and
Mill. Bagehot had the measure of it as well as anyone in detecting
this 'instinct of revision . . . abroad in human opinion, of which
thinking men want to know the direction' and, more important,
'the end'.[9] Such apprehensions and protests against an enlarged
franchise moved in two ill-defined waves running before the
1867[10] and 1884[11] Reform Acts, with Carlyle and Mill looking
largely to the earlier and others, like Arnold, Bagehot and Stephen
to both and with Henry Maine's principal anti-democratic lament,
Popular Government, just post-dating the 1884 reforms.

   Their reactions to this apparent headlong rush towards increased
democracy and to the general questions of identifying the sources
and conditions of progress differed enormously. Carlyle and
Ruskin regarded laissez-faire industrialism with the strongest distaste; it produced a 'mercenary, venal, and unheroic'[12] lifestyle,
spawning a 'world of mere Patent-Digesters' and degrading and
dehumanising the working masses; it was a 'Midas-eared
Mammonism' that turned a worker's life into a gambler's existence: today prosperity, tomorrow starvation. Laissez-faire was
mutual hostility named 'fair competition'; it left the poor to perish
from poverty and, worse, from the risk of idleness.[13] The absolute
antithesis of a remedy for these evils was liberal democratic utilitarianism, Carlyle's congenital hostility to which spills out in the
Latter-Day Pamphlets (1850) with his matchless satirical creation of
'Pigdom', where:

The Universe, as far as swine conjecture can go, is an immeasurable swine's
trough, consisting of solids and liquids, and other contrasts and kinds; especially
consisting of attainable and unattainable, the latter in immensely large proportion for most pigs . . . Moral evil is unattainability of pig's-wash; moral good
attainability of ditto . . . It is the mission of universal pighood, and the duty of
all pigs at all times, to diminish the quantity of unattainable, and increase that of
attainable. What is justice? Your own share of the general swine's trough, not
any portion of my share . . . But what is my share? Ah there, in fact, lies the
grand difficulty . . . My share is on the whole whatever I can contrive to get
without being hanged or sent to the hulks.

Yet even Carlyle was able to acknowledge Benthamism's effectiveness in the 'laying down of cant'. For Carlyle and Ruskin the way
ahead (or back) lay in extensive state intervention in both matters
of employment and property ownership.[14] Fuller democracy
offered many only the freedom to go without; democracy was at

odds with the fundamental 'right of the ignorant man to be guided by the wiser, [for] to be gently and forcibly held in the true course by him is the indisputablest'.[15] Democracy would be little more than the rule of 'hoofs and hobnails',[16] 'of blockheadism, gullibility, bribeability, amenability to beer and balderdash'.[17] The true and proper course was benevolent autocratic rule by an aristocracy of 'hero-kings', with the 'puddle' of Parliament relegated to an advisory role. But even though 'the atmospheric effect' of such 'insistence on personality, immaterial values, and leadership was immense',[18] Carlyle's compelling invective amounted to merely the 'stupendous growls from a misanthropic recluse',[19] winning over few converts, and constituting no more than a brilliant literary side-show to the main political events.

Stephen's most thorough-going examination of Carlyle's views on parliamentary democracy dates from 1865,[20] when Stephen's own commitment to franchise reforms was at best one of guarded scepticism. Published in *Fraser's Magazine*, the article is a valuable indication of Stephen's state of mind at the time, not least because it involves taking the rare (for him) posture of positive, almost enthusiastic advocate of a democratic system. Carlyle's diagnosis of the country's ills and desperate need for a supreme leader left Stephen unimpressed: 'Downing Street, Westminster Hall, and the Houses of Parliament, with all their babblements [and] janglements . . . are collectively a far better king than any Cromwell or Frederick could possibly be.'[21] For all its faults there was something eminently 'satisfactory in the slow irresistible elephantine manner in which the English Parliament and cognitive institutions' did their work.[22] And even if within a decade his views of the parliamentary process had grown measurably less sanguine, he still never developed the rich Carlylean taste for completely sweeping away 'constitutional, sentimental and other cobwebberies' in exchange for heroes or kings.

Anxiety with a different emphasis afflicted Matthew Arnold. Although not directly focused on the distribution of political power it was, nevertheless, very much part of the broader concern for the nation's intellectual climate and the threat of future decline that a wider franchise seemed to pose. Though Carlyle and Ruskin were right in regarding the ethos of industrialism as degrading, leading to intellectual enervation, for Arnold national spiritual and artistic regeneration would come not through any heroic leadership but from a revitalised and educated middle class acting from within the

administration of government, the universities and principal professions. Arnold's was a call for postponing the plunge into a wider
franchise until its likely consequences became more predictable; a
plea which, whilst agreeable to those like Stephen, others such as
Henry Sidgwick saw as resting on no more than the threadbare
'external excuse of indolence', though in the past served up not in
the 'name of culture but in the name of religion and self-sacrifice'.[23]

Much of the essence of Arnold's concern for his country's political
and spiritual health appears in his essays 'The Function of Criticism
at the Present Time' (1864) and 'My Countrymen' (1866); the first
of which provoked Stephen's 'Mr Matthew Arnold and His Countrymen' (1864), the second, 'Mr Arnold on the Middle Classes' (1866).
These literary encounters were set off by Arnold's assertion in 'The
Function of Criticism' that the English were far too inclined
towards a practical or parochial perception of culture and politics;
that in unflattering contrast with the French (similar to Mill's
Francophilia of a few years earlier in *Dissertations and Discussions*)[24] the English were unreceptive to broader, more general
conceptualising. Stephen's response, according to one modern
commentator, 'was of central importance in shaping the course of
Arnold's social and political comments for the next several years'.[25]
The core of his Macaulayan[26] reply to Arnold was that far from
neglecting any grand 'transcendental theory of philosophy' ('transcendental' being the favoured utilitarian term of philosophic
abuse) the English since the time of Hobbes had positively rejected
it and developed a superior, empirically based, tradition whereby
political institutions were solidly set in experience and concrete
action, firmly ignoring matters such as, in Bagehot's words, 'historic
twaddle about the rise of liberty . . . '[27] Moreover, Arnold simply
deluded himself in believing that he could influence events from
such a remote and detached critical eyrie, so far removed from the
hot polemic of practical political and social issues,[28] 'always using a
moral smelling bottle, like those beloved countrymen, who at foreign
tables d'hote delighted to hold forth on the vulgarity of "those
English" '.[29]

Arnold, having acknowledged the criticism of Stephen and others in
the preface to *Essays in Criticism*,[30] published in the following year,
eventually came back at Stephen in 'My Countrymen'; once more
portraying England's intellectual character as becoming ever more
insulated from the great currents of European thought. Carlyle,
amongst others, approved of such sentiments; Stephen did not. In

'Mr Arnold on the Middle Classes',[31] allegations of intellectual parochialism were beaten aside, the reader being invited to ponder the realities of England's unrivalled political and religious freedoms with its 'honest attempt to use its power for good', and if then 'you still sneer at the general result and fail to see the lines of greatness through the dust and sweat and noise and turmoil which obscure what they develop, you despise human life itself'.

Yet, Stephen's slightly overblown Podsnappian pride apart, the difference of view between Arnold and Stephen on the state of the nation's intellectual well-being was less in substance than these and other exchanges might initially suggest. They shared a deep anxiety over the outcome of an enlarged franchise, particularly whether the result of a political levelling would truly be a general cultural levelling too. Both eventually favoured a strong meritocracy to provide firm enlightened leadership, for, as Arnold neatly concluded in *Culture and Anarchy*, 'without order there can be no society, and without society there can be no human perfection'. Common ground was the insubstantial and unsatisfying nature of materialism, the importance of achieving, of becoming rather than possessing something. And although easy to overstate, there is a discernible resemblance of cadence and substance between elements of Arnold's definition of 'Culture' and Stephen's understanding of 'Liberalism'. 'Culture' was the enemy of the 'vulgar and all immaturities of the ignorant'; it was to 'know the best that had ever been done and said' yet 'still to see things as they really are'. 'Liberalism' was a 'large-minded and impartial intellect' that looked to elevating the 'general tone of life'. And, as with Arnold, 'Culture' was also for Stephen the embodiment of the nation's spiritual existence transmuted into its artistic, religious and political activities. Certainly Stephen's review of 'Culture and Its Enemies' was amongst those few broadly sympathetic, agreeing that Arnold's was 'just the lesson which in an age and country like our own men have the least inclination and the greatest need to learn'.[32]

'Mr Matthew Arnold on Culture' (1867) saw Stephen returning once more to belabour Arnold's critical stance as too impractical, too removed from the fray to be effective in counteracting the tendencies which they both found so disturbing. Of course charges of foppishness, 'rococo' mindedness, or 'intellectual dandyism' were commonly thrown at Arnold, and in most cases with far more animosity and far less sympathy than accompanied Stephen's own complaints. But, as Stephen no doubt eventually understood, this was Arnold's chosen and calculated way of pursuing an 'Idea of the world in order not to be prevailed over by the world's multitudinousness': a 'sinuous, easy unpolemical mode of proceeding' away from the 'rougher and coarser movements' and stylistically the far side of the moon for Stephen.[33]

Set against this disparate collection of those frankly hostile to or strongly suspicious of franchise reform was a range, almost as diverse, of pro-reform opinion. Inside Parliament, Russell, Gladstone and their train of followers saw the controlled admission of the working man to the electoral club as a moral gesture of trust, combined with the hope that it would peacefully lead to a more representative government and harmonious nation; or, for Disraeli, that the existing social order would at least not be seriously imperilled and the reassuring deference of the lower classes not greatly altered. Beyond Parliament, a valuable reflection of the broadly progressive arguments favouring the apparently imminent 1867 reforms was *Essays on Reform* (1867).[34] As the preface suggests, the collection of essays came from a group of authors 'drawn together by general similarity of ideas and by a comon desire to contribute . . . to the solution of the great problem which at present occupies the mind of the nation'. More openly, to a substantial degree *Essays* constituted an attempt to head off the opposing case that Lowe in particular had so powerfully been putting across in Parliament and up and down the country.

Amongst the contributors to this influential collection[35] were R. H. Hutton, Albert Dicey, Leslie Stephen, Goldwin Smith and James Bryce. Although they displayed a common sympathy for reform there were marked contrasts in the justifications offered for it. On one side, distinctly tinged with radicalism (but not, according to Morley, 'windy, transcendental talk'),[36] was the case put by G. C. Brodrick, along with Lowe a *Times* leader-writer, and a fellow and later Warden of Merton College. Brodrick's essay was largely a direct attack on Lowe and the inadequacy of using utility as the sole basis of testing the desirability of franchise changes. For Brodrick it was quite insufficient to view the question as one of the tendency of any change to contribute towards good or bad government; equally important were matters of intuitive justice and morality which conferred 'a presumptive title to a share of political power' – effectively a rights of man claim; and, despite Morley's denial, very much 'windy, transcendental talk'. Yet looking back from 1900 Brodrick felt able to offer a partial but, nevertheless, handsomely frank recantation of these views. He not only saw Lowe's speeches

on the Reform Bill as 'the most brilliant and argumentative series
of Parliamentary orations delivered in that decade' but believed
'later experience has verified too many of the predictions contained
in them . . . He knew that men of ability and professing high principles would not scruple to flatter the prejudices, pander to the
passions, and inflame class antipathies . . . for the sake of winning
support. This is exactly what has happened . . . '[37] For Fitzjames
Stephen, and others such as Henry Maine,[38] there were few if any
such initial optimistic illusions later to turn sour. And even Arnold
saw hypocrisy lurking within the political hearts of generally unimpeachable radicals like Frederic Harrison; detecting 'a sort of motion of Mr Frederic Harrison's tongue towards his cheek when he
tells the working class that "theirs are the brightest powers of sympathy and the readiest powers of action" '.

Leslie Stephen's contribution[39] was of quite a different nature
from Brodrick's, openly agreeing with Lowe – and implicitly with
his brother – that the ultimate test must be one of utility, of judging
the legislature as 'we judge an artist, by the quality of his work; not
by asking whether he works in his court suit and ruffles, or in his
shirt sleeves and with a pipe in his mouth'.[40] But Stephen, like
Brodrick and Hutton, concluded that the working masses excluded
from parliamentary representation would look (and were already
looking) to alternative ways of gaining and exercising political
influence, most ominously, through the formation of trade unions.
Denied the 'self-respect' as well as the power of parliamentary
access, such social forces were 'compelled to grow in the dark,
instead of the daylight'.[41] His cousin, Albert Dicey, turned in a
more enthusiastic performance. Dicey's 'The Balance of Classes',
an elaborate argument against rigid 'class' representation, was singled
out by Morley as the 'most unflinchingly democratic' of all the essays.

James Bryce, with his acclaimed *Holy Roman Empire* already
launched on a career as one of the century's great constitutional
and political historians, reached much the same conclusion as Leslie
Stephen, though via a somewhat different and more polished pragmatic route. In arguably the most perceptive analysis of the collection, Bryce stressed that the basis of political power – knowledge,
self-respect, the capacity for combined action – having been formerly possessed by a few, now rested in the hands of many who
were yet to enjoy civic privileges; in effect 'the social progress of
democracy [had] outrun its political progress'.[42] This was a decidedly
risky state of affairs bringing to mind Macaulay's warning issued
during the First Reform Bill debates that a 'great cause of revolution' was where 'while nations move onwards, constitutions stand

still'.[43] For Bryce, these threatening developments were to be contained by the enfranchisement of such classes, who once within 'the pale of the Constitution . . . will themselves become its defenders'. Gloomily, Fitzjames Stephen predicted, mainly in the *Pall Mall Gazette* leader columns, that the constitution and culture that these newcomers might well stoutly defend would, because of their membership, inevitably be changed and inferior.[44] English institutions would be transformed into a 'sort of exaggerated Whiteley's shop, smirking to all its customers, and specially anxious not to offend anybody'.[45]

MILL AND THE TWO FACES OF POPULISM

In this ocean of opinions favouring and opposing the wider distribution of political power and responsibility it was John Stuart Mill's task to shoulder the formidable intellectual burden of Bentham's democratic legacy. Mill's problem was that the Benthamite belief that the pursuit of individual self-interest could be harnessed for the community's benefit through the device of self-government needed to be reconciled with the patent incapacity of the majority to know just what was in their best long-term interests. His broad acceptance of Benthamite principles of government was vitally qualified. Bentham's and James Mill's assumptions – that the behaviour of 'average rulers' was determined solely by self-interest, and that majority rule was for the general good – were viewed as misleadingly simplistic. Mill's fears for the 'rule of an ignorant, miserable and vicious democracy'[46] and the 'despotism of public opinion' were possibilities that never seriously troubled Bentham.[47] Moreover, Mill's assessment of the collective character and ethos of the working classes was hardly over-generous: they were 'habitual liars', though usually 'ashamed of lying',[48] and 'As soon as any idea of equality enters the mind of an uneducated English working man, his head is turned by it. When he ceases to be servile he becomes insolent.'[49]

At bottom, the problem was 'how the rule of numbers [was] to be reconciled with the rule of sage judgment'.[50] Those of John Morley's persuasion held dear the belief that the 'best guarantee for justice in public dealings is the participation in their own government of the people most likely to suffer from injustice'.[51] Yet even to radicals such as Morley and Harrison, 'Governing is one thing; but electors of any class cannot, or ought not, to govern', if only, as Arnold suggests, for no other reason than that the minds of the masses were mostly absorbed in the 'necessity of constantly struggling for the little things'.[52] Stephen,[53] like Mill and the *Reform* essayists, hoped that when finally enfranchised the working classes would recognise the wisdom of being led by their social and intellectual betters, through, according to Bagehot, the 'daily play of the higher mind upon the lower'. Or, as Mill described the process: being 'guided by the counsels and influence of a more highly gifted and instructed few'; adding with as much hope as conviction that 'The honour and glory of the average man is that he is capable of following that initiative; that he can respond internally to wise and noble things, and be led to them with his eyes open.'[54] Doubtless Mill's belief in this was strengthened by his 1865 election as MP for Westminster. Certainly a leader in the *Pall Mall Gazette* (possibly by Stephen) saw the event as evidence of an 'entente cordiale between the educated middle class and the more enterprising leaders in the great underlying masses of society'.[55] However, even when supporting the cause of a wider franchise Mill wished to hedge his bets with various qualifications. His answer to Bagehot's call for 'power' to be 'proportionate to capacity' was that votes should be weighted in accord with a voter's attributes. Under these 'fancy franchises', as Bright termed them, weight should correspond with a voter's worth, judged largely by education and the ownership of property.

Such 'fancy' devices aside, it is in his essay *On Liberty* that Mill offered his main philosophic defence against the perceived threat of increasingly oppressive authority, whether from government or public opinion: a threat to the country's social and intellectual vitality made especially potent by the likelihood of a reformed franchise which could translate the tyranny of public opinion into legislative form. As a bulwark against materialisation of some of these possibilities, Mill offer on one 'very simple' principle to set limits on the use of any coercive power which the state and society might properly exercise over an individual:

that the sole end for which mankind are warranted, individually or collectively, in interfering with the liberty of action of any of their number, is self protection. That the only purpose for which power can be rightfully exercised over any member of a civilised community, against his will, is to prevent harm to others. His own good, either physical or moral is not a sufficient warrant. He cannot rightfully be compelled to do or forbear because it will be better for him to do so, because it will make him happier, because, in the opinions of others, to do so would be wise or even right.[56]

Stephen's initial reaction to *On Liberty* appeared in February 1859 in the *Saturday Review*, soon after publication of Mill's essay. Enthusing that 'The general tone of the book . . . coincides . . . essentially with [our] temper of mind in respect to political institutions', he agreed it was 'impossible to overvalue' the importance of 'individuality as one of the elements of well-being', comparing (as Frederic Harrison later did)[57] Mill with Milton, finding 'nothing in English literature since the *Areopagitica* more strong, noble, better worthy of the most profound and earnest meditation than these two chapters of Mr Mill's essay'.

Yet even in these early reviews of *On Liberty*, planted firmly amongst Stephen's lavish praise were two substantial reservations. The first related to Mill's charge that self-satisfied mediocrity was already pervasive in an intellectually moribund climate; this being coupled with a well-advanced creeping anti-individualism. Although never easily assuming optimistic garb, Stephen found all this excessively pessimistic. True, such risks and tendencies towards 'molluscous' natures were evident, but Mill was 'distinctly wrong' in his assessment of the current state and forms of individuality, for there clearly existed the freedom to read, think and worship according to inclination. And nothing resembling the insidious effects of the flaccid intellectualism of the Roman Empire, seen by Gibbon as a 'slow and secret poison', was now being witnessed in England. This and the claim of a decline in individuality Stephen eccentrically met with an example of 'outstanding' civilian resistance and self-defence during the Indian Mutiny by

People who, at any common English dinner-table, or on the platform of some local Missionary Society, would have drawled out the dreariest of all incoherent twaddle, and have impressed Mr Mill with the notion that they were not only on their way to an intellectual China, but had absolutely reached it, and given themselves over to spiritual pigtails, started into heroes at the approach of real danger . . . met and generally conquered it with that desperate courage which is the great constituent element of individuality.[58]

The view that Mill had wildly overstated his case on the decay of individuality, far from being confirmed to a few like Stephen, was common currency amongst contemporary critics,[59] though Arnold too had perceived much 'running blindly together in herds'. Even Herbert Spencer,[60] arguably 'the most consistent individualist and laissez-fairest of the epoch', had a decade before seen the time as one of great individualism;[61] and Mill himself later admitted that this pessimism was perhaps more appropriately directed at future generations.[62]

Stephen's other point of dissent was the attribution by Mill of the decline of individuality to Calvinism. It was also to figure most contentiously in *Liberty, Equality, Fraternity*, but at this earlier stage Stephen contented himself with suggesting that Mill had failed to distinguish the crushing of will and slavish submission from the encouragement of self-control or discipline, 'the greatest of all agents in ennobling and developing the character'.[63] If proof of this were required one had to do no more than compare the 'Scotch' with 'French shopkeepers [who] are . . . as feeble a folk as any class of Englishman and their worst enemies would not accuse them of having been degraded by Calvinism'. With such passages Stephen signals his own predisposition in what has been elegantly described as the coexistence within most Victorians of the ethics of 'moral earnestness and enthusiasm': the latter 'assumes that human nature is good; that the organ of virtue is the sensibility rather than the conscience; and that the moral life depends, not on the arduous struggle to master the passions and compel the will to a life of duty, but on the vitality of the noble emotions, inspiring the delighted service of a high ideal'.[64] Nevertheless, particularly in Stephen's case, inclinations towards moral earnestness were by no means constant or consistent; neither were oscillations in mood predictable or always conscious.

Much that was implicit in, or in the spirit of, *On Liberty* appeared earlier as separate essays, usually in the *Edinburgh Review* or *Westminster Review*, which were eventually collected and republished soon after *On Liberty* as *Dissertations and Discussions, Political, Philosophical and Historical*. In his 1859 *Saturday* review of this collection the thirty-year-old Stephen provided further glimpses into the state of his maturing political philosophy, much of which was recognisably to emerge thirteen years later in *Liberty, Equality, Fraternity*. Again, as with the treatment of *On Liberty*, the general tone was favourable, verging on the adulatory; extensive praise was awarded for a more sophisticated account of human nature which embraced powerful feelings and notions, either neglected or only 'very slightly noticed' by Bentham when formulating his calculus of action. Mill's enlarged view of human nature was seen as greatly ameliorating the 'harsh one-sided dogmatism' imputable to crude forms of utilitarianism – an allegation Stephen himself would one day face.

Stephen was similarly at one with Mill in adopting de Tocqueville's insight that democracy may come in the 'shape of democratic freedom or in that of democratic slavery'. Taking his cue from Mill's review of de Tocqueville's *Democracy in America* (1835–40), Stephen agreed that the

characteristic evils which may be apprehended from democracy – the slavery exercised not so much over the body as over the mind by the tyranny of multitude – the general dead level to which democratic governments . . . would tend to reduce all merit and all intellect – the pettiness of the pursuits to which they would infallibly condemn or seduce the great majority of mankind. . .[65]

Other than a repetition of the criticism of Mill's pessimism on the uniform state of English individualism and intellectualism, only one expressed area of dissent surfaced; it was, however, one which, although of limited significance as a single issue, was based on what was the most serious charge Stephen could have levelled against Mill: lack of analytical objectivity. This challenge was provoked by Mill's support for the general equality of the sexes, an idea which struck Stephen as an aberration, where heart had overridden head and led Mill dangerously close to the arch heresy of intuitionism. Of course Mill was

no believer in abstract rights, the law of nature, the inherent equality of all men, and the other doctrines from which Republican opinions are usually deduced; but though he is a Benthamite of the severest kind, he does not write like one upon these subjects. Like smaller men, he takes his side and allows his views to be determined by his sympathies and antipathies as well as by his reason. There is something very remarkable in the degree in which he is obviously influenced by such considerations in several of his opinions. Perhaps the most striking illustration of this is to be found in the view which he takes of the rights of woman.[66]

It was an allegation that strongly resembled one made against Mill's *Representative Government* by Henry Sidgwick years later in his *Elements of Politics* (1891), revealing that the seeds of doubt about the consistency of Mill's adherence to utilitarian empiricism, which were ultimately to grow into *Liberty, Equality, Fraternity*, had already germinated in Stephen's mind many years previously and well before his Indian interlude.

HOBBESIAN ANTECEDENTS

Closely allied and complementary to Stephen's early attitudes on the proper shape and distribution of political power were those he developed on the nature of the state and political society – views which in maturer form were to shine forth prominently in *Liberty, Equality, Fraternity*. As might have been expected of any young intellectual of the day, Stephen's attentions propelled themselves in the direction of Burke, Locke, Hume,[67] Paine and Rousseau. Far less commonplace was his study and admiration of Hobbes. In the works of Burke and Hobbes, and particularly the latter, can be found the pedigree of a good deal of Stephen's thinking on a range of questions relating to the creational and sustaining forces of any modern state. It was these formative excursions into the writings of Burke and Hobbes that laid the foundations of much of *Liberty, Equality, Fraternity*; and although a few ideas were jettisoned along the way, and a few others trimmed, the direction and outline of Stephen's thoughts on liberty and equality are not difficult to discern in those early *Saturday Review* essays.[68]

One such important source of speculation which greatly preoccupied Stephen was the relationship of religion and the state. For Burke, Christianity was an essential ingredient of political stability. Stephen agreed with this and was later to make a good deal of it, but parted company with Burke in believing that the truth of religion was 'at least as important as that of its [political] utility; for truth is the highest form of utility, and grapes will grow on thorns, and figs on thistles, before all human life can be founded on a lie'.[69] Hobbes' treatment of religion was rather more ambivalent in so far as it related to his own beliefs; was his whole discourse in *Leviathan* suggesting that the Sovereign should declare the attributes of God no more than an ironic ruse to fend off possibly dangerous charges of atheism?[70] Clearer and more significant than Hobbes' personal beliefs was his conclusion that church and state are identical – a 'unity of government, not . . . of doctrine'. Hobbes, argued Stephen, was right in believing that government must be 'in one hand', and, anticipating his own strenuous dismissal of the 'Religion of Humanity' in *Liberty, Equality, Fraternity*, Stephen denied the value of distinguishing between spiritual and temporal sanctions to morality: the ultimate question was 'Who, by any threats, whether of punishment here or damnation hereafter, can secure obedience?'[71] Locke was wrong in his belief that church and state were 'independent societies, having perfectly distinct objects in view, each of which is to be attained by the use of means altogether unfit for an attainment of the other'. But, significantly to Stephen, Locke, unlike Hume or Bentham, did understand that the mere chance of a future life and punishment was quite enough to 'make vice a losing bargain'.[72] Religion as a 'supernatural sanction to natural morality'[73] was the 'steam of Locke's engine' and a version of utilitarianism that would power one of the central arguments in *Liberty, Equality, Fraternity*.

Taking much the same view later adopted by John Morley in his two studies of Burke,[74] Stephen estimated Burke to be a liberal constitutionalist[75] and a 'utilitarian of the strongest kind' in the sense that expediency was the basis of all his speculation.[76] Burke correctly understood that social and political institutions were less a product of calculated endeavour than the consequence of the chance and unforeseeability of human society. Thus Burke arrived at the proper conclusion that 'constitutional questions, if fully thought out, are all questions not of law, but of power'.[77] Therefore, on the rationales of expediency and power, Stephen granted that Burke was right in believing the secession of the American state was justified and that compromise was the appropriate solution to this rebellion.[78]

In *Reflections on the Revolution in France* Burke's contemptuous denunciation of the Revolution involved a rejection of what he saw as a new political order formulated on a defective philosophy: the abstraction of liberty was an 'object stripped of all concrete relations' standing 'in all the solitude of a metaphysical idea'; notions of equality were socially divisive, inspiring (as Hume had also argued) 'false hopes and vain expectations'; and fraternity was simply 'cant and gibberish'. Stephen, however, whilst far from objecting to these sentiments, saw the Revolution in a different, more expedient light and, applying de Tocqueville's estimate in *L'Ancien Régime* (1856) of the political and social condition of pre-Revolutionary France, believed the Revolution not just inevitable but necessary.[79] Indeed Stephen was more sympathetic towards the events of 1789 than those, like Bentham, who saw this form of republicanism as the 'raging pestilence of the times'. For Stephen, Burke's most telling failure was in omitting to explain why a revolution occurred.[80] It was de Tocqueville's assessment that reform of the existing institutions was impossible because of their feudal nature and incapacity to provide the foundations of any modern political order. Burke, as Stephen understood, had quite misconceived the difference between the political histories of France and Britain, not sensing that evolutionary or gradualist change in France had become an impossibility. And to have produced anything resembling a British constitutional change 'the history of France ought to have been the history of England'.[81]

Furthermore, Stephen realised that Burke was far from being uncontaminated by metaphysics: theories of natural rights had established a clear foothold in some elements of his thinking. Most notably in his 'Tract on the Popery Laws', Burke could be seen embracing the idea of 'justice antecedent to, and by right formative of all law';[82] conduct which, for Stephen, placed Burke closer to Rousseau or Voltaire than to Hobbes and Bentham, with the essential political distinction between Burke and Rousseau and Voltaire being 'not whether men had natural rights, but whether they had the rights which were claimed by the Revolutionists'.[83] Burke's writings have, since the nineteenth century, attracted a sizeable heap of accusations of fundamental philosophic inconsistency along with strenuous counter-assertions of Burke's unswerving intellectual consistency.[84] Stephen's primary concern was not so much to condemn the substance of Burke's beliefs, but rather to censure any employment of natural rights as the foundational assumptions of a political philosophy.[85]

For utilitarians, especially of the Stephen variety, a far surer philosophic footing was provided by Hobbes.[86] As Leslie Stephen suggested in his English Men of Letters study *Hobbes* (1904), Hobbes had passed out of general notice by the end of the seventeenth century,[87] being principally replaced by Locke on the centre stage of political philosophy. Resurrected in the nineteenth century by the utilitarians, particularly James Mill and John Austin, Hobbes' theory of sovereignty offered an intellectually convincing account of modern popular government as well as of the autocratic tyranny with which his works had previously been associated. Incorporated into the theory of sovereignty were Hobbes' notions of human psychology, many of which anticipated Bentham's own assessment of the central importance of egoism in human nature. Human nature was made up of appetites and aversions; Hobbesian man was both rational and afraid of death; 'All society is either for gain or for glory, that is, not so much for love of our fellows as for love of ourselves'; the state of nature is one of war and the life of man – in Hobbes' famous phrase – 'solitary, poor, nasty, brutish and short'. Man's innate tendency was towards self-assertion and the seeking of power; but fear of death was the great counterpoise to this egocentricity and for this reason man accepted social order. Law is valid because it is enforced and enforceable by a supreme authority; Leviathan was the alternative to social and political anarchy, and this 'thing itself will always remain, just as there will always be a centre of gravity in every mass of matter'.[88] For Fitzjames Stephen this was the 'central' idea of Hobbes' *Leviathan*, a severely mutated version of which would surface eventually in *Liberty, Equality, Fraternity*.

Although understanding that Hobbes seriously underrated the 'social parts' of human nature and overestimated the rationality of man in being able to reconcile wants and the means of satisfying them, Stephen still believed *Leviathan* to be 'full of the shrewdest and most profound observation'.[89] And as Stephen rightly acknowledged, Hobbes' propositions on sovereignty and human nature were, in any case, not intended to be taken as completely literal truths – rather a 'thought experiment' or abstractions 'suggested to the imagination by facts'; there being in nature no society in which men acted solely with a view to gain, neither was there absolute sovereignty. They were abstractions from underlying predominant tendencies on which general explanatory principles could be posited.[90] Moreover as Stephen, unlike most, seemed to grasp, Hobbes' egocentric account of human behaviour was not based on immediately selfish acts; for although Hobbes argued that man acts for the 'good' of himself, 'good' meant more than the object of his desire. Therefore generally benevolent motives were recognised by Hobbes as within the ambit of possible springs of action; however, although Hobbes had little doubt that selfishness predominated, for him, unlike the utilitarians, the greatest social happiness was not the ultimate goal.

Sovereignty was to Hobbes a necessary means of providing conditions conducive to individual happiness, not, as for utilitarians, the means of creating a greater sum of human happiness through harmonisation of opposing interests. But Stephen recognised that the potential for true sovereign power, in the form of a 'man or a body of men', was itself limited by human nature, being 'always more or less ignorant, weak and irresolute'. The sovereign might be 'deceived, or avoided, or dissuaded from his purpose'.[91] Threats, therefore, lost some of their force because of the real prospects of 'impunity'. Additionally Stephen (as Mill had, years before, argued in his *Logic*) believed Hobbes exaggerated the need and extent to which people were capable of being affected by threats; there being a 'point beyond which you cannot terrify . . . [for] the mass of mankind are not of the opinion that death is the greatest of evils, and they are moreover actuated by a singular propensity to disbelieve in the reality of that which is exceedingly disagreeable'. Just how far then might people be coerced by a sovereign power to follow laws contrary to their general interests? Here Stephen was confident that 'Let laws be complicated and punishments as severe as you please, nothing will ever make that useful to mankind which in point of fact is injurious, or that injurious which in point of fact is useful . . . no amount of punishment . . . will ever make [bad] laws good' or make people obey them in the long run.[92]

On a different front, adopting an essentially Humean view,[93] Stephen credited Hobbes with having failed to separate government and society or to understand that if laws ceased to exist society, albeit 'in a much less comfortable manner than at present . . . would carry on the main affairs of life'. Social forces and not laws were the great binding powers of society:

The number of actions in which any particular individual is in any degree restrained by law is almost infinitesimally small. The social desires are, after all, much stronger and much commoner than those which are anti-social . . . Society is the work of law in some proportion, but in a much greater proportion it is the work of . . . love of companionship, curiosity, the desire of all sorts of advantages which are to be derived from mutual assistance . . .[94]

Part of Hobbes' general insistence on knowledge from experience entailed his effective preclusion in *Leviathan* of natural rights or laws of nature. The state existed to reconcile individual and opposing self-interest, not to assert or protect immutable natural rights. Liberty, Stephen agreed with Hobbes, was a negative idea, being that part of our lives free of legal restraint; the real distinction between an autocracy and a democracy lay not in the amount of liberty enjoyed by subjects, but in the distribution of power: a simple but important political truth whose recognition, Stephen believed, would 'tend considerably to clear up various matters connected with the question of extension of the suffrage'.[95]

For Stephen, Hobbes' supreme contribution to political philosophy was his secularisation of it. He insisted that notions of state were based on the ultimate need for order and security; that matters of right and wrong were relative, not absolute; and that whether a political objective was good or not turned on its propensity towards maintaining peace and security. Yet at the same time Stephen recognised that (like Burke's) Hobbes' account of government amounted to an 'Essay on Political Statics',[96] for both assumed a state of political equilibrium,[97] ignoring the dynamics of government and making no provision for political change.[98] Burke's limpet-like adherence to the political institutions of the time and his scepticism of the utility of their scrutiny Stephen attributed to the then recent horrors of the French Revolution.[99] In Hobbes' case, this state of mind was seen as resulting from the lingering trauma of the civil war, though, as Stephen noted, generally man had had more to fear from oppressive neighbours than from government. Burke and Hobbes viewed change as dangerous, 'permanent tranquillity' the essence of a political society;[100] contrastingly, rather than anarchy, Benthamites feared incompetent or bungled government. Stephen understood, and at least professed to accept, that political institutions must always reflect social conditions; that the world was not a multitude of ready-made fixed institutions, but rather a mass of developing processes and that permanence of any state of society was undesirable and impossible: 'the only question is whether [political changes] shall be more or less abrupt, and more or less violent'.[101] Yet when it came to the reality of change, although critical of Hobbes' and Burke's static perception of a political and social society, in *Liberty, Equality, Fraternity*, Stephen himself was partly to lose sight of this distressing insurmountable truth.

Despite its many patent deficiencies Stephen had no doubts about the merits of *Leviathan*, 'one of the greatest of all books, and the very oddest of all great books in English literature'.[102] Though a modern commonplace, such lavish nineteenth-century praise of Hobbes was rare; yet Stephen's enthusiasm was paralleled by a few, particularly Austin and Frederick Pollock, lawyers of quite distinctive jurisprudential make-up. Ranking Hobbes alongside Bentham, Austin knew of 'no other writer who has uttered so many truths, at once new and important, concerning the necessary structure of supreme government'.[103] And as Austin recognised, his own theory of sovereignty owed much to Hobbes'. But Hobbes' appeal was not confined to dyed-in-the-wool Austinians like Stephen, a fact demonstrated by Pollock, who, though decidedly not a follower of that analytical school, eagerly acknowledged his intellectual debt to Hobbes in law and politics. In his *First Book of Jurisprudence* (1876) Pollock held that 'acquaintance with [Hobbes'] work at first hand [was] indispensible for all English speaking men who give any serious consideration to the theoretical part of either politics or law'.[104] And following Stephen, he credited Hobbes, in the *History of the Science of Politics* (1890), with the analytical separation of positive law from ethical and social considerations, a task later theoretically completed by Austin. Indeed Pollock, in *Essays in Jurisprudence and Ethics* (1882), appears to outstrip Stephen in the powers he is willing to concede to any sovereign authority. Here Pollock says, or at least comes perilously close to suggesting, that government may legitimately hold and exercise an arbitrary or discretionary power in the interests of maintaining administrative efficiency and uniformity,[105] a flirtation with the fringes of Hegelian statism – the monolith of the state being almost an end in itself – which never shows up in Stephen's philosophies.

As a brief coda to Stephen's views on the subject, a reading of his essay on Tom Paine provides a check against any precipitate conclusions on the content of Stephen's political philosophy in the 1860s and his degree of attachment to Hobbesian thinking. If any home-bred political philosopher was likely to produce a generous flow of vitriol from Stephen then Paine, Burke's arch-enemy, had to be the strongest contender. Certainly to Stephen he was indeed a 'real live monster',[106] 'coarse, violent, ignorant and unmannerly',[107] and guilty of 'Old Bailey brutality',[108] with his *Age of Reason* (1794–1807) containing much to justify a reputation for stupid and gross vulgarity and profanity.[109] Yet clearly elements of both Paine and his preachings attracted as well as repelled Stephen. The *Rights of Man* (1791–2) was a 'solid, lawyerlike theory to which he sticks like a leech', and which Paine contrasted with 'considerable effectiveness with the state of things then existing in England'. And so long as calls for the Rights of Man were seen not as claims to fundamental inalienability, but as practical rules for legislators, then they 'contain a good wholesome doctrine'. Furthermore, declarations of the Rights of Man in the eighteenth century had to be viewed as levelled at 'gross tyrannies', not at 'English constitutional lawyers nourished on the Bill of Rights and . . . Habeas Corpus . . . ' .[110] All in all, Paine was coarse but 'thoroughly sincere', coupled with a 'magnanimity . . . by no means destitute of impressiveness'. And if pressed, Stephen was ready to admit to 'infinitely prefer[ring] the Rights of Man' to the 'violent and scarcely intelligible affirmations' of the ultra-conservative philosopher Joseph de Maistre, for whom religion was the vital social controlling agent, and the pope God's terrestrial sovereign.[111]

It is an untaxing exercise, at least with the advantage of hindsight, to stand back and point out the constituent opinions, prejudices, strengths and failings of *Liberty, Equality, Fraternity* to be found amongst the body of essays written by Stephen between the late 1850s and 1860s; prejudices and insights that India was, by and large, to bolster and develop and in some cases coarsen, in others refine. Parliament, for Stephen, never ceased to be the great glory of England, but with the advancement of democratic accessibility he progressively conceived it more as a debating forum and less as a leading component of the legislative and executive machinery of government. Instead an elite of highly talented administrators and advisers should, if not exactly take up the reins of power, show the right legislative way ahead; a cast iron recognition by Stephen of the truth of the adage that 'he who administers, governs'. Indeed, on occasion Stephen's strong utilitarian conviction of the great worth of efficient government almost suggests a belief that the art of governing was as 'mechanical . . . as . . . laying drain-pipes, to be acquired through a similar routine of instruction and apprenticeship'.[112]

It was, however, a view of government that took time in maturing. His reaction to Northcote-Trevelyan's withering condemnation of the Civil Service was muted.[113] The 1854 Report's scorching critique of the patronage-ridden recruitment of incompetents left Stephen awkwardly placed. Everyone – except Dickens – understood that Sir James was of high ability and had been a generally effective administrator; yet he had undeniably flourished within a system now roundly exposed as rotten. Personal factors aside, Stephen's reticence may have been the product of a general uncertainty over other possible latent ramifications within the Report. The whole tenor of the Report and its proposals was overtly meritocratic rather than democratic; but although neither intended by Trevelyan nor necessarily logically following, many saw a natural and inevitable confluence between administrative and broader political reforms. This was certainly initially true of the Administrative Reform Association[114] and individuals such as Henry Maine. Maine's carping[115] at the Report's claimed collectivistic tendencies was, if anything, more motivated by this believed connection than by any of its intrinsic deficiencies. Stephen too, at that stage, had probably not fully appreciated what Macaulay,[116] in particular, so well understood: that open recruitment on merit of a desirably skilled administrative elite was a road to superior government that could be travelled independently of objections to popular democracy, a truth which had permitted Macaulay to be one of the age's great meritocrats without ever endorsing wider democratic reforms.

Not until after India does Stephen reveal his hand, partly in *Liberty, Equality, Fraternity*, but largely in two 1873 lectures given to the Edinburgh Philosophical Society, subsequently published in the *Contemporary Review* as 'Parliamentary Government'.[117] Mill's earlier call in *Representative Government*[118] for a revitalised Civil Service was given even stronger emphasis by Stephen, whose solution for 'considerably alleviating' parliamentary paralysis and administrative lethargy was a combination of a revamped professionalised service alongside the establishment of de-politicised permanent committees or commissions charged with the 'management of those public affairs which can be severed from party struggles'[119] – that part of the government Bagehot associated with 'wrinkles on the forehead and figures on the tongue'.[120] Permanent heads of departments needed to be placed on a 'totally different footing in regard to . . . pay, rank and responsibility'. They 'ought to be the ablest men in their own lines who are to be found in the country' and paid as much as judges, 'whose duties are, generally speaking, much less important'. And, no doubt with 'Mr Over-Secretary Stephen' in mind, rather than be 'mere clerks to Cabinet Ministers, who, in many instances are, greatly their inferiors both in knowledge and power [they] should be . . . councillors'. Most radical of all, not to say revolutionary, was Stephen's advocacy of a system, as with the Indian Council, whereby professional advice to ministers was recorded and open to parliamentary inspection. Overall, the permanent Civil Service needed to be recognised 'as one of the most important professions in the country' and made 'lucrative and honourable in a corresponding degree'.[121]

Moving from government to the role of the individual, along with Mill, Stephen comprehended that unmodified Benthamite utilitarianism was incapable of offering a tolerably satisfying moral account of man the social being. Each in his own quite different way graduated to a 'higher utilitarianism', seeking to deny Carlyle's taunt that the 'Soul' in 'Utilitarian philosophy' was 'a kind of stomach' and 'Spiritual Union but an Eating together . . .'.[122] But both claimed a continued fidelity to Bentham's great intellectual legacy of empirical rationalism. The obsessive individualism at the heart of On Liberty at the same time appealed to and repelled Stephen. The excesses of the creed of classical liberalism which accepted self-seeking com-mercialism seem to pass beyond the serious notice of Stephen and,[123] in some ways, Mill too; unlike those such as Carlyle and Arnold. Yet Stephen unquestionably shared their distaste for the crude mean materialism built on Mammon, wanting instead a national consciousness of 'high tone' with 'freedom from frivolity' with its 'pettiness purged away'; not so much an electoral but more a 'Spiritual enfranchisement'. However, Arnold's scepticism as to the attainability of this sweetness and light – by making the 'best thought . . . current everywhere' – was matched in Stephen by an unyielding disbelief that the 'ignorant armies' inhabiting Arnold's 'darkling plain'[124] could ever be so enlightened.

6

INDIA AND THE IMPERIAL ETHIC

Between 1855 and 1869 Stephen poured out a great volume of articles, initially in a variety of journals and latterly in the *Pall Mall Gazette*. Yet wide-ranging success and an enviable reputation in higher journalism were not matched by an equally steep ascent in his career at the Bar. Certainly the normal signposts of progress soon appeared, with a Recordership at Newark in 1859 and the taking of silk in 1868. However, not only had the steady gale[1] of absorbing and lucrative work refused to blow, but Stephen was also experiencing an increasing restlessness and desire for involvement in something of greater substance than life on circuit – despite its promise of eventual high financial reward. The opening of 1869 had brought some disappointment when he failed to secure election to Cambridge's Whewell Chair of International Law, with victory going to his old rival Vernon Harcourt; although of the six electors Stephen received the votes of the Millite Henry Fawcett and theologian F. D. Maurice.[2] Therefore when the possibility of legislative work in India turned up Stephen was fairly receptive to the scheme.

Quite when he was first alerted to the chance of replacing Maine as Legal Member of the Viceroy's Council is unclear. Stephen was formally offered the position by the Duke of Argyll, Secretary of State for India, in July 1869;[3] although Leslie Stephen recalls that Maine had approached his brother the previous year.[4] Somewhat coyly, almost misleadingly, Stephen had written to Mill in late April 1869 that

A kind of rumour has grown up, I hardly know how, or why, to the effect that I am to have the offer of Maine's place when he vacates it. The whole matter is quite in the clouds as it appears to me quite uncertain whether Maine will return or not for several years to come, equally unlikely whether if he did I should have the offer of his place and equally uncertain as to whether if I had I should accept it.[5]

The only real uncertainty, it seems, was in Stephen's mind. In favour of going was the epic scale of the adventure. The prospect of being, professionally speaking, a lineal descendant of Macaulay and Maine could only have been immediately and immensely tempting for someone of Stephen's temperament.[6] As he remarked to his mother in March 1869, India appeared 'Legally, morally, politically and religiously . . . nearly the most curious thing in the world.'[7] But pulling in the opposite direction were two similarly powerful considerations against the idea: the possibility of five years of disrupted and fragmented domestic life,[8] and the real risk that he would be exposing his legal career to a period of damaging neglect by opting out of more conventional ways of advancement. Finally in May, after months of dispiriting indecision, Stephen concluded that it was 'the part of a wise and brave man' to take hold of such a chance.[9] Shirking the opportunity and responsibility would have meant forfeiting self-respect and the right 'to profess the doctrines I have always held and preached about the duty of doing the highest thing one can and of not making an idol of domestic comfort'.[10]

Writing in May to their mutual friend Grant Duff, Under-Secretary for India since 1868, Maine confirmed that he intended to vacate office on or about 9 October.[11] One of his concerns was the desirability of meeting up with his successor before handing over his seat in Council. Considerately mindful that the Red Sea at the end of August would be 'simply awful' for the new man, Maine had settled on his own departure date by calculating that the voyage out to India would be pleasanter in September. However, Stephen was prevented from leaving until mid November, just a few days after Maine's arrival back in London.[12]

Seen off at Dover on a bleak 'wet through morning'[13] by Leslie, Minny and Anny Thackeray, Stephen undertook the long journey in optimistic good spirits. Soon after its beginning, a buoyed up, liberated Stephen was able to write 'how perfectly happy I feel in all my prospects . . . never . . . more sure in my life of being right . . . A whole ocean of small worries and cares has fallen away and I can let my mind loose . . . on matters I really care about.'[14] A month later, however, when finally approaching Calcutta, writing to Minny and Anny ('my dearest sisters') Stephen admits to being smitten by a wave of homesickness in attempting 'to utter thoughts that fill my eyes'.[15] Predictably, in addition to a whole series of letters home, Stephen amused himself between England and Bombay by composing – 'like a steam engine' – [16] a healthy crop of *Pall Mall Gazette* articles.[17] Precisely when his Pall Mall Gazetting ceased during his Indian period is uncertain. It is a small but interesting question, for in autumn 1870 Stephen was accused by the Bombay press of unconstitutionally being the *Pall Mall Gazette*'s 'our Indian correspondent'. Leslie Stephen records that his brother's contribution to the paper in that year was fourteen articles, without specifying what they were or exactly when they were published, although commenting elsewhere that 'For the first three or four months he still yielded to the temptation of turning out a few articles on the sly; but he telegraphs home to stop the appearance of some.'[18] Sir Alfred Lyall, then a rising light in Indian officialdom and later a close friend of Stephen's, refers to the allegations in a letter to his sister but, without revealing his evidence, declares them groundless.[19] Yet in December the same year Stephen disclosed to Grant Duff that following Mayo's keenness to have government policy publicly explained it was 'decided that I should take up my old trade at the old shop, and accordingly . . . be devil's advocate in the Pall Mall', in which would soon appear in 'various forms and divers places . . . the touch of a vanished hand'.[20] However, this irregular scheme was nipped in the bud with Grant Duff informing Stephen of the Secretary of State's disapproval of a principal member of the Indian government acting in this fashion.[21]

On the social side, Stephen found most of Anglo-Indian society a little lack-lustre:

passing the winter . . . in Calcutta he finds evening parties are a bore, does not care for the opera, and has nobody with whom to carry on a flirtation – the chief resource of many people. He has therefore nothing to do but to take his morning ride, work all day, and read his books in the evening. He is afraid that he will be considered unsociable or stingy, and is . . . aware of being regarded as an exceptional being; people ask him to 'very quiet' parties.[22]

No doubt many found Stephen's energetic intellect somewhat intimidating, with an Indian colleague noting how he 'fairly dazzled or overwhelmed the exceedingly able coteries among whom he was thrown by a sense of his own transcendent powers'.[23] But, though finding them in the main socially tedious, Stephen had few reservations as to the moral fibre of the British community. Their work-hardened toughness was impressive: 'I am continually reminded of the old saying that it is a society in which there are no old people and no young people. It is the most masculine middle-aged, busy society that ever I saw, and, as you may imagine, I don't like to fall behind the rest in that particular.'[24]

A CODIFICATORY HARVEST

The task of bringing new legal machinery and law to British India had been shared between an Indian Law Commission, eventually sited in London, and the Viceroy's Legislative Council sitting in Calcutta – two bodies sometimes oceans apart in more than a literal sense. It was the function of the Council's legislative department to take up such of the Law Commission's proposals as seemed politically and administratively desirable to the Viceroy's government, and draft enabling bills for eventual enactment. Each bill was required to survive a process of critical evaluation by local government bodies, district officials and other interested parties; after which followed the appointment of a special scrutiny committee, usually including the Legal Member, charged with a detailed examination of both bill and any responses elicited. Depending on the nature and substance of the bill's defects, it would return to the Viceroy's Council for further discussion and possible modification before enactment.[25]

In all these proceedings the most decisive influences on the nature of any legislative programme were the personalities of the Viceroy and the Legal Member and their relationship. Revelling in the central importance of the Legal Member's role, Stephen compared himself to a 'schoolboy let loose into a pastry cook's shop with unlimited credit. The dainties provided, in the way of legislative business, are attractive in kind and boundless in quantity.'[26] All in all, the work was 'perfectly magnificent . . . which I would not have missed to be Lord Chancellor'.[27] Quite what he was required to do and able to achieve as Legal Member was also in large part pre-determined by the immediate history of Maine's occupation of the post. And, in turn the character of Maine's seven-year tenure owed much to political and constitutional antecedents running back over a quarter of a century to Macaulay.

With his appointment in 1834, Macaulay, as head of the first Indian Law Commission, began what was to be a succession of meandering attempts to convert into clear codes a complex and jumbled amalgam of administrative regulations and native laws, the nature of both having been settled overwhelmingly by geography and accident. It was a state of law combining 'nearly every defect': 'exceedingly voluminous and intricate in regard to the matters for which it did provide [and leaving] a vast number of matters of the utmost importance practically unprovided for'.[28] The pace and impetus of reform fell with Macaulay's departure in 1838, energies then being diverted by a succession of external military engage-

ments and internal conquests and annexations. Further
efforts to lift the rate of change came with the appointment of a
second and third Indian Law Commission in 1853 and 1861.[29] By
1861, three years after the Crown had relieved the East India Company of its governance of India, Macaulay's Penal Code had finally
been enacted, along with civil and criminal codes of procedure.

The final phase of Maine's period in India, and the first few
months of Stephen's were soured by a festering conflict with the
Law Commission. During Maine's term of office (1862–9) the Law
Commission had laboured away, producing seven reports ranging
over matters including[30] evidence, criminal procedure and the law
of contracts, all of which were to be the legislative building-blocks
of Stephen's almost frenzied two and a half years in India. On 2 July
1870 the third Law Commission resigned from the process of Indian
legislation expressly on the grounds of Maine's 'systematic' and
'persistent inaction' whilst Legal Member. In their letter of resignation the Commissioners concluded that 'Whatever may be the
cause of this continued inaction, its existence defeats the hope
which we entertained that we were laying the foundation of a system which, when completed, would be alike honourable to the
English Government and beneficial to the people of India.'[31]

From Maine's side the issue had been brought to a head by a
dispute over the Commissioners' report on contracts. Like all
previous reports, it originated solely from London without consultation or liaison with the Legal Member, a practice which Maine
fairly saw as inevitably leading to conflict over the practicality and
relevance of proposed Indian legislation. Writing to Grant Duff,[32]
Maine regarded the central question as whether policy decisions
should 'be shifted from the Indian government to the Indian law
commissioners, a perfectly irresponsible body, sitting once a week
for two hours and including only two gentlemen who have ever
been in India . . . '. On top of this, Maine lacked enthusiasm for
the Benthamite hue of the Commissioners' offerings:

I am greatly afraid that the law commissioners have formed a radically false
notion of the India of the present day. I admit that in the various papers written
by Macaulay and his colleagues on the subject of the first Code, the Penal Code,
there is much to countenance an impression that India is a field for the application
of a diluted Benthamism. It is also true that the Codes and parts of Codes
framed hitherto by the various Commissions have quite succeeded. But the
explanation is to be sought in their subject matter. As to the Penal Code, nobody cares about criminal law except theorists and habitual criminals. The
Codes of Civil & Criminal Procedure affected only functionaries and lawyers,
& the first chapter of the Civil Code, the Indian Succession Act, merely applied

to Europeans. But a substantive Civil Law, applying to everybody and cutting across every transaction of everyday life, is a very different matter.[33]

The dispute rumbled on until July 1870, with Stephen warning Argyll (a supporter of the Commission's position) that the legislative autonomy of the Indian government was indirectly being challenged by the Commissioners.[34] Moreover, like Maine, Stephen complained of having 'very little belief in the opinion that you can properly frame systems of . . . substantive law upon abstract principles as if they were mathematical theories at a distance from the places and people affected by them'.[35] Stephen, even more jealous of the Legal Member's authority than worried about the Commission's legislative insensitivity, was not going to be 'their clerk, but I will do as I like and think right'.[36] By February it was clear to him that there would have to be a 'Desperate fight with this Indian Law Commission . . . like it or not'.[37] The real possibility of his resignation and return from India within the following twelve months was raised;[38] but this prospect died with the Commission's self-extinguishment.

Ahead of Stephen lay two heavy years of capitalising on the Law Commission's efforts, though now in a fashion dictated by Calcutta rather than London. Within a few days of the Law Commission's demise Stephen was able to boast that 'Practically and substantially I am a sort of king in my own department for nobody interferes with me and I can bring in . . . pretty well whatever I choose',[39] and if 'allowed to try my hand' would be able to 'pass all the substantive law they will want to have for many years'.[40] However, time was limited, for he had, from early days, the intention of serving less than a full term:

I felt that for family reasons my time in India must be short . . . I determined to make the most of my opportunity. I worked night and day, cut up . . . drafts and redrew them after my devices and by ways and means and in particular by incessant labour, passed so many Acts that Hobhouse [his successor] and Lord Northbrook looked on me as a sort of revolutionist and did little or nothing in that direction.[41]

By his departure Stephen had piloted through three provisions of principal importance – the Evidence Act,[42] the Contract Act[43] and a revised Code of Criminal Procedure[44] – along with a very substantial cluster of other enactments.[45] Each unselfconsciously and unhesitatingly embodied European juristic and moral notions, the broad ethic of individual rights sweeping aside a culture of collectivistic beliefs and customs. Through circumstances and personality Stephen presided over probably the most legislatively dense period of any Legal Member. Sir Courtenay Ilbert (Legal Member from 1882 to 1886) vividly captured the nature and style of Stephen's activities in India:

His tenure of office lasted only half the ordinary span but he compressed into it enough work for five law members – He left the Legislative Council breathless and staggering, conscious that they had accomplished unprecedented labours.[46]

Soon after returning to England Stephen was able to claim without exaggeration that in the course of thirteen years between 1859 and 1872 'the law of India [was] all but completely codified'.[47] If anything, Stephen modestly understated the force of his performance between 1870 and 1872. Both the role of the Law Commission's formerly fruitless labours and Maine's preparatory work were generously and openly acknowledged. It was, in Stephen's view, 'undoubtedly true that every one of the great laws which collectively form what may be called the Indian codes, was originated, and the first drafts of them were prepared, by the Indian Law Commissioners'.[48] Neither was Maine's contribution, or that of Stephen's officials, overlooked, with Stephen declaring his good fortune in being able to 'reap where others had sown'.[49]

The scale of Stephen's formidable energy and industry in India has never been contested, but the quality of the product has. Criticism has come from two directions: one concentrating on the substantive worth of the legislation, the other arising from the school of colonial thought critical of excessively rapid or 'over-legislation' in India.

As for the instrinsic merits of Stephen's principal works, Maine, amongst other close friends, pronounced the Indian codes in 'form and comprehensiveness' as able to 'stand against all competition'.[50] Pollock's judgement was similarly approving, subject to some reservations over the lack of 'harmony' amongst certain elements of the Contract Act; though they were not faults affecting its serviceability.[51] Bryce tartly suggested that Stephen's 'capacity for . . . drafting was . . . not equal to his fondness for it'.[52] The skilled draftsman's eye of Courtenay Ilbert drew him to a critical yet more sympathetic assessment. Ilbert detected in Stephen an impatience with 'technicalities' and 'minute details', where he compared unfavourably with those like 'his gifted colleague [Lord Justice] Bowen, a legal archangel who danced with ease on the point of a needle'. Whilst Bowen elaborated his arguments 'with the finest camel-hair pencils', Stephen, 'in laying on his colours, preferred a mop'.[53] Nevertheless, in Ilbert's overall judgement Stephen's codes, despite the raw edges, met Indian needs,[54] both practically and educationally.[55]

Suggestions, such as Ilbert's, of Stephen's unwillingness to devote more effort in refining legislative drafts also came from Leslie Stephen. He endorsed the view of his brother's resistance to taking a 'sufficient interest in the more technical parts of his profession . . . and a readiness to be too easily satisfied before the whole structure had received the best possible degree of polish',[56] claiming that Fitzjames too readily saw criticism as 'superfine' with the 'errata pointed out such as concerned a mere corrector of the press rather than a serious legislator'.[57] It is in this last observation that the truth and defensibility of Fitzjames' position lie. Before his arrival in India there had built up a log jam of legislative proposals and an extensive need for the enactment of new measures. Stephen's likely assessment was that this dithering was best met by generating a strenuous legislative momentum, great enough to sweep before it years of prevarication and resistance wedged firmly between London and Calcutta. To believe Stephen was incapable of meticulous attention to legal minutiae when convinced of its appropriateness is to push aside the evidence of his numerous legal digests, prepared, as Stephen reminded his readers, at the cost of long periods of numbing boredom. In India Stephen conceived his task as primarily laying sufficiently solid legislative foundations which, where necessary, could later receive amendment and revision. As Pollock rightly noted,[58] Stephen often declared himself as favouring the (Benthamite) argument for frequent code revisions as a matter of good legislative practice: 'a very laborious business, but . . . essential to the real utility of a code and to maintenance of the simplicity which it is intended to produce'.[59] Unlike Ilbert, who saw codes as being best built of materials with the enduring qualities of 'brass or stone', Stephen may well have chosen the 'brick and stucco of Lower Bengal' as much through preference as perforce.

Coupled with questions relating to the quality of the codes were charges of over-legislation. Certainly Stephen's intensive activity had produced uneasiness in India and England, with his successor Arthur Hobhouse on taking office receiving 'strong hints that it would be desirable to slacken the pace of the legislative machine'.[60] Even Maine had more than once been similarly cautioned by the Secretary of State in the mid 1860s.[61] At heart, the question was political: just how speedily should the Westernisation of Indian institutions progress? From the 1860s to the 1890s a succession of governments blew hot and cold on the issue. Within two years of being warned off over-energetic legislative activity, a resistant Hobhouse was being urged to greater efforts by Lord Salisbury,[62] then Secretary of State for India. Yet, as Ilbert recalls, the pendulum swung back again in the early 1880s when he, as the new Legal Member, was advised to 'hold my oars'.[63] In truth Stephen's tenure represented a cyclical peak, albeit a particularly high one, in Indian legislation. Though when it came to Whitley Stokes' Legal Membership of Lord Lytton's Council, his substantial civil law codifying schemes were enacted under the modifying and restraining influences of Stephen and Maine[64] acting as government consultants;[65] Stephen's primary concern was to maintain Benthamite clarity and accessibility.

Beyond the substance of his legislation, a particularly powerful and lasting impression was made on Stephen by the whole mode of law-making, which contrasted more than favourably with the hit and miss of competitive party squabbling back in England. Moreover, all the participants in the Indian legislative process knew what they were talking about. The passing of the Criminal Procedure Code exemplified this enviably logical way of conducting affairs. After preliminary consultation with a wide body of interested parties

the Code was referred to a Committee of the Legislative Council, consisting, I think, of fourteen or fifteen members, comprising men of the largest experience and highest position from every part of India. The committee met five days in the week, and sat usually for five hours a day. We discussed successively both the substance and the style of every section, and different members assigned for the purpose brought before the committee every criticism which had been made on every section, and all the cases which had been decided by the High Courts on the corresponding sections of the Code of 1861. These discussions were all by way of conversation round a table, in a private room. When the report was presented the Code was passed into law after some little unimportant speaking at a public meeting of the Council. This was possible because in India there are neither political parties nor popular constituencies to be considered, and hardly any reputation is to be got by making speeches. Moreover, every one is a man under authority having others under him. The point which made an ineffaceable impression on my mind was the wonderfully minute and exact acquaintance with every detail of the system displayed by the civilian members of the committee. They knew to a nicety the history, the origin, and the object of every provision in the Code which we were recasting. Such a section, they would say, represented such a regulation or such an act. It was passed in the time of such a Governor-General in order to provide for such and such a state of things, and we must be careful to preserve its effect. To be present at, and take part in, these discussions was an education not only in the history of British India, but in the history of laws and institutions in general. I do not believe that one act of

parliament in fifty is considered with anything approaching to the care or discussed with anything approaching to the mastery of the subject with which
Indian acts are considered and discussed.[66]

The qualified application of such lessons to the English political
scene was obvious and appears fleetingly in *Liberty, Equality,
Fraternity*, with a fuller development of ideas and prescriptions
mapped out in his *Contemporary Review* articles 'Parliamentary
Government' (1873 and 1874).[67]

ADMINISTRATIVE EFFICIENCY AND THE RULE OF LAW – A 'BLENDING OF SOMERSET HOUSE AND THE OLD BAILEY'

Macaulay understood that the basis of any policy of imposing
Western culture and its accompanying institutions on the Indian
states was a strong and well-developed legal infrastructure. He
accepted that the Benthamite aims of 'suppressing crime with the
smallest possible infliction of suffering, and ascertaining truth at
the smallest possible cost of time and money' could be achieved by
clear codes effectively enforced by a well-trained judiciary. Only
with this apparatus could there be reasonable hope of engrafting
'on despotism those blessings which are the natural fruits of liberty'[68]
and appeasing any Whiggish scruples over the general expectation
of free institutions. A sound efficient system of laws was an obvious
prerequisite of any civilised nation, for as James Mill frequently
argued,[69] without such machinery there could be no economic regeneration or advance; law was the sole guarantor of the security of
the rewards of individual and commercial endeavour.[70]

But whose laws? Macaulay saw as clearly as any that if British
rule was to be an enlightened despotism the laws and the system
must be Western in nature, coinciding with our own political
instincts and expectations though falling short of producing self-
government. Yet when it came to framing laws and establishing the
institutions of justice, Macaulay, determined to resist English models,
practised an unhampered eclecticism in settling general principles
of liability. This was the declared basis of his Penal Code,
Macaulay's most lasting contribution to Indian law. In this limited
respect he was, unlike Stephen, a thorough-going Benthamite.
However, although the introduction to the Penal Code proclaims
its conceptual independence of other systems,[71] almost inevitably
much of the content of English common law insinuated itself into
the Code. Yet Stephen was somewhat misleading in describing the
substance of Macaulay's great work as the common law 'freed from

all technicalities and superfluities, systematically arranged and modified in some few particulars . . . to suit the circumstances of . . . India',[72] even if he did expressly recognise its form to be 'an entirely new and original method of legislative expression'.[73] Contrastingly his own approach to codification in India lacked Macaulay's de novo originality, and indeed much more resembled English common law 'freed from all technicalities and super-fluities'.[74] They shared a pragmatic approach to law-making, but rather than seeing India as a testing ground for radical theories of substantive criminal responsibility, evidence and procedure, Stephen's imagination was in many ways more taken up by the broader political and social significance of his legislative work.

For as Stephen soon discovered, even in the 1870s the relevance of and justification for a Westernised legal system in India was far from fully accepted at all levels of Indian government: 'They have an opinion which I have in some instances heard very distinctly ex-pressed by persons of high authority, that the state of things throughout India is such that law ought in all cases be overridden by what is called equity in the loose popular sense of the word'; that the executive power vested in government representatives should not be fettered by complex systems of laws only appropriate to a self-governing nation; that lawyers were their 'natural enemies' and law a 'mysterious power', the special function of which was to prevent or 'embarrass and retard anything like vigorous executive action'.[75] Put in the starkest terms, it amounted to the desire for discretionary power when it was thought necessary 'to put people to death without any trial . . . on secret information for which the persons who give it are not to be responsible'. These beliefs in the opposing demands of law and vigorous administration rested on a confusion of ideas and traditions which were 'super-annuated and ought to be forgotten'.[76] Such a common hankering after rule by discretion exhibited to Stephen a compelling need for him to make out a principled justification in favour of government by law; this he did in a lengthy dissertation innocently entitled a 'Minute on the Administration of Justice in British India' (1872),[77] and later in a chapter contributed to Sir William Hunter's *Life of the Earl of Mayo* (1875).

Stephen's initial ground for the supremacy of the rule of law, like James Mill's, was the obvious need for security of life and property, 'the indispensible condition of the growth of wealth'. That conceded, there was no halfway house of mixing law and 'personal government'; any compromise between law and despotism 'is like a compromise between straight and crooked'. Indian history was unassailable proof of the truth of this. Government by the whim and caprice of 'innumerable rulers' had worn Indian society down 'to the bone'. At best the country had become a 'mass of village communities, presided over by perhaps the most inorganic, ill-defined aristocracies and monarchies that ever existed'.[78] The outcome of this absence of legal institutions had been a state of affairs hostile to the 'growth of wealth, political experience and the moral and intellectual changes which are implied in these processes' – Hobbesian misery rather than Rousseauesque natural bliss. These village communities were 'a crude form of socialism, paralysing the growth of individual energy and all its consequences'. Continuation of this state of soceity was 'radically inconsistent with the fundamental principles of our rule both in theory and in practice'.[79] Disputes between individuals or communities were necessarily settled by violence, a primitiveness that could only be eliminated by 'laws in the full sense of the word':

If Government does not allow a man to assemble his friends, arm them with bludgeons and axes, and march out against a set of neighbouring villagers who have interfered with his pasture or his watercourse, it must determine whether he or his antagonist is in the right; and it must determine this according to rules which must be made distinct for the purpose of getting to a decision: and this is law. In a word, peace and law go together, just as elastic custom and violence go together. But every one admits that, whatever else we do in India, we must keep the peace; and this is strictly equivalent to saying that we must rule by law.[80]

The Penal Code, the Code of Criminal Procedure and the institutions which they regulate, are somewhat grim presents for one people to make to another, and are little calculated to excite affection; but they are eminently well calculated to protect peaceable men and to beat down wrong-doers, to extort respect, and to enforce obedience.[81]

Good law provided not merely the benefits of peace but 'vigorous administration'. Moreover, sensible laws soundly administered constituted a 'moral conquest more striking, more durable and far more solid, than the physical conquest which renders it possible' – in many ways an influence comparable to that of a 'new religion'. Our law was the 'sum and substance of what we have to teach'. It was the 'gospel of the English'; though in this case, a 'compulsory gospel which admits to no dissent and no disobedience'.[82]

This was Stephen's Benthamite answer to those seduced by the appetising prospect of government by discretion. Additionally, there was a different objection to the importation of English legal institutions not wholly met by these arguments. There was considerable scepticism from some quarters as to the appropriateness of (essentially) undiluted English law for India: more particularly, whether Macaulay's emphasis on Western jurisprudence was right. The matter struck Stephen as one of 'time, season, and opportunity'.[83] Less cryptically, reliance on native law and structures, where they existed, would be a demonstrable absurdity. Indian notions of government had been disastrous, for they had led to 'general anarchy and [national] degradation'. Their long-term effect had produced a race and collection of institutions incapable of effective self-government. In any case, if native ideas were adopted, would we rule on the basis of Hindu or Muhammadan principles, or by both? No; history, theory and practical experience resoundingly excluded government by native principles.[84] Was the whole ramshackle body of indigenous laws and customs to be mercilessly swept away and a policy of complete Europeanisation to be instituted? Stephen's answer was susbstantially the one given in Bentham's 'Essay on the Influence of Time and Place':[85] that the elimination of native law was legitimate so far as it was necessary for the 'firm establishment of British power [and] the principles which it represents'.[86] Beyond these admittedly vague restrictions any other interference was 'speculative, mischievous and dangerous'.

However, despite this, Stephen confessed to believing that native laws and customs though not directly struck at 'by legislation would eventually be overwhelmed by the social revolution' spawned by the introduction of a new regime of 'peace, law, order, unrestricted competition for wealth, knowledge and honours and an education to match'. It was a social revolution likely to modify every part of the daily life of India, 'changing every article of all their creeds'. The duty of the British in India was to ensure that this revolution ran in 'proper channels' and produced 'good results'. Quite what the final outcome would be was 'impossible to fortell', though it seemed to Stephen most unlikely that, as regards politics, religion or morals, India would 'reproduce Europe'.[87]

THE JAMAICA COMMITTEE AND IMPEY

Two famous incidents in colonial history which in different ways detained Stephen were the Governor Eyre case and the impeachment of Warren Hastings. Both affairs further illustrate Stephen's strong interest in and insistence on the key function of law as the basis of all legitimate and wholesome government.

The Eyre case came into Stephen's life more than three years before his departure for India when political unrest in Jamaica culminated in widespread rioting and the deaths of a number of white residents. On the command of Governor Edward Eyre the disorder was savagely suppressed, with almost 100 blacks killed by troops; a further 300 or so were executed following Eyre's imposition of martial law and trial by courts martial.[88] Though no direct participant in the rioting, George Gordon, a mixed race member of the Jamaican legislature, was arrested at Eyre's instigation, tried by a court martial on General Nelson's orders, and executed for his complicity in the insurrection.

The Jamaican events fuelled a national controversy, 'conducted', as Leslie Stephen describes, 'with a bitterness not often paralleled'.[89] A special commission, including Stephen's cousin Russell Gurney, was dispatched to Jamaica in late 1865. Produced the following April, the commission's report found that Eyre had used excessive measures in putting down the riot. The division of national opinion on the whole issue came to be represented in two campaigning bodies. Those critical of Eyre rallied behind John Stuart Mill as chairman of the Jamaica Committee. Supporters of the Governor countered with the Eyre Defence Committee. The former grouping included Bright, Harrison, Spencer and Huxley; the latter, Dickens, Tennyson and Carlyle, who later[90] typically labelled the opposition as that 'knot of rabid Nigger Philanthropists'.

To view the opposing camps as at odds on clear-cut principle would be an oversimplification,[91] for their differences were those of emphasis or predisposition to accept a particular interpretation of events. Those, like Bright and Harrison, who had long suffered an uneasy conscience over British colonialism were not unready to believe that allegations of brutal repression were true, whereas the starting-point of the pro-Eyre camp was acceptance of the Empire as a glorious achievement, to be defended with all expedient firmness. Therefore it was to be assumed, subject to the strongest rebutting evidence, that Eyre had done no more than was essential to protect national interests. Rapidly, almost accidentally and misleadingly, the two committees also became focuses for the broader contemporary question of franchise reforms, Mill's movement being associated with the progressive and the Defence Committee coming to represent the forces of conservatism.

Against such a backdrop in January 1866 Stephen[92] was approached by Mill on behalf of the Jamaica Committee for a legal opinion on whether, and how, prosecutions might be brought. Stephen advised that Eyre and General Nelson (amongst others) were triable for murder.[93] Further study of the special commission's findings and evidence left Stephen in little doubt that Eyre had acted in a manner that was 'violent, tyrannical and imprudent to a degree which I hardly imagined possible'.[94] Gordon appeared to have been hanged not in order to maintain immediate peace, but in the interests of longer-term political expediency.

Stephen appeared twice as counsel for the Committee. In January 1867 he successfully applied to Bow Street Magistrates' Court for an order committing General Nelson[95] for trial on a charge of murdering Gordon. Stephen's legal argument was well laced with the sentiment that riding on the back of the Court's decision was the larger issue of how far the rule of law was to prevail over arbitrary government in the Empire. But the Committee's initial success was terminated three months later by an unconvinced Grand Jury. During March 1867, Stephen made a further appearance for the Committee at Market Drayton in an attempt to have Eyre himself indicted for murder. On this occasion, despite Stephen's five-hour presentation, the action immediately foundered, with the Shropshire Bench finding that the evidence failed to make out even a prima facie case. Against Stephen's advice, Mill and the Committee continued into the following year with further fruitless efforts to start up prosecutions. As Leslie Stephen observed, and as is attested to by Fitzjames' court performances, Mill felt more keenly the moral dimensions to the cases; whereas Stephen, though hardly condoning the conduct of Eyre and Nelson, believed it was at least understandable in the heat of the rebellion. It was this personal detachment of Stephen, with his concern focusing principally on the wider question of the dependency of good government on strictly enforced law, that separated him from Mill and the Jamaica Committee. And if Leslie is to be believed, it was his brother's want of committed ardour for the cause which did not endear him to Mill.[96]

Coming well after his period in India, and of quite a different order, was Stephen's scholarly connection with the great eighteenth-century scandal of Warren Hasting's impeachment, an interest which sprang (according to Stephen) from the way important events in British history had frequently been linked to the administration of criminal justice. In the *Story of Nuncomar* (1885) Stephen selected for his study the role of Sir Elijah Impey in the Hastings affair. His choice turned partly on the intrinsic importance of this incident, and also on the fact that Impey was Chief Justice of the Supreme Court of Calcutta. As Stephen owned, it was very natural that a former Legal Member of the Viceroy's Council should feel an interest in the 'history of a Chief Justice charged with judicial murder, alleged to have been committed in order to shield his old friend Hastings the first Governor-General of Bengal from detection [for] corruption'.[97]

With an analytical mind honed to slice through irrelevancies and to sift and weigh evidence, Stephen was obviously admirably suited for a task of this nature. On completion of his historical post mortem he entertained no doubts (nor did many others afterwards) that Macaulay's claim that 'Impey, sitting as a judge, put a man . . . to death in order to serve a political purpose' was, at best, an example of 'fancy' doing the work of logic, or, put more fairly, an 'audacious inference from a few hints and indications'.[98] However, as Stephen admitted, rewriting a part of history so vigorously and spectacularly created by Macaulay was attended by keen regret at having to expose the reputation of the great man to such a tarnishing rebuttal.[99] Not only was there the strong kinship of their common Indian experiences, but Macaulay was 'my own friend, my father's and my grandfather's friend also, and there are few injunctions which I am more disposed to observe than the one which bids us not to forget such persons'.[100] Yet Stephen dutifully presented his damning evidence,[101] condeming Macaulay, James Mill[102] and Burke as having miscreated history either through a miserable absence of political objectivity or plain slipshod scholarship.

As a literary venture, Stephen honestly confessed to doubts over whether it was worth the 'infinity of trouble' it had demanded, concluding that the 'public will say of it as Carlyle said of something or someone "Dog won't eat it."' [103] But, at least, as Goldwin Smith later noted, 'Thanks to Sir James Stephen we know that the judicial murder of Nuncomar is a fiction [and] a tissue of falsehoods.'[104]

MAINTAINING THE INDIAN CONNECTION

With his return to England in April 1872 Stephen was terminating the physical link with India, but his absorption in that country's affairs actively endured for the remainder of his life. It was an interest and involvement that would operate through intimate friendships with high-ranking Anglo-Indian officials and dignitaries, and through public campaigning.

Before the 1870s, colonial, and particularly Indian, matters had not figured prominently in party politics. The 1858 post-mutiny change-over of responsibility for the administration of India from the East India Company to the British government was a predictable yet not wholly welcomed development, though disagreement was not party based. Many had seen, and still saw, the system of shared or double government as the most effective apparatus for controlling Indian administration. Macaulay, both Mills and Maine[105] had all favoured the approach because of their common belief that good government required a level of sympathy and knowledge only possessed by those in the field. Even after 1858, Mill still doggedly promoted the case for the old system in *Representative Government*. Only through a delegated body, like the East India Company, composed of committed and informed professionals, would India be likely to receive enlightened rule, well insulated from the 'vortex of party and parliamentary jobbing'. For above all in a country like India 'everything depends on the personal qualities and capacities of the agents of government. This truth is the cardinal principle of Indian administration.'[106]

But by the 1870s hopes of keeping India detached from domestic politics were fast fading; political minds had turned to the question of the ends to which India was being ruled. For some the answer was tied up in the larger issue of the general philosophy and posture of Britain's foreign policy. Originally an appointee of Disraeli, Lord Mayo, as Viceroy from 1869 to 1872, began the open espousal of Conservative imperialism with India as its centrepiece and forward base. The Conservatives, according to Mayo, were 'determined as long as the sun shines in heaven to hold India. Our national character, our commerce, demand it; and we have, one way or another, two hundred and fifty millions of English capital fixed in the country'; though, remembering higher duties, 'we have no right to be here at all unless we use all our power for the good of the blacks'.[107]

Until Disraeli's 'new' Conservatism, the political and moral basis of Indian rule was not a serious source of division between party dogmatists. There was no expressed deviation from Burke's notions of colonial trusteeship; that power was to be exercised over native races principally for the welfare of those races, coupled with an implicit expectation of ultimate self-government. In the meantime few had doubts about the general rectitude of colonial rude. As Mill explained: 'The sacred duties which civilized nations owe to the independence and nationality of each other, are not binding towards those to whom nationality and independence are a certain evil, or at least a questionable good.'[108] Differences between and within parties had centred on the best means of achieving good government rather than on longer-term objectives. And even though a long line of theoretical anti-colonialists from Bentham to Bright could each produce a bag of arguments against our overseas presence,[109] their political consciences were reassured by the belief that having taken on the burden it was our national duty to complete the task; for precipitate withdrawal would be equivalent to 'scuttling the ships we had ourselves launched'.[110]

Additionally, the direct issue of self-government was obscured and avoided by fanciful schemes for the pan-continental settlement of Britain's population overflow. The essence of such projects, earlier entertained by Bentham and Molesworth, was revitalised and propagated particularly by the likes of Charles Dilke and James Froude, with Dilke's *Greater Britain* (1868) offering a cocktail of federalism and Anglo-Saxon leadership,[111] and Froude, from the vantage-point of his editorship of *Fraser's Magazine*, joining in efforts to bring about a political and cultural expansionist mood within the country.[112] It was partly these sentiments of looking abroad for national development and glory, intellectually represented by those such as Dilke and Froude, that Disraeli rendered into political policies and, eventually, action.

Stephen's connection with Disraeli's early imperialism came about through his close friendship with Lord Lytton, elegant littérateur and Viceroy from 1876 to 1880. Lytton and Stephen first met on 26 January 1876 at a dinner party given by Lady Arthur Russell, leaving later 'to spend the rest of the evening at the Cosmopolitan Club, [after which they] spent half the night walking each other home, too absorbed in their subject [of India] to feel fatigue or the wish to separate'.[113] Lytton obviously felt that here was someone who might authoritatively help counteract the 'absolute ignorance of every fact and question concerning India' which he had admitted to Disraeli when accepting the viceroyalty.[114] On the eve of his departure, Stephen provided Lytton with a written discourse on Indian government, described by the recipient as 'a policeman's bull's-eye', which had given him 'the master-key to the magnificent mystery of Indian administration'. In Lytton Stephen had found a man of positive and direct power who paid him the 'one compliment which goes straight to my heart – the compliment of caring to hear what I have to say and seeing the point of it'.[115] There followed an almost daily correspondence during Lytton's period as Viceroy, Stephen's letters being rated by Lytton as 'chief among the greatest comforts and enjoyments' of life in India.[116] Stephen became Lytton's great moral support – stability and dependability at times when other alliances sagged; in turn Lytton was the 'gleam of poetry shed over the close of Stephen's life'.[117] By contrast, during the four years of the viceroyalty, Lytton's firm friendship with John Morley ran downhill almost as rapidly as his one with Stephen had become established.[118] The three formed a sort of political ménage à trois, with Lytton receiving opposing counsel from each and being quickly won over by Stephen's instinctively more appealing advice, with Stephen's position approximating to Salisbury/Disraeli expansionism, and Morley's to Gladstone's 'Little Englandism'.

Lytton's viceroyalty was to be a prominent failure and source of heated party dispute for both its internal policies and frontier exploits. To Salisbury (then playing the role of a strongly interventionist Secretary of State for India) a powerful recommendation for Lytton's appointment was his presumed willingness to take up Disraeli's 'forward' Afghan policy; something which Lytton's predecessor, the Liberal Lord Northbrook, had shown some reluctance to do.[119] Lytton adopted his brief with a degree of enthusiasm that required Salisbury to rein in his Viceroy from a policy that was developing into pure adventurism. But with a less diligent Lord Cranbrook replacing Salisbury in 1878, the relatively unsupervised Lytton moved through a successful popular opening campaign of the second Afghan War to the sourness of the quickly ensuing setbacks which became an embarrassing political liability at home for Disraeli.

Throughout the political storms over Afghanistan Lytton had few non-governmental defenders. In England, Stephen shared the burden of fighting Lytton's corner in the columns of *The Times*. During October[120] and November 1878 *The Times* published a series of letters from Stephen, mostly of considerable length, with some exceeding three full-page columns, and on practically every occasion accompanied by careful editorial analysis. Ranging over a combination of political, diplomatic, legal and military questions, they displayed, in *The Times'* opinion, formidable analytical cogency.[121] Overall, his position was, essentially, that Lytton's measures were justifiable as self-defence of India, whose care and control we were duty bound to safeguard – actions motivated by national honour rather than avaricious ambition: a stance provoking a flurry of rejoinders and surrejoinders. Most distinguished among Stephen's opponents were Lord Lawrence, Lord Northbrook and Vernon Harcourt, the last of whom had vigorously set about Stephen on a question of international law. Harcourt,[122] who had the year before given up the Whewell Chair of International Law at Cambridge, was on home ground. Stephen's thesis entailed the proposition that the rights of autonomous states to freedom from external interference were graduated in accordance with the degree of civilisation each had attained: developed Westernised states enjoyed total protection under international law, while completely barbarous states had none. Harcourt ridiculed the theory as untenable and absurd; but T. E. Holland, the late Austinian jurist and occupant of the Chichele Chair of International Law at Oxford, thought otherwise and wrote strongly in Stephen's defence,[123] doubtless to Stephen's considerable satisfaction.

Lytton was naturally grateful for Stephen's steadfast support, writing in December 1878: 'My two and a half years of life in India have had their fair share of anxiety and discouragement, . . . but they have given me two friends, whose friendship I prize infinitely beyond every other gift, yourself and John Strachey.'[124] In respect of Morley, after his highly critical letters and hostile treatment in the *Fortnightly Review*[125] Lytton was driven to

recognis[ing] as irremediable, all that is involved, to my lasting loss, in the fundamental difference between our respective views and feelings about which no Englishman should be indifferent, and which both of us deeply take to heart . . . How can I find any comfort in intimate intercourse with one who conscientiously regards me as the willing, or witless instrument of a wicked betrayal, or abominable mismanagement, of the highest public interest?[126]

In the deflated atmosphere of his final few months in India, a weary Lytton felt compelled to express the extent of his debt to Stephen:

You can have no idea what a help your letters are to me . . . I . . . swear to God, and to all the gods ever swearable at, that from . . . occasional suicidal failures of heart and hope I am more than rescued, I am exalted – and for all anxiety or unmerited abuse more than recompensed – glorified – by the continued esteem and sympathy with which I find myself still honoured by you, whose good opinion of my work in India I value more than that of any man living, and much more than that of posterity, which so rarely has a fair chance of justly judging the dead, and in whose eyes I shall assuredly cut a sorry figure if the history of my Indian administration comes to be written by Liberal pens.[127]

Lytton's internal policies earned him no more friends than the Afghan campaign. His early period in office had basked in the brilliance and imperial showiness of the 1877 Delhi durbar, at which the Viceroy had proclaimed his Sovereign Empress of India. And although at the time he was a continent away, Stephen's presence and influence were very much in evidence, for Lytton's durbar speech was saturated with suggestions eagerly drafted by Stephen's 'itching fingers'.[128] Stephen even received express acknowledgement as 'One of the wisest, and most eminent' advocates of the funadamental necessity of the impartial adherence to the Rule of Law in India.[129] Though in general terms unremarkable, with its policy of firm but even-handed administration, the Lytton viceroyalty earned from many an indelible black mark for its enactment of the repressive Vernacular Press Act (1878), under which native language newspapers could be censored where thought potentially seditious or likely to generate political disaffection. Lytton saw only administrative advantage in the provisions of the 'muzzling Act'.[130] Unlike his predecessors, he discounted the value that a free Indian press might have in providing the government with some open channel of information on the direction of current educated Indian thought.[131] And it was this particular measure, along with the adventurism of Afghanistan, that gave Gladstone a firm political purchase on Disraeli's Indian policy, used to damaging effect in the late 1870s and during the 1880 election campaign.[132]

Prior to Lytton there had been no serious open party division on the issue of where British Indian rule was or should be leading, or more directly, whether self-government was to be consciously worked towards, or whether it was a possibility that a less engineered form of political evolution should be left to take care of. However, during Lytton's tenure, and even more so in that of his successor, Lord Ripon, the question came to the surface in the wake of the general political turbulence caused by Tory imperial inclinations meeting Gladstonian conscientious objections. With Gladstone's 1880 election success, Lytton resigned to be replaced by Lord Ripon , who saw as a priority both undoing the harm he believed Lytton's rule had caused to good Indian government and erasing the overpowering impression that native interests were to be sacrificed to those of Britain.[133] Most particularly, Ripon was bent on implementing Gladstone's policy of politically educating the native population for eventual self-rule, progress towards which meant replacing Lytton's firm paternalism with moves towards a consensual partnership in government.

By the second year of his viceroyalty Ripon felt justified in boasting of getting 'more radical every day and am rejoiced to say that the effect of despotic power has so far been to strengthen and deepen my liberal convictions'.[134] However, the fruits of this unashamed radicalism were not so quick in coming, with even Lytton's 'detestable' Vernacular Press Act remaining unrepealed until 1882.[135] Ripon's efforts in the area of increased provincial native administration met with Gladstone's warm approval: Gladstone agreed that the political benefits of local self-government outweighed the apparent administrative inefficiency that the policy seemed to entail.[136] Such subordination of governmental efficiency to other more far-reaching objectives was proclaimed in an Indian government resolution on 'Local Self-Government' (1882), under which native involvement in local government was declared as 'chiefly desirable as an instrument of political and popular education'.[137] Speaking for some members of the Indian Council in London, Maine warned of the widespread disquiet that Ripon's activities were generating.[138] This and consequential legislation following the Ripon resolution agitated British officialdom in India, doing much to feed suspicions that Ripon and the Liberals were set hard on an accelerating policy of the general Indianisation of government.

In such a climate of growing Anglo-Indian unease the then Legal Member, Sir Courtenay Ilbert, introduced what quickly became known as the Ilbert Bill, whose object was the removal of race as a basis for jurisdiction in certain criminal trials.[139] This unremarkable attempt to rationalise the administration of criminal justice was substantively quite free of any radical taint, yet its proposal convulsed the Anglo-Indian community, sending massive political reverberations from Calcutta to Westminster. The irrationality and unexpectedness of the outcry can be gauged from the fact that native judges had for some time exercised civil jurisdiction over Europeans and non-Europeans alike without serious dissent. At home, the only substantial cautionary note recorded before the bill's publication came from Maine. But Maine's warning, conveyed to Lord Hartington, Secretary of State for India, never reached Ripon, and so the latter unsuspectingly 'put his hand deep into this hornets' nest'.[140] Not that Ripon would have been overimpressed by Maine's apprehensions even if he had received notice of them.[141] For Maine had, from early on in Ripon's tenure of office, harboured the gravest doubts about its general direction. According to Stephen, Maine frequently referred to Ripon as 'that bloody little fool', whose policies were 'six times more rash and dangerous than anything [Lytton was] ever accused of'.[142] It was the style as much as or more than the content of Ripon's policies that most upset Stephen; and as a punishment for these sins and the throwing out of grand 'rhetorical resolutions' to show a 'great Liberal Viceroy is come in as an Avatar of Liberal Justice',[143] Ripon 'deserve[d] to be hugged to death by the greatest Baboos in Calcutta'.[144]

Along with Maine, both Stephen and Lytton engaged themselves in opposing the bill. Lytton's contribution was made primarily in the Upper House,[145] Maine's through his membership of the Indian Council, and Stephen's, naturally, by a dose of hard-hitting journalism – first in the correspondence columns of *The Times*[146] and later at greater length in 'Foundations of the Government of India', published in the *Nineteenth Century*. But, as Stephen soon realised, the apocalyptic tone of his opening letter to *The Times* was miscalculated. Though in no way altering the substance and logic of his case against the bill, Stephen sensed the need to explain the provocative use of terms such as 'conquest . . . heathenism and barbarian', which larded his first *Times* contribution, – where 'I may have yielded to the temptation of expressing my opinions in a needlessly trenchant and unpopular style.'[147] This sliver of tactical repentance was in good part brought about by Sir Arthur Hobhouse's *Contemporary Review* defence of the bill in which he had spoken, with obvious allusion to Stephen's letter (and *Liberty, Equality, Fraternity*), of the 'recrudescence of the doctrine of force, and the doctrine that mankind are mostly fools who require the strong and wise Ruler to break their heads if they do not conduct themselves as he thinks fit'.[148]

Stephen's interventionary style even irritated close friends still serving the Empire, whose lives during the affair had become rather stressful and politically uncomfortable. Sir Alfred Lyall, Lieutenant-Governor of the North-West Provinces, told Stephen[149] that the *Times* letter had 'mightily strengthened and encouraged Anglo-Indian opposition to the Bill'. It was a source of regret to Lyall that Stephen had reached for his 'formidable cudgel at quite so awkward a moment'. Lyall readily admitted, however, that the 'very high degree and temperature of race feeling . . . exhibited, proves now that we all miscalculated the political bearings of the measure'.[150] Grant Duff, then Governor-General of Madras, was blunter, informing Ripon that 'Personally I am devoted to Stephen, but I have just sent him a message through Arthur Russell to the effect that he is politically "a child of the devil and getting more silly every day" '.[151] Even Sir John Strachey, Stephen's intellectual comrade since Mayo's viceroyalty, sympathised with the object of the bill, whilst agreeing that the form of the proposals and tactics of enactment could have been more discreetly managed.[152] By 1884 the whole salutory episode, as distinct from the broader issue, had fizzled out with the adoption of a change which granted Indian magistrates extended jurisdiction, whilst retaining the entitlement of European British subjects to be tried by jury. As Strachey noted,[153] this was a 'virtual though not avowed abandonment of the original bill'.

The political lesson, both for emerging Indian nationalists and progressive governments, was plain: even with strong support at home and from a sympathetic Viceroy, the rate of change could not overtake that permitted by the confidence of the Anglo-Indian establishment – much as Gladstone believed it was 'right and needful to chasten [its] saucy pride'.[154] With the prospect of such unattractive domestic political consequences, any serious re-distribution of political and administrative power looked unlikely to come from British governmental initiatives. The message, if there was one, for Indians was to look to their own resources for any realisation of political hopes and ambitions.

Stephen's detailed response to being 'challenged by Arthur Hobhouse who blasphemed against me in a rather pointed way'[155] appeared in the *Nineteenth Century* a few months after his full-blooded *Times* letters. As the cooler, more measured 'Foundations of the Government of India' explains:

The question between my friend Sir Arthur Hobhouse and myself is indeed a question rather of general theory, of tendency, and of sentiment, than a question as to the particular measures. I do not approve of Mr Ilbert's Bill, but I think its instrinsic importance has been exaggerated . . . [Though it constituted a] truckling to popular prejudices and commonplaces and to measures which are of no use except to annoy Europeans and hold out all sorts of delusive expectations to natives.[156]

Stephen was right insofar as he saw the bill as symptomatic and symbolic of a Gladstonian inclination to take seriously the possibility of a programme of Indian political education with self-rule sitting on a discernible, albeit distant, horizon. At the heart of Stephen's argument was a call for openness and absence of hypocrisy in discussions on the nature and legitimacy of British government in India. As a starting-point we should cease all humbug or anxious wringing of hands over the reality of our dominion there. Force, as Stephen had said at some length in *Liberty, Equality, Fraternity*, was the presupposed basis of all governments. 'Justice' in the sense of an impartial striving to promote the lasting good of the population was, without force, a 'weak aspiration after an unattainable end'.[157] All governments must decide 'how and how far is collective force of any given community to be organised? in which hands is it, when organised, to be vested? to what ends shall it be directed? by what means shall it be made to effect those ends?'[158] On this Stephen took Lord Salisbury's line, that although 'We are told to secure ourselves by their affections, not by force, [our] great-grandchildren may be privileged to do so, but not we'.[159] In short, Indian government rested on conquest, not consent. But it was a conquest that was neither 'insulting nor humiliating' to either conqueror or conquered: 'conquest in India had in no case meant anything more than the transfer by military force of political power from one hand to another', a transfer sanctioned in many subsequent Acts of Parliament and paralleled by the whole history of Europe. So to 'stigmatise conquest as robbery[160] and describe conquerors as criminals' was a worthless analogy 'fit only for rhetorical purposes'.[161]

From these unchallengeable truths of British rule in India, certain 'practical inferences' followed, the most central of which was that such government could not be representative of its subjects. The basis of rule was European morality and notions of civilisation, a reality that was 'supremely useful to India and honourable to England'. We had imposed a superior civilisation on an inferior one; by force we had largely eliminated cruel and inhuman religious and social practices. Europeanisation of India, once our presence had been established, was a 'moral necessity'. For Stephen, just as with James Mill and Macaulay, keeping India in its undeveloped condition would have been 'rightly regarded' with abhorrence both on moral and economical grounds. Besides, politically it would have been suicidal. If the British had tried to govern India by Indian ideas they would have been fatally swallowed up by the disputes which had in the past fragmented and demolished Indian society. Refusal to recognise this was 'dangerous in the highest degree, and . . . a long step to the destruction of the Empire'. Granted the indisputability of this, what voice might Indians have in the country's destiny? Were they to be permanently excluded from self-government? Here Stephen offers no more than principles of good government appropriate to India, advocating neither perpetual British rule nor Indian self-government.[162]

The task of providing effective government of India was undeniably awesome, truly 'gigantic', but achievable through the introduction of the essential elements of European civilisation:

peace, order, the supremacy of law, the prevention of crime, the redress of wrong, the enforcement of contracts, the development and concentration of the military force of the state, the construction of public works, the collection and expenditure of the revenue required for these objects in such a way as to promote to the utmost the public interest, interfering as little as possible with the comfort or wealth of the inhabitants and improvement of the people. [In effect] the laws and institutes of the country are to be founded on European secular morality, on European views of political economy, and on the principle that man ought to be entitled by law, irrespective of religion, race, caste and similar considerations, to enjoy securely whatever property they have, to get rich if they can by legal means, and to be protected in doing as they please, so long as they do not hurt others.[163]

As a classical statement of Whig/Liberal political and economic doctrine, Stephen's 'European' ideals might easily have been drafted by Macaulay. By the steady and firm pursuance of this political evangelism there was the hope of working a gradual and permanent transformation in the indigenous character, beliefs and culture of a country still 'grossly ignorant, steeped in idolatrous superstition, unenergetic, fatalistic, indifferent to most of what we regard as the evils of life, and preferring the repose of submitting to them to the trouble of encountering and trying to remove them' – all aspects of spiritual sloth so deeply despised by those well imbued with the Calvinist ethic. But the history of India suggested such progress was unachievable in the absence of an external intervention of the nature and scale then being experienced. In making these judgements Stephen, in obvious contrast to Maine,[164] was unencumbered by any elements of social Darwinian or evolutionary theory[165] – that the whole of mankind was at different stages of progress towards common civilised ends – though Stephen had no doubts as to the universal validity and relevance of European institutions and morality. Along with J. S. Mill and the broad utilitarian school, Stephen's deductions and prescriptions largely rested on the near events of modern history and the realities of what could be seen and experienced. Most specifically, as *Liberty, Equality, Fraternity* shows, Stephen invested no faith in any form of historical determinism, whether of a Comtean of Spencerian variety.

Assuming the success of this gigantic enterprise, what would be the eventual political outcome? How, and by whose hand, should a remodelled, a recreated, India with all the principal attributes of European nationhood be governed? Certainly, Stephen fairly confidently foresaw a wealthy India with immense trade accompanied by fundamental changes in religion, morals and politics, but 'with what specific result no one who does not claim the power of prophecy can pretend to say'.[166] The likelihood and time scale for this intellectual and moral metamorphosis was obviously of immediate political consequence in that it could colour current government policy. Awareness of this was no doubt responsible for Stephen's caution, if not downright evasiveness, in speculating on the matter. First thoughts suggest change was reasonably certain within 'due time' if present policies were followed, though a few paragraphs later the odds seem to lengthen in favour of change being 'not improbable' in the 'course of time'.[167] In private, at least, he saw no obstacle to the indefinite continuation of the existing situation.[168]

But putting aside the difficulties associated with anticipating the speed of this social revolution, what would or should happen when it finally arrived? This Stephen side-stepped with a denial that any one could sensibly answer it. Were, then, all forms of political education, like that spoken of by Ripon, futile? Was there nothing favouring education through co-involvement in the country's management? Such questions Stephen answered with a 'qualified affirmative'. The process of political education could be taken 'to whatever extent is consistent with keeping the principal direction of affairs in the hands of Europeans'; a more precise indication was impossible. Without any great display of enthusiasm, Stephen accepted that in local government experiments should continue to the possible advantage of all parties without serious risk to efficient government; although failures should be anticipated for a considerable time, with the 'principal value of such measures' lying 'in their educational effect'.[169] Here, as he doubtlessly well appreciated, Stephen was with others, painfully caught between two ultimately conflicting goals: the Mill/Macaulay objective of bringing India to full national adulthood through a progression of relentless Europeanisation, set against the growing imperialistic appeal of perpetual British rule of the subcontinent. Yet this irreconcilability was never directly confronted by him, presumably because he believed fitness for independence was so remote a state as to be of negligible importance for all practical political purpose.

How, then, did Stephen see his views on India as differing from what he called 'English Radicalism'? Rather than any particular measure, it was its 'temper and tone of mind', most especially the belief that it was Britain's moral duty eventually to lead India into a democratic form of government administered by representative assemblies. Such an operation, Stephen believed, was 'so difficult and dangerous that it is morally impossible that it should succeed'. Moreover, it would be 'entirely gratutious', undertaken solely on unsound theoretical grounds by those, in Strachey's words, who 'accept with composure any political folly provided that it involves some triumph of sentiment over sense'.[170] Why, asked Stephen, stir up discontent against a form of government that functions so effectively, and where there is no widespread native desire for anything other than absolute government?[171] The 'root' of the answer was that an absolute government of this type operating in India was a 'rock of offence to English Radicalism', a persuasion that wished to sacrifice proven government to democratic theory.[172] As Stephen had said elsewhere at different times and in a variety of ways, the appropriate form of government for India (or any country) ought to be determined by 'circumstances of time, place, and person': essentially, whether it

will keep the peace, protect person and property, enable men to think, speak, write, and live as they please, so long as they do not disturb the peace or hurt others, [and provide a] firm foundation for the growth of every kind of virtue of all forms of knowledge, of all the solid advantages which make civilised life possible, and all the graces which adorn it. . .[173]

In Stephen's view, what should be kept uppermost in mind was the whole avalanche of tangible benefits showered on India by British rule. Why jeopardise them by the indulgence of political ideals which in any case were misinformed and misplaced? Besides, the prevailing conditions promised not the slightest utility in moves towards representative government. How could they? Indians were totally without experience of anything beyond absolute government. Excepting a tiny fragment 'too trifling to mention', the population were 'ignorant to the last degree according to any European standard of knowledge'. Most were 'under the dominion of grovelling superstitions', with the majority 'divided into castes, each man's caste forming his world'. To these features of Indian culture could be added the stunting presence of a practical fatalism 'impatient . . . of the burden of existence', and the racial and religious divisions which demanded a 'common superior' to maintain a stable peace.[174]

However, Stephen conceded that if in the distant future when the time for self-government had finally arrived, the Indian population, for one reason or another, showed a desire for a variety of representative government, then he 'for one should say by all means let them by degrees, as they can use them' have the necessary institutions. But failing that, he would not give the slightest encouragement in that direction, for the present form of government suited all parties.[175] To 'try to tease' a people accustomed to absolute government into dissatisfaction 'which might at any moment produce frightful catastrophes, but is utterly unlikely to produce anything else' was pure madness.[176]

Quite how far these sentiments were at variance with 'English Radicalism' can be gauged by the stance adopted by Gladstone before and during Lytton's viceroyalty and throughout the 1880 election campaign. Back in 1858, Gladstone had been ready to suggest that India should be governed by Indians as far as practicable.[177]

There was an open sympathy with the Cobdenite belief that rather than an enobling experience, empire-building was not only economically foolish but morally compromising. Discomfort at the circumstances of the continent's acquisition was frequently paraded, provoking assorted references to the need to 'redeem from discredit' our past.[178] India was a 'capital demand upon the national honour',[179] and one to be eventually paid off. An appropriate occasion for progress in that direction had been Lytton's great Delhi durbar, when some 'increase of franchise' might have been delivered or promised;[180] but until then we must accept India as the 'most arduous and perhaps the noblest trust, that ever was undertaken by a nation'.[181] We should 'make common cause with her people; let them feel that we are there to give more than we can receive; that their interests are not traversed and frustrated by selfish aims of ours . . . ' .[182] Most of all, we should emphatically reject the notion of 'Liberty for ourselves, Empire over the rest of mankind'.[183] 'National honour' depended upon a 'firm decision to accord to others the rights you claim for yourselves' and the 'everlasting principle of equal rights for all'.[184] Stephen's private response to such progressive moralising appears in a stingingly sarcastic parody written to Grant Duff.

Dearest India, we have shamefully wronged you. Our wicked Hastings and Clive were sad, sad heathens. We govern you for your own good and not for our own sinful sakes. All our efforts are directed dearest India towards & oh let us humbly hope not away from your eternal welfare. What will it profit you or us if we gain the whole world and lose our own souls. May we earn your forgiveness here and may we meet in a happier (and if possible a cooler) world hereafter.[185]

IRELAND AND THE GROWTH OF IMPERIALISM

Ripon's replacement in 1884 by the anodyne Lord Dufferin was intended to smooth ruffled feathers in the Anglo-Indian community. Politically Ripon and his successor shared little other than membership of the Liberal party. Four years later, on completion of his term of office, Dufferin seemed well pleased at being able to quit India 'without any very deep scratches on my credit and reputation'.[186] Stephen, ever anxious to maintain links with India, took up a cordial correspondence with the new Viceroy, something which Ripon's outlook and policies had made quite unthinkable. Well aware of Dufferin's conservative inclinations, Stephen felt no inhibition in attempting to reinforce that aspect of the Viceroy's character. On his side, Dufferin provided Stephen with lengthy accounts of Indian gossip and politics, frequently complimenting Stephen for the effects of his letters, likened by their recipient to the 'wholesome blast of a sea breeze, full of freshness, salt and vigour'.[187]

It was during Dufferin's relatively passive viceroyalty that Gladstone's first Irish home rule manoeuvres began. Naturally, for Stephen and many others, India, the Empire and Ireland rested on common political assumptions[188] relating to the role and legitimacy of central rule and authority. As Stephen predicted early in January 1886, unity of the United Kingdom and Empire was a feeling powerful enough to split the Liberals and change the old party lines 'almost beyond recognition'.[189] It was a realignment which pressed him and the 'old' Intellectual Liberals cheek by political jowl against longstanding more Radical Liberals such as Dicey, Sidgwick, Brodrick, Huxley and Seeley; a time when Unionism became 'the prevailing creed of . . . highly educated Englishmen',[190] with Bryce, Harcourt and Morley (the last behaving in a way, according to Stephen, 'worthy of Robespierre')[191] amongst those remaining loyal to Gladstone.

Though hardly rivalling the future obsessional scale it was to assume for Dicey, Irish home rule truly stuck in Stephen's craw, dominating his correspondence with Dufferin before, during and for some fair time after the defeat of Gladstone's bill; a dispiriting time, causing Stephen to be 'sadder than a man ought to be, who has everything else on earth to make him perfectly happy'.[192] A few weeks before the bill's initial introduction, Stephen had left the Viceroy in little doubt where he stood:

the abject folly, the gross stupid arrogance, the silly lightheartedness with which huge masses of silly people talk and vote and act and think about Ireland reminds me of a crowd of immigrants in a steamer electing their officers and deciding on the course to be steered by universal suffrage disposed to try the experiment of not keeping the boilers properly supplied with water, and thinking seriously of cutting holes in the bottom of the ship, proper precautions and simple guarantees being taken of course against bursting the boilers and the entry of the waters in inconvenient quantities.[193]

In early May 1886, at the feverish height of the national debate, Stephen admits that 'like all the rest of the world, [I am] so absorbed in the Irish controversy that it is difficult for me to write or think about other things;'[194] though his healthy sardonic streak is never entirely absent:

It seems to me that Gladstone's whole conduct in the matter is bad to a degree incomprehensible with anything but venerable age and great holiness. A man must feel himself close to the gates of heaven and on strange terms of familiarity with the Almighty before he could betray his country and lay the fire of civil war in order to keep in office, persuading himself that it is all heavenly good-ness.[195]

At the same time, his public voice was, once more, being very clearly heard in the *Times* correspondence columns. Between January and May five letters from Stephen on Ireland were pub-lished. Most, as in the past, occupied a full half page, and each, as before, attracted leader comment. *The Times*, not always Glad-stone's most devoted follower, found that Stephen's 'close and searching analysis' with its 'vigorous intrepid logic' had swept away 'a whole mass of illusions and fallacies'.[196]

The core of Stephen's opposition to home rule was an amalgam of constitutional, Empire and domestic political concerns. Proposals leaving the British Parliament with guarantees and residual controls over a provincial assembly in Dublin were valueless; equivalent to complete 'Irish independence restrained by a thread, and veiled with a fig leaf'.[197] Stephen, like Mill before him, saw the strategic connection between England and Ireland as so close that 'we cannot each take our own path and yet live in peace'.[198] In the company of those such as Dicey,[199] Stephen hammered away at the consti-tutional and social[200] threat posed to the unity of the United Kingdom by conceding even limited Irish autonomy, seeing the dangerous advancing forces of Jacobinism in action.[201] With Benthamite assurance he rejected Gladstone's thesis that the whole history of Ireland argued for its independence, dismissing such matters as of interest only to 'historians and antiquaries'. Attempting to rewrite history was futile. 'What is is, and we have got to make the best of it. . . '[202] Still holding fresh memories of the Pheonix Park assassin-ations,[203] nationalist rural terror campaigns and mainland dyna-miters,[204] Stephen advocated the reimposition of Lord Spencer's latterly successful Crimes Act. It was a case of lawful coercion being the proper immediate solution to the murderous coercion of the nationalists.[205] As for the long simmering agrarian grievances of tenants which fed much nationalist sentiment, Stephen, without denying their political relevance, believed it to be a matter for sub-sequent settlement rather than something to be demeaningly bar-gained for by the government – the restoration of peace and order had to come first.[206]

Later in the year, Stephen revealed plans to write a 'piece called "Justice to Ireland" ', but, as anticipated, they came to nothing, partly through the 'physical disinclination to hard work[207] . . .

[and] partly scepticism, which, however, is a base cowardly feeling which ought to be trampled on'.[208] Ireland was still gnawing away at Stephen in April 1887, even though Gladstone's third cabinet had been turned out of office a few months back, with Salisbury comfortably sitting on a (combined) majority of over 100 seats. But Irish nationalist rumblings were

reducing Parliamentary Government to a practical absurdity, which I see with the utmost horror, not the least because I love Parliamentary Government, but because the alternative attitude practically lies between this imbecile system – which reduces the ablest men of the day to a life of talk which . . . at best is only defensive and self explanatory – and a really vigorous government of the revolutionary order.[209]

Ireland, if only by diverting Radical Liberalism's political energies, had the general indirect effect of boosting Empire and imperial inclinations. Stephen's involvement in the development of imperial theory and policies came in two forms: through his close association with Lord Lytton, Sir John Strachey, Sir M. E. Grant Duff[210] and Sir Alfred Lyall; and by virtue of his occasional but prominent journalistic sorties. The likely effect of the latter, whilst impossible to gauge, was probably not without significance. Stephen's presence in the Anglo-Indian milieu was substantial and relatively longstanding, with his *Times* correspondence over Afghanistan and Irish home rule receiving the most careful, even respectful, editorial analysis. Rather less open to speculation is Stephen's influence on events through his friendship with prominent figures in Indian government. Beyond Lytton and Grant Duff, his strong friendships with Strachey and Lyall are by far the most noteworthy.

During Stephen's period in India, Strachey was probably more influential than any other single member of the Viceroy's Council – a position later maintained under Lytton.[211] Strachey and Stephen soon developed the highest regard for the other's abilities and character. Strachey was the dedicatee of *Liberty, Equality, Fraternity*,[212] with Stephen similarly honoured by Strachey in his work *India*.[213] If anything, Strachey was less sanguine than Stephen over the prospects of native advancement to the higher echelons of government. In 1888 Strachey denied that there had been any true substantial change in the Indian mentality: Western views still only touched the 'merest fringe of ideas and beliefs of the population'.[214] Barbaric practices suppressed by British rule were still culturally acceptable even amongst educated Indians, ready to 'instantly spring into vigorous life if our watchfulness' were relaxed.[215] It was Britain's 'highest duty towards India . . . to maintain our dominion', and the time when cessation of British rule would not be a 'signal for universal anarchy and ruin' was almost unforeseeable. Our national duty and India's only hope lay in the 'long continuance of the benevolent but strong government of Englishmen'[216] pursued 'with unflinching determination on principles which our superior knowledge tells us are right, although they may be unpopular'. The general similarity of outlook and tone of expression between Strachey and Stephen are expressly confirmed in *India*, with the use on the book's concluding page of an extensive quotation from Stephen's 1883 article 'The Government of India', where Stephen epigrammatically reminds the reader that 'The English in India are the representatives of peace compelled by force.'

Lyall presented a contrast with Strachey's forceful utilitarian purposefulness. A friend of John Morley through his *Fortnightly Review* contributions, Lyall gained a fair degree of eminence as a scholar of Indian and Middle Eastern culture,[217] with an Indian career ranging from cavalry action during the Indian mutiny, to Home Secretary (1873–4) and Foreign Secretary in the Indian government (1878–81) and finally Lieutenant-Governor of the North-Western Provinces until 1887. The personal attachment was strong, with Lyall expressing considerable distress at the illness of 'one of the firmest friends I have in the world' when Stephen was incapacitated in 1885.[218] Stephen's and Lyall's likemindedness on Indian affairs was extensive, and, if Lyall's earlier determination to cultivate Stephen's acquaintance is remembered, it seems reasonable to assume a fair measure of influence by Stephen in Indian affairs. During Lytton's Afghan campaign Lyall had noted how it was 'curious to observe how minds, equal in apparent clearness and knowledge, differ entirely upon political questions – Lord Lytton and Fitzjames Stephen certain that their views are right, which Lord Northbrook and Grant Duff denounce to me as utterly wrong. I go with former.'[219]

Probably the most accurate indication of Lyall's thinking on the political future of India is found in his extensive *Edinburgh Review* essay 'Government of the Indian Empire' (1884),[220] where Lyall reflects on the conflict faced by Liberals with their devotion to free institutions and the necessity for their absence in India. Regulating the pace of change of the 'Leviathan' of English rule in India became ever more difficult; the 'finer springs of political sentiment and social prepossessions' were now being touched and the 'general law of the motion of political bodies afforded . . . no certain data for calculating the future course into which this immense region may be drawn'.[221]

Lyall's prescription for this unsteadiness required the open acknowl-edgement of the nature of our title to India: 'Conquest and direct inheritance from actual possessors are the title deeds . . . the only valid and recognized title known to Asia'. Withdrawal within a foreseeable period would generate a 'political earthquake'. To treat the 'morality of our rule . . . as an open question of ethics will only lead the dis-cussion away into a region of fallacies, illusions and disappointment'. Political stability demanded the acceptance of a paradox: we might properly entertain the possibility of eventual transfer to Indian self-rule, but constant public proclamation would inhibit the process likely to lead to it. Therefore, the 'permanency and indisputable right of . . . dominion in India' must be resolutely held to.[222] In substance and final direction, Lyall had put Stephen's case in 'Foundations of the Government of India', published a few months before.[223]

Intellectual Liberalism's response to India,[224] as articulated by Stephen and, to a lesser extent, by Strachey, Lyall and Maine, was, on the surface at least, quite distinct from and hostile to Gladstonian or Radical Liberalism; yet just how far did it coincide with and provide a theoretical account of full-blown (Tory) imperialism? Essentially, two strands of thought combined to produce the imperial ethic: the increasing geo-political nature of foreign policy brought on by the competing threats of other growing colonial empires; and national pride in the supposed special nature of English character and insti-tutions, typified by Lord Rosebery's reminder that it was 'our responsibility and heritage to take care that the world as far as it could be moulded, shall receive an English-speaking complexion and not that of other nations [and our responsibility] to look for-ward . . . to the future of the race, of which we are at present the trustees':[225] imperialism was just a 'larger patriotism'. For those like Salisbury, the former imperial element, in so far as it was separ-able from the latter, was of principal importance. His was an over-riding concern for 'power, privilege, and strategy', one that blew up into a militaristic 'Jingo hurricane' by the turn of the century.[226] But it was in Curzon's viceroyalty that the clearest and closest identi-fication can be found between Stephen's notions of colonial rule and the imperial ethic. For with Curzon came a very late flowering of nineteenth-century Intellectual Liberalism.[227]

Stephen's link with Curzon began in 1877, when the eighteen-year-old George Nathanial, as President of the Eton Literary Society, invited Stephen along to speak on India. The effect on Curzon and the audience was mesmeric. Over thirty years later Curzon still held 'a vivid recollection [of] the vast head, the heavy pendulous jaw, the long and curling locks of Sir James Fitzjames Stephen as he stood at the desk'.[228] Curzon on more than one occasion after recalled 'Ever since that day . . . the fascination and if I may so, the sacredness of India have grown upon me.'[229] With Curzon there was the same powerful sense of mission and keenness to impart what were seen as the fine innate features of English character and England's institutions and to bring firm effective government, justice and civilised order to India: an open, unfaltering belief in rightness of cause and faith in racial destiny, reminiscent of Stephen's own confident ringing certainties. For both, efficiency was their administrative 'gospel',[230] English conduct the moral example: 'Everyone of our actions should be open to inspection: every deed a duty . . . I decline to wink at all the little jobs and naughtinesses and pranks. Above all I see, oh so clearly, that we can only hold this country by our superior standards of honour and virtue.'[231] There was also a shared marvelling in the ability of the few tens of thousands of English to hold such an empire, with 'so mild a restraint that the rulers are the merest handful amongst the ruled, a tiny speck of white foam upon a dark and thunderous ocean'.[232] It is difficult to believe that Stephen would for a moment have dissented from Curzon's claim that in 'Empire we have found not merely the key to glory and wealth, but the call to duty, and a means of service to mankind'.[233]

For Stephen, along with others like Strachey and Lyall, self-government was a conceivable abstraction, though negligible as a practical reality. The chances of Indians reaching the higher ranks of government were shut out largely by the standard belief that the necessary hereditary character was not to be discovered amongst the indigenous population.[234] Since Dufferin's viceroyalty and annexation of Upper Burma, the Tory and Liberal attitudes towards India were hardly distinguishable, with the Liberals forced to choose between maintaining either a policy that encouraged moves to self-rule (as seen under Ripon) or the security of the Empire against real and imagined threats posed by the imperial ambitions of others.[235] By the end of the century Stephen's imperial outpourings of the late 1870s and early 1880s had grown from representing Intellectual Liberalism's analytical support for 'Dizzy's suit of imperial spangles'[236] into the general political consensus. It is a development amply illustrated by the gradually shifting stance over more than thirty years of John Morley, Stephen's almost inevitable opponent on practically all matters philosophical and political. In 1905 his career in politics was topped off with the appointment as Secretary of State for India – for Morley a crown woven out of laurel leaves and thorns. Morley's liberal credentials were immaculate: his defence of Millism, *On Compromise*, was almost required reading amongst Indian intellectuals; and two terms as Gladstone's Chief Secretary for Ireland during the home rule periods further sharpened the radical image.

With Bright and other radicals, Morley, probably Gladstone's loyalist acolyte, had shared the view that the circumstances of Britain's acquisition of India were such as to require not just Burkean trusteeship but something resembling national atonement. Yet like many accused of 'Little Englandism', Morely was far from untouched by the extensive party political consensus over the legitimacy of Empire developing after the mid 1880s.[237] As Stephen had urged in 1883, Morley, as Secretary of State, later conceded that it would be 'criminal folly' to feel 'bound to apply the catch-words of our European liberalism as principles fit for . . . India'.[238] Such 'simple ideas and absolute principles' were now eyed with creeping scepticism.[239] Parliamentary institutions were no longer seen as appropriate to all nations.[240] Increasingly India appeared to Morley as never likely to be suited to anything like Western representative government.[241] Even on self-rule, Morley had, in practical terms, come to see this as a retreating prospect. Alfred Lyall, who had adhered to his view from Stephen's time,[242] became, according to Morley, the 'one man to whom I must look for counsel in decisions of real moment'.[243] The political wheel came full circle when, during his Secretary of Stateship, Morley, faced with fierce waves of nationalistic unrest and terrorism, was forced to introduce repressive measures similar to Lytton's Vernacular Press Act – a supremely distasteful move which invited and received charges of political hypocrisy.[244]

By 1911 Morley felt no shame in admitting that 'the more I read and think about British rule in India, the more stupendous and the more glorious it appears'.[245] His criticisms of Curzon's reign were directed more at the insensitive high-handed manner of implementation than the substance of policies; the truth of this being particularly borne out by Morley's acceptance of Curzon's widely unpopular partition of Bengal.[246] Moreover, Curzonian beliefs in racial superiority were almost as common amongst radicals as elsewhere. Goldwin Smith, Dilke and Morley shared few doubts as to the high inherent qualities of Anglo-Saxons and the absence of such qualities in colonised races.[247] However, much as Morely had by the end of his period of Indian government moved towards attitudes not so far removed from Stephen's of the 1880s, there always persisted a crucial distinction. Morley never completely deserted at least an abstract commitment to Midlothianism: a mentality that embraced those political and moral axioms of Radical Liberalism well represented by Morley's 1885 claim that, regardless of the violent autocratic cruelty of many native governments, their subjects still enjoyed from the fact of self-rule a quality that 'they could never derive from boons conferred upon them by the cast-iron benevolence of foreigners and aliens'.[248] Whether Morley ever had a clear political strategy for India is questionable,[249] though for him the Raj, for all its undeniable splendours, always remained 'intensely artificial and unnatural', and unlikely to endure.[250] But Stephen, despite passing ritual[251] acknowledgements of the ultimate possibility of native government, would not have found objectionable a single element of Curzon's desire to 'infuse principle, direction, consistency, into our policy . . to make our administration equitable, and our dominion permanent'.[252]

7

LIBERTY, EQUALITY, FRATERNITY: REFUTATION AND APOLOGIA

In April 1864 Stephen wrote seeking Mill's advice as to whether his recently published *General View of the Criminal Law of England* and other writing showed the intellectual promise able to produce a significant work on religion and morals. Mill's response to this slightly curious request was to suggest that if he 'threw [his] whole mind' into the venture Stephen was likely to write something of value; although a critical discussion of particular legislative or practical questions, for which Mill thought Stephen had a 'decided talent', would possibly be of greater use than a treatise of abstractions.[1] During the following half-dozen years Mill and Stephen corresponded cordially,[2] if spasmodically, occasionally meeting at the Political Economy Club, of which they were both members. Their correspondence and contact appear to have ended with a letter written at the beginning of August 1871, over a year before Stephen's return from India, in which he issued Mill a form of friendly warning of the impending appearance of *Liberty, Equality, Fraternity*. After soliciting Mill's 'marginal notes' on a draft of what was to be the Indian Evidence Act, Stephen casually expressed the hope 'some day to set forth certain qualifications to your essay on Liberty' confirmed by his experiences in India.[3]

In the weeks steaming home,[4] relieved of the administrative burdens of the subcontinent and having sorted out the vital matter of his seating arrangements,[5] Stephen fully indulged a sizeable appetite for reading and composition:

With my library on the deck by my side, the days seem only too short. I hate the saloon in the evenings too much to read there, so that after sunset I lie down in my clothes in a long chair, and sleep without undressing till daylight. Then I get up and bathe and dress and when the decks are washed I write my árticle, then a bit of a letter, then I have a German lesson, or an Italian lesson, i.e. a quantity of reading.[6]

However, the great part of Stephen's study was devoted to a rereading and rethinking of Mill:

I have not written an article today. My excuse is that I have been loading my guns by reading two of Mill's later pamphlets . . . – Liberty and Utilitarianism. I don't agree with them. Mill seems to me to be one of those people whose logical and thinking power is quite out of all proportion to his seeing power. For the purpose of arranging his thoughts and putting them all in proper relations to each other, he is incomparable and unapproachable, but the quality of the thought itself seems to me, in many cases, exceedingly poor and thin. His whole concept of human nature appears to me to be a sort of unattractive romance, yet it is the romance of a man who, in some aspects, is very good.[7]

First appearing as a series of articles in the *Pall Mall Gazette*,[8] late in 1872, *Liberty, Equality, Fraternity* was published in March 1873. It constituted, as John Morley later conceded, the 'first effective attack on Mill's pontifical authority'[9] and was rightly identified by Ernest Barker as the 'finest exposition of conservative thought in the latter half of the nineteenth century'.[10]

The aim of *Liberty, Equality, Fraternity* was considerably wider than an attempt to explode some of the basic premises of *On Liberty*. It's object, as Stephen owns,[11] was to examine the 'doctrines rather hinted at than expressed by the phrase "Liberty, Equality, Fraternity" ', doctrines that were part of what came to be known as 'The Religion of Humanity', of which Auguste Comte's 'Positivism' was the 'best known of our generation',[12] and with which sentiments Mill shared a considerable sympathy, as demonstrated in his essays *On Liberty, Utilitarianism* (1863) and *The Subjection of Women* (1869).

For Stephen the essence of the Religion of Humanity, or Comtist positivism, was the dangerously naive tripartite optimism that the human race

collectively has before it splendid destinies and that the road to them is to be found in the removal of all restraints on human conduct, in the recognition of a substantial equality . . . and in fraternity or general love . . . Such . . . is the religion of which I take 'Liberty, Equality, Fraternity'[13] to be the creed. I do not believe it.

I am not the advocate of Slavery, Caste, and Hatred, nor do I deny sense may be given to the words, Liberty, Equality, and Fraternity, in which they may be regarded as good. I wish to assert with respect to them two propositions.

First, that in the present day even those who use those words most rationally – that is to say, as the names of elements of social life which, like others, have their advantages and disadvantages according to time, place, and circumstance – have a great disposition to exaggerate their advantages and to deny the existence, or at any rate to underrate the importance, of their disadvantages.

Next, that whatever signification be attached to them, these words are ill-adapted to be the creed of a religion, that the things which they denote are not ends in themselves, and that when used collectively the words do not typify, however vaguely, any state of society which a reasonable man ought to regard with enthusiasm or self-devotion.[14]

Liberty, Equality, Fraternity was at one and the same time Stephen's refutation of this creed and an 'Apologia'[15] of his own beliefs on the interdependency of law, politics, religion and morality. It was a classical, sustained and single-minded exercise in rationalism, with its author almost brutally anxious to demonstrate that reason should be the supreme regulator of belief and actions, and that we should not 'shrink from accepting the logical consequences of such truth, however remote or unwelcome they may be'.[16] Above all, the dominant recurring mood of *Liberty, Equality, Fraternity* is a dark Hobbesian disbelief in the perfectibility of mankind, an un-suppressed incredulity that Mill with his impeccable philosophic lineage could propagandise such alien humanistic and optimistic doctrines.

LIBERTY AND COERCION: DEPENDENT OPPOSITES

Mill's solution to the threat to intellectual and personal individualism – the 'simple principle' of permitting interference with 'liberty of action' only for reasons of self-protection[17] – had been the declaration of a new moral principle: one based on 'utility in the largest sense grounded on the permanent interests of a man as a progressive being', but uncontaminated by any 'idea of abstract right as a thing independent of utility'.[18] It was a broad and generous conception of liberty that embraced liberty of conscience, thought, opinion, expression and action, whether pursued singly or in combination with others; in John Morley's eyes, a principle representing the 'larger expediences', preferring the 'wider utility to the narrower'.[19]

The cornerstone of Stephen's assault on this central tenet of Mill's case was his belief in the universal necessity of 'coercion' as the underlying basis of society – 'coercion' in the broadest sense, for even 'persuasion is a form of force'.[20] In unexceptional utilitarian fashion, Stephen reasoned that voluntary actions are caused by 'hope and fear, pleasure or pain', and only acts motivated by the hopes of pleasure are regarded as free. When this was incorporated into Mill's principle two conclusions followed: that 'No one is every justified in trying to affect any one's conduct by exciting his fears, except for the sake of self-protection'; and, taking Mill's word that his was a utilitarian principle, that 'It can never promote the general happiness . . . that conduct of any persons should be affected by an appeal to their fears except in the cases excepted.'[21] Such consequences, argued Stephen, were hostile to the existence of both morality and religion, for they were largely 'coercive systems' whose contents were regulated by notions other than self-protection. Their importance exceeded the criminal law in that far more were restrained by the fear of social censure, religious sanction or their own conscience. Therefore *principled* opposition to coercion was opposition to the binding forces of society, and a theory that would tend to 'unmoralise' society.

More tangibly, Mill's theory was antithetical to the continuation of, or to changes in, existing forms of government or social institutions; it floated on the assumption of a static or ideal state of affairs. Even taxation, for example, whose revenues were not laid out on purposes in some way self-protective – 'to the support of the British Museum' – was as 'distinct a violation of Mr Mill's principle as religious persecution'.[22] Undeniably compulsion and persuasion 'go hand in hand but the lion's share' of progress had fallen to the use of compulsion.[23] Liberty, from the very nature of society, is dependent upon power and coercion for, as Hobbes knew so well, it is only under the protection of a powerful, well-organised, and intelligent government that any liberty can exist at all.[24] And although the form of coercion changes as any society develops, it always remains the ultimate guarantee of social institutions.

Parliamentary government is simply a mild and disguised form of compulsion. We agree to try strength by counting heads instead of breaking heads, but the principle is essentially the same. It is not the wisest side which wins but the one which for the time being shows its superior strength . . . or by enlisting the largest amount of active support. The minority gives way not because it is convinced that it is wrong, but because it is convinced that it is a minority. The difference between a rough and a civilized society is not that force is used in one case and persuasion in the other, but that force is (or ought to be) guided with greater care in the second case than in the first.[25] . . . Men are so constructed that whatever theory as to goodness and badness we choose to adopt, there are and always will be in the world an enormous mass of bad and indifferent people – people who deliberately do all sorts of things which they ought not to do, and leave undone all sorts of things which they ought to do. Estimate the proportion of men and women who are selfish, sensual, frivolous, idle, absolutely commonplace and wrapped up in the smallest of petty routines, and consider how far the freest of free discussion is likely to improve them. The only way by which it is practically possible to act upon them at all is by compulsion or restraint. Whether it is worth while to apply to them both or either I do not now inquire: I confine myself to saying that the utmost conceivable liberty which could be bestowed upon them would not in the least degree tend to improve them.[26]

Liberty, Stephen claimed, was imbued with no absolute value. In itself it was neither good nor bad but, chameleonlike, took either quality depending on the particular circumstances and consequences: its desirability was determined by its utility. Similarly force – or the absence of liberty – was good when the objective was good and the means employed were efficient without excessive human cost; again, the question was always one of expediency.

Stephen's Benthamite suspicions were aroused by Mill's insistence on the generality, not to say the absolutism, of the principle of self-protection. Crucially, was Mill asserting the principle as a means (to 'happiness') or an end in itself? On some occasions he appeared to Stephen to use liberty as a means to knowledge, rationality, social progress and self-development, which in turn led to the ultimate goal of happiness. Yet at other times Mill expanded happiness to include liberty as an end, as the 'highest good'. And although Mill, anticipating charges of heresy, had claimed his principle was squarely founded on the bedrock of empiricism, Stephen believed that Mill had committed the philosophic sin of leaning more on abstractions than experience. As his brother Leslie perfectly put it, Mill 'had, as his opponent thought, been coquetting with the common adversary and seduced into grievous error'.[27]

Mill's non-interference principle – 'That the only purpose for which power can be rightfully exercised over any member of a civilised community, against his will, is to prevent harm to others' – only applied to so-called 'self-regarding' acts. This Stephen and many others found a soft target for criticism.[28] Most acts having a social as well as immediate impact, the distinction was unworkable.[29] Furthermore, queried his critics, what had Mill meant by 'harm'? Was it limited to physical harm, or was moral harm also included? Again, Mill talked of nuisance as a form of harm, but what was a 'nuisance'? Even Mill admitted that self-regarding acts may 'affect others through himself'[30] and society at large.[31] Moreover, the principle was only intended to apply to mature adults inhabiting a developed society. How, asked Stephen, were we to determine such levels of individual and social development, for 'maturity and civilisation are matters of degree'?[32] Was there any society anywhere where free discussion might substantially supersede compulsion? 'What proportion of human misconduct in any department of life is due to ignorance, and what to wickedness or weakness?'[33] Few had the capacity or inclination to be improved by discussion – 'mankind at large are in a state of ignorance which in favourable cases is just beginning to be conscious [of its own] ignorance'.[34] Mill's opposition was, though, not only to legal but to extra-legal public sanctions, perceived by him as more threatening because they left 'fewer means of escape', penetrating 'much more deeply into the details of life and enslaving the soul itself'. Just how, then, might social disapproval be exercised? Advice, entreaty and exhortation were acceptable to Mill because they were unorganised, simply natural and spontaneous. But to Stephen, and many later critics,[35] such a distinction between acceptable and impermissible forms of social coercion was without significance or value as a proposition meant to guide social behaviour.

Moving from generalities to liberty of thought and discussion, Stephen was at particular pains to emphasise that it was Mill's theory from which he dissented, not his 'practical conclusions'.[36] Mill's case for freedom of opinion and expression was that censorship or suppression amounted to an assumption of infallibility by the suppressors; that only through the 'collision of adverse opinions' would the complete truth in any situation ever be likely to emerge; that only by vigorous and open discussion would true opinions be rationally comprehended rather than simply held; and only by such a process could truths remain living and personally experienced truths[37] – a somewhat drastic change of prescription from that offered to the world by a rather less tolerant and much younger Mill who had heaped contempt on 'Every dabbler [who] thinks his opinion as good as another's', tearing 'headlong into opinions, always shallow, and as often wrong as right'.[38]

As an assertion of the vital importance of free and open discussion of the 'great questions of morals and theology' Stephen found Mill's stance unimpeachable,[39] but the theoretical route by which Mill reached this agreeable destination was unacceptable and potentially 'a serious embarrassment to rational legislation'.[40] Stephen rejected both the individual elements and the totality of Mill's argument: suppression of another's opinion may or may not amount to a claim of infallibility or an assertion of untruth; suppression may be based on grounds of political expediency or social harmony; rather than by 'collision' of views, most opinions emerge through self-selecting principles largely dictated by personal temperament; and instead of invigorating truth, the more frequent consequence of unhampered freedom of discussion was a 'general scepticism[41] . . . in the vast majority of minds'. For the bulk of mankind most truths 'came home' not through disputation but through direct interest and immediate experience.[42] Mill's was an idealised, generally unachievable system of reasoning and the formation of opinion – his *Logic* reduced to daily application. Stephen's was one of unoptimistic realism, that most of mankind were quite incapable of even establishing the superstructure of their beliefs by independent and untutored reasoning. In this Stephen was further removed from Bentham than Mill was, for Bentham also saw the ability (or even duty) 'to censure freely' as strongly conducive to good government, though unlike Mill, he saw no 'intrinsic human[ising] value' in it.

Mill's appeal for liberty and toleration involved freedom not simply of opinion but of action. A healthy open society sustained by a free exchange of opinion was to be populated with well-formed intellects. For not only did an advanced society depend on that, but the happiness – the 'well-being' – of all individuals demanded the opportunity to develop originality and individuality facilitated by freedom.[43] 'The only unfailing and permanent source of improvement is Liberty, since by it there are as many possible independent centres of improvement as there are individuals.'

Surveying the beginning of the second half of the nineteenth century, Mill was gloomily pessimistic about the future of individuality, sensing the stifling embrace of a 'despotism of custom'. Opportunities and impulses for experiments in lifestyles were withering away. 'Energetic characters on any large scale [were] becoming merely traditional.' Much of the blame for this lay with Calvinism, a creed demanding 'no capacity but that of surrendering to the will of God'; and one that cramped, stunted and changed characters in the way trees are clipped into pollards.[44] Along with this process the rich diversity of European culture was fading: the same books were read, similar sermons heard, like ends pursued; public opinion grew ever more clear and homogeneous; and all this amounted to 'a mass of influence hostile to individuality'. We were, as Stephen summarised Mill's forebodings, on our way to 'a Chinese uniformity'.[45] Though here was a great paradox in Mill's position: the social and democratic advances he had campaigned for were close to realisation, but at the same time they were seen by him as unsympathetic to the very forces that had led to them and which he valued so highly. Yet, as Leslie Stephen observed, half a dozen years later 'when Mill became a politician, he gave his vote as heartily as the blindest enthusiast for measures which inaugurated a great step towards democracy'.[46]

As already seen,[47] it was in the *Saturday Review* thirteen years earlier that Stephen first registered his dissent from much of Mill's diagnosis of an intellectually declining nation, malnourished by an inadequate diet of liberty and individuality. *Liberty, Equality, Fraternity* both offered new criticisms and amplified earlier ones,[48] with the source of a good part of Stephen's disagreement with Mill, as Stephen admitted, being their differing expectations of human nature: Mill had far 'too favourable an estimate' of it.[49] For Mill, removal of restraints could lead to an invigoration of character, 'the free development of individuality' and realisation of potentialities. Stephen believed the opposite more likely, with originality often the product of exertion of which danger, vicissitude, restraint and coercion were great stimulants. The assumption or hope that character would be invigorated simply by stripping away restraints lacked historical foundation. Moreover, neither was variety intrinsically good; a country in which everybody was uniformly sober would be 'a better and more progressive, though less diversified nation than one of which half the members were sober and the other half habitual drunkards'.[50] In the way that Mill overstated the worth of opposition or contradiction, similarly for conduct he seemed to place a premium on eccentricity, for Stephen 'more often a mark of weakness than . . . of strength'.[51]

Mill's portrayal of the crushing weight of Calvinism was dismissed by a host of critics[52] as a grossly misleading caricature, though a few, like Hazlitt,[53] were much in agreement with him. Rather than converting its followers into spiritual automata, Stephen saw Calvin's belief in self-restraint and discipline as a means for achieving the supremacy of each individual's better nature over their baser elements – a true 'freedom to be good and wise'. How could Mill be right in requiring 'us to believe that such a man as John Knox was a poor heartbroken creature with no will of his own?' Given the opportunity, Mill might, of course, have suggested the fiery Knox was what he was despite rather than because of his creed. But as some have since suggested,[54] the balance of history, if anything, favours Stephen in that individualism seems to have flourished as well in disciplined Calvinist communities, like Scotland and New England, as in more tolerant or indifferent societies. And to round off his general rebuttal, Stephen raised the clever and not insubstantial charge that the logic as well as the historical substance of Mill's argument was suspect; for if, as Mill claimed, 'whilst a doctrine is struggling for ascendancy it is full of meaning, and that when it has become a received opinion

its living power begins to decline, surely prove that coercion and
not liberty is favourable to its appreciation'.[55]

If, as Stephen thought, Mill was on a fool's errand chasing a
general principle of liberty – a preoccupation as irrational as asking
'whether fire is a good or a bad thing' – then just how were we to
recognise its proper limits? The answer lay in the ad hocery of
expediency: for

> a complete answer to the question, In what cases is liberty good and in what
> cases is it bad? would involve not merely a universal history of mankind, but a
> complete solution of the problems which such a history would offer. I do not
> believe that the state of our knowledge is such as to enable us to enunciate any
> 'very simple principle as entitled to govern absolutely the dealings of society
> with the individual in the way of compulsion and control'. We must proceed in
> a far more cautious way, and confine ourselves to such remarks as experience
> suggests about the advantages and disadvantages of compulsion and liberty
> respectively in particular cases. . . Discussions about liberty are in truth dis-
> cussions about a negation. Attempts to solve the problems of government and
> society by such discussions are like attempts to discover the nature of light and
> heat by inquiries into darkness and cold. The phenomenon which requires and
> will repay study is the direction and nature of the various forces, individual and
> collective, which in their combination or collision with each other and with the
> outer world make up human life. . . The result is that discussions about liberty
> are either misleading or idle, unless we know who wants what, by what restraint
> he is prevented from doing it, and for what reasons it is proposed to remove that
> restraint.[56]

As with liberty, compulsion was good or bad according to the particular circumstances; everything was susceptible to the standard
test of utility. Utility in the 'highest sense' was truth; to believe
true statements and disbelieve untrue ones, and 'to give to probable
or improbable statements a degree of credit proportionate to their
apparent probability or improbability, would be the greatest of
intellectual blessings'.[57]

PRINCIPLES AND PRACTICE: RELIGIOUS AND MORAL LIBERTY

Principles clearly did not exist simply for the abstract satisfaction
involved in their formulation; they were, especially for the utilitarian, to be a genuine guide to life and legislation. Therefore,
argued Stephen, 'Government ought to take the responsibility of
acting upon such principles, religious, political and moral, as they
may from time to time regard as most likely to be true, and this
they cannot do without exercising a very considerable degree of
coercion.' With this reflection on the possible limitations of the

expression and practice of religious and moral opinions Stephen attracted (and has continued to draw) more widespread hostility than for any other element of *Liberty, Equality, Fraternity*. At least in part, this was fuelled by a fair measure of misconception, some credit for which must go to the ill-organised presentation of many of Stephen's contentions, a likely consequence of too rapid and insufficiently careful conversion from article to book form.[58]

For Stephen, the light in which religion should be regarded by the state was determined by its intimate and (for him) vital connection with morality. Sequentially his logic ran: morals were the main bonding forces of a society; morality substantially rested upon religious conviction;[59] therefore no government could stand detached and aloof from general questions of religious belief, for 'Whether Christianity is true or false, and whether European morality is good or bad, European morality is in fact founded upon religion, and the destruction of the one must of necessity involve the reconstruction of the other.'[60] Because life, both temporal and spiritual, was an indivisible whole it ought, as Hobbes had asserted, to be 'regulated by one set of principles'; church and state differed only in their sanctions; consequently principled legislative neutrality on religious matters was politically impossible.[61]

The truth of Christianity was, then, *the* 'vital question', for on that hung morality, politics, and all legislation. The religious legislative stance of any government, Stephen argued, was dictated by the 'nature of the [religious] view which happens to be dominant for the time being'.[62] Quite what a government might in practice do in encouraging and reinforcing current religious beliefs turned on the utility of any possible action, not, as Mill argued, on an absolutist prohibition on interference with individual religious beliefs. When it came to practicalities, however, Stephen had no doubt that any attempt at legal prosecution of religious nonconformity would be socially 'absolutely destructive and paralysing'. Yet, as Stephen keenly noted, in states where Christianity was not established but where Christian government was dominant, such as in India, Millite principles of religious freedom were ignored 'without any [opposing] demand from those who would generally espouse them'.[63] And while rival religions were not persecuted as such, they were overridden when contrary to European Christian ethics. The government of India was based on the assumption that Christianity was true and the native religion untrue. Effectively, that 'I am right and you are wrong, and your view shall give way to mine, quietly, gradually and peacefully; but one of us must rule and the other must obey; and I mean to rule.'[64]

Although legal penalties were 'quite out of the question', because of their disutility, social intolerance was 'morally right in so far as [Christian] opinions are true'. But would not even public intolerance of non-(orthodox) Christian religions promote social division and friction? Yes, discord might be inevitable; however,

Upon the whole, it appears to me quite certain that if our notions of moral good and evil are substantially true, and if the doctrines of God and a future state are true, the object of causing people to believe in them is good, and that social intolerance on the behalf of those who do towards those who do not believe in them cannot be regarded as involving evils of any great importance in comparison with the results at which it aims.

Taken at face value, here indeed was a raw doctrine of intolerant repression. Yet Stephen was not to be swept away by his own insulated principled logic. It was, he agreed, 'not a pleasant doctrine' and 'liable to great abuse'. How, then, might we at the same time accept its essential truth but avoid its all too obvious risks of abuse? Stephen's unconvincing solution was self-recognition by most people of their own ignorance in such matters.

No one has a right to be morally intolerant of doctrines which he has not carefully studied . . . The true ground of moral tolerance in the common sense of the words appears to me to lie in this – that most people have no right to any opinions whatever upon these questions, except in so far as they are necessary for the regulation of their own affairs. When some ignorant preacher calls his betters atheists and the like, his fault is not intolerance, but impudence and rudeness. If this principle were properly carried out, it would leave little room for moral intolerance in most cases; but I think it highly important that men who really study these matters should feel themselves at liberty not merely to dissent from but to disapprove of opinions which appear to them to require it, and should express that disapprobation.[65]

Assuming that religious bigots were open to self-appraisal and self-restraint, rather than being divisive, if anything, the net effect of Stephen's strictures would have meant greater day-to-day social tolerance of rival religious views.

Certainly Stephen the man of action was on the side of the angels in the great religious controversies of the times. As has been seen, the storm centring on the allegedly heretical *Essays and Reviews* led to Stephen acting as defence counsel at Rowland Williams' trial for heresy, as well as causing a bitter and lengthy rift between the *Saturday Review* and some of its more freethinking contributors like Stephen. And, along with Leslie, Fitzjames was a strenuous advocate and supporter of the campaign to repeal the religious 'Tests' that restricted university appointments at Oxford and Cambridge to their Anglican graduates.[66]

The law of blasphemy also received more than one pummelling from Stephen. In 'The Laws [and] Religious Opinions (1874)'[67] he likened the prosecutorial history of the offence to a process of 'straining at gnats and swallowing camels'. Inevitably the law could never in practice produce a worthwhile outcome. 'It can effect nothing but scandal – the scandal of ruining and crushing some poor, helpless, defenceless creature . . . , or the scandal of producing a conflict between the law and a man of spirit and courage in which the law must of necessity get the worst of the encounter.' Consequently, 'the whole of the law which can possibly be applied to the punishment of the expression of religious opinion should be abolished'.[68]

Neither did the combination of maturity and elevation to the bench alter these attitudes. A decade later, following the Foote blasphemy trial, Stephen took the rare step for a High Court judge of publishing in the *Fortnightly Review* (1884)[69] a fierce criticism of Lord Chief Justice Coleridge's[70] judgment in the case. The ruling that 'If the decencies of controversy are observed, even the fundamentals of religion may be attacked' showed the law to be 'essentially and fundamentally bad'. Contrary to general opinion,[71] Stephen argued the law did not unchallengeably 'secure full liberty of discussion upon religious subjects' as the law would, because of its concern with the mode of expression 'in practice send a man to gaol for not writing like a scholar and a gentleman'. Calling for amending legislation, Stephen characterised the existing blasphemy law as largely facilitating the 'gratification of private malice under the cloak of religion'.

Reducing the dispute to its bare bones, Mill and Stephen agreed on the need for informed and vigorous self-criticism by any society, with Stephen (a little in the mood of *Past and Present*) [72] seeing the process as one of 'intellectual warfare . . . from which no institution, no family, no individual man is free', resulting in the 'weaker . . . less robust and deeply seated feeling' being 'rooted out to the last fibre'.[73] In all practical senses Stephen accepted Mill's views on religious toleration almost completely, 'though not quite'.[74] And to illustrate where his theory would have clashed with Mill's, Stephen chose (for him) the supremely uncomfortable case of Pontius Pilate, arguing that if Pilate had followed Mill's views there would have been the gravest risk of serious civil disorder, and therefore in principle his actions were correct. It was not Pilate's persecution that was criticisable, but rather the 'clumsy and brutal' nature of its application. What then did Stephen favour? Did he oppose the 'whole current of civilised opinion for the last 300–400 years?' Did he wish to return to the Inquisition? To such questions he answered 'most emphatically, No'. The practice of 'modern Liberals' was unobjectionable. On the concrete issues of the day he accepted their course of actions, and their grounds too, so long as they were founded on expediency and not absolute and unbending principles conjured out of intuition.

Was this state of theoretical discord and practical harmony on religious liberty between Mill and Stephen carried through to matters of morality? In relation to immorality Mill was by no means blithely unaware of the difficulties of sustaining his self-regarding distinction, openly conceding that most individual acts in one way or another touched the lives of others. To accommodate this reality Mill refined his basic principle with the notion of a 'distinct and assignable obligation': 'Whenever, in short, there is a definite danger or . . . risk of danger, either to an individual or to the public, the case is taken out of the province of liberty, and placed in that of morality or law.' So, if a man through 'intemperance or extravagance' is unable to support and educate his family he may be properly censured for breach of his duty to his family, but not solely for his debauched state. Though beyond this 'with regard to the merely contingent or . . . constructive injury which a person causes to society, by conduct which neither violates any specific duty to the public, nor occasions perceptible hurt to any assignable individual except himself, the inconvenience is one which society can afford to bear, for the sake of the greater good of human freedom'. But what, inquired Stephen, would constitute a 'contingent injury'? Rather than an ascertainable fact, it was something of variable quality, turning almost exclusively on the viewpoint of the observer; for the tolerance threshold of the licentious libertarian would naturally tower over that of a priggish busybody: a very remote contingency for the former might be perceived as an immediate harm by the latter. Moreover, identification of these 'assignable obligations' could not be carried out automatically by anything resembling guiding principles, which (along with other balancing concerns of Mill's) showed Mill's simple principle of self-protection was hardly 'simple' or 'single'. At the same time as taking a little of the gloss off the principle's appeal, more significantly, this lack of simplicity made Stephen's target less distinct.

Yet for all this, their final positions were within close hailing distance. Mill's strong libertarian arguments are qualified by the realities of social life; Stephen's initial purist utilitarian stance is greatly tempered by his own liberal freethinking tendencies and practicality. For Stephen, although it was impossible to pronounce in absolute terms whether any government policy was right, there was, nevertheless, a sufficient working consensus on what was good or bad to make the promotion of 'virtue and preventing of vice . . . sufficiently intelligible for legislative purposes'.[75] But the great trimmer was utility: the efficiency of means and the overall social cost. In encouraging virtue and suppressing evil society has the options of law or public opinion. As the 'roughest engine' of social control available, use of the criminal law required the greatest of care: 'every sort of precaution against abuse or mistake is essential'. Before behaviour was treated as criminal it ought to be 'capable of distinct definition, and of specific proof, and . . . of such a nature that it is worth while to prevent it at the risk of inflicting great damage . . . upon those who commit it. The conditions are seldom, if ever, fulfilled by mere vices.' On top of this, enforcement would mean 'an infinite number of deliberate and subtle inquiries which would tear off all privacy from the lives of a large number of people, . . . considerations [which] are . . . conclusive reasons against treating vice in general as a crime'.[76] However, Mill's insistence that the coercive influence of public opinion ought to be exercised only for self-protection was 'a paradox so startling that it is almost impossible to argue about it'.[77] The force of public opinion was 'incalculably great' and, though more powerful an influence than the law, was, as Mill argued, 'infinitely less well instructed [and] exceedingly liable to abuse'.[78]

Where, then, did Stephen's limits to the enforcement of morality, either by law or the exercise of public censure, run? Extensive and incapable of precise formulation they approximated to the following:

'(1) Neither legislation nor public opinion ought to be meddlesome. A very large proportion of the matters upon which people wish to interfere with their neighbours are trumpery little things which are of no real importance at all. The busybody and world-betterer who will never let things alone, or trust people to take care of themselves, is a common and a contemptible character. The commonplaces directed against these small creatures are perfectly just, but to try to put them down by denying the connection between law and morals is like shutting all light and air out of a house in order to keep out gnats and blue-bottle flies.

(2) Both legislation and public opinion, but especially the latter,

are apt to be most mischievous and cruelly unjust if they proceed upon imperfect evidence. To form and express strong opinions about the wickedness of a man whom you do not know, the immorality or impiety of a book you have not read, the merits of a question on which you are uninformed, is to run a great risk of inflicting a great wrong. It is hanging first and trying afterwards, or more frequently not trying at all. This, however, is no argument against hanging after a fair trial.

(3) Legislation ought in all cases to be graduated to the existing level of morals in the time and country in which it is employed. You cannot punish anything which public opinion, as expressed in the common practice of society, does not strenuously and unequivocally condemn. To try to do so is a sure way to produce gross hypocrisy and furious reaction. To be able to punish, a moral majority must be overwhelming. Law cannot be better than the nation in which it exists, though it may and can protect an acknowledged moral standard and may gradually be increased in strictness as the standard rises . . .

(4) Legislation and public opinion ought in all cases whatever scrupulously to respect privacy. To define the province of privacy distinctly is impossible, but it can be described in general terms. All the more intimate and delicate relations of life are of such a nature that to submit them to unsympathetic observation, or to observation which is sympathetic in the wrong way, inflicts great pain, and may inflict lasting moral injury. Privacy may be violated not only by the intrusion of a stranger, but by compelling or persuading a person to direct too much attention to his own feelings and to attach too much importance to their analysis. The common usage of language affords a practical test which is almost perfect upon this subject. Conduct which can be described as indecent is always in one way or another a violation of privacy.'[79]

All in all, despite lengthy bursts of ferocious and seemingly hardhearted rhetoric Stephen clearly conceded that (at least as a matter of utility) there was an undefinable yet real sphere within which law and public opinion were unacceptable intruders, likely to do more harm than good, cause more misery than happiness: 'To try to regulate the internal affairs of a family, the relations of love or friendship, or many other things of the same sort by law or by the coercion of public opinion is like trying to pull an eyelash out of a man's eye with a pair of tongs. They may put out the eye, but they will never get hold of the eyelash.'[80]

Stephen's case for what may loosely be called the enforcement of morality carried within it at least two separate strands of argument or types of rationale, aptly described by H.L.A. Hart as the 'disintegration' and 'conservative' thesis.[81] The 'disintegration' theory argues that a shared morality is the binding force of society, enforcement of the former preventing collapse or at least a dangerous weakening of the latter.[82] The 'conservative' thesis maintains that the majority have the right to choose their moral environment and protect it from changes of which they disapprove. This second theory is possibly a lurking subordinate argument in *Liberty, Equality, Fraternity* and is non-utilitarian in character, unless regarded as resting on the assumption that the collective displeasure of the majority will necessarily outweigh the misery of the oppressed minority. It is an interpretation given some credence by Stephen's occasional emphasis on the majority's feelings of disgust, intolerance and indignation.

Mill for his part was accused by Stephen, and others, of underrating the essential cohesive effects that only a shared morality could supply; although in his essay on Coleridge, and later in *Representative Government*, Mill showed that he was fully alive to the key function of shared values in any stable society. But what was the necessary level of common agreement, and over which matters? Obviously without a core of shared morality there can be no 'society';[83] yet, unless moral ossification is contemplated, a sufficient degree of tolerance capable of accommodating change is necessary. Moreover, neither Mill nor Stephen offer historical or psychological evidence to support or refute the disintegration thesis. But even accepting that any society risked disintegration by tolerating opposing moralities, where (as Locke asked in relation to religious unorthodoxy)[84] would be the lasting value of enforcing external compliance? What is the worth of outward conformity without inner conviction? One answer, suggested Stephen, was that 'your children will be brought up in the truth', and 'your neighbours' will not be seduced from it'.[85] Additionally, coupled with the effects of propaganda and the exclusion of alternative opinions, there was the Aristotelian argument, implicitly taken up by Stephen, that minds can be educated through coerced action and example. On Mill's side was the strong inclination towards Rousseau's belief that enforced inculcation of views impedes a higher natural development; that internal judgement should not lightly be overlaid by an external one.[86]

In modern times the issue of the legitimate degree of enforcement of morality has been most notably revived and fought over, once again, by a philosopher and a lawyer, the two eminent protagonists roughly occupying Mill's and Stephen's positions being Professor Hart and Lord Devlin.[87] Rather than directly set off by the great nineteenth-century encounter, the principal responsibility for this reopening of the debate lay in the more prosaic pages of the Wolfenden Committee Report on homosexual offences and prostitution.[88] As with the Report, Lord Devlin's and Professor Hart's major concern was the narrower, question of sexual morality and its possible legal superintendence. The Committee contended that there was a 'realm of morality and immorality which is not the law's business', although, unlike Mill, it did not also except such behaviour from strong public censure. Contrary to the Committee's view, Lord Devlin maintained that the 'suppression of vice is as much the law's business as the suppression of subversive activities'; that private morality might properly be regulated 'if society . . . in its collective judgement . . . is affected'. Protection of society from disintegratory immoral forces is an important common thesis of Stephen and Devlin, resting largely on the highly questionable assumption that society's morality 'forms a single seamless web', deviation from part of which threatens the whole. However, despite shared features, significant distinctions exist between the two lawyers – principally that Lord Devlin in presenting his case does not directly express himself as pursuing the utilitarian goal of 'the greatest happiness'; and, most obviously, Stephen's objective was the consideration of the much larger question raised by Mill of the legitimate coercive role unformalised public opinion might play in shaping society.

Though obscure in certain passages, Stephen seemed to justify both legal and social intervention on two grounds: as a necessary reinforcement of key social values and cohesive forces and, additionally, on the paternalistic[89] basis that the wise should look after and govern the foolish. But the significance of his repeated emphasis on the force and value of public or majority opinion lacks clarity and possibly harbours contradictions. It is a difficulty generated by frequent assertions that public exchanges on the proper content of religion and morality should be left to the cognoscenti, set against the claim that the moral majority should dictate such matters. That the

real difference between Mr Mill's doctrine and mine is this. We agree that the minority are wise and the majority foolish, but Mr Mill denies that the wise minority are ever justified in coercing the foolish majority for their own good, whereas I affirm that under circumstances, they may be justified in doing so.[90]

However,

You cannot punish anything which public opinion, as expressed in the common practice of society, does not strenuously and unequivocally condemn. To try to do so is a sure way to produce gross hypocrisy and furious reaction. To be able to punish, a moral majority must be overwhelming.[91]

Suggestions that the content of both legislation and public opinion should be reliant on or defer to the enlightened few stand uneasily alongside calls to accede to moral majorities. Was Stephen for a moral democracy even though opposed to a political one? Only by the most strenuous efforts can it be believed that he really intended the army of public opinion to be led by the informed elite from behind. Furthermore, uncertainty arises from Stephen's stance on the relationship of moral majorities and minorities with utility. At times he approaches identifying current moral values with utility, often smudging the distinction between existing and desirable moral standards. All of which creates a suspicion, hard to suppress completely, that Stephen was particularly ready to look to majority views when they happily coincided with those of the educated and right-thinking, but considerably less willing to do so when they did not.

LIBERTY AND UTILITARIAN ORTHODOXY

How faithful was Stephen to utilitarian reasoning, and how extensive was Mill's heterodoxy? After reading the third volume of Hume's *Treatise of Human Nature* (1740) Bentham recorded: 'I learnt to see that utility was the test and measure of all virtues . . . and that the obligation to minister to general happiness was an obligation paramount to and inclusive of every other.'[92] His broad-fronted hostility to vague notions of liberty was manifest: 'Whose liberty? . . . the liberty in rulers to oppress subjects and to lawyers to plunder suitors?'[93] Talk of the 'rights of man' or the 'ideas of 1789' were pure 'jargon'. For Bentham, as with Hume, liberty as an absolute right 'annihilates' law because every law supposes coercion. Happiness came from benevolence and utility, not abstract justice and liberty. Yet, support from Bentham for some principle of liberty or reasoned basis for excluding law and public opinion from private morality does, at first glance, seem to exist. For although Bentham insisted that utility governed the content of both morals and law, some elements particularly of his *Introduction to the Principles of Morals and Legislation* (1789) appear to suggest that in the realm of private morality the standard of utility is the maximisation not of general happiness but of the individual's,[94] 'principles' which he termed the 'art of self government or private ethics'.[95] Here, Bentham accepted that not every act which promises to be 'beneficial' or 'pernicious' to the community should be the subject of legislation. 'Where then is the line to be drawn?' For Bentham, activity was beyond legitimate legislative intervention if there were no discernible mischief, or if intervention would prove inefficacious, unprofitable, or needless because the harm was preventable in some less forceful way, for example 'by instruction'.[96] Public opinion would not condemn acts where there was no mischief, but would operate when a legal sanction was inefficacious, unprofitable or needless.

Furthermore, Bentham recognised 'intransitive' or 'self-regarding' offences,[97] acts which were only directly 'detrimental to the offender himself'. For 'intransitive' offences, such as 'drunkenness and fornication', Bentham admitted severe doubts as to the possible effectiveness of a legal sanction, believing that it would cause 'such a mass of evil . . . as would exceed a thousand-fold the utmost possible mischief of the offence'.[98] Even in the most notorious cases Bentham could see only 'slight censure' as being possibly advantageous, so 'thereby to cover them with a slight state of artificial disrepute'. Far from being concerned with the law neglecting such behaviour, Bentham saw the 'great difficulty' as one of persuading legislators 'to confine themselves within bounds' for 'A thousand little passions and prejudices have led them to narrow the liberty of the subject in this line, in cases in which the punishment is either attained with no profit at all, or with none that will make up for the experience.'[99]

Yet ultimately Bentham returned to his base point, restating the question always as one of utility or expediency, with freedom from interference never offered as even a vital means to happiness, let alone an end in itself. Unlike Stephen, though, Bentham never directly underwrote moral and social cohesion (as distinct from political stability) by restrictions on individual liberty. Custom, instinct and passion are recognised but undervalued by Bentham; whereas Stephen was fully alive to their strength and significance. Bentham's was a largely Hobbesian and external account of action, to which Mill added the sanction of morality – the internal sanction of the 'conscientious feelings of mankind'.[100] Such were notions of duty in a properly cultivated moral nature that were acquired not innate: one view of Mill's from which Stephen did not dissent.

When it came to questions of how far coercion might rightly be used, Mill's general principled rejection of paternalism[101] and more limited conception of harm crucially separated him from Bentham and Stephen. Whilst not swallowing Kantian assertions that the paternalistic removal of self-determination was the 'greatest despotism imaginable', Mill emphatically denied that a person's 'physical or moral good' was a sufficient warrant for interference, for 'Over himself . . . the individual is sovereign.'[102] Few such qualms disturbed Stephen's belief that many people required protection against the consequences of their own weakness, ignorance or imprudence.[103] Mill's claimed differences between prohibition and indirect means of discouraging socially unacceptable behaviour meant that drunkenness might be suppressed by heavy taxes or restrictions on availability, and that gambling and fornication could be met by outlawing gambling houses and brothels, distinctions which not only Fitzjames but Leslie Stephen too saw as sheer 'dexterous casuistry'.[104] Reinforcing this hostility to paternalism was Mill's restricted notion of the 'harms' that were capable of justifying coercive intervention. The types of harm accepted as worthy of enforced avoidance were based on the recognised interests of others – normative tests judged objectively. Yet even though in Mill's assessment disgust and revulsion were real sources of unhappiness, and therefore strictly relevant to utilitarian calculation, he still, in contrast with Stephen and Bentham, discounted them as recognised interests or harm.

In other directions Mill held closer than Stephen to the more Benthamite view of the nature of society and the individual in the social process. Bentham's neglect of the reciprocity of influence and reaction between individuals and society was in good measure perpetuated by Mill. Mill's model of society was atomistic, more an aggregate of independent units than an organism. But although some elements of Mill's individualistic conception of society were unmistakably Benthamite, a belief in and emphasis on the personal development of the individual was decidedly not. Mill's notions of the enrichment of individuality constituted a middle way between Bentham's utilitarianism, with its monochromatic concentration on satisfying desires for happiness, and T. H. Green's 'Idealists', with their collectivistic concern for what social man *ought* to be doing and thinking, and their perception of liberty's strong 'positive capacity' to develop the 'social self'.

In horticultural terms, Mill 'graft[ed] idealist concepts on to a utilitarian stock'.[105] For dull, two-dimensional Benthamite man

honesty is the best policy; he has enough sympathy to be kind to his old mother, and help a friend in distress; but the need of romantic and elevated conduct rarely occurs to him; and the heroic, if he meets it appears . . . an exception, not so far removed from the silly; [never reflecting on] what unsuspected capacities may lurk in his own commonplace character.[106]

With Mill, 'utility in the largest sense' signified the development of individuality, a fuller comprehension of the differences in the needs and ambitions of humans; liberty was not simply a condition of this, it was intrinsically valuable and a means to discovering new truths. Freedom was a prerequisite of individuality because individuality involved choosing for oneself. Freedom generated a climate of toleration receptive to personal and social innovation. Benthamism looked to the passivity of man; to conditioning and stimulating rather than the dynamics of human development. Stephen never displayed a convinced belief in the power of social forces to work any permanent and truly significant effect on the characters and souls of the bulk of mankind; yet of the desirability of romantic and elevated conduct he had not the slightest doubt.

Challenges to Mill's gospel of individualism sprang from many quarters, though never approaching the scale of Stephen's. Some saw Mill as encouraging an aimless eccentricity, seeking to substitute 'bohemian nonsense for bourgeois nonsense'.[107] Others, such as Leslie Stephen and T. H. Huxley, in relation to freedom of expression, accused Mill of advocating what amounted to a 'perpetual state of revolution and fermentation'.[108] Similarly, Arnold, in 'Doing as One Likes' (*Culture and Anarchy*) perceived in Mill's individuality a franchise for lawlessness and social anarchy, for anyone to 'hoot as he likes, threaten as he likes, smash as he likes'; dissent for its own sake – a 'Dissidence of Dissent'.[109] Though Arnold pursued as earnestly (and even more single-mindedly) as Mill the ideal of every man's highest self-development, the path chosen by each for its realisation ran some way from the other. Even possibly outdistancing Stephen, Arnold contends in *Culture and Anarchy* that neither freedom of expression nor action is an essential of individual enlightenment. Rather than liberty, it was state leadership and authority that would deliver Arnold's cultural renaissance; he believed, along with Stephen, that 'all the liberty . . . in the world will not ensure . . . high reason and a fine culture'.[110]

From the content of his own lengthy catalogue of restrictions on social and legal intervention into human activity, it is obvious that

Stephen would have agreed that Mill's distinction between self-regarding and 'other'-regarding acts at least had a rule-of-thumb value in predicting the likely efficacy of interference. But the great ideological wrangle focused on whether Mill's invocation of a distinct principle of liberty, not derivative of utility, really could be utilitarian. Was not this great principle of liberty an absolute moral fetter on the pursuit of general happiness? Could the connection between happiness and individuality be made out in utilitarian terms? How could the 'tone of militant individualism' of *On Liberty* be reconciled with the 'tone of enthusiastic altruism' issuing from *Utilitarianism*?[111] The question just how far Mill strayed from the utilitarian fold – and how justified Stephen's claims were – still contentiously survives amongst political historians, with the predominant view probably favouring Stephen.[112] However, Mill has not lacked defenders claiming his fidelity to a coherent body of utilitarian principles, who offer constructions of considerable subtlety and ingenuity, seeing *On Liberty*, *Logic*, and *Utilitarianism* as a sort of integrated treatise on justice, obligations and values.[113] Such arguments maintain that utility, rather than a moral principle from which direct judgements may be derived as to the rightness of action, is instead a fundamental principle specifying that happiness alone has intrinsic value. Liberty as a principle of critical morality assists the process of determining the correctness of actions; but quite what the relationship is between utility and liberty appears to defy anything resembling unanimity amongst Mill's supporters.

Perhaps Stephen's most powerful ally is the failure of any of Mill's immediate circle to protect their leader's reputation by resorting to interpretations of the nature of those set up in recent times. Modern claimants of Mill's coherence and consistency only enjoy meagre pickings from John Morley's *On Compromise* (1874), written partly in defence of Mill and as a rejoinder to *Liberty, Equality, Fraternity*. Indeed in some sections[114] Morley seeks to cut back the acceptable forms of liberty; and as one critic observed, *On Compromise* contains 'no sign of compromise except on the title page'.[115] Whilst easy to overrate, the failure of Mill's intimates, like Morley, to dispatch Stephen with arguments of the variety currently used does require explanation.

EQUALITY: JUSTICE AND SUFFRAGE

Alongside 'Liberty' lay 'Equality', the 'second great article of the modern creed' which, like liberty, was little more than a 'big name for a small thing', being at the same time the 'most emphatic and least distinct' of the three doctrines of 'Liberty, Equality and Fraternity'.[116] As with liberty, Mill was again selected by Stephen as the most cogent contemporary representative of those who preached, in one form or another, theories of egalitarianism. In this instance the offending opinions were implicit in chapter V of *Utilitarianism* (1861) – 'On the Connection between Justice and Utility' – and openly propagated in Mill's essay *The Subjection of Women* (1869). Together these two works were rightly seen by Stephen as forming a 'powerful and striking . . . condensation' of the sentiment of equality.

The most obvious and, particularly for the well-to-do, most disturbing ramification of theories of equality was the danger they posed to the private ownership of property, a risk later generating much of the concern that powered Maine's *Popular Government* (1885) and Lecky's *Democracy and Liberty* (1896). Both Maine and Lecky in their own ways warned that the populist democratic movement threatened the propertied classes with eventually being forced to 'disgorge' the source of their superiority. However, as a first line of defence there stood the powerful and fundamental tenet of classical liberalism showing equality to be in basic opposition to liberty; for, as Stephen observed, 'of all items of liberty, none is either so important or so universally recognised as the liberty of acquiring property'. Exclude a man from this entitlement and it would be 'difficult to see what liberty you have. . . ' .[117] Moreover, went Stephen's argument, if all restraints were minimised and the largest possible measure of liberty given to everyone, the eventual outcome would be inequality. Leave distinctions of ability and power 'to find their own level by unrestricted competition, and they will display themselves in their most naked and their harshest forms'.[118] Private property was the result of and reward for industry; private property was the 'very essence of inequality'. Whether Stephen intended this to be a rare oblique glimpse of his own economic theory is unclear. Certainly there seems to be a hint of dissatisfaction with the undiluted free-market doctrines of Smith, Malthus and Ricardo, but nothing of real substance emerges, perhaps confirming Mill's own unflattering judgement of his fellow Political Economy Club member's command of the subject: 'exceedingly ignorant, but nonetheless presumptuous'.[119]

Of course, in alleging the incompatibility of liberty and equality Stephen was doing little more than looking back to Austin,[120] Bentham, Hume and Locke; although their several views rested on quite different philosophical premises. For Bentham, inequality was a source of evil because 'by the inferior more is lost in the account of happiness than is gained by the superior'.[121] However, inequality was an inescapable evil, as without inequality of power there could be no political society. Furthermore, inequality of wealth was a necessary consequence of the right to property and essential if man were to be encouraged to work and save. Any substantial equalisation of wealth would, as Hume had suggested,[122] endanger general stability and security, particularly of property.[123] Though contrastingly, Locke's attachment to liberty of ownership and retention of property originated not so much from utility as from a framework of natural rights.

Mill's conclusions on equality were initially derived from the related but hardly less elusive concept of justice; Stephen traced Mill's steps. In the context of 'legal justice', Stephen agreed with Mill that 'justice' could refer either to the judge who applies the law, or to the legislator who makes it, or to the law itself. 'The judge is just if he enforces the law impartially. The Legislator is just if he enacts the law with an honest intention to promote public good. When the law itself is called just or unjust, what is meant is that it does or does not . . . promote the interests of those whom it affects.'[124] This was similarly true of moral justice, for a rule of positive morality may also be called unjust. As in the case of legal justice so also for moral justice, expediency and justice were the same thing; in both cases it was impossible to discuss the question of 'their justice or injustice apart from that of their expediency or inexpediency'.[125] For Stephen, Mill had 'irresistibly' demonstrated that justice meant the impartial administration of rules (legal or moral) founded on expediency. In this sense equality was just insofar as it was expedient, and only in the narrow sense of judicial impartiality did equality have a special connection with justice. All of which was sound utilitarian doctrine in accord with Bentham's portrayal of 'justice' as a 'phantom' or 'imaginary personage, feigned for the convenience of discourse, whose dictates are the dictates of utility'.[126]

Although Mill and (especially) Stephen professed allegiance to the premise that justice was utility, both were in varying degrees discomforted by its patent inability to account for many intuitive and self-evident expectations of 'justice': most centrally, that what may be regarded as expedient is not necessarily accepted as just. Rather remarkably, particularly for a criminal jurist, Stephen made no direct attempt to reconcile the conflict between utility and commonly accepted principles of distributive justice – governing such issues as how individuals are singled out for punishment, or how they are treated. These matters and questions of equality in the distribution of a community's benefits and burdens were, however, tackled by Mill who, like Hume,[127] recognised the need to account for them in utilitarian terms. But in 'On the Connection between Justice and Utility',[128] Mill was able to achieve little beyond unconvincingly concluding that all major instances of distributive justice were explicable on the basis of Bentham's equality of treatment principle. Yet this provided no obvious solution to the conflict between individual justice and general social expediency as in cases such as exemplary punishment. Moreover, application of a broad test of overall social benefit ignores the sense of fairness or value attached to truth-telling or promise-keeping. Thus if two possible courses of action have equal social utility the fact that one may involve the fair and just honouring of promises would not in itself be a factor relevant in its preference over the other, 'unfair' action.[129]

If, then, any distinction between justice or equality and expediency were to be maintained this could only be accomplished through recognition of equality as an end in itself – by the 'mouthing' of 'eternal and immutable justice',[130] as Austin disparagingly put it. It was the 'foundation' of just such a suggestion that Stephen believed Mill had laid in *Utilitarianism* and *The Subjection of Women*. Here Mill gave equality a 'character different from other ideas connected with justice', claiming 'justice is a name for certain moral requirements which regarded collectively stand higher in the scale of social utility, and are therefore of more paramount obligation than others'. Furthermore, each man's share of the 'labour and sacrifice incurred for defending the society or its members' ought to be determined on 'some equitable principle'. And turning to the basic utilitarian objective of the greatest happiness, Mill maintained.

The equal claim of everybody to happiness in the estimation of the moralist and the legislator involves an equal claim to all the means of happiness, except in so far as the inevitable conditions of human life, and the general interest in which that of every individual is included, sets limits to the maximum, and those limits ought to be strictly construed. As every other maxim of justice, so this is by no means to be held applicable universally. On the contrary, as I have already remarked, it bends to every person's ideas of social expediency. But in whatever case it is deemed applicable at all it is held to be the dictate of justice. All persons are deemed to have a right to equality of treatment except where some recognized social expediency requires the reverse, and hence all social inequalities which have ceased to be considered expedient assume the character not of simple inexpediency but of injustice, and appear so tyrannical that people are apt to wonder how they ever could have been tolerated.[131]

Stephen spotted this for what it was: a dangerous reversal of the onus of utilitarian logic, a case of putting the theoretical cart before the practical horse; and whether it was a rebuttable or irrebuttable presumption in favour of equality, the whole empirical basis of utilitarian reasoning was being thrown over. Experience was the starting-point of reasoning and Mill seemed, albeit with less than his 'usual transparent vigour', to be twisting out of sentiment an a priori assumption of the goodness of equality in all cases, subject to its dislodgement by the countervailing evidence of experience. As Stephen realised, it was placing in every case of inequality the 'burden of proof on those who justify its maintenance'.[132]

From Mill's supporting arguments Stephen drew out the general proposition that history showed human progress had been one from a 'law of force' to a state in which command and obedience were exceptional. Even assuming that all progress in Western European civilisation had been true advance (Stephen grudgingly would neither 'bless . . . nor curse them all'), was this to be fairly associated with a phased abandonment of the law of the strongest – with the view that the importance of force in human affairs had greatly declined? And if so, was this equivalent to the growth of equality? Stephen disputed both propositions.[133] Mill's enlistment of Maine's historical observation in *Ancient Law*, that the movement of 'progressive societies has hitherto been a movement from status to contract', proved no more than that 'force changes its form'. True, it was now less apparent, better organised and worked generally discreetly, but this was because no one doubted its existence, or its direction or its 'crushing superiority'. Men, for Stephen from his classical liberal viewpoint,[134] were 'fundamentally unequal', materially, intellectually and spiritually; an ineradicable inequality that would show through whatever way society was organised, and attempts to achieve equality by restrictive social arrangements were likely to be as effective as trying to make 'cards of equal value by shuffling the pack'.[135] Legally recognised rights and duties should reflect the realities of this natural inequality in society; efforts to establish equality where none existed would be as inefficacious as attempting to make 'clumsy feet look handsome by the help of tight boots'.[136]

The primary focus and illustration of Stephen's dissent from Mill's stand on equality was the issue of women's rights. These 'pet opinions', as Stephen acidly termed them, achieved fame and notoriety as amongst the most radical of the nineteenth century. Such views were advanced in a number of Mill's works including *Political Economy* (1848), *Representative Government* (1861) and, most prominently, *The Subjection of Women*, in which both the economic and political equality of women were advocated. No mere pale theoretical recluse, Mill was a strenuous platform campaigner for the cause into the early 1870s with his pamphleted speeches showing him well able to fire off effective and rousing rhetoric.[137] And whilst Mill unsuccessfully proposed a women's suffrage amendment to the Second Reform Bill, professional radicals like Bright became noticeably faint-hearted.

Although not always clear, rather than proposing a principle of 'perfect equality', Mill looked for a liberation of the means whereby women would enjoy an equality of opportunity to achieve fuller self-realisation and development. Equality was a vital step towards achieving the liberation spoken of in *On Liberty*. Women's inequality was a restriction of freedom, drying up the 'principal fountain of human happiness'.[138] Here, perhaps more than anywhere, Mill assumed the role of 'moral coach, keeping the national conscience in trim, shaming it out of flabbiness, urging it on to yet more strenuous efforts'.[139]

The extremity of the moral exertion urged in *The Subjection of Women* can be gauged from its reception amongst Mill's own friends and intellectual circle, with his 'biographer' Alexander Bain recording much upset and hostility.[140] Many of a generally enlightened outlook, like T. H. Huxley, railed against what they saw as the 'new woman-worship which so many sentimentalists and some philosophers are desirous of setting up'.[141] Even prominent progressives such as Frederic Harrison scoffed at the notion of sexual equality well into the next century,[142] comparing *The Subjection of Women* with the 'fanatical extravagance found in Abolitionists, Vegetarians and Free Lovers'.[143] Unsurprisingly Stephen too disagreed with Mill's essay from the 'first sentence to the last', believing it to express the 'most ignoble and mischievous of social sentiments of the time'. As they both well understood, Mill was seeking to undermine the most fundamental single condition of the existing social order.[144] Mill saw the social and legal subordination of women as quite at variance with the progressive movement of the age, and such as to place the onus on those who wished to defend the existing state of affairs. At the heart of the issue was the institution of marriage:

The equality of married persons before the law . . . is the only means of rendering the daily life of mankind in any high sense a school of moral cultivation . . . We have had the morality of submission and the morality of chivalry and generosity; the time is now come for the morality of justice . . . [Equality would bring] the advantage of having the most universal and prevailing of all human relations regulated by justice instead of injustice.[145]

All this was, for Stephen, unsound history combined with a 'grotesquely disturbed' view of reality. Incontrovertibly, men had not only superior physical power, but greater 'nervous force, greater intellectual force [and] greater vigour of character'.[146] For another *Saturday* reviewer, also expressing this general Benthamite[147] sentiment, evidence of the intellectual inferiority of women was plain from their striking under-representation in the history of literature and the arts, where those of highest reputation were only on the rarest occasions women.[148] However, the writer did concede in passing that social forces and other such disabilities might just have had some measure of influence on this pattern of achievement.

But even if women were inherently inferior in the ways supposed, should they, nevertheless, be treated as equals? Might there be some social utility in ignoring these differences? Far from it: Stephen saw the reverse as true. Rather than being disadvantaged, women benefited from the existing social and legal arrangements. Regard parties to a marriage contract as equals and then, logically, like other partnerships it should be dissoluble at the instance of either: an arrangement likely to operate most unfavourably for women, the weaker party. Moreover, women, having lost the bloom of youth earlier[149] and abandoned career prospects for marriage and children, were more vulnerable to desertion than the better-preserved, more independent male.[150] If two people were (effectively) indissolubly committed, then ultimately the stronger party would decide matters of great moment, although, of course, a man would have been a complete fool to deprive himself of his wife's advice. Undeniably, the relationship was sometimes abused; the existing laws governing the effects of marriage on property exhibited a 'stupid coarseness',[151] and most certainly acts of domestic violence called for the severest measures. But treat men and women similarly, socially and legally, and allow unrestricted competition, and the result would be that women would truly become 'men's slaves and drudges'.[152]

Mill's account of marriage was somewhat different: more often a form of social tyranny, with the family as a 'school of despotism . . . , a double-dyed and idealized selfishness', the happiness of the wife and children being 'immolated' in every shape to the husband's 'smallest of preferences'. To Stephen, Mill's assessment of family life involved the logic that 'good fruit grows on a bad tree', whereas for Stephen the natural consequence of a sound institution was good results – a case of Stephen inferring a good cause from good results. Naturally their respective childhoods were not completely foreign to their opinions of domestic life. And certainly in Stephen's characterising the nature of marriage in terms of the ultimate supremacy (or sovereignty) of one party, there was much, as Frederic Harrison quipped, of the 'tone of Petruchio taming the shrew'.[153] Yet as Leslie Stephen almost anxiously observes, Fitzjames' pugnaciousness put a 'misleadingly harsh face on his opinions', and his brother had admitted that 'When a beast is stirred up he roars rather too loud [and] this particular beast loves and honours . . . women more than he can express, and owes most of the happiness of his life to them.'[154]

Stephen's attitude to the education and entry into the professions of women was undogmatic: he regarded the matter as one of 'sentiment', not of practical importance. Oddly, though, he failed to register the likely impact on the institution of marriage following the educational and professional advancement of women. For his part, Mill too readily dismissed the social forces responsible for the position of women, placing an excessive explanatory reliance on coercion, and too easily departing from his Coleridgean[155] belief that whatever has long subsisted probably (but not unchallengeably) contains a measure of significant truth.

But forceful as Stephen's diatribe was, in substance the harsher elements were, of course, completely representative of his time and class. The *Saturday Review*'s stance was typical in seeing much of the 'Women's Question' as of an 'hysterico-sentimental' character, and the principal objective of a woman's life as the 'married state'. Opening up the major professions or universities to women lacked any obvious utility. More unimaginable was exposing women to the 'saturnalia' of active politics, where 'beer, banknotes, and Fescennic ribaldry are the most conspicuous elements'.[156] Even educated womanhood was divided on the franchise question, one powerful manifestation of anti-female suffrage being 'An Appeal against Female Suffrage' in the *Nineteenth Century*,[157] endorsed by a hundred or so women, including Mrs Leslie Stephen and Mrs Matthew Arnold. Only those very few like Mill with subtler perceptions of the deep effects of social education and conditioning saw the 'nature of women' as 'eminently artificial', largely the consequence of 'hothouse cultivation' carried on for the benefit of men.[158]

Predictably Stephen's flamboyant uncompromising stance set off a heavy barrage of criticism from the Women's Suffrage movement, drawing fire from, amongst others, Millicent Fawcett and Lydia Becker, two of its best-known members. The latter's sharp analytical criticisms of Stephen struck home on more than one occasion. For example, why, Becker asked, did Stephen conclude that if parties to a marriage were treated as equals it was impossible to avoid the inference that marriage like other partnerships might be dissolved at pleasure? There was no made out logical connection, for permanence of a marriage contract did not depend upon the strength or whim of either party, but upon the law. Enforceability was unaffected whether the law regarded it as between 'equals or between persons of unequal antecedent rights'.[159] Most telling of all, Becker noted that although Stephen emphatically denied that any man should have the right to beat his wife for disobedience, the logic of his case carried with it such an entitlement. If force were the ultimate source and sanction of all power both within and outside the home, where was the limit if a wife refused to defer to her husband's judgement? That it was contrary to the criminal law still begged the question why. Perhaps it was not unanswerable on utilitarian terms, but Stephen's stance was clearly inadequately argued.

Mrs Fawcett's[160] pamphlet, 'Mr Fitzjames Stephen on the Position of Women' (1873), was of a more general and grander sweep, mocking the tone and language of *Liberty, Equality, Fraternity* as much as disputing its contents. With *Liberty, Equality, Fraternity* the 'English-speaking nations' had received the latest revelation of the 'Gospel according to St Stephen'. She felt that ' "This is the way, walk ye in it" ought to have been printed in letters an inch high on the top of every page', an impression reinforced by the reader's feeling that the author was shouting in his ear. Stephen's discussion of woman is challenged at every stage: he was excessively naive in respect of the actual derisory punishments handed out to brutal husbands; the benefits of marriage seen from Stephen's privileged position ill equipped him to make generalisations beyond his class; and his view that 'submission and protection are correlative' was met with a catalogue of substantial disabilities suffered by married women. Nevertheless despite her profound disagreement with Stephen, Mrs Fawcett felt compelled to acknowledge his 'intelligible and honest arguments', which raised the standard of debate of the anti-suffrage case above the puerile level employed in the 'House of Commons by the Home Secretary'. In 'contrast with such pea-shooting we welcome the attack of Mr Stephen's heavy artillery'.[161]

Looking steadily at the wider question of political equality – 'the equal distribution of political power' – Stephen conceded, half fatalistically, half deterministically, the irreversible nature of the movement towards a broader-based democracy: the waters were out and no human force could turn them back, but nothing would enjoin him to associate with those who viewed the advent of eventual universal suffrage with 'something approaching . . . religious enthusiasm'. The current might be irresistible, but there was no reason 'why as we go with the stream we need sing Hallelujahs to the river god'.[162] Increased democracy was delusive, more a matter of appearance than substance; cutting up political power 'into little bits' meant that we were governed by 'the man who can sweep the greatest number of them into one heap'.[163] Democracy embodied a substantial element of chicanery whereby the ruling group would be the party 'wire pullers and their friends'; the subdivision of political power had 'no more to do with equality than with liberty'. And, just as with liberty, the question whether it was good or bad must be determined by 'direct reference to its effects'.

Stephen viewed the theory and practices of universal suffrage as a hopeless inversion of the real and natural relationship between wisdom and folly, preventing government by those who were wise and good of those who were foolish and bad. To believe that the populace would somehow by its collective understanding and voting power produce effective government was the 'wildest romance that ever got possession of any considerable number of minds'.[164] How could Mill, Stephen asked, with all his own forebodings and reservations advocate 'liberty in the sense of the negation of all government, and equality in any sense at all?' As Stephen well knew, having read *Representative Government*,[165] Mill looked on the coming of political age of a wider section of the nation as a means of awaken-

ing a fuller sense of personal responsibility and self-discipline, en-
riching both individual character and society. For Stephen, this
grand scheme was inflated with self-defeating delusion:

> We are told that it fosters noble qualities, that it is a splendid education, that it
> teaches men lessons of independence and self-reliance, gives vast numbers of
> persons an immediate interest in public affairs, and enables the government of
> the country to be carried on by the general consent of the persons governed. All
> this and much more of the same sort is continually repeated amongst us in every
> tone and on all possible occasions.
>
> There must be many ears in which such commonplaces have a very false and
> hollow sound. I have on general grounds the greatest possible reluctance to be-
> lieve in the good moral effects on any one whatever of habitually doing things
> ill. If there is (and how can there fail to be?) a right and a wrong way of doing
> every sort of important business, the moral effects of doing it well and in the
> right way are pretty sure to be better than those of doing it the wrong way. If
> there are – and hereby there must be – such things as true and false principles in
> politics, and good and bad kinds of political establishments, it would be contrary
> to all experience to believe that it is a matter of little importance whether those
> principles are not understood and applied, and whether those establishments are
> or are not set on foot.[166]

As Mill had frequently accepted, his was a social and political strategy
not without risks. Stephen, with his severely limited faith in the
general educability of the masses towards wholesome political
judgements, was at a loss for convincing reasons for making this
leap into the dark: it was a venture that offered little and
jeopardised much. Mill perceived the dangers, but with considerably
fewer doubts that there really was clear light on the other side.

However, having strenuously acquitted himself of any dogmatic
or theoretical endorsement of a wider franchise, Stephen was far
from ready to slouch away from its practical implications; rather he
threw his bulk behind schemes which promised at least to extract
the best advantage from this change. Or, more cynically, Stephen
hoped to neutralise the worst effects of greater political equality by
attempting to ensure that democracy was firmly guided by an able
and enlightened bureaucracy. Here he was often at one with Mill's
approach laid out in *Representative Government*. This was hardly surprising as they both wished to make parliamentary government
better at the job of governing, agreeing that it was then 'radically
unfit' for this function, and that following increased political equality
the task was to ensure that the administration of government was
entrusted to those who possessed the necessary high skills.[167] Con-

trol and criticism needed to be 'disjoined' from the actual conduct of affairs; some 'human contrivance' was required to avoid the dangers associated with 'popular stupidity' and (working-) 'class based' legislation.[168] Others, and especially Morley, pinned their hopes on political rather than administrative elitism; on the 'necessity of giving supreme political power to supreme political intelligence',[169] which through 'constitution or training find their chief happiness in thinking in a disciplined and serious manner how things can be better done'.[170] Stephen's extensive and innovatory organisational reforms in government sketched out in Liberty, Equality, Fraternity were more fully explored in two papers on 'Parliamentary Government' delivered to the 'Edinburgh Philosophical Society' soon after the book's publication. However, whereas Mill's schemes were meant to enhance and refine the rough elective element of representative government, the pervasive tone of Stephen's objectives was of a faintly optimistic damage limitation exercise.

Though the subsequent history of the Civil Service in many respects showed Mill's and Stephen's far-sightedness, at the time of his Edinburgh lectures Stephen attracted an unappreciative if largely predicatable reaction from Carlyle, who

found it a very curious piece indeed, delineating one of the most perfect dust whirls of Administrative Nihilism, and absolute absurdities and impotences, more like an electric government apparatus for Bedlam, elected and submitted by Bedlam, than any sane apparatus ever known before. And strangely enough, it is intended with the loyalist assurances every now and then that it is the one form of government for us for an indefinite period and that no change for the better can be possibly contemplated.[171]

Bearing in mind the lack of popular appeal of Carlyle's own political dreaming, Stephen doubtless would have found his friend's lampoonery heartening as well as entertaining.

Stephen's administrative schemes were not purely the fruits of the imaginative theorising of a concerned but detached observer of Britain's political structure. For as well as being conceptually unappealing, the demeaning reality of electioneering and the hustings had vividly reinforced this progressively developing antipathy towards the populist element of parliamentary democracy. At the general election of 1865, Stephen had unsuccessfully attempted to secure Harwich for the Liberals, a failure which his brother put down to 'indifference and want of familiarity with the small talk of politics', demonstrating to all including the voters of Harwich that Stephen was 'rather out of his element'.[172] It was, however, his

1873 candidature for Dundee that created the most powerful and distasteful impressions. With the considerable practical incentive of possibly securing the Attorney or Solicitor Generalship,[173] Stephen this time approached the whole enterprise with a fair degree of commitment. But, as a consequence of three 'Liberals' standing, the proclaimed policies and personality of each hopeful gained particular significance – with Stephen suffering in both respects. His espoused manifesto of uncompromising 'self-help' and 'individualism' was matched by the comfortable 'stolid middle class prejudices' of Yeaman (former provost of the town) and the 'sentimental socialism' of Jenkins, overflowing with unctuous 'philanthropic enthusiasm'. Publication in a local paper of extracts from *Liberty, Equality, Fraternity* doubtless, as its author feared, hardly helped his cause. Stephen's constitutional inability to dress up his policies, let alone sell himself as a congenial servant of the people, was painfully apparent; as was his 'disgust'[174] for the whole sordid business. It was truly 'hateful work – such noise, such waste of time, such unbusinesslike, raging, noisy, irregular ways, and such intolerable smallness in the minds of the people, that I wonder I do not do it even worse. The S.G. ship would no doubt be a prize worth getting, but I really think heaven itself would hardly tempt me to go through a month of this.'[175] Even supporters saw him as 'over-defiant', 'almost rude'; speeches extolling his oratorical and parliamentary virtues were found 'so unspeakably fulsome' as to 'nearly [make] him sick'.[176] Inevitably Stephen was, in the most unmistakable fashion, 'given a by'[177] by Dundee's voters.[178] The whole episode had confirmed pre-existing prejudices, and with just a forgivable touch of pique, lingering on from his electoral bruising, he later declared himself 'neither Tory or Liberal. I simply hate English politics and do not concern myself with them at all'.[179]

Beyond the immediate objections to political levelling, two sizeable omissions from Stephen's account of liberty and equality were the issues of economic freedom and equality, and the possible economic consequences of moves towards social and political equality. Stephen's apprehensions were largely confined to social fragmentation, fears for the absence of a high-minded and sound political philosophy and the rule of a generally ignorant and philistine culture. Worries of economic catastrophe, or at least stagnation and the threat to property were given rather more emphasis by Stephen's friend Henry Maine in *Popular Government* (1885), and by the historian, and fellow cohort of Carlyle, William Lecky in *Democracy and Liberty* (1896).

In *Popular Government*, Maine analysed the nuts and bolts of democratic advance and, unlike Stephen in *Liberty, Equality, Fraternity*, only marginally concerned himself with great ethical questions. Neither was Maine much worried by the threat to religious beliefs. Rather it was an interest in and knowledge of the evolutionary forces in society which suggested to him that a rapid democratic levelling posed a threat to long-established and vital values. As Dicey[180] remarked, Maine's historical studies bred a great scepticism as to the value of popular government. Such investigations combined with Darwin's evolutionary theories confirmed his beliefs in the validity of laissez-faire individualism and the notion of inherited human characteristics,[181] a view that Mill had earlier frequently rejected.[182] For Maine, democratic government was a fragile mechanism, fraught with organisational difficulties, having no necessary connection with human improvement and which had always been the work of the few, usually against the inertia of man's inherent hostility to change. As with Stephen, India was for Maine a great political awakening: 'India and the India Office make one judge public men by standards which have little to do with public opinion.'[183] In common with Stephen, he viewed the mass of mankind as open to little change, holding that ignorance twinned with limited intelligence could only be partially alleviated by education. But in believing the finest qualities of natural leadership and government were best found within the hereditary aristocracy, Maine was politically far closer to Carlyle than Stephen was. For him, unlike Stephen, salvation was not to be found in any intellectual or meritocratic elite.

Whilst Maine turned to history to show that neither democracy nor political equality was inevitable or stable, Stephen looked to the logic of utilitarian ethics and human nature to say the same. From being representatives, Maine feared Members of Parliament were becoming sectional delegates.[184] Along with Stephen, Maine was repelled by thoughts of strict party control and 'wire-pullers', actually openly borrowing Stephen's expression.[185] Again echoing Stephen, Maine saw the morality and intellect of the country's rulers being enfeebled by having to mouth meaningless generalities to capture and retain political power.[186] Rousseau's claims that democracy[187] was the only legitimate form of government were dismissed as flying in the face of the great weight of historical experience. Democratic equality led not to progress but to a widespread disillusioning stagnation; one of uniform mediocrity and vulgarity. Maine scoffed at Bentham's belief that most men knew their own best interests, because most were incapable of understanding them. And reproducing Macaulay's reaction to James Mill's 'Essay on Government' more than half a century before, Maine predicted political and economic equality would see 'a mutinous crew feasting on a ship's provisions, gorging themselves on the meat and intoxicating themselves with the liquor, but refusing to navigate the vessel to port'.[188] It is the spectre of socialism that haunts much of *Popular Government*, with the introduction of widespread state benefits seen as likely to decrease the willingness to work and save – the vital Benthamite 'springs of action' for the production of wealth. For Maine and Lecky, as for Macaulay, notions of equality were, because of their hostility to the concentrated ownership of property, 'incompatible with civilization' itself.

In many ways a more traditional performance than *Liberty, Equality, Fraternity, Popular Government* was also a longer-lasting one, runing to six editions by 1909. Yet successful as Maine's book was, its intellectual integrity and impartiality were searchingly questioned by many, notably John Morley and James Bryce, who suggested that Maine's claim to have applied the 'Historical Method' to political institutions was little more than an ill-disguised effort to clothe personal political fears and prejudices[189] in the respectability accorded to his earlier works. Bryce declared a 'low opinion of everything in it but its style', finding Maine's 'historical instances . . . one sided and flimsy'.[190] Morley, with some cause, cuttingly likened parts to the 'drone of a dowager in the Faubourg Saint-Germain',[191] and, more seriously, faulted Maine's method of judging and comparing forms of government in isolation from 'other deeper forces of the time'.

Stephen, though, loyally confessed a liking for his friend's work, probably finding the agreeability of the sentiments more than adequate compensation for any methodological shortcomings.[192] Indeed, in the early 1880s Stephen often spoke of his own inclination to write a further work on 'Democracy', on one occasion confessing to Lord Lytton that 'at 53½ I am still capable of falling in love and I have been flirting with a variety of nymphs of a less grim nature than the Principles of English law'.[193] However, even more intriguing than speculating on how different such a book would have been from *Popular Government* is imagining how it would have looked alongside *Liberty, Equality, Fraternity*. The democratic liberal Morley would have had few doubts, believing that when the 'scientific lawyer is doubled with the Indian bureaucrat, we are pretty sure . . . that in such a tribunal it will go hard with democracy'. And when characterising *Popular Government* as 'exclusively critical and negative' – a sort of 'philosophical cul-de-sac'[194] – Morley could easily have been repeating his views, from more than a decade before, of *Liberty, Equality, Fraternity*.

FRATERNITY OR CALVINISM 'WITH THE BOTTOM KNOCKED OUT'

As a legislative and ethical theory, utilitarianism provides a formula for explaining why and how certain outcomes should be morally preferred to others. Rather than with the morality of individual acts, Bentham and Austin had primarily occupied themselves with systems of legislation and law – with the question of the general tendency of acts for good or bad. Although accepting the essential premises of Benthamite utilitarianism, neither Mill nor Stephen was satisfied with its neglect of individual morality or its crude incomplete account of society and human nature. In their separate responses to these deficiencies the single most important distinguishing feature was that Stephen's conception of a higher moral framework, unlike Mill's, still clung to notions of sanction and coercion.

In 1865 Stephen used his *Fraser's Magazine* essay on Carlyle to combine an explanation of his preference for utilitarian empiricism with a form of vindication for some of the attractions of Carlyle's 'intuitionism' or 'transcendentalism'. Stephen conceded that empiricism was morally and religiously inadequate in its inability thoroughly to answer the questions 'why men should be virtuous? what virtue consists of? and how one is to know whether this is right or wrong'. The 'Virtue and Justice offered by the transcendentalist [was] the voice of the Eternities'; for hard-headed empiricists or utilitarians, virtue was compliance with a system of rules calculated to produce happiness. But the question why promote pleasure or happiness? (as Mill and Bentham recognised) admitted no absolute answer because they were ends in themselves. Indisputably, there was no serious alternative to utilitarianism's reverence for evidence and truth, which must be 'pursued unflinchingly to all lengths' because the widest experience proves that they alone are 'useful and good in the long run'. Yet, at the same time, it had to be admitted that not everything could be revealed by an 'anatomical photo' or a 'geological section'; truth was a 'beauty' that was incapable of being wholly represented by the 'anatomist' or 'geologist'. Men understandably succumbed to the soft emotional appeal of the transcendentalism practised by those like Carlyle for whom the need to prove and find reasons gave way to the greater necessity 'to know and believe'.[195] But despite their earth-bound prosaic image, utilitarians were not mere pigs, with 'no souls to speak of above the trough and its contents. . . ' . And for all its inadequacies, utilitarianism contained 'most of the truth' and actually achieved desirable goals. The prominent position of utilitarianism in nineteenth-century reforms hardly needed defending. Benthamites had, for example, preached law and educational reform 'in season and out of season, till they became positive bores to mankind',[196] carrying such measures in 'the teeth of all sorts of stupid, arrogant and ignorant opposition'.[197] And despite admitted shortcomings, for Stephen, its plain prescription for getting things done was *the* great recommendation of Bentham's creed.

Mill was no more impervious to the appeal of 'transcendentalism', at least in filling up Benthamism's philosophic holes; so much so that his essay on Coleridge caused more rigid Benthamites to dub him a kind of 'German metaphysical mystic'. Stephen's regard for and treatment of the Carlylean outlook bears an obvious resemblance to Mill's assessment of Coleridge. Just as Mill in his comparative essays on Bentham and Coleridge acknowledged that utilitarians might enhance and deepen their philosophy by taking from Coleridge, Stephen likewise understood that Carlyle's intuitionism was not to be brushed aside as totally worthless; although quite how its value might usefully be realised was perplexing.

Mill's *Utilitarianism* attempted to particularise utility's application and describe the relationships of the individual and society, and of utility with morality. However, his defence of Bentham's pain and pleasure calculus succeeded more in undermining than shoring up Bentham's credibility. For in attempting to show it as the measure of utility and the basis of morality, Mill actually demonstrated that pleasure was not the sole object of action, that all pleasures were not equal, and that individuals and their needs were not identical. One of the particular failings of utilitarianism addressed by Mill was the apparent assumption that individual and general social interests would always coincide sufficiently for there to be no invidious choice facing a person when deciding on a course of action. Though it was fraught with interpretational difficulties, Bentham's approach seemed to take for granted that self-interest would always coincide with the long-term general happiness of all. Mill's redefinition and refinements of utilitarian ethics stressed that in achieving the greatest general happiness the social effects of individual actions were of the highest importance, and that with the advance of civilisation came an accompanying 'feeling of unity with all of the rest' of mankind.[198] Certainly happiness, Mill later affirmed in his *Autobiography*, was the ultimate goal of life, but rather than individual gratification it was 'the happiness of others, [and] the improvement of mankind'. Submerging himself in a glowing Comtean optimism, Mill foresaw almost limitless potential for the cause of humanity in the cultivation of such natural social benevolence.

This 'Comtist positivism' offered, to those whose Christian faith had foundered, a substitute moral order and the spiritual conviction capable of providing a steady coherent explanation of existence, of man the social being and the process of social evolution. Through a claimed assimilation of morals with physical science, it supplied a blueprint of ordered progress and inevitable improvement, and could, as John Morley suggested, like a true religion, be the 'supreme, penetrating, controlling, decisive part of a man's life'.[199] Others, like T. H. Huxley, felt able sharply to write it off as simply 'Catholicism minus Christianity'.[200] But if the whole order of morality was to be replaced by this superior, more ethereal, version of utilitarianism – the 'religion of humanity' – what would be the answer to the question 'why should I do right, why should I act morally?' Having 'abolished hell', or at least put it in mothballs, utilitarianism lacked a supernatural sanction.[201]

Mill's substitute was the 'subjective feeling in our minds, [the] conscientious feelings of mankind . . . , the desire to be in unity with our fellow creatures'.[202] Stephen had something rather different in mind. Fraternity in the shape of this abstract 'worship and service of humanity', particularly during the 1860s and 1870s, was a constant source of 'hot debate'[203] and deeply repulsed Stephen. Rousseau's general 'expressions of love for mankind were nauseous', a 'cloud castle of sweet illusions and darling lies'. Undeniably, agreed Stephen, the greater part of the happiness of mankind arose from all levels of friendship, yet beyond 'me and mine' it was not 'love that one wants from the great mass of mankind, but respect and justice'.[204] As Stephen recognised, the single strongest source

of his disagreement with Mill and the 'positivists'' religion of
humanity was the different assessment of the characteristics of
mankind; a difference 'beyond the reach of argument'.[205] Mill
believed that were men to be freed from restraints and given a fair
measure of equality there would develop a harmonious fellowship
of mankind. But in the world inhabited by Stephen, while many
men were bad and many good the vast majority were merely
uncommitted, spinning like weather cocks 'this way or that according to the dominant current of goodness or evil'.

Rather than Rousseauesque or Comtean fraternal love, for
Stephen, the natural and inevitable state of society was Calvinistic
strife, with even good men brought into collision by conflicting
interests or by their different conceptions of goodness. How then
could such conflict be turned to mankind's benefit? Neither Bentham's
nor Mill's solution was convincing. It was true that happiness was
the most significant and least misleading word by which any moral
order might properly be tested. And certainly morality could not
be 'twisted out of pure reason'. Instead it was to be founded on an
objective standard against which its results could be measured and
happiness might be that standard. But happiness was not fixed in
meaning, so neither did morality have an absolute quality.[206]
'Happiness' was another name for the general and permanent
objectives of human existence which turned on the individual spectator's conception of the world and of the nature of life.[207] Whose
happiness was more worthwhile and to whom? Was it 'Lord
Eldon's or . . . Shelley's' or 'a very stupid prosperous farmer who
dies after a life of perfect health or an accomplished delicate woman
of passionate sensibility and brilliant genius who dies worn out
before her youth is passed, after an alternation of rapturous happiness with agonies of distress?' Such questions might as easily be
answered as stating the 'distance from one o'clock to London
Bridge'. Mill's exercise[208] of grading pleasure in moral terms
amounted to the illogicality of proposing a standard for a standard.
Happiness, for Stephen, had no abstract value which could be
detached from the consumer, agreeing in this sense, at least, with
Bentham that because of the relativity of happiness any qualitative
test was futile, therefore making 'push-pin . . . of equal value with
. . . poetry' in any purely utilitarian calculation.

Stephen saw that attempting to base a universal moral system on
a belief in the collective consensus of a brotherhood of man
'denoted by the word happiness is to build on sand'.[209] The legislature says 'you shall'; the moralist, 'I advise you.' Love of mankind

was just one of a range of motives; it had its place but it neither stood alone nor dominated.[210] Though Mill had never denied the self-centred nature of most people, he had, optimistically, anticipated a transition from this state to one of a highly developed social sense of such strength that it even risked swamping human liberty and individuality. However, this transformation entailed accepting altruism as a major human characteristic; something which utilitarians had never quite sorted out. Certainly Bentham recognised social motives, such as benevolence, which sometimes led men to seek their own happiness in the happiness of others;[211] yet whilst confident in 'his power of constructing a happy society as the most ardent believer in the perfectibility of mankind, he [was] as convinced of the unqualified selfishness of the vast majority of human beings as the bitterest cynic!'[212]

Like Mill, the late utilitarian theorist Henry Sidgwick[213] was troubled by this apparently deep conflict between private happiness and general happiness. Just how could egoistic hedonism be reconciled with the ethic of general happiness when each emotion often encouraged opposing courses of action? Sidgwick was driven to admitting that without the existence of God and Providence, providing an unchallengeable reason for altruism was virtually impossible. In his *Methods of Ethics* (1874), however, by a half-convincing synthesis of intuitionism and utilitarianism, Sidgwick concluded that egoistic instincts could be overborne to recognise the greater worth of social good. No such doctrinal dilemma afflicted Stephen; to him the notion of self-sacrifice was illusory: self was 'each man's centre from which he can no more displace himself than leap off his own shadow'.[214] How could love of humanity serve as the foundation of morality, when 'Humanity is only I writ large'? Love for humanity generally meant 'zeal for my notions as to what men should be and how they should live'.[215] A safer, surer and more realistic route to general happiness than this vacuous love of humanity as practised by any 'moral Don Quixote who is always liable to sacrifice himself and his neighbours' was that followed by the man whose acts are governed by ordinary motives and who works for the 'advantage of himself and his own'.[216] Put in this stark fashion it was a philosophy uncomfortably resembling one pilloried by Mill in his St Andrews inaugural address, of the man 'all whose ambition is self-regarding; who has no higher purpose in life than to enrich or raise in the world himself and his family'.[217]

For Stephen, the religion of humanity was empty of meaning in two critical ways: in a political and moral sense it was incapable of providing the (coercive) basis of any higher moral order; in a spiritual

sense it was an anaemic substitute for what Christianity offered its
followers. Reacting to the first edition of *Liberty, Equality, Fraternity*, Frederic Harrison, as a staunch positivist propagandist,[218] had
maintained that a practical religion could be founded on the 'vast
collective development in the energies of man ever more distinctly
knitting up in one the spirit of races, and forming the dominant
influence which ultimately shapes the life of societies and of men'.
Quite reasonably, all this struck Stephen as no more than a 'bag of
words', meaning 'anything, everything or nothing just as you
choose'.[219] Exactly what spiritual comfort could this vapid humanism
offer? Harrison's tribute to the memory of the recently dead Mill
had asserted that his death carried no 'sting' and that 'victory' had
been denied the grave, for 'the soul, the sum of moral powers,
live[d] eternally', although not a 'life of sensation or consciousness'.[220] Stephen castigated such talk as 'empty and unsatisfying as
undertaker's plumes', providing no spiritual solace and 'essentially
a mockery'. In truth

[t]he death of a friend admits of no consolation at all. Its sting to the survivors
lies in the hopeless separation which it produces, and in the destruction of a
world of common interests, feelings, and recollections which nothing can replace. The amount of suffering it inflicts depends on the temperament of the
survivors, but it impoverishes them more or less for the rest of their lives, like
the loss of a limb or a sense. The lapse of time no doubt accustoms and recon-
ciles us to everything, but I do not believe anything can blunt the sting of death
or qualify the victory of the grave, except a belief of some sort as to a future
state; and that, for obvious reasons, does little enough. The common views upon
the subject are anything but consolatory, and the more rational views are of
necessity vague. Their importance lies not in creating definite posthumous fears,
or in applying definite hopes or consolations to definite suffering, but in the fact
that they give to life, and especially to that which is most permanent in life, a
degree of dignity which could hardly attach to anything so transient and uncertain as the time which we pass upon this earth, if it is viewed as the whole of our
existence.[221]

When thinking through the consequences for morality of an exchange of Christianity for humanism, Stephen felt obliged first to
present his reader with the strongest case for belief in an after life
as a foundation for his subsequent thesis of a higher morality, for
the answer to moral and social problems lay in 'What am I? How
am I related to others? Are my body and I one and the same
thing?'[222] Employing a parallel form of Cartesian logic and using
self-perception as the base argument of existence, Stephen took it
also as the best evidence of the soul. Glancing towards Mill and
Carlyle, his intellectual and 'poetic' mentors, Stephen saw the 'final

inexplicability' of self-awareness as something separate from the physicality of existence, as an unchanging fixed point in the midst of constant change, rendering probable the prior and future existence of such a separate consciousness. However, the great limitations of language frustrated expression and communication between humans of these deeper truths:

It seems to me that we are spirits in our prison, able only to make signals to each other, but with a world of things to think and to say which our signals cannot describe at all. It is this necessity for working with tools which break in your hand when any really powerful strain is put upon them which so often gives an advantage in argument to the inferior over the superior, to the man who can answer to the purpose easy things to understand over the man whose thoughts split the seams of the dress in which he has to clothe them.[223]

Underscoring the direction of his argument, Stephen speculated that if 'my organs are not I . . . then my happiness and their well-being are different and maybe incoinsistent with each other'. Quite how a man should and will behave on earth turns on his belief (or absence of it) in some form of after life; something completely neglected by positivists, whose sanctionless moral creed was really no more than an insipid matter of 'individual taste'. Those who had a well-developed taste for the good of humanity could do no more than condemn the selfish as 'brutes'; but the 'brutes' could reply 'you are fools' and neither party would advance one bit further.[224] For sorting out the sheep from the goats 'Mr Harrison's religion [did] not even provide a sheep-dog to bark at them. . . '[225] Comte, Stephen had long thought, was 'mad',[226] with Comtist philosophy not much beyond social and metaphysical quackery. As an organised religion positivism was 'superfluous' to its adherents, and little more than a toothless 'Ritualistic Social Science Society' to all others.[227] Undeniably the 'commonplace morality' of utilitarianism and Comtist positivism espoused the cultivation of benevolence and sympathy, but a 'higher' quality in the scale of morality was dependent upon belief in a future life – 'a Providence'. Virtue then ceased to be mere fact and became the law of society; 'law' rather than 'fact' because, in utilitarian terminology, there was the sanction of the 'hopes and fears' excited by Providence. In this Stephen adopted or borrowed much from Paley's 'other-worldly Benthamism' or 'theological utilitarianism': 'doing good for the sake of everlasting happiness'. Indeed, Stephen had in the past registered his affection for Paley, noting that 'with all its defects, Paley's *Evidences* is worth a cartload of (Seeley's) *Ecce Homos*',[228] which strongly gave 'the impression of being written by a sheep in wolf's clothing'.[229]

Both this quasi-Paleyan and positivistic way of looking at the
world and morality were 'complete, consistent, intelligible and
based upon fact'; but only with the inclusion of the sanction of a
future state could a 'rational account of the feeling that it is a duty
to be virtuous' be provided. Without such a reason virtue was
reduced from a duty to a matter of taste – just like the buttons in
the small of the back on a frock coat: so long as they appealed they
could stay, though if found inconvenient they would be 'snipped
off without mercy'.[230] The only absolute justification for the inconvenience of duty in all forms was that 'God is a legislator and virtue
a law in the proper sense of the word' – conduct enforced by a
sanction.[231] Thus, in short, 'problems of government, law, and
morals revolve round the questions which lie at the root of religion
– What? Whence? Whither?'[232]

Stephen was fully alive to the likely reception of this full-blooded
treatment of 'Fraternity', expecting it to 'pain some of my friends,
. . . but I cannot help it for it is now a case of over shoes, over
boots with me. I must either say what I have got to say on such subjects or I must hold my tongue altogether, and that I cannot do.'[233]
On top of the overall harshness of the doctrine were the more
detailed interpretational difficulties. Even Stephen's staunchest
defenders would be bound to admit that some features of his case
for a 'higher morality' severely test the reader's powers of comprehension.[234] How, for instance, does any man ever progress from
being self-centred and self-seeking? If virtue were more of the natural
essence of higher man then was there a real need for the supernatural sanction – unless supernatural belief had the concomitant
effect of erasing or suppressing self-centredness? Moreover, just
how did Stephen know that the higher and spiritual mode of life
would lead to greater happiness for all or most? Had he followed
his own strictures and found the empirical basis for this assertion?
   Still more interpretational problems were dug out by Frederic
Harrison. In 'The Religion of Inhumanity' Harrison labelled
Stephen's rationalistic account of the relationship of morality and
religion as 'Stephenism' with hell at its centre from his 'new edition
of Bentham'. Although remarking that 'hell is an essential part of
the whole Christian scheme', Stephen strongly denied that one
word of *Liberty, Equality, Fraternity* implied his own belief in hell in
the sense of 'any place or state of infinite torture reserved for the
wicked after death'. But, with considerable cause, Harrison made
the telling point that Stephen was acutely obscure – not to say

verging on the opaque – when it came to settling quite what the Providential sanction was. As Harrison asked, 'What are the hopes and fears you appeal to? Is your heaven and hell a transcendental state of feeling, or is it intense human pleasure and acute human pain, and, if so, pleasure of what sort, and pain of what sort? For on your answer . . . the influence it will exert . . . entirely depends.'[235]

Conceding that *Liberty, Equality, Fraternity* was 'incomplete and negative' in this area, Stephen met Harrison's inquiry by reaffirming that his simple objective had been to demonstrate that the content of our morality could not be independent of our belief or disbelief in God; that the prudence or wisdom of virtue turned on whether there was a future state. As a matter of record, Stephen owned that he saw the 'common doctrines about heaven and hell' as unsupported by 'adequate evidence'; although it was 'highly probable' that our 'personal consciousness in some shape survives death'.[236] To Harrison's highly germane question 'what sort of future state?', Stephen was driven to speculating that 'if there is a future state, it is natural to suppose that that which survives death will be that which is most permanent in life. . . That is to say, mind, self-consciousness, conscience or our opinion of ourselves'. Bodily pleasures and sufferings could hardly be part of this after a man's body has been 'dispersed to the elements, but so long as a man can be said to be himself in any intelligible sense of the word, he must more or less remember and pass judgment on his past existence, and the only standard which we can imagine as being used for that purpose is the one with which we are acquainted'. It followed, then, that a calculating and rational man believing in the possibility of an after life would cultivate those 'feelings and powers . . . most advantageous to him [as] such a permanent being'.[237]

Hence the supposition that this life is not all, but only a part of something wider, is important, not exclusively, perhaps not even principally, because it tends to heighten the importance of moral distinctions . . . but because it supplies a reason for attaching more importance than we should attach, if this life were all, to those elements of our nature which though permanent and deep-seated, are often weak in comparison with others of a more transient kind.[238]

All this was a great distance from substantiating the hell and damnation allegations thrown at Stephen then and since. Indeed, it is tempting to suggest that his preface to the second edition of *Liberty, Equality, Fraternity* is more a reinterpretation, or rethinking, of earlier thoughts than a clarification and textual expansion.

As will be seen, Stephen's religious convictions faded with the years and even the short period between completion of the first edition and the preface of the second no doubt took its toll on the strength of already heavily eroded beliefs. So much so that the vital and unavoidable question is whether Stephen redefined his religious sanction out of existence and came in sight of upending his thesis that morality necessarily leaned heavily on belief in God and a future life. There is an unmistakable hint of intellectual helplessness, or at least unease; of someone who was arguing the case for the necessity of a belief to which he himself could not even loosely adhere.

Yet, however insubstantial and unsatisfying Stephen's beliefs then were, the truth of a future state remained the central inescapable issue. But uncertainty was the essence of life; we are all compelled to make this choice, one that should be accepted with an upright stoicism[239] – recognising in a fashion, after Luther, 'Here stand I, I can do no other.'

Each must act as he thinks best, and if he is wrong so much the worse for him. We stand on a mountain pass in the midst of whirling snow and blinding mist, through which we get glimpses now and then of paths which may be deceptive. If we stand still, we shall be frozen to death. If we take the wrong road, we shall be dashed to pieces. We do not certainly know whether there is any right one. What must we do? 'Be strong and of a good courage.' Act for the best, hope for the best, and take what comes. Above all, let us dream no dreams, and tell no lies, but go our way, wherever it may lead, with our eyes open and our heads erect. If death ends all, we cannot meet it better. If not, let us enter whatever may be the next scene like honest men, with no sophistry in our mouths and no masks on our faces.[240]

Thin as his own beliefs were, and true as the contemporary jibe was that Stephen was essentially a 'Calvinist with the bottom knocked out',[241] he had few doubts that positivist notions of fraternity, if not undiluted sophistry, were little more than an elaborate but irrelevant avoidance of the real questions posed by existence.

With Mill's death in 1873 it was left to his outstanding and ambitious lieutenant, John Morley, then editor of the *Fortnightly Review*, to organise the slaying of Stephen 'the monstrous Goliath' lest 'the uncritical public will suppose that he has fairly knocked the wind out of . . . Comte, Mill, you and the whole band of us. . .'.[242] The 'you', and Morley's David, was to be his friend the astute Frederic Harrison. Doubtless to Morley's surprise[243] and annoyance, Harrison was forced to admit that he agreed with much

of the substance of *Liberty, Equality, Fraternity*: 'Stephen is a big bul-
ly, and a Philistine down to the end (the blunt end) of the spear that
is in his hand, but it is a strong spear often rightly guided at the
right mark . . . , as against Mill he is successful and even triumphant . . . ; of Liberty [he] is right . . . ' ; Mill's talk of abstract
and absolute rights was 'metaphysical nonsense and . . . anarchical'.
Stephen was 'as near the truth as a politician or lawyer need be,
though not as clear as a philosopher should be'. His argument on
'Equality' was brutal but admirable; yet stylistically, Harrison
found the 'closing paragraphs of the work really fine, almost poetic'.
Even in respect of 'Fraternity' Harrison felt Stephen was 'fairly
right', though sufficiently wrong to warrant a rejoinder in that
quarter at least.[244] Morley himself was left to perform the major
role of attempting to smite this 'bluster[ing]' and 'swagger[ing]'
Goliath, as well as showing that Millists and Comtists were equally
committed to firm order and effective government. Both found it a
testing task. From April to August 1873 correspondence between
Harrison and Morley hummed with references on how most effectively to 'skin', 'hit', 'smash', or 'stamp on' 'Old Fitzjames', 'J.F.S.'
or 'Goliath',[245] with both admitting to difficulties over the style
and tactics best suited to carrying out these various mutilations. July
found Harrison still 'full of the Stephen controversy', having just
discussed it with Archbishop Manning, who was likewise 'full of
it'.[246] A month later a less exuberant and resilient Morley confesses
to being 'haunted' by 'Fitzjames Stephen, Gladstone and all other
things infinitely great and infinitely better'.[247] Harrison's 'The
Religion of Inhumanity' appeared in June 1873, followed by Morley's
'Mr Mill's Doctrine of Liberty' in August.

In the second edition of *Liberty, Equality, Fraternity*, Morley's and
Harrison's critiques were taken by Stephen as representative of the
'Radical' and 'Positivist' views respectively. Their arguments
formed the subject matter of an extensive preface and textual notes
throughout the body of the book, with Morley's response provoking
seven and Harrison's eighteen prefatory pages: possible evidence of
the strengths of their cases and the relative weaknesses of parts of
Stephen's. Harrison, in 'The Religion of Inhumanity', though unable
to retrieve much of positivism's credibility blown away by Stephen,
nevertheless still effectively demonstrated some of the shortcomings of Stephen's own position: the confusing and confused
mingling of physical and moral power, the foggy vagueness of
'Providence', and the hopes and fears to which Stephen was appeal-

ing as a means of achieving a higher level of moral consciousness were all justifiably important targets of Harrison's.

Morley's 'Mr Mill's Doctrine of Liberty', by comparison, was surprisingly slight, more of a eulogy for the recently dead Mill and failing to find Stephen's vulnerable points. Beyond emphasising Mill's central themes and denying the contaminating presence of any 'abstract' rights, it turned little of substance against Stephen's weighty though hardly watertight challenge. Morley's real and hefty reply came a few months later in the form of *On Compromise*. Here he set down an 'elitist manifesto' on the intellectual's role in politics; how an elite enthused with what is right and best in ideas could lead the enfranchised masses. Throughout *On Compromise* Morley tilts and jabs at 'Stephenism', sometimes by direct reference, sometimes by scarcely disguised allusion. According to Morley, a good part of Stephen's problem was the disability of a lawyer's mentality. Because a lawyer must deal 'mainly with acts . . . by way of repression . . . a habit of thought is created which treats opinion as something equally in the sphere of coercion with actions. At the same time it favours coercive ways of affecting opinion. . . Exertion of power on one hand, and compliance on the other – this is his type of the conditions of the social union'. Particularly in 'criminal lawyers' this attitude sprang from 'a very shallow kind of impatience, heated in some of them by the addition of a cynical contempt for human nature and the worth of human existence'.[248] Yet, as Stephen might reasonably have asked, if the intellectual impatiently pressed to know what his course should be if the masses had no appetite for what is right and best, he would find that at this point *On Compromise* unsatisfyingly slides away from specifying the appropriate role of coercive authority.

At a more personal level Morley, Harrison and Stephen seemed to have much enjoyed their philosophic tussle, at least in retrospect, with Morley writing to Harrison in August 1873:

I had a letter from our good Fitzjames yesterday – very genial; he is going, he says, like Warburton, to erect a gallows in the notes of the Second Edition, in which you and I are to take our turn. I hinted to him that it was against all usage for dead men to turn hangman; and we have slain him; or at least you slew him, and I went and fired an old blunderbuss into his ear by 'way of a coup de grace; yet he is a good fellow of the Johnsonian way of thinking.[249]

Many years later Harrison recalled how 'Fitzjames forgave, and Leslie enjoyed my little caricature of Fitz's "Liberty and Equality" ', and what 'memories of energy, sterling sense and downright bonhomie Fitzjames left to his friends'.[250] On his side, Stephen's obituary of Mill in the *Pall Mall Gazette* concluded that with the great man's death 'one of the tenderest and most passionate hearts that ever set to work an intellect of iron was laid to rest'.[251] Mill's opinion of Stephen had been considerably less generous. Writing to T. E. Cliffe Leslie in May 1869, Mill made no attempt to conceal his dislike for the

insolent domineering affectations of Fitzjames Stephen. In pol. economy he is exceedingly ignorant. On other matters, however, he is able to do some useful work and he is undoubtedly a clever man. . . It is certain that he is very vain . . . full of . . . fanfaronade, which is offensive enough, but which we may excuse if he is earnest about anything. One cannot help hoping he is because he is clever enough to do a good deal of good or of mischief.[252]

Beyond Morley and Harrison, the critical reception of *Liberty, Equality, Fraternity* was mixed though largely in agreement that Stephen had severely dented Millite doctrines.[253] Mill's friend, Alexander Bain, identified Stephen's as the 'best sustained attack' on *Liberty*, 'often irresistible'.[254] Even Henry Sidgwick, whilst expressing the strongest distaste for Stephen's literary manners, accepted Stephen's case that Mill had fatally twisted 'absolute practical axioms' out of utilitarian theory.[255] Frederick Pollock admitted to agreeing with 'nearly all [Stephen] says concerning Liberty, most of what he says concerning Equality, and much, though not so much, of what he says concerning Fraternity'. As for the dispute over theoretical methodology, Pollock saw Mill's 'technique' as starting with a 'comprehensive' statement while Stephen 'proceeds step by step . . . not laying down universals for perpetuity'; however, 'Mr Mill's subtractions from his generalities and Mr Stephen's cautious addition of his particulars not infrequently end in finding much the same level.'[256] More narrowly focused, but perhaps the ablest and most perceptive contemporary reading came from the *Spectator*'s gifted critic and editor, R. H. Hutton. Hutton, although believing Stephen had 'the best of the argument' with Morley and Harrison, was still unable to swallow Stephen's 'somewhat remarkable' moral and religious creed: a 'strong and manly, though wonderfully maimed religion . . . , breaking down suddenly into the most unexpected and abrupt chasms, misshapen here, stunted there, and elsewhere again exhibiting the most massive and even pathetic grandeur'. For Hutton, such beliefs consisted of a 'few huge, almost Cyclopean masses of moral conviction, impressive and striking enough, but broken off just at the most critical points, and as striking from their apparently almost wilful insufficiency and isolation, as from their solidity and strength'.[257]

'BILL SIKES CONVERTED BY BENTHAM'?

In alleging his cousin Fitzjames was 'always trying to show somebody else's error',[258] Albert Dicey struck a note already unfamiliar to Stephen. Undeniably the greater part of *Liberty, Equality, Fraternity* is a destructive combination of fine anatomical dissection and sledgehammer rhetoric. But to regard Stephen's performance as purely combative or negative would be mistaken, for, as Pollock suggested, so much of it was 'entangled with transitory polemic that its real merit is obscured in the eyes of a younger generation'.[259] The period running from the early 1860s to the mid 1880s was one when the political and moral landscapes were exposed to the eroding forces of popular democracy and the strengthening religious doubts bred by Darwinism; in Morley's words, a time of 'hesitation and shivering expectancy of multiplied doubts and shaken beliefs'.[260] Though it hardly merited Carlyle's description as an age 'at once destitute of faith and terrified at scepticism',[261] with religion's social cohesive power alarmingly seen as seeping away, the necessity of a substitute was obvious. Henry Sidgwick, like Stephen, spoke for many in fearing the consequences of removing belief in Providence from 'the minds of average human beings . . . , an evil of which I cannot pretend to measure the extent'.[262] And according to Kingsley, the Bible had served as a 'special constable's handbook'; but what in coming years would function as the alternative great pacifying agent of the populace?

At a higher remove this unease sharpened the anxieties of those who already felt the need to identify agreed standards of morality and to construct a satisfying account of the individual's place in society and history; for, as Lecky suggests, developing a 'working hypothesis of life [was] the indispensible sanction of moral obligation'.[263] Some, including Bagehot and Leslie Stephen, incorporated Darwinistic evolutionary theory in their response. For Bagehot, in *Physics and Politics* (1872), social, moral and political outlooks were the product of heredity and imitation; the principles of natural selection applied to political society. Leslie Stephen's *The Science of Ethics* (1873) argued that moral rules are prerequisites of social welfare. Thus 'courage, benevolence . . . truthfulness and justice are logical necessities. All are essential conditions of social

existence. Reason and morality are linked . . . [Effectively]
Stephen marries Darwinism to John Stuart Mill.'[264] Closer to
Fitzjames was T. H. Huxley's critique of such 'absurd' attempts to
employ evolutionary theory in this fashion: social progress meant
'checking the cosmic process at every step' and putting in its place
an ethical process whose end is not 'the survival of those who may
happen to be the fittest . . . but of those who are ethically the best';
for the rules of morality were discoverable 'by observation and experiment, and only in that way'.[265]

More specifically, for some such as the young F. H. Maitland,
the topicality of liberty and equality made them fitting subjects for
a fellowship dissertation;[266] for Stephen and Mill, a broader audience
and a weightier objective was the motivation. Mill's undisputed
pre-eminence as the nation's prince amongst philosophers provided
a secure platform for his preaching on liberty and equality, a message
which fell (and falls) agreeably on the ear. As Harrison recounted,
On Liberty 'had an extraordinary success with the public . . . , read
by hundreds of thousands, and to some . . . a sort of gospel – much
as for a time Rousseau's *Social Contract* or Bentham's *Principles of
Legislation*'. It was a popularity, at one level, which rested on Mill
'defying reality and denying complexity'[267] – a liberation from
grey pettifogging philosophising. For Stephen to confront Mill
with a doctrine as bleak as Mill's was attractive was inevitably going
to be an uphill struggle, unlikely easily to win converts. Yet
Stephen succeeded critically, sometimes resoundingly, in many
localised battles even though, in the long term, he failed to overrun
Mill's positions completely. At the most immediate level of understanding, Mill offered humanity, hope, enlightenment. In opposition Stephen pointed to a grim incurable self-centredness checked
by an all-pervasive and multi-faceted coercion, at times coming
perilously close to eliminating liberty as something of any intrinsic
worth in establishing human identity and self: a performance that
Hutton likened to 'trampl[ing] over the most delicate blossoms of
human life and character with a heavy elephantine tread'.[268] At its
darkest, here seemed to be an unmistakable manifestation of
Arnold's 'Hebraism', the rigid seizing 'upon certain plain, capital
imitations of the universal order, and rivet[ing] itself . . . with
unequalled grandeur of earnestness and intensity on the study and
observance of them'.[269] Except that rather than religious dogmatism, Stephen's 'capital imitations' were coercion and utility.

Mill's winning underlying optimism lay primarily in his belief in
the general educability and changeability of the common man.

Realisation of this would come through a more generous toleration of alternative philosophies, reinforced by a national maturation brought on by wider franchise responsibility and the removal of the constraints that hindered greater, if not absolute, equality of opportunity. For Mill, though, such a process was to take place in a society of principally independent self-regarding individuals. Certainly Dicey interpreted *On Liberty* as espousing classical 'Benthamite Individualism'[270] and an important ally against later moves favouring increased state intervention, or 'collectivism', as Dicey would have it. Stephen's perception of the individual and society was in many ways the converse of Mill's. In contrast to Mill's misleadingly atomistic emphasis, Stephen came up with an exaggerated view of the interdependency of social insitutions and moral norms. And, curiously, by highlighting the harshness of untrammelled economic liberty, he indirectly embraced a larger toleration of interventionism than Mill's more doctrinaire laissez-fairism, although Stephen gave very little direct indication of quite what the state should do for the individual.

Human nature, in the large, was essentially unalterable for Stephen; certainly no amount of liberty or artificially imposed equality could change the unchangeable. Vigour and independence of character were not commodities obtained by Mill's 'mere rhetoric dressed out to look like logic'. Yet Stephen's hard-shelled individualism was somewhat Janus-faced, seeing great virtue in strenuous independence whilst at the same time viewing the mass of humanity as largely open only to the effects of restraints. But how were the finer human qualities, which even Stephen conceded existed, to be encouraged? On his own admission he agreed with Mill that the greatest coercive forces were informal and social; were these in no way the product of the better forces in mankind's common character? Were these benevolent characteristics of social existence incapable of consolidation if not enhancement? Certainly, if Stephen's Hobbesian-cum-Calvinistic estimates of human character were correct then the prominence he gives to all varieties of coercion would be more convincing.

As for Stephen's brand of 'higher utilitarianism', a form of intellectual duplicity might, as first sight, reasonably be suspected. And, indeed, Frederic Harrison said as much in claiming that Stephen had 'clung to Hell for its utility as a moralising agent in deterring the weak and the vicious from sin and crime'.[271] Yet to accept this as anything more than an oversimplification of Stephen's case would be a considerable injustice. These suspicions of double-dealing in *Liberty, Equality, Fraternity* were publicly dealt with four years later in his article 'A Modern Symposium' on 'The Influence Upon Morality of a Decline in Religious Belief'.[272] Here Stephen roundly declared that although the opinion that belief in God and a future state influences human conduct was a 'proposition too plain to be proved', the basing of morality on a theological falsehood would be as productive as 'legislation based on a mistaken view of facts'.[273]

Mill's own ambivalent final views on the moralising role of religion caused a contemporary outcry. His posthumously published essay 'Theism'[274] provoked Morley's description an 'intellectual scandal';[275] Stephen himself labelled it a 'diet of anaesthetic'. In 'Theism' Mill expressly recognised the human need for spirituality – Christ was the 'ideal representative and guide of humanity'. Here Mill, for many of his friends, fell foul of an inclination which he had earlier warned of in the 'Utility of Religion': that 'such belief as men have is much more determined by their wish to believe than by any mental appreciation of evidence'. As Mill well knew, the great dilemma for rationalists was that 'truth and the general good' sometimes seem to pull in opposite directions.[276] However, for Mill, religious belief could be 'morally useful' although intellectually unfounded. George Eliot too was prepared to concede that there was value in observing the formalism of the church provided it was taken as symbolic of belief in a higher morality.[277] And although mental athleticism of this sort looked like 'theosophic moonshine' to Carlyle,[278] it was, nevertheless, falseness 'with consciousness of being sincere'. An incisively unbelieving Leslie Stephen, in 'An Apology for Plainspeaking' (1873),[279] was also prepared to grant that 'even the most genuine lovers of truth may doubt whether the time has come at which the decayed scaffolding can be swept away without injuring the foundations of the edifice'. Only the more robust, less compromising, like Morley, had few such qualms about writing off the possible 'utility of error'. 'Any embarrassment in dealing with it, due to a semi-latent notion that it may be useful to some one else is a weakness that hinders social progress.'[280] On this Morley and Fitzjames Stephen appeared to agree, at least in their public pronouncements.

Carlyle's long, passionate and perplexing crusade for a deeper moral earnestness touched many, like Stephen, who broadly accepted the diagnosis though resisting the prescribed cure. For them there was no seriously contesting the Carlylean view that we had 'quietly closed our eyes to the eternal substance of things, and opened them only to the Shows and Shams of things'.[281] In his own way Stephen was visibly groping for a rational basis for what may be inaccessible to rationalistic explanation, having in mind something that justified those moral hopes which 'commonplace' utilitarian calculation was incapable of doing; a species of idealism essential to the complete man with an inescapable spirituality that the flat blandness of utilitarian ethics could not accommodate. Quite what this additional justification is never openly emerges in *Liberty, Equality, Fraternity*, though its shadowy form can be briefly glimpsed soon after in a *Contemporary Review* article entitled 'Caesarism and Ultramontanism'.[282] Here, in the course of lambasting Archbishop Manning's claim to absolute moral authority for the papacy – the 'Grand Lama of Mankind' – Stephen seems to hint at a retreat from the value previously attached to a supernatural sanction. Instead

Human reason, pure and simple, and undisguised, acting within convenient local limits, through the best representatives of it that can be found, is the best and highest authority we have on all subjects whatever, and, fallible as it is, is most likely to be right . . . It cannot be too strongly asserted that the end at which laws should aim, and by their attaining which they must be judged, is their conformity with the permanent principles of human nature and society; principles which are antecedent to and independent of all laws whatever, whatever may have been their origin.[283]

Although this is construable as nothing beyond a reaffirmation of the fundamental tenets of utilitarianism, from the context a more promising interpretation is that 'permanent' and 'antecedent' principles look equally towards the intuitive immutability of certain values much in the fashion suggested by Mill;[284] an acceptance, according to Leslie Stephen, that 'men have believed in hell *because* they were virtuous',[285] or, in Hutton's version, that morality was the 'base rather than [the] superstructure' of religion.[286]

Clearer corroboration of Stephen's downgrading of the significance of religion to morality followed in succeeding years, and by 1884 he had travelled some distance from his initial point of departure. In 'The Unknowable and the Unknown',[287] while still contending that belief in God and a future life was a 'most powerful motive to virtue' and that a special 'class of motives and feelings' affect a Christian's conduct, Stephen admits that 'We can get on very well without' religion. Without it most of what was worthwhile in life would remain untouched:

Love, friendship, ambition, science, literature, art, politics, commerce, and a thousand other matters will go equally well . . . whether there is or is not a God or a future state . . . [moreover] men can never associate together without honouring and rewarding and protecting in various ways temperance, fortitude, benevolence, and justice.[288]

Was this a total recantation of the claims in 'Fraternity' of the central importance to morality of religious belief? Undeniably it was the severest of compromises but not quite a complete abandonment of his earlier stance, for Stephen persisted in claiming that we would still lose the 'mystical, emotional part of morality' and that element of Christianity which has 'deified self-sacrifice'. It was true that 'Love, friendship, good-nature, kindness, carried to the heights of sincere and devoted affection will always be the chief pleasures of life, but Christian charity is not the same as any of them or all of them put together.'[289] This remnant of Christianity was, then, the surviving portion of Stephen's 'higher morality' which would perish if morality lost the reinforcing effect of belief in God and Providence.[290] So, to return to Stephen's own 'great' question, why be virtuous? What remaining incentive was there to strive for a 'higher morality'? Everyday commonplace social order and morality were maintained, as Stephen again argued in his *History of the Criminal Law*, by public censure affirmed and reinforced by the criminal law. But beyond such moral ordinariness, for the individual lacking a belief in Providence, the choice whether to reject or embrace a higher morality seemed to be no more than a matter of 'individual taste' – just as with Harrison's positivism.

In later life Morley recollected that his own saying, 'that love of truth is often a true name for temper',[291] was very much a favourite of Stephen; doubtless, equally acceptable to Stephen would have been Locke's observation that temperament is the great governor of perceptions.[292] As in the *History of the Criminal Law*, so also in *Liberty, Equality, Fraternity*, the confessional style reveals much of the conflict between intellect and imagination, the struggle of the 'emancipated head' with the 'traditional heart': the most impressive and the least appealing sides of Stephen.[293] Yet only in the occasional brutality of bombast did he ever approach seriously deserving the epithet of 'Bill Sikes converted by Bentham'.[294] It was true that Stephen sympathised with Carlyle's attachment to 'Might is right', but only in the sense of its being 'the assertion of the ultimate identity of truth and utility'; that finally only good institutions and sound social practices can endure; that in the long run 'truth and justice prevail'.[295] Though, of course, as was notably demonstrated by Carlyle,[296] 'truth' and especially 'justice' are far from completely objective substances and, consequently, quite open to the most personal of interpretations.

8

RATIONALISM'S BURDEN

SCEPTICISM IN THE MAKING – TESTING THE EVIDENCE

Not long after completing *Liberty, Equality, Fraternity*, Stephen prepared a 'statement of my religious opinions' for his children,[1] partly to explain his 'unnatural degree of reserve to you all on these matters', and also to deal with their 'surprise at my taking no part either in family prayers, or in the services at church on Sundays'. This concern to ensure his children approached religious understanding with a semblance of open-mindedness reveals something of Stephen's own progression from initial acceptance of the primary tenets of Anglicanism to eventual unbelief. It was a journey not altogether willingly undertaken, but one which a fiercely rationalistic cast of mind made largely inevitable. And, like the progression of his political and social philosophy, it mirrored to flattering advantage and disadvantage the character and obsessions of both Stephen and his era.

In the company of a good many of his peers, Stephen applauded the run of liberalising measures leading towards institutional secularisation whilst at the same time anxiously looking to the likely consequences for a society where religious beliefs appeared to be fast sliding away. An eighteenth-century rationalism, reinvigorated by a sympathetic climate of political advance and scholastic and scientific enlightenment, pressed hard for an adjustment or scaling down of spiritual sympathies in favour of purer intellectual demands. At least by the 1850s, for the educated believer religious scepticism was something to be confronted and, where temperament allowed, passed through like any other unholy spectre. The duration and eventual outcome of this ordeal was infinitely variable. Some, like Leslie Stephen, John Morley[2] and Thomas Huxley with a 'conscious, clear-eyed endurance'[3] briskly abandoned the 'shifting phantasmagoria'[4] of Christian theology without any overpowering desire to settle on a substitute. Although equally speedy in casting off Christian belief, others, such as Frederic Harrison and Herbert Spencer, moved to varieties of challengingly abstract spiritualism which more orthodox Humean[5] contemporaries found almost as indigestible as conventional theism. Some, most notably Matthew Arnold and (possibly) Benjamin Jowett, jettisoned the multi-layered accretions of Christian theology quite as vigorously as any thorough-going rationalist, yet intuitively held to what they saw as its immutable core of spiritual truth – a 'morality touched by emotion'.[6]

In so far as comparisons are possible and useful, Fitzjames Stephen followed in his brother's general direction, though taking a more circuitous route made unavoidable by his particular mentality and entailing rather greater emotional buffeting and abrasions. The common formative influences on the Stephen brothers – evangelicalism,[7] utilitarianism, rationalism and a relatively liberal intellectual upbringing – combined to produce a large measure of self-dependence, introspection and belief in private judgement as vital functions in seeking out salvation. Metaphysical juggling and theological dogma (most especially of the Roman Catholic kind) were at the very best wasteful misleading distractions, likely to obscure the vital truth of each individual's own spiritual self-responsibility; for each man was to hold on firmly to the 'fee-simple' title of his conscience.[8] The principal features of Fitzjames' formal and informal religious education owed most to Sir James Stephen, with many of the impressions left by his father on Stephen's early theological beliefs recorded in the 'Autobiographic Fragment', written between 1884 and 1887, and 'Choice of Profession' (1850). However, such autobiographic reflections on past states of mind and beliefs held by the subject's young self are obviously open to the unconscious inaccuracies, reinterpretations and refractive effects of nearly half a lifetime.

Of no mean or closed variety, Sir James' evangelicalism was of a healthy breadth having, according to Leslie,[9] 'discovered that Clapham was not the world, and that the conditions of salvation could hardly include residence on the sacred common'. Certainly his *Essays in Ecclesiastical Biography*,[10] in which is expressed a comparative tolerance of Catholicism and scepticism over the nature and existence of hell, generated hostility in both Clapham and Cambridge.[11] Yet Sir James was no serious renegade, being willing to accept the counsel of less worthy, more conventional, intellects such as that of his brother-in-law and prominent Claphamite, Henry Venn.[12] Religious fervour was alien to the Stephen household,[13] for whilst there was a 'full allowance of sermons and Church services', these were not obligatory.[14] Indeed beyond daily prayers there was very little talk of religion: apparently the consequence of an unspoken acceptance that 'needless revelation of the deeper feelings [was] a kind of spiritual indelicacy'.[15] However, with the maturing of Fitzjames' intellectual faculties, particular features of his father's faith began to puzzle and then to chafe. Doubts as to the basis of belief that seeped from the father's mind were detected by the son, who sensed 'an odd sort of uneasiness . . . which lasted, more or less, all his life. He was in the world, but not of the world, he was half in the church but not quite.'[16] For Sir James, reason alone was no royal road to religious truth. 'Cold blooded animals' like Hume were 'mere reasoning machines';[17] religious truth was in part self-revelatory: 'one must begin by taking Christianity for granted, throwing oneself into the system – praying and so forth, and then, as a reward, you would get to see how true it was'. Fitzjames gave the system a 'thoroughly fair trial', but found it failed to 'answer . . . at all'.

Requests from son to father for something approaching an authoritative declaration on the nature of belief surfaced in correspondence. In response to one such invitation, Sir James informed the 25-year-old Fitzjames that 'I am not here to speculate but to repent, to believe and to obey; and I find no difficulty whatsoever in believing each in turn of two or more doctrines which yet seem to me incompatible with each other . . . I adopt [evangelicalism] as a regulator of the affections, as a rule of life, and as a quietus, not a stimulant to enquiry. So, I gather, do you.'[18] Mixed with the hint of self-defensive tetchiness was a degree of humility seen by Fitzjames as almost running into irony.[19] It was a trait corroborated in the final years of his father's life, when Fitzjames sought an opinion on the Bible's historical accuracy and whether Sir James conceded that disbelief in substantial elements of it made acceptance of its supernatural character impossible. Sir James, 'pained and embarrassed', could only reply 'Well, well, my dear boy – perhaps it is as you say – but don't tell your mother and sister': a response causing Fitzjames the deepest of unconcealed disillusionment:

Nothing could make a deeper impression on me than these reluctant admissions, torn from him as they were by arguments of which he was too honest to deny the force, though not bold or truth loving enough to measure the full force. He had a genuine distrust of the powers of his own mind in reference to such subjects, or rather a genuine reluctance to be guided by his own reason. I watched the outward signs of his mental struggle for many years without fully understanding them. I understand them well enough now, and much as I reverence his memory, I wish he had been bolder and more decisive.[20]

Beyond home and Sir James, schooling, first at the Reverend Guest's establishment in Brighton and afterwards as a day boy at Eton, made no great religious impression on Stephen. At Brighton the boys were exposed to an 'immense deal of Evangelical theology', the greatest effect of which was permanently to lodge many hymns in Stephen's memory.[21] Religious education at Eton was totally form without substance, an atmosphere characterised by a 'complete absence of moral and religious enthusiasm'.[22] The two years spent at King's College, London, immediately prior to going up to Cambridge brought Stephen into contact with the Christian socialist theologian F. D. Maurice. Maurice, then professor of English literature and history, struck Stephen as a sort of 'refined and highly sensitive Luther'[23] whose attraction lay mostly in his gospel of religious tolerance and open sincerity. However, his attachment to nebulous beliefs in the infinite love of God and unorthodoxy on eternal punishment[24] failed to impress Stephen, who in any case doubted whether Maurice himself ever truly arrived at 'any clear conception of his own meaning'.[25] His talent lay in being a 'great theological rhetorician' whose works 'did their utmost . . . to make one squint intellectually, but I never learnt the trick'.[26] Cambridge appears to have carried forward Stephen's religious thinking little if any. Leslie summed up his brother's state at the time as that of a 'zealous and reverential witness on behalf of dogma, and that in the straitest school of the Evangelicals'.[27] Apparent disparities between this view[28] and Fitzjames' memories may be accounted for possibly by Fitzjames' unwillingness openly to reveal early doubts, or his simply later crediting himself with a more rapid rate of maturation than was due.

THEOLOGY ON TRIAL

Having rejected a clerical career, Stephen was nevertheless eager to air his theological opinions in print and be paid for the privilege. After his production of a few 'poor little articles' for the *Christian Observer*, styled on a combination of 'conveyancing' and special pleading',[29] came the birth of the *Saturday Review* and his entrée to a wider world of journalism. The *Review*'s generally chilly posture towards anything smacking of distasteful enthusiasm or extremism soon showed itself in religious matters. Stephen's frame of mind[30] typified the *Review*'s stance. An intolerance of intolerance, an unflagging concern with the evidence for belief and a deep-seated aversion to the Roman Catholic mentality all appear in the first half-dozen years of the *Review*'s life.

The rival bigotry of the Catholic *Tablet* and evangelical *Record* was an early target of Stephen's: 'We have vulgar papers, we have unprincipled papers, we have disingenuous papers, and we have imbecile papers; but the full bitterness which the human heart is capable of feeling, the full ferocity which it is capable of expressing, is to be met with nowhere but in religious papers.'[31] In similar temper nearly ten years on, crude anti-papist propagandists are dismissed as a group of 'absurd street curs barking with all their little souls'.[32] Equally keen was Stephen's participation in the *Review*'s long-running campaign[33] to discredit popular revivalist preachers busy inflaming souls and devaluing the faith. Chief amongst the offenders of sound clerical manners were the Baptist Charles Spurgeon and Presbyterian John Cumming. Spurgeon was 'quite unable to understand the commonest principles of either logic or of interpretation', reducing the Scriptures to a 'kind of book of puzzles'. Worse was Cumming, who perverted theology into an instrument for excitement and gratification of some of the 'meanest appetites of human nature – the grovelling superstition which finds its aliment in omens from the howling of a dog or the spilling of a salt cellar. . .'. Though as an 'established butt' of the *Review*, Cumming had his uses, and, like a 'bag-fox of huntsmen', could be turned out for a 'day's sport whenever game was scarce'.[34]

Putting down a marker for future more extended debates, in 'Save me from my Friends', Stephen unmercifully laid into a Christian dogmatist who had attacked sceptics as an 'unmanly . . . credulous . . . totally abandoned and sensual class'. Invoking, as he was to frequently over the years, the authority of Bishop Butler, Stephen held up the logic of probability fed by tangible evidence as the proper basis of Christian belief; any claims for a doctrine of truth through the senses were rejected as an absurdity.[35] Within a month, in 'Bunkum', criticism in the *British Quarterly Review*[36] of his 'scribbling' is used to reiterate the arguments of the earlier article.[37] Such questioning of the basis of belief and methodology of assembling supporting evidence inevitably brought Roman Catholicism under scrutiny. And naturally the reasoning of John Henry Newman was given greatest attention: a double-edged compliment Stephen was to pay on many occasions over the following thirty years.

Though never remotely proposing intolerance, the *Review* had no great affection for Catholicism or Newmanism whose 'queer fit of unreason' converted young men into old women.[38] The general tenor of Stephen's early *Review* comments were reasonably predictable from someone who had recently firmly adopted the empirical mode of reasoning elaborated in Mill's *Logic*. In 'Dr Newman on Universities',[39] Newman's whole career and thought are described as distinguished by 'giving excellent reasons for untenable opinions', and reducible to: 'You must believe something because peace of mind is the reward of belief, and uneasiness is inseparable from doubt. . . Unless this is truth, there is no truth; but as I cannot do without truth, this must be true.' Strongly characteristic as this early review of Newman was, it took the publication of his *Apologia* (1864) and *Grammar of Assent* (1870) to expose fully Stephen's philosophic objections to Newman's elaborate intellectual constructs. Also of distinct but far lesser importance during the *Saturday Review*'s first few years was a bluff scornful rejection of attempts to manufacture secular religions, and most particularly positivism; Comte and his English apologists were written off as getting up a 'sort of atheistical parody of the Roman Catholic ritual'.[40] As with Newmanism, Comtean positivism was a tendency that Stephen was to make determined efforts to discredit as an empty sham over the coming two decades or so.

A rising reputation, gained through Saturday Reviewing, as a general controversialist and one also at home in ecclesiastical affairs no doubt helped recommend Stephen for the task of defending Rowland Williams. Stephen's involvement in Williams' trial for his heretical contribution to *Essays and Reviews* (1860) represented a singularly happy coincidence of professional and intellectual interests. Not only did Stephen's legal career enjoy the exposure given by the case's public prominence,[41] but his literary inclinations were also gratified by publication of the rapidly executed *Defence of the Reverend Rowland Williams* (1862)[42] along with a healthy crop of derivative articles over succeeding years. All in all, the *Essays and Reviews* controversy might have been specially designed to exercise Stephen's talents and engage personal intellectual concerns. Stephen was particularly sympathetic towards the Essayists' collective anxiety that for growing sections of the educated classes biblical and doctrinal authority could no longer convincingly support the

Christian church in its existing form, with the aloof obstinacy of rigid orthodoxy being seen as responsible for discrediting the church and engendering a dishonest and destructive cynicism. In the face of thirty years of scientific[43] and historical developments some sort of retrenchment and discarding of the non-essentials of the faith was viewed as pressingly overdue. As representatives of the Broad Church movement, the Essayists, by openly declaring the entitlement to and necessity of free religious inquiry, looked towards closing this widening schism between orthodox belief and the intelligentsia. Though others, including Stephen, had already frequently preached from this gospel, the great novelty and dangerous nature of *Essays* lay in the fact that its authorship was largely clerical. Now the very cohesion of the English church was seen by the guardians of orthodoxy as being internally subverted, with many outsiders viewing 'radical' doctrine-shedding Protestantism as beginning to resemble 'simply rationalism still running about with the shell on its head'.[44]

The substance of the charges against Williams[45] were: his denial of the divine inspiration of the Bible, described instead as just the 'written down voice of the congregation';[46] his assertion that much of the early chapters of Genesis were historically untrue; and his suggestion that 'Prophesy [meant] moral and spiritual teaching not secular prognostication.' Stephen framed the issue in legal and stark rationalistic terms, asking whether the 'Law of England forbade the Clergy of the Church of England to use their mind'.[47] Whether they were so entitled, he argued, was purely a question of civil law to be found in the ʼ39 Articles, the rubrics and formularies', which had 'designedly' entitled the clergy to declare the Bible 'contains' rather than 'constitutes' divine revelation. What's more, ecclesiastical history well demonstrated that Anglican clergy and theologians had exercised this interpretational liberty from Hooker to Paley and Archbishop Whately. And, in a forgivable lawyer's rhetorical flourish, Stephen left the Court in no doubt as to the gravity of the matter; at stake, according to this 'obscure advocate', was the 'cause of learning, of freedom, and of reason – the learning of the most learned, the freedom of the freest, and the reason of the most rational church in the world'.[48]

At first instance Stephen only partly won the day, but a final appeal judgment by Lord Chancellor Westbury for the Privy Council gave the English clergy almost the 'freedom of the freest': a popular verdict except with those like Carlyle who perversely suggested that, as with sentries, such clergy should be shot for

deserting their posts.[49] Oppositionally more constructive was the
rearguard campaign led by Dr Pusey for the creation of an exclusively ecclesiastical Court of Appeal, stocked with bishops to adjudi-
cate on all religious disputes. Part of Pusey's activities involved
publication of a pamphlet containing a 'virulent personal attack'
on Westbury. On behalf of liberalised theology and the Lord
Chancellor, Stephen obliged by cataloguing the undesirable features of the proposed system, taking the opportunity along the way
of returning in kind some of the invective Pusey had turned on
Westbury.[50] Not unfairly, Stephen found Pusey's whole performance 'singularly clumsy', 'positively indecent and hardly gentle-
manlike', showing an 'almost grotesque' incapacity to understand
basic legal principles. Practically, the proposals would be 'monstrous, giving the English Church judicial and legislative powers akin
to the Catholic Church'. Freethinking meant that the moral sanction was the only proper means of enforcing doctrine. Unless Dr
Pusey wished the Church of England to become an 'arena for jug-
glers' tricks', he should not try and 'convert moral obligations into
legal ones'.[51]

How then should the clergy cope with disbelief in the Bible's
historical truth? Stephen probably reveals his own hand in answering
through the device of a fictitious clergyman, who speculates that
whilst in the future it 'may be necessary to have a new Reformation
. . . I have to act . . . for today, upon the best of my knowledge
and belief . . . I can still honestly preach out of this book [but] I do
not bind myself for the future . . . How I may think or act in twenty
years hence, is a question which I will answer in 1884. . . '[52] The
only certainty was uncertainty; and that there remained a 'vast deal
more to be said . . . than has been said yet'.[53] Stephen's role in this
process was narrow, destructive but distinctive; one of attempting
to ensure that metaphysics was purged and kept a safe distance
from English theology, and that whatever beliefs might survive
could be honestly held without intellectual gymnastics.

HOUSETOP PREACHING AND NEWMANISM

Before *Essays and Reviews*, when reviewing Buckle's *History of
Civilization in England* and whilst expressing disgust at the severity
of social penalties for 'unorthodox opinions', Stephen made his own
plea for plainspeaking on religious topics: that 'philosophy, criticism, and science itself too often speak amongst us in ambiguous
whispers what ought to be proclaimed from the housetops'.[54]

Enlisted as an important aid in this campaign of 'housetop' preaching was J. A. Froude, editor of *Fraser's Magazine* between 1860 and 1874. The author of *Nemesis of Faith* (1849) had made an early break with Christian orthodoxy and soon ensured that *Fraser's* was one of the most sympathetic homes for freethinkers.[55] In *Fraser's*, Stephen revelled in the facility of gloriously generous stretches of column inches for saying 'all sorts of things that had been cooking up in my mind for years'.[56] An early product was 'Women and Scepticism', the genesis of which was 'The Nature of Belief' (1862), a painstaking religious guide written for his sister-in-law, Emily Cunningham,[57] containing a candid description of the mode of thought and reasoning which Stephen brought to theological investigation. As well as Bishop Butler's *Analogy of Religion* (1736) thesis – that probability was the guide both to life and faith – obvious utilitarian influences were well to the fore: the ultimate reason for believing was to increase happiness; what should we believe? only that which is true, for universal experience shows that only truth is useful in increasing happiness;[58] usefulness and longevity were evidence of the truth of any institution, including the church; instinct alone was no more than a way of 'recording our ignorance'. In its marked utilitarian colouring Stephen's appraisal is Millite, owing nothing of substance to Bentham's and George Grote's primitive bludgeoning of Christianity in *Analysis of the Influence of Natural Religion on the Temporal Happiness of Mankind* (1822).[59] Here the object was to demonstrate that natural religion was not only valueless but positively socially harmful. That weighing up the primary features of Christianity, there was a considerable surplus of pain over happiness: belief in eternity of which we can know nothing brought more fear than comfort; and religion frowned on or forbade a whole range of harmless pleasures. However, Stephen would not have objected very strongly to Bentham's and Grote's vituperative scorn for a 'standing army' of 'wonder-working priests', busy encouraging superstition and blocking intellectual advance by detaching reason from the truth of experience.

Applying the measured principles of reasoning set out for his sister-in-law, drawing 'natural inferences from credible . . . history related to you on good authority', Stephen concluded that it would be reasonable to believe in spiritual immortality, the existence of a 'just and good God', and that Jesus was the 'revealer of God's will to man'.[60] Yet perplexingly, when turning to his own beliefs, Stephen almost completely throws empiricism aside by admitting that:

As a matter of feeling all the arguments on the existence of God that I ever heard or read, have not weighed with me half or a quarter as much as my own personal experience [which] I think . . . fairly justifies my personal belief in the doctrines of a superintending Providence, though of course it could supply no evidence . . . to anyone else.[61]

It is a conscious lingering ambivalence emphasised by Stephen's closing warning to his pupil of the highly subjective nature of religious belief; that the answer to the question 'what am I to think true?' must inevitably be 'personal, and always depend on the circumstances of the individual who asks it'. Any ability to furnish grounds which 'ought to convince everyone . . . of the truth of Christianity' was firmly disclaimed.[62] Present throughout the final passages of 'The Nature of Belief' is a disinclination to let rationalism take its unhampered course; intuitive beliefs and revealed truth cohabit uncomfortably with an intellectual philosophy whose whole nature is explicitly hostile to such modes of thought. Either Stephen had been less than totally honest in his brief *Saturday Review* critiques of Newman half a dozen years before when deploring the transcendental style of reasoning, or the early 1860s witnessed a fleeting revival of his belief in the possible validity of such thinking.

At first sight it appears surprising that Stephen's progress towards some form of unbelief – whether agnosticism or atheism – should have been relatively so delayed. For as much or more than most of his rationalist contemporaries, he had in the mid and late 1850s pressed the cause for fearless openness in investigating the truth of Christianity. But within Stephen's mentality existed a sizeable knot of resistance to embracing what Carlyle[63] called the 'mad joy of Denial'. And even Leslie, still preaching in 1863,[64] had yet to show Fitzjames' passion for proselytising rationalism's virtues. Only a few, such as Harrison,[65] Spencer, Morley and Huxley, had publicly exchanged belief for the fruits of rationalism. For as Alfred Benn suggested, at the time there remained a powerful sense that 'aggressive infidelity was ill-bred; and to ignore the pretensions of the Churches was wiser as well as more mannerly than to dispute them'.[66]

Eventually, Stephen's combative and controversialist instincts located their most distinguished theological foil in John Henry Newman. And in unravelling the nature of Newman's system of reasoning Stephen peeled away dead or dying layers of his own beliefs. Newman's great sin, in Stephen's eyes, was to threaten the process of religious scarification which the Zeitgeist of scientific rationalism was helping bring about; though to what ultimate end Stephen had no clear idea. Seeing that historical scriptural analysis was steadily eating away at the foundations of Christian dogma, Newman had sought to shift belief to a position less vulnerable to 'all corroding, all dissolving scepticism'; one where proof rested on the internal witness and evidence supplied by the moral senses. But Newmanism was unlike the harmless woolly mysticism peddled by Carlyle and Coleridge. By virtue of claiming to distinguish faith from mere raw intuition through a separate reasoning process complementary to conventional rationalism, Newman appeared to his opponents dangerously equipped to win over whole flocks of waverers who, 'blinded by their very terror [of faithlessness], might plunge into the opposite gulph-stream, which hurries them along in the direction of Rome'.[67]

Stephen's first serious attempt to explode the convolutions of Newmanism followed in the afterwash of the great dispute set off by Charles Kingsley's brutally provocative comment that 'Truth for its own sake had never been a virtue with the Roman clergy' and that Newman had suggested it 'need not and on the whole ought not to be' such – 'cunning' being a far better 'weapon'.[68] Newman's eventual response, his *Apologia*, a subtle Coleridgean 'concrete representation of things invisible', was intended to act as a superior supplement to rationalism, which had revealed itself to be a barren creed. The 'current of the Reformation had run its course, and its spent energies were losing themselves in the flats and shallows of worldliness and unbelief';[69] and rather than the 'suicidal excesses' of pure empty reason, Newman's most powerful evidence for faith lay in the internal witness of the individual's moral sense.

Kingsley's and Newman's 'little passage of arms' attracted Stephen's initial comments in the *Saturday Review* during February 1864; his full considered analysis of *Apologia*, by far the most thorough of all contemporary reviews, appeared a few months later in *Fraser's*. From the *Saturday Review* it is obvious that Stephen, although almost totally behind Kingsley's sentiments, was irritated by his bungling ineptitude in presenting the case. Kingsley, though a 'brilliant partisan' and holder of a 'great broad moral truth', was a 'very unsafe teacher', whose inaccuracy had enabled Newman to hold him in a 'hard, biting, grammatical and logical vice'.[70] Stephen waited for the manoeuvring space of well over 20,000 words provided in *Fraser's* before attempting to break this 'logical vice'. Prefatory assurances were carefully laid out: '*Apologia* is a winning, . . . in some ways a touching book . . . full of courage'; the 'simple dignity' with which Newman 'tells the story of his life [goes] straight to the heart of his readers'. Yet Newman's theology is plain – though decidedly not simple – 'dangerous sophistry, calculated to serve no other purpose than that of drugging the minds of men who care more for peace of mind than for truth, and whose *ultima ratio* is found not in their reason, but in their fears or their fancies';[71] an 'intellectual dishonesty' flowing in large measure from 'Hatred to liberals and liberalism' – an antipathy to open modes of thought espoused in his confession that 'dogma has been the fundamental principle of my religion'.[72] And making dogma the foundation rather than the superstructure of a creed was, to Stephen, the most monumental example of begging the question.

All this aside, Stephen's main target was Newman's 'canon of proof' in religious matters, his 'doctrine of probability': that . . . the cumulative force of belief in 'God', 'Christianity' and Catholicism provided religious certitude. Taken purely as an exercise in conventional logic, destruction of this assertion was easy meat for Stephen, as for such beliefs to have the force suggested they would need to be independent, not dependent probabilities, as Newman's trinity of beliefs appeared to be:

Dr Newman can have his probabilities whichever way he pleases; and in either he gets a result fatal to his theories. If the probability of the existence of a God, of the truth of Christianity, and of the truth of Romanism, are dependent on each other, then it must be less probable that Romanism is true than that Theism or the fact of the divine mission of Christ is true. If, on the other hand, the probabilities are independent, what becomes of the argument that every consistent man who is not a Romanist, must be an Atheist? If independently of the probability of Romanism, there is a separate probability in favour of Theism and of Christianity, [they] may be believed on the ground of those probabilities, and that without resorting to Rome.[73]

Newman's whole system was a series of a priori assumptions; a partial selection of evidence not remotely resting on any 'honest balancing' of probabilities, but rather a 'castle in the air built in defiance of probabilities' to suit the architect's taste. Newman's honesty was sometimes impugned, Stephen suggested, because if he seriously took probability to heart he might quite reasonably believe in God,[74] yet such probabilities were hardly adequate to support a claim on behalf of the 'Pope to moral and religious sovereignty'. It was a mentality that put Stephen in mind of

a man who, having been infatuated by a woman neither young, lovely, nor virtuous, marries her at the expense of destroying all his prospects in life, and of throwing up all his connexions, and who then exhausts every resource of his mind in proving that she combines, in ideal perfection, eternal youth, perfect beauty, and every moral and mental grace which could adorn such a person.[75]

But even though he regarded Newman's whole edifice of belief and pseudo-logic as corrupting sophistry, Stephen felt impelled to conclude that the man was 'better than his opinions', capable of 'wring[ing] . . . from a hostile critic a degree of regard and respect'.[76]

At the time, the compliment wasn't entirely hollow, for Stephen had years before made Newman's personal acquaintance through an introduction effected by Grant Duff. And later in October 1865 and 1866 Stephen called on Newman at the Oratory.[77] Newman regarded the *Fraser's* critique as 'more like a lawyer's argument . . . than the writing of a philosopher'. 'I had turned over the pages of his review and had said to myself "This is shallow", "this is unfair", "this is shameful".' Consequently, Newman assumed the object of Stephen's 1865 visit was primarily conciliatory:

So the first thing I did, was to draw his attention to the fact of his severity, which he took very well, and made a sort of apology. Then we talked of many things at random but as I perfectly well knew that any real controversy would be like a fight between a dog and a fish, it never occurred to me to *argue* . . . the amusing thing is that I thought, and still think that what I said did on the whole *soften* him, and I thought I had gained a victory.[78]

But Stephen's steady flow of criticism in the coming years unsurprisingly rankled with Newman. When Stepehen noted in 'Caesarism and Ultramontanism' (1874) that Newman had never answered the case against *Apologia* put in *Fraser's*, Newman complained that 'for ten years he has been at me [but] I have no intention to controvert with him'.[79] Again, in February 1876, Stephen wrote suggesting that he might call at the Oratory to 'talk over some subjects on which we formerly conversed' and on which the intervening years had 'considerably matured and extended my views'.[80] Newman declined primarily because debate would be futile: 'in matters of religion we unhappily differ in first principle; that each of us assumes . . . what the other will not grant and . . . in consequence discussion [would be] a melancholy waste of time'.[81] Rather Newman had a particular and more graphic fate in mind for his inquisitor's assertions: the 'seizing by the collar and carrying off to the Police Court all assumed first principles in the works of Huxley, Mill, Fitzjames Stephen etc. etc. Their arrogance in assumptions, and superciliousness towards any one who will not admit them, is in the most provoking degree; and they ought to be brought to book.'[82]

Six years after *Apologia* Newman published *A Grammar of Assent* (1870), his most refined and subtle attempt to use faith to transmute probabilities into certainties. Privately, Stephen admitted to a longing to begin his review of the *Grammar*, 'This book gives me a contempt for its author's intellect and confirms the opinion which I had always held that he is a systematic and shameless liar.'[83] However, Stephen's more temperate public assessment[84] of the work broadly corresponded with Alfred Benn's later description of it as having posited 'new canons of inference in an endeavour to win acceptance for what the old logic had flung away as incredible'.[85] Newman's *Grammar* argued that religious truth could be proved by evidence falling short of the 'severe requisites of science', that all reasoning rested on a combination of temperament and objective evidence which often lead to conclusions beyond the natural limits of the proof adduced. The ability to disentangle historical truths from such conclusions and reach religious certitude was supplied by the supernatural 'illative sense', a faculty to be assiduously cultivated and trusted above all, for the right spiritual and moral attitudes fostered the right intellectual attitudes.[86] As in *Apologia*, Newman was attempting to construct a theory of belief; a theory of the process by which certitude of conviction is achieved. Yet as Stephen saw, this was distinct from a tenable account of *how* doctrines were proved – conviction or certitude not being conclusive of truth: giving an explanation of the genealogy of faith was not to demonstrate its truth.[87] To Stephen, 'illative' reasoning was equivalent to arguing that a

certain feeling in your own mind can produce an effect upon the facts outside of you; that your certitude can convert a probability into a certainty; that is, can cause a given set of facts to fulfil conditions which they would not otherwise fulfil. It seems . . . just as rational to say that if you saw an object through a mist, which might be either a man or a bush, your conviction that it was a man could make it into a man.[88]

Effectively, the Kantian contrast between the separate truths of 'It is certain' and 'I am certain.'

The intellectual stances represented by Stephen and Newman were (and are)[89] irreconcilable. However respectably or ingeniously they might be dressed up, rationalists regarded claims of being able to know, to have knowledge, without analysable reasons as intellectual savagery. Newmanism looked to an unquiet conscience as the underlying basis of faith – the 'moral imperative'. And no matter how much those like Stephen tunnelled away into the verbal representation of Newman's faith, the honeycombed edifice held firm, bonded by beliefs quite impregnable to conventional logic. As Newman's first theological lieutenant, W. G. Ward, explained, 'Knowledge of phenomena is obtained by the intellect, knowledge of realities by the conscience; knowledge of phenomena by enquiry, knowledge of reality by obedience':[90] for the rationalist another way of saying that what could be intellectually wrong could be morally and intuitively right.

Truth was the vital substance on which all depended and of which everything of value was constructed. Christianity was useless unless true; its truthfulness must precede the question of its goodness. Catholicism, in Stephen's eyes, never ceased to play fast and loose with truth. Christian morality if untrue was equivalent to teaching people to fasten 'wings to their shoulders and to hop instead of walking, because hopping is more like flying and flying is nobler than walking'.[91] Religious truth, Stephen endlessly insisted, was discovered by the same process of investigation as all other matters of fact – by evaluation of evidence. Doubtless Strauss, Renan and Newman might for their separate reasons revolt at this 'petty and narrow mode' of investigation of something of such vast importance, but their reasoning was addressed largely to the imagination, whereas the decisive issue was a 'dry question of fact'.[92] Catholics were engaged in a 'perpetual game of leap-frogging between tortoise and elephant. . . The explanation supports the mystery and the mystery supports the explanation, and faith supports both.'[93] Protestantism, in the 'form stated by Paley and others . . . of that school' was the only form of Christianity which 'rational men' could seriously consider.

These were all binding realities which, in Stephen's world, could not be uttered too often or too emphatically; though it was something on which Lecky's popular and acclaimed *History of Rationalism in Europe* (1865) had been badly remiss. Lecky's highly industrious and painstaking effort to trace public sentiments on reason and religion over three centuries had been needlessly hesitant in declaring allegience to and defence of the 'only test of truth'. Why, asked Stephen, be content with merely uncovering what was current thought at any particular stage of civilisation? More important was the theoretical basis of the sentiments. On this, Lecky's central thesis argued that theological dogmas alter[94] as a consequence of progressive changes in the general intellectual climate. To Stephen, and others including his brother,[95] this appeared to be needlessly understating the direct force and efficacy of rationality in dismembering unsound beliefs – including religious ones. And for Lecky to suggest

that 'conscience' was the test of theological truth merely bolstered
the impression of his inadequate understanding of the universal
applicability and effect of reasoned analysis.[96] In Stephen's eyes, by
this overscrupulous acknowledgement of the force and value of
intuitionism, Lecky had squandered the opportunity to contribute
to eliminating the credibility of a mode of reasoning of which
Newmanism was an outstandingly superfine product.

With his brother, Stephen shared the role of setting out the
strongest purely rationalistic case mounted against Newman's
Apologia and *Grammar*; and of attempting to expose Newman's
apparent theological fastidiousness as fakery, if not downright
intellectual fraud. Most of Newman's other critics[97] of the time
confined their objections to private or smaller-scale assaults. 'In
speculations' Jowett found Newman 'habitually untruthful and not
much better in practice. His conscience had been taken out and the
Church put in its place.'[98] As a 'reasoner' Sidgwick was 'never . . .
disposed to take [Newman] seriously'.[99] Not a person to mince
words, Huxley labelled Newman as the 'slipperiest sophist I have
ever met with'.[100] Even the liberal Anglican Hutton, strongly personally sympathetic to Newman as he was,[101] felt unable to concede that 'any accumulation of mere probabilities [could] amount
to mathematical certitude'.[102]

It was not just Newmanism that carried the clear and instantly
recognisable indelible taint of religious sophism. For Stephen,
Newman's velvet logic simply represented the intellectual pinnacle
of English Catholic theology. Therefore at the same time as
attempting to unpick *Apologia* and the *Grammar*, Stephen thought it
desirable to consider broader questions related to the Catholic
mode of thought, especially concerning science, papal infallibility
and political allegiance.

December 1864 witnessed the issue of Pius IX's *Syllabus of Errors*,
expressly rejecting papal need to reconcile itself to liberal inquiry
and scientific achievement.[103] Stephen's attitude to the *Syllabus* and
the 1870 Vatican Council proclamation of papal infallibility was
strongly indicative of the bad odour in which these measures put
this 'aggressive' form of Catholicism[104] with a large element of the
English intelligentsia, whether believers or not. Benn described the
contemporary reactive literature as unexampled in English history
for 'copiousness, ardour, eloquence and outspoken hostility to all
theological belief'.[105] Protestantism, at least in its liberal garb, represented the Enlightenment, Catholicism the incarnation of

reaction and the Dark Ages. Gladstone's two bitterly anti-Roman pam-phlets, *The Vatican Decrees in their Bearing on Civil Allegiance* (1874) and *Vaticanism* (1875), though coming somewhat late in the day, provide a strong flavour of the suspicion of spiritual imperialism and resentment aroused amongst the Anglican establishment. The same is true of *The Times'* reaction to Lord Ripon's conversion to Catholicism: an act seen as forfeiting political esteem and renouncing moral and mental freedom.[106] Stephen's responses to the *Syllabus* are largely contained in a short *Saturday Review* article, 'An Ultramontane View Of The Temporal Power' (1865), and two successive *Fraser's Magazine* pieces entitled 'English Ultramontanism' (1865), with the propagandistic activities of Archbishop Manning provoking Stephen's 'Caesarism and Ultramontanism' eight years later.[107]

Stephen's earlier criticisms focused on the significance of essays by Wiseman and Manning appearing in *Essays on Religion and Literature*. Manning and Wiseman never qualified for the relative respect and civilities accorded to Newman: Wiseman's contribution was 'turgid and pompous'; Manning's able enough if it was 'proof of ability to be able to rest with perfect satisfaction upon transparent sophistry'.[108] Obligatory tartness aside, Stephen set out two of his principal objectives: consideration of the relation of Catholicism to modern science and to modern society.

As for the first, Cardinal Wiseman, who had in the past been abused in the *Saturday Review* as an author of work 'so greasy and slobbering . . . that it very nearly turns a man's stomach',[109] was seen by Stephen as a splendid example of Catholic opposition to scientific investigation.

Cardinal Wiseman does take a line about science which differs only in phrase and style (and the difference is not in favour of the Cardinal) from the passionate appeal of an Old Bailey or Middlesex Sessions orator to a British jury not to convict a man who calls a dozen respectable witnesses to his character, merely because a few scientific detectives have found somebody else's plate buried in odd corners of his cellar, and have traced his footmarks to the place where it was stolen. Why is this? How is it that so many and such respectable and virtuous people consider lying so wicked, and yet care so little for truth on a large scale?

While Stephen agreed that such reactionary tendencies were not absent from Protestantism – witness Puseyite campaigning – he took them to be practically synonymous with Catholicism. The general poisonous effects of this seeped far beyond the confines of religion, polluting a society's moral and intellectual climate. It worked against men being accepted as beings who had it in their power to 'improve the condition in which they lived, to strengthen their faculties, to enlarge their whole sphere of action, to put out to interest a vast variety of talents of different kinds and degrees. . . ' .[110] Achievement of all these desirable ends largely rested on viewing truth and its pursuits as the 'highest, the most universal, and the most entire of all obligations'. Manning and Wiseman claimed themselves genuine lovers of science on the apparent footing that different types of human knowledge were subject to variable standards of truth and methods of verification; an absurdity enabling the Catholic Church to affirm that science and theology were not in opposition. Consequently, 'the sun may go round the earth in a theological sense, and the earth round the sun in a scientific sense. . . What is true whilst you are praying becomes false when you leave church . . . one creed for Sunday, another for Saturday.' Cardinal Wiseman even had the 'unspeakable audacity to say the Bible "created geology" . . . what in the world [did] he mean?' The reality was that the Catholic Church had long been the 'deadliest antagonist of science, though it persisted in claiming to be the "mother of intellectual culture" because a thousand years ago it nursed the infancy of the sciences, which it wished to strangle in their youth, and now curses in their maturity'.[111]

What, then, was the relation of Catholicism to modern society? Stephen found that views in *Essays on Religion and Literature* openly demonstrated the 'utter irreconcilable hostility' which existed between Ultramontanism and the English state. It was the old question, stretching back beyond the Reformation: of 'double allegiance' – to pope and Crown; of suspected Jesuitical meddling, or even subversion, in state affairs. Stephen's view classically stated these fears in nineteenth-century form, seeing an Ultramontanist as under the 'strongest possible temptation to be false to his country'; a 'stranger and sojourner amongst us . . . the subject of a foreign priest'.[112] Further ammunition for such sentiments came in Archbishop Manning's pamphlet *Caesarism and Ultramontanism* (1873), where Manning vigorously argued the consequences of absolute papal authority to be spiritual supremacy, 'independent of all civil powers, the guardian and interpreter of the Divine Law. The proper judge of men and of nations in all things touching . . faith and morals'.[113] As Newman understood, Manning's outspokenness gave the opposition stout rods with which to beat all Catholics; impolitic behaviour by the Archbishop to a degree quite 'incomprehensible' to the more wary Newman.[114] Stephen was doubtless greatly obliged to Manning for openly setting out the theory and manifesto of one of the 'busiest and most conspicuous religions and political parties of the day'. Bearing in mind the huge dimensions of his claim, Manning needed to adduce powerful substantiating evidence: that God existed, the Apostles' Creed was true, and that Christ established a church with the constitution and powers which was the Catholic Church. Turning over the testimony of centuries, Stephen found the weight of evidence quite incapable of supporting the vast claims laid upon it. The 'institution' which Manning represented had totally failed to make out a 'clear title' to the powers claimed. In truth Manning and his clients had no superior entitlement, being 'just like other men, not much worse or better than [their] neighbours, and assuredly not much wiser'.

Although falling well short of Lytton Strachey's level of cruelty, Manning's 'almost jaunty self-confidence' gave Stephen an excuse for polished snidery concerning the Archbishop's 'sincerity'. Claims that the pope had made him a 'part of the Holy Ghost' needed to be judged in the light of the Archbishop's change of religion in mature life; a fact which tended to diminish the value of 'his own assertion of his own infallibility'.[115] Moreover, Manning possessed little of Newman's polished polemical technique, making much of his reasoning, almost embarrassingly susceptible to the analytical skills of a determined persecutor such as Stephen. In many passages of Manning's response[116] to Stephen's 'Caesarism and Ultramontanism', terms such as 'Evidence', 'Source of Evidence' and 'Authority' were with apparent obliviousness, used seemingly interchangeably. Manning, insisted Stephen, had entangled himself in a 'network of words, which, at best, to use Lord Macaulay's expression, mark time instead of marching and sometimes trip themselves up instead of marking time'.[117]

Imperfections of reasoning aside, Stephen's primary quarry remained Manning's claim for church authority, for moral and spiritual dominion. Manning had denounced as 'Paganism Revived' a *Pall Mall Gazette* claim that 'a nation as such is essentially a better thing than a Church, [the] most sacred . . . most deeply rooted in human nature and . . . best fitted to engage the affections of a rational man'; to Stephen a quite unimpeachable stance.[118] And after discoursing over Roman law, Hobbes and Austin's notions of sovereignty, he naturally concluded that far greater wisdom lay with secular supremacy – offering classical Erastian grounds for this belief and preference.

The real question between Churches and States is like all other questions between conflicting authorities. The question is, Which of the two sorts of institutions is the better, the healthier, the wiser? Which has most of a hold upon the principles upon which political and social life depend, and which every good Government, whether ecclesiastical or lay, must recognise and depend upon? I say States for the following reasons: They are more honest than Churches. The objects at which they aim are more rational. The means of which they dispose are better in every respect. Their leading men are, as a rule, abler and wiser than the leading main Churches. The results which they produce admit to being from time to time tested by visible results. They have in every way less nonsense about them.[119]

CHRISTIANITY'S SUBSTITUTE

The 1870s and 1880s were marked by a proliferation of religious and ethical exchanges and controversies. Unlike the 1860s, where formalistic questions of ecclesiastical freedom were uppermost, the following two decades witnessed the fully fledged intellectual response of an entrenched scepticism with which large portions of Christian theology were now viewed. By the early 1870s institutional secularisation had progressed to the abolition of University Tests (1871), Irish disestablishment (1868), giving atheists the right to testify in legal proceedings,[120] and the removal of much sectarianism from schooling with the enacting of the Education Act (1870). Religious speculation (given a fresh impetus by Darwin's *Descent of Man* (1871)) not only packed out most existing journals, but was in large measure responsible for the founding of the *Nineteenth Century* (1877) and the *Contemporary Review* (1866). Beyond these two journals one of the most quintessential creations of the era was the Metaphysical Society, established in 1869.[121]

Although surviving only eleven years, this illustrious debating society, with a founding membership which included Gladstone, Bagehot, Froude, Manning and Harrison, inspired a wealth of theological argument often eventually published in the *Nineteenth Century* or *Contemporary Review*. With the notable exceptions of Mill, Newman, Spencer and Arnold,[122] most religious controversialists of the day eventually became society members. Stephen joined on returning from India. His brother, a little superciliously, saw the Society's 'talk' as that of 'amateurs' with only 'a small minority' who had 'ever really looked into Kant'; and Hegal 'was a name standing for an unknown region wrapped in hopeless mist'. Yet Leslie too joined in 1877 after acknowledging that the amateurishness was 'perhaps, [one] of dialect than of substance'.[123] With philosophical differences of the most fundamental nature 'embedded in the very texture' of each participant's intellect, no conquest or converts were made, yet the process at least often clarified the core of division between combatants. In rough terms, Fitzjames Stephen sat on the agnostic benches alongside Huxley, W. K. Clifford and other 'scientifics', facing the Christian front benches ranging from the Ultramontanists Manning and W. G. Ward to rationalist theologians such as Hutton[124] and James Martineau; with Comtists like Harrison sitting on the agnostics' side, though not with them, and Sidgwick[125] hovering uncomfortably over the cross benches.

Undoubtedly a debating society suited the talents of some better than others. Those like Huxley, Clifford, Ward and Stephen, as accomplished stand-up dialecticians, were at home with such a forum. Rome's interests were powerfully defended by Ward, then editor of the *Dublin Review*, whose metaphysics 'were as sharp cut as crystal' according to Hutton.[126] Half admiringly, Huxley dubbed Ward a 'philosophical and theological Quixote'.[127] But the polemical powers of Ward's less able clerical brother and society member, Archbishop Manning, were all too obviously vulnerable to predators like Stephen, 'whose attacks . . . were the terror of Christian theists both in and out of . . . the society'.[128] Leslie Stephen clearly relished the memory of Manning, as a 'fluent popular preacher, clutched by a powerful logician, and put into a witness box to be thoroughly cross-examined'.[129] However, the combination of Stephen's 'mighty base that always exercised a sort of physical authority over us',[130] and his advocate's style did not appeal to all. Harrison complained that

I fear the Society lost something of its urbanity, and more of its cohesion when Stephen introduced into metaphysics the style of the *Saturday Review* or a court of law. He would return upon his favourite thesis that a Catholic was psychologically incapacitated from attaining to the pure truth of any problem. He abstained from accusing . . . Cardinal [Manning] of direct mendacity, but he gave him to understand that his own standard of veracity was somewhat higher.[131]

Stephen's religious beliefs on joining the Society in the early 1870s are more easily stated in a negative rather than a direct positive fashion. Leslie implies his brother had ceased believing in the 'historical truth' of Christianity before departing for India.[132] And whilst there, writing to Minny Thackeray and his mother, Stephen admitted to believing in a god, though not in Mount Sinai and the Ten Commandments[133] or in the supernatural side of Christianity.[134] Yet in 1873, though denying the New Testament to be true and taking the history of Christ as merely legendary, Stephen still found the 'two great doctrines' of natural religion – 'God and a future state – more probable than not'.[135]

The outward manifestation of this severely restricted belief was his ceasing to participate in religious rites. Family prayers were attended by Stephen, but read by his wife. On Sundays the children were escorted by both parents to church services,[136] with Stephen taking no active part in proceedings;[137] thus neatly circumventing Trollope's Mr Quickenham, Q.C.'s dilemma of experiencing the 'sting of conscience . . . in neglecting a duty' by not attending church and 'feelings of imposture' when he did.[138] However, the Stephen children had been put on express notice:

I have told them in the very plainest words that our object in our religious teachings had been to give them feelings of reverence and a sense of duty toward God, that we had taken the only means in our power to do so, but that these means were very imperfect, that a great part of what they heard in church and in the Bible was not true, and that much of the teaching founded upon it by clergymen and others was most immoral and dangerous.[139]

As others, like Harrison, were not slow to point out – particularly after *Liberty, Equality, Fraternity*[140] – Stephen's beliefs were obscure beyond inclining towards holding to the existence of *a* god and some sort of Providence: seeming to hang suspended between a form of basic lay Christianity and agnosticism. Applying the Butlerian[141] formula and performing the delicate psychological feat of rationing belief in proportion to the state of evidence at any given time became steadily more demanding. But, however vaguely, Stephen still believed that the 'soul must survive the body', which for him implied the existence of *some* god.[142] Without biblical foundations, however, belief was largely thrown on to a naturalistic[143] or final cause basis. In someone of Stephen's mentality the durability of such beliefs was surprising, though their ultimate demise was reasonably predictable. Yet in the same way that the initial source of revelatory truth along with the reasons for its decline and eventual total evaporation defy serious investigation, so also does Stephen's ultimate abandonment of final cause reasoning. In William Hale White's *Autobiography of Mark Rutherford* (1881) loss of faith is dramatic: 'silently the foundation is sapped while the building stands fronting the sun, . . . but at last it falls suddenly with a crash'.[144] With Stephen both the process and final outcome were without spectacle; no sudden catharsis expelled Stephen's faith; instead there grew a contained yet clear sustained resentment. Hutton detected this mood in Stephen's Metaphysical Society performances, where he some-times appeared to be 'revenging himself on what he could not believe, for the disappointment he had felt in not being able to retain the beliefs of his youth'.[145]

The relatively isolated nature of Stephen's position during the 1870s creates difficulties in firmly categorising his beliefs alongside other religious controversialists. His brother's road to unbelief was shorter, more direct and, apparently, subject to little resistance – more akin to being 'relieved of a cumbrous burden'.[146] But they shared much. Rationalistic intensity was a common character trait, with Leslie declaring just as keen as 'unflinching respect for ration-alism' and the zealous pursuit of religious truth.[147] For both straight talking was everything; symbolism and metaphor simply confused and obscured. Leslie spoke for his brother too in claiming 'I stick to Spinoza . . . and Hume and all really clear-headed people.'[148] Yet they parted company in the different forms of rationalism adopted. Rather than swallow the full exclusive diet of Humean theological analysis, Fitzjames also ingested portions of Paley's *Evidences* and Butler's *Analogy*[149] which led to much concern with biblical veracity and the evidential value of natural phenomena. Of course, for him, Hume's empirical premises and 'mental workmanship' could not seriously be faulted; however, complete suspension of belief was impracticable; religious truth should shape our conduct, therefore the unavoidable question must be 'how was man to proceed?' 'Ought he, or not, to teach his children to say their prayers and go to church?' Being an 'anatomist and not [a] physician' Hume failed to prescribe 'what is it desirable for me . . . to act upon as true' on a specific occasion.[150] Leslie saw no escape from the great central truth of Humean logic:[151] that the limits of human intelligence were such as to exclude religious knowledge[152] and consequently Christian beliefs were unverifiable. But although agnosticism was the abstaining from religious opinion Leslie was far from inhibited in seeking to expose Christian theology as a 'mere edifice of moonshine'.[153] Was there, he asked on Minny Thackeray's death, a more 'cutting piece of satire in the language than the reference . . . to the "sure and certain hope of a blessed resurrection"?'[154]

Yet, in one sense, Fitzjames finally overtook his brother by not settling merely for the agnostic's plea of no knowledge of god, but by positively denying the existence of that which could not be proved. It was an eventual impiety of an angry, almost challenging nature, following in part from his inability to adopt Leslie's pro-claimed stance of resisting provocation from the 'empty bray of

charlatans and humbugs' in favour of cultivating one's own 'little
area of garden'.[155] And, paradoxically, it was also a consequence of
surviving religious resonances within Fitzjames; particularly that
self *had* to be more than a mere bundle of perceptions, that the
answer to the question whether there was *a* god was the Carlylean
'Yes though No'.

It was a mentality seen in a far more pronounced form in Carlyle
and Matthew Arnold.[156] Carlyle's disbelief in historical Christianity
leant hard against an inarticulated faith in the 'eternal verities'. For
him, agnosticism engendered by scientific analysis produced the
'sand blind Pedant'.[157] The truth of Darwinism was 'dreaded', for if
man was 'no more than a developed animal, and conscience and
intellect just functional developments', then 'God and religion
[were] no more than inferences [which] might be lawfully disputed.'[158] Together with Stephen, the desire to believe owed much
to their common membership of the company of 'escaped Puri-
tans'.[159] Except whereas Stephen saw stainless rationalism as the
means to true enlightenment, Carlyle believed it threatened to expose the universe as 'dead and mechanical'.[160]

Arnold, though far more elaborate in his attempts to retain
Christian spirituality and benevolence after removing the doctrinal
supports, was ultimately hardly much more successful than Carlyle.
For Arnold, aggressive agnosticism like that of W. K. Clifford's
was as useful as filling the 'air with one's own whooping to start the
echo'.[161] Man could not do without religion; yet neither could he
'do with it as it is'.[162] The necessary substitute was the co-operation
of man with a 'beneficent power'.[163] According to *Literature and
Dogma* (1873), rather than for literal translation, the Bible was to be
treated as an inspirational source – a move to resting theology on
the emotional and imaginative instead of the cognitive. Religious
belief was 'morality touched by emotion'; effectively, God was a
'literary term'.[164] Doubtless Stephen endorsed both Morley's
description of Arnold as an 'eminent divine not in holy orders';[165]
and, more damning, F. H. Bradley's suggestion that the Arnoldian
spiritual order might be reduced to ' "Honesty is the best policy"
or "Handsome is that handsome does." '[166]

Beyond providing both a personal insight into the nature of existence, most felt social ethics were, to a greater or lesser degree,
linked with religious beliefs. Whether a reasonable hold on some
sort of divine belief could be retained affected both the inner man
and the social man. Many saw as self-evident that living the

'Christian' life without its concomitant faith needed justification: more than *why* be virtuous, rather, *what* was virtue? What were the origins and basis of moral sentiment? On 12 December, 1876, Stephen treated the Metaphysical Society to a paper on the 'Effect of a Decline of Religious Belief on Morality', the likely progenitor of a 'Modern Symposium' on the same topic which appeared in the following April and May numbers of the *Nineteenth Century*. The contributors to the 'Modern Symposium' were all drawn from the Metaphysical Society and calculatedly included the full spread of belief and unbelief: from Ward, through high-church Lord Chancellor Selborne, Hutton and Martineau to Harrison, Huxley and Clifford; with Stephen, as 'proposer' of the subject, providing the introduction and 'summing up'. In differing degrees, almost all were optimistic enough to believe that morals would survive the extinction of individual belief, though overall social standards would decline, and in particular truthfulness or feelings of duty would weaken.

Adopting a softer tone than that found three years earlier in *Liberty, Equality, Fraternity*, Stephen accepted that although morality had its own basis, the extinction of religious beliefs would involve a 'moral revolution'.[167] Huxley took the effects of religion to be two-sided, seeing the 'lover of moral beauty as personally strengthened by his faith in ultimate perfect peace and goodness'; but theology representing God as 'glorious, irritable and revengeful – as a sort of pedantic drill sergeant of mankind' – simply corrupted personal morality. For his own part, Huxley estimated that present morality without the prop of religion could, with some possibly significant slippage, hold its own; though it was likely that the slightest scintilla of truth in religious dogma would be held on to more tenaciously than any 'drowning sailor ever clutched a hencoop'.[168] Ward, with Selborne no great distance behind, unhesitatingly declared that the absence of religious belief more than simply injured 'Christian' morality; it utterly destroyed it.[169] Harrison agreed with Stephen that without religious faith morality could be expected to decline; but for him there was a ready substitute in positivism, charged with power to kindle the 'feelings which are the impulse to duty'.[170] Of the group, Clifford stood alone in denying the likely worsening of morality with the fading of religious belief, maintaining innate moral sense to be of supreme and overriding influence – a case of a severe scientific rationalist resting easy on intuitive belief.

Few,[171] whether in or out of the Metaphysical Society, took

Clifford's sanguine view for the prospects of a morally wholesome world without religious inspiration or some substitute for it. If theology could no longer offer a working ethical basis for life, what could? For some the solution lay in the move from serving God to serving society.[172] The objective of most was to retain Christian morality even though its theology might be dead; an a posteriori justification for what social history seemed to have shown was right. All this was as true of Leslie Stephen's naturalistic *Science of Ethics* as of Matthew Arnold's bewildering mystical 'eternal not ourselves'[173] or Mill's 'Theism'. For those such as Arnold, Mill and Jowett,[174] Christ symbolised high Christian virtues, with works like the *Science of Ethics* marking out the scientific/secular route to upholding the same moral status quo. Considering their rationalistic fervour, Huxley and Fitzjames Stephen were particularly conspicuous amongst this group for failing to offer a developed alternative ethical basis to Christian theology, although both were blisteringly critical of the efforts of others to do so. Huxley saw attempts to tie ethics to evolution as futile; evolution said no more than how good and evil tendencies developed, not why good was preferable to bad.[175] Unlike Leslie Stephen, Huxley (and implicitly Fitzjames) viewed evolutionary theory as opposed to ethical laws; above all, social progress involved checking the 'cosmic process'. However, where it came to positivism's Religion of Humanity and Herbert Spencer's Physiological Theory of Knowledge, Leslie and Fitzjames were largely at one in scornfully dismissing these 'feather-headed enthusiasts' who so thankfully grabbed the 'first will-o'-the-wisp for a safe guide', each patching up a new religion out of 'scraps and tatters of half-understood science'.[176] Leslie easily wrote off Spencer – the 'prophet of the unknowable' – as getting less than nowhere in the most tryingly complex fashion.[177] And as for Comtean positivism, 'a man who fancies that he can dictate a complete system to the world only shows that he is arrogant to the verge of insanity'.[178] Fitzjames expended rather more time and effort in ridiculing Spencerian and especially Comtean notions of a universal spirit; the last sustained example of such attacks was the 'Unknowable and the Unknown' (1884).

Spencer had postulated the existence of an unknowable and infinite universal power – an 'Infinite Eternal Energy' – which, through inherited ancestral experience, mankind had constantly been aware of. Unlike Arnold's 'Eternal not ourselves', Spencer offered no intelligible practical employment of these sensations.

Stephen, hardly unfairly, ruled out Spencer's elaborate speculations as meaningless; so abstract as to assert nothing; a string of metaphors ending where they began; like a 'gigantic soap bubble not burst, but blown thinner and thinner 'till it has become absolutely imperceptible'. So much so, that the truth or falsehood of Spencer's 'Eternal Energy' was a matter of absolute indifference.[179]

In all essentials such conclusions were those of Harrison also.[180] But Harrison's quasi-spiritual Comtist brew and Spencer's offering to the spiritually bereft were much of a muchness: for Stephen, a 'question as to the comparative blackness of the pot and the kettle'.[181] This was more damning for positivists than for Spencer, for he, unlike them, had never seen his 'Unknowable' as an important governing force amongst mankind. True, the 'Religion of Humanity' had a terrestrial structure – 'Popery conducted upon atheistical principles'[182] – but as a religion it remained, as Stephen had so often charged in the past, a barren abstraction. 'Humanity', the object of Comtean 'awe and gratitude', was the term for all who had 'contributed to the improvement of the human race'. Quite how, asked Stephen, could an indefinite number of diverse characters combine into a 'single object of thought'? Anything which hoped to perform a spiritual function – 'to be the object of worship' – needed an element of the concrete, such as was common to the Roman Catholic Church or the Great Western Railway. For Stephen, *they* at least both entailed comprehensible attributes – the Pope led the former, declaring a dividend was a characteristic of the latter. But just what could be confidently affixed to 'humanity'? Talk of 'awe and gratitude to humanity' represented nothing beyond 'yearning after some object of affection, like a childless woman's love for a lap dog'.[183] To Stephen, it was an undeniable stark truth that efforts to unite and govern men by religion lacking 'a supernatural basis' were as likely to succeed as 'attempts to fly without air and without wings':[184] axiomatic to any worthwhile religion was a fulcrum outside present life. Ignoring this produced no more than 'miserable little abortions like positivism',[185] or a 'half-breed' between science and theology endowed with the 'faults of both parents and the virtues of neither'.[186]

By 1884 Stephen felt able to put a tolerably optimistic public face on the changed and changing spiritual order of things. Although scientific advance had still not made complete nonsense of all theistical beliefs, it appeared to be a question of *when*, rather than *if*, the irresistible case for unbelief would be made out. Ungrudgingly,

Stephen accepted that religious faith could be a deeply ennobling experience, carrying its possessor far above the petty and vulgar side of existence. However, it was a state many more might enjoy only 'if the truth of propositions depended not upon the evidence by which they can be supported, but by their intrinsic beauty and utility'; then, of course, under such unreal conditions they might 'vindicate their creed against all others'.[187] Looking to the likely course of social ethics, Stephen anticipated no thunderous crash of existing morality following the exit of belief; instead, more or less strong changes of emphasis would evolve, with the Christian deification of self-sacrifice most vulnerable of all if Christ were a 'mere dead man'. An uninviting process of moral 'brutalisation' loomed, making many elements of life 'smaller-meaner-fiercer',[188] swelling the burden of social regulation to be performed by the criminal law's crude machine as religious influence faded[189] – as Frederick Pollock said of G. E. Moore's *Ethics*, 'Not much catching the tail of the Cosmos there.'[190] Stephen's was a powerful example, typical of the time, of an obsessive concern with and clamour for standards, of a moral rigidity and severity well exhibited in Carlyle's references to the '*infinite* difference . . . between a Good man and a Bad', the second of whom we must 'abhor and avoid infinitely'.[191] Yet Stephen believed that in a purely secular society most would find no insurmountable problem in turning their minds away from the transient character of existence. And, with an almost bitter-sweet flippancy, he saw the 'chief difference' as falling on the 'respectable man of the world, the lukewarm nominal Christian who believed as much of his creed as happened to suit him and led an easy life, will turn out to have been right after all, and enthusiastic believers of all creeds to have been quite wrong'.[192]

The defensible middle ground between what Stephen always regarded as the sinister blind faith of Catholicism and complete disbelief had by now disappeared;[193] pretending otherwise was dishonest cowardice. It was a feeling typified in and implicitly colouring his assessment of Jowett, whom Stephen had been acquainted with at least since the *Essays and Reviews* affair. On one occasion, having stayed overnight at Balliol, Stephen, as the willing recipient of a discourse on Hegel, listened to Jowett with

that uncomfortable conviction which one often gets from such conversations, that the great attraction of Hegel's speculation was that in some super superlative sense . . . the same statement may be both true or false at the same time, and to the same person, especially if it relates to Christian religion. There is something so meek, so gentle, so lovable in every way about Jowett, that I for one would never say a word that would censure or wound him, but I always look upon him as a man under a terribly heavy burden, bearing it not perhaps with perfect courage and frankness, but still with a very large share of both and infinitely more honest in every way than the people who force their minds into believing that they believe in Popery. I have a most sincere regard for him, but somehow, I do not wish to see very much of him or of people of his way of thinking.[194]

For along with his brother,[195] Stephen's senses had detected the most delicate but, as they perceived it, unmistakable scent of sophism; an ultimate evasiveness or inability firmly to grab hold of and vigorously shake one's beliefs regardless of the risk of their disintegration.

Looking back in his 'Autobiograpahic Frgament', the subject recalls how the full course of belief to unbelief had run: 'one bit broke away, and by degrees, when I had reached middle age, I gave it up, and now that I am on the verge of old age, I feel altogether estranged from it and convinced in a quiet way without any conscious indirect motive that it is not true at all'.[196] By the late 1870s Stephen appears to have achieved an emotional and intellectual accommodation with faithlessness; though it is impossible to be certain whether he drew the bleak Carlylean inference that without belief the universe would be just 'one huge, dead, immeasurable steam engine rolling on, in its deadly indifference'.[197] Most likely, there never ceased to flicker some inextinguishable inchoate feeling poignantly admitted in *Liberty, Equality, Fraternity* that we are all imprisoned spirits, 'able only to make signals to each other, but with a world of things to say which our signals cannot describe'; that 'things which cannot be adequately represented by words are more important than those which can' – almost an admission of the dangerous heresy that the truth of what words are incapable of expressing, rationalistic analysis cannot penetrate.

Stephen's unpleasant practical dilemma stared him in the face: belief that acceptance of many Christian virtues was valuable at a public level though in '[his] own room' he rejected them. And whilst aware of possible charges of some sort of nihilistic hypocrisy, he felt compelled not to be over-zealous in undermining belief 'as a whole or without some serious necessity';[198] a peculiarly painful concession for anyone who had spent half a lifetime strenuously preaching the overriding value of public truth and candour. Stephen had finally arrived at a stage where not only was Christianity both intellectually and historically unacceptable,[199] but a large part of its morality too; though his distaste for the sermon on the mount and the Christ portrayed by Seeley[200] or Renan carried a very long pedigree:

> My dear father . . . used habitually to speak of Christ as the 'The Master', with a sort of pathetic accent over the a. This is just what I have never been able to feel. It seems to me that the character of Christ embodies only one type or variety of beauty, it is one which does not attract me at all. . . I cannot in any way accept Christ as a master or a pattern, or an example of perfect goodness [as shown in his] resigned socialistic temper. Christianity [was] to common everyday morality what medicine is to food and I think that Christ, like many physicians . . . dealt so much with sick people that he hardly believed in the existence of the healthy. . . [He] was a most extraordinary person [and] probably influenced this world more deeply than any other . . . but lawyers and soldiers and butchers and bakers have a basis of their own in human affairs, just as much as saints and heroes and poets and artists, and I and my friends have legs of our own to stand upon and I do not feel the least need of leaning upon or acting as disciple to anyone, living or dead; past, present or future.[201]

And as if to underline his spiritual autonomy, this 'defiant pride of intellect',[202] in the following week Stephen took off for a fort-night's winter holiday quite alone in Switzerland, with Christmas Day 1884 spent steaming down Lake Constance.[203]

9

THE BENCH AND BEYOND

The final phase of Stephen's legal career opened in 1870 with elevation to the High Court Bench, an appointment long coveted by him. It was an event which came about in spite of the unconventionality of both the appointee's character and his activities over the two previous decades or so. Stephen's regard for professional advance and preferment had always been a curious mixture of the keenest ambition married to an unwillingness to expend much effort in cultivating the right alliances and a winning public persona. From the early years he spent as a jobbing barrister, moderate success came despite a gruff, generally unsolicitous professional demeanour. Establishing a solid practice hung a good deal on courting solicitors' favour and constant vigilance against creating the slightest impression of being 'dangerously clever'. Yet Stephen held himself out for business in a largely negative manner,[1] being as 'capable of making himself agreeable to an attorney as dancing on the tightrope' and giving off an aura of 'downright honesty [which] must have struck dismay into many of his clients'.[2] It was also a background and bearing that normally hardly recommended a man for public recognition or election to office, something that the electors of Harwich and Dundee had unequivocally testified to. But partly through the friendships of Maine and Grant Duff, Stephen's appetite for office – for being able to influence the course of events and register concrete success – had been both satisfied and sharpened by the great adventure of India.

On returning to England Stephen had faced the humdrum practicality of earning a living, and putting to best use law-reforming energies and schemes that had been fermenting away over the previous ten years or more. One person of influence well placed to employ such talents was John Duke Coleridge, Attorney-General

245

since 1871 and Chief Justice (Common Pleas) from 1873. As well as being instrumental in commissioning the drafting of an Evidence Bill, Coleridge was an enthusiastic advocate of making wider and more substantial use of Stephen. Writing to Gladstone in September 1873,[3] after Stephen's rejection by the voters of Dundee, Coleridge set out the case for Stephen's appointment as Solicitor-General:

I regard it as of real importance to the party even to the public service to put such a man as Stephen into office and make him an adherent of the Liberal Party. He is a very remarkable man with many elements of greatness in him and I am very confident could be in all ways a great gain to us . . . I think if I were in your place with my own strong sense of Stephen's powers I should run the risque of appointing him. But it is a great risque which with *your* knowledge of Stephen it is almost impossible to think of your running and Selborne tells me he is very strongly against it.

Whether or not Lord Chancellor Selborne was truly averse to the idea is unclear; certainly in correspondence[4] with Gladstone he leant in Stephen's direction in preference to Harcourt, the eventual choice. Quite what decided Gladstone in Harcourt's favour is obscure. With the reverberations of *Liberty, Equality, Fraternity* still very much in the air, along with Stephen's awkward Dundee performance, Harcourt's more straightforward political profile must have looked distinctly less chancy.[5] On top of this, Stephen's close identification with the increasingly frequent anti-Gladstonian tone of the *Pall Mall Gazette* could have done nothing to advance his suit.[6] Doubtless the pangs of disappointment felt by Stephen on hearing of Harcourt's good fortune can only have been heightened by the realisation that his old Apostle friend and antagonist had once again deprived him of a desirable professional prize.

Surprisingly, bearing in mind Stephen's age and unorthodox experience, hopes if not expectations of a High Court judgeship were alive as early as 1873. But by the beginning of the following January his little 'bubble about the judgeship, which looked a very bright bubble indeed, had gone where all bubbles go'.[7] Yet there was no doubting the growth in Stephen's hankering after such an appointment, with Maine reporting to Lytton that their mutual friend 'oddly enough, appears to wish for a Judgeship more than anything else in the world'. And when, in 1876, two seats on the Bench became vacant, Stephen believed that the 'crisis of his future had arrived'.[8] Satisfaction of the ambition finally came three years later. Rumour and surprise hung around the motivating forces responsible for lifting Stephen to the grand position of a High Court judgeship and enviable financial security of £5,000 per annum.[9] Indisputably Stephen lacked anything resembling the standard credentials,[10] a fact which naturally set in motion the oily wheels of professional and journalistic speculation. Less generous parties looked to Stephen's fierce public defence of the Lytton-Disraeli, Indian-Afghan policies.[11] However, the limited and accessible positive evidence that survives points to the more laudable reason for Stephen's service on the 1878 Code Commission: that acceptance of the position rested on the understanding that the first vacant judgeship would go to him,[12] with confirmation of Stephen's being 'rewarded' for Commission duties coming in correspondence between the Attorney-General, Sir John Holker, and Lord Chancellor Cairns.[13] Whatever the principal reasons were which brought him to the bench, his manifest intellectual qualities and unrivalled wide-ranging (if somewhat unconventional) professional achievements made the appointment objectively imaginative and thoroughly defensible.[14]

Stephen was quite open, at least amongst friends, that he saw judicial office as offering the marvellous combination of an absorbing professional existence, financial security and, not least, the opportunity to appease ever-present literary cravings. The daily routine was soon established: a working session before breakfast, court half past ten to four, then three hours' labour at home – 'I cannot tell you how much I enjoy this . . . If I keep it up long enough, I really hope I may ultimately be able to realise some of the dreams of my earlier life as to the writing of books.'[15] Predictably, though, within two or three years the novelty of that part of the day spent on judicial duties wore thin, a 'great part' of it becoming 'exceedingly dull and petty'.[16] Life on circuit could be desperately tedious, sometimes involving 'sitting 10 hours a day trying all kinds of abominations', even 'corrupting' the judicial mind so as to cause it to try long cases overnight in its sleep.[17] And occasionally trial tedium was such as to demand alleviation by spells of surreptitious letter-writing, 'with a bit of my mind' on the correspondence and 'listening with the rest'.[18]

Though generally mundane, judicial routine at one time was given the added frisson of death threats. In common with some of his brethren, Stephen was responsible for trying Fenian terrorists. Frequent public pledges by the 'Dynamiters' to kill judges and other principals involved in the prosecution process meant periods in the constant companionship of armed guards. Quite which was the bigger irritant, the permanent fear of shooting himself with the heavy-calibre revolver that Stephen was obliged to carry in his greatcoat or the self-conscious embarrassment of being shadowed by policemen with 'loaded carbines',[19] he was unable to decide. Naturally, Stephen's annual summer holiday in Ireland offered no relief from such attentions, with strolls taken in the company of 'two smart green coated police . . . gliding . . . some 20 or 30 yards off'. But at least their presence gave a 'little zest to the practice of rifle and pistol shooting' at which the Stephen family seemed 'decidedly better' than their protectors.[20]

By common consent, Stephen's thirteen years on the bench were unimpressive when put alongside the intellectual vigour and achievements he displayed in other directions: a measurable shortfall existed between expectations and outcome. As some contemporary commentators observed, first-rate intellects do not automatically conduce to first-rate judges; often 'Fine jurists [make] second best lawyers.'[21] Stephen's failure as a judge was of a relative rather than an absolute nature: relative to the high hopes held by many – possibly including himself. Failure lay in being unremarkable, in not being extraordinary. A succinct modern assessment fairly suggests:

There are undoubtedly some judgments of Stephen's which stand out as important in the development of criminal law: important because he always grasped what was the central issue, because of the decisions he reached and the principles he laid down. The very quality which he so conspicuously displayed in his writings, namely, an uncanny faculty for sifting the grain from the chaff, for brushing aside a multitude of details, irrelevant, inconsistent and confusing, and for dissecting out the nucleus of a legal argument, is also manifest in his judgments. . . Yet Stephen's judgments of high significance are few . . . no more than half a dozen, and none is prominent enough to be a landmark in English criminal law.[22]

Some contributory causes to Stephen's generally undistinguished judicial career are more apparent than others. A widespread impression[23] that he shared out his time and energies over too large a range of pursuits was not without substance; the first three years on the bench were accompanied by the heavy labour of producing the *History of the Criminal Law*. On its completion Stephen was torn between literary ventures which fully engaged intellectual interests – particularly 'politics and morals and religion' – and writing 'law-books', which he viewed as an unappetising duty 'so horribly dull and laborious that I cannot bring myself to give my whole strength and time to it'.[24] *Nuncomar*, the outcome of such havering, represented an unfortunate and unrewarding compromise: it was neither legal scholarship of compelling general interest nor an enterprise much enjoyed by the author. But this and occasional journalistic excursions more than filled Stephen's free time until his illness of 1885 led to a permanent diminution in physical capacity and appetite for work.

Literary distractions aside, an uncompromising temperament and low boredom threshold marked Stephen out as not altogether well fitted for a comfortable, controversy-free, career on the bench:

> The irritating intricacies of our technical procedure annoyed him; the jargon of the middle ages in which is wrapped up the law of real property offended him, he refused to assimilate it. The arts of the advocate employed upon a common jury aroused his indignation, which he was not slow to express, and in weightier matters he found it difficult to patiently endure the thrashing out of minute detail.[25]

Moreover, some saw him as 'ponderous and unhappy' with the steady flow of trial details; lacking any lightness of touch, he dealt with 'every question with the tremendous precision of a Nasmyth hammer', projecting the awkward image of 'a philosopher among lawyers and a lawyer among philosophers'.[26] Lord Birkenhead was not alone in claiming that the 'real truth' was that Stephen should have been a 'Judge of Appeal'[27] or was better suited to the 'Senate than the Bench'.[28]

Rather more relevant to the comparative lack of notable judgments from Stephen was his attitude towards judicial creativity in law-making. A fairly rigid view on the impropriety and inadvisability of judges taking upon themselves an openly creative function shows up both in his writing and in certain judicial observations, most particularly in *Coney* (1882):[29]

> It seems to me . . . that in exercising the narrowly qualified power of *quasi* legislation which the very nature of our position confers upon us, we ought to confine ourselves as far as possible . . . to applying well-known principles and analyis to new combinations of facts, and supplying to general definitions and maxims, or to general statutory expressions, qualifications which though not expressed, are in our opinion, implied . . . I think . . . that the court would exceed its power if it were to remove by judicial decisions . . . defects in the criminal law . . . which have caused so many failures of justice. To abolish a well-established rule of law because it is a bad rule, is the business of the legislature.

Yet even within such self-imposed limitations, Stephen produced a very respectable collection of criminal first instance and appeal judgments whose quality of analysis and exposition were often of a high order.

Beyond the juristical standing of Stephen's criminal judgments, there is little evidence to suggest the extent to which a morally forceful character translated itself into any pronounced sentencing practices; although Leslie Stephen alludes to his brother's reputation, 'among careless observers', for severity.[30] Whether generally true or not, certainly where it came to capital cases and questions of reprieves Stephen felt greatly the full chilling burden of judicial duty, which sometimes took on an almost surreal quality:

I have had a ghastly experience today – talking over with Harcourt [as Home Secretary] the question whether a woman I sentenced to death, a fortnight or more ago, is to be hanged or not on Tuesday morning. I know nothing so horrible as those life and death conversations, and there is something, I know not exactly what it is, in one's old intimacy with Harcourt, which makes it peculiarly ghastly. In this particular case he was doubtful – I was against the woman, who as I think, most cruelly poisoned her friend. . . The decision rests with him – and I am heartily glad of it. But it is a dreadful feeling to vote for death, when a word, spoken in a private room, between two old friends would mean life. In the midst of our talk, Lady Harcourt and her little boy, looking as radiant and handsome and full of life as possible, came in and talked . . . for a minute or two, and Harcourt played with the child, neither of them once having the faintest idea of the subject of our conversation. It was very strange too to see the difference of our manner to each other, from what is natural to us both when we talk even on business. As a rule we are as familiar as possible – interrupt each other – both talk at once, and stand on no ceremony at all, as men do, who have known each other all their lives – but on this occasion we were as polite and measured and diplomatic as possible and for once talked with no shade of talking.[31]

In one sense the Lipski (1887) murder trial can be viewed as an example of Stephen's considerable care and scrupulousness in trying to ensure properly based convictions. Despite a guilty verdict, Lipski's solicitor, John Hayward, convinced of his client's innocence, organised a national campaign supported by the *Pall Mall Gazette* which succeeded in inducing the Home Secretary to stay the execution pending a review of the evidence. Stephen's efforts were exceptionally painstaking, going so far as the very unusual measure of discussions with Hayward. Even so, the vindication of rejecting the appeal provided by Lipski's last-minute confession still came as a clear relief to both Stephen and the Home Secretary.[32]

The one case which did injure Stephen's judicial reputation was Mrs Maybrick's, albeit rather unfairly and beyond anything justified by the events. In August 1889 Stephen presided over the trial and conviction of Florence Maybrick for murdering her husband by poisoning. The verdict's immediate unpopularity caused a 'large mob' to surround the court buildings, with counsel and witnesses 'hooted' at and Stephen needing to be driven away under a police guard.[33] Extensive public and parliamentary[34] unease resulted in the commutation of Maybrick's death sentence to penal servitude on the declared grounds that though there was no doubt poison had been administered by the defendant, uncertainty remained as to the actual cause of Mr Maybrick's death. Much criticism was levelled at Stephen's trial conduct: that he had been irrelevantly censorious of the defendant's recent adultery and offered it as a possible motive for murder; that he had made errors as to a number of relevant dates; and that he had wrongly attributed certain medical evidence. Certainly although Stephen's summing-up shows all proper concern with defence submissions, elements of it do display an untypical and disquieting 'slackness'.[35] But, overall, nothing in the complete record of Stephen's two-day summing-up suggests any need to disagree with Lord Birkenhead's conclusion that it was 'fair and impartial', containing 'slips', but none more than 'incidental'.[36] Evidence of Stephen's own perceptions of the case is mixed. Anecdotal, yet of some substance, is Sir Henry Dickens' claim that the night before completing his summing-up, Stephen awoke a fellow judge by pacing up and down his room repeating 'That woman is guilty . . . '[37] Better documented is his comment in the second edition of the *General View of the Criminal Law* that of the 28 cases he tried between 1885 and 1889 referred to the Home Secretary, Maybrick was the only one where there 'could be any doubt about the facts'.[38]

However competent Stephen then was to carry out judicial duties, by the end of the decade the decline in his physical vigour and mental endurance had become marked.[39] Completion of a greatly revised second edition of the *General View* was something which lay 'heavy' on the author.[40] Within a year, Stephen's capacity and ability to execute his judicial functions effectively had become a matter of press debate;[41] first through general observations, and then through increasingly pointed discussions of judicial incapacity and the appropriate mechanism for meeting the problem. Inexplicably Stephen appeared to have remained unaware of this swell of public concern until March 1891,[42] when Lord Coleridge is said to have eventually brought matters to Stephen's notice.[43] Following immediate medical consultation with Sir Andrew Clark, Stephen announced his early resignation, trying his last case at Bristol Assizes on 23 March, 1891.[44] The retirement was formally marked by an affecting ceremony attended by the Bench and leading members of the Bar held in the Lord Chief Justice's Court on Tuesday 11 April, the beginning of the Easter law sitting. Stephen, sitting in the Lord Chief Justice's chair flanked by Lord Coleridge and Lord Justice Bowen, heard a handsome laudation delivered by the Attorney-General. 'The learned judge at the conclusion of this address remained some moments silent, evidently unable to find immediate utterance for [his] feelings.'[45] Then, speaking 'slowly in a subdued voice with some emotion', Stephen bade farewell to his profession, ending a moving speech with a small self-perceived irony: 'I will only add these words, which are more sincere than you perhaps may think, "God bless you all and everyone." '[46]

With retirement the darkness of bereavement and an inexorable general decline steadily closed in. Maine had died three years earlier,[47] and Lytton's death came in November 1891, an event 'felt deeply by the survivor'.[48] Most devastating of all was the mental breakdown and death in February 1892 of Stephen's gifted and admired son James Kenneth.[49] James Fitzjames Stephen died at Red House Park, Ipswich on 11 March 1894.[50]

Attempts to label any individual neatly must necessarily always be of dubious value. Lytton Strachey, however, found the mark in summing up Stephen the public man as one who 'preponderated with a character of formidable grandeur, with a massive and rugged intellectual sanity and colossal commonsense'.[51] But in describing Stephen, as *The Times* obituary chose, as 'the last of the Benthamites' was to graze the truth in the lightest manner. In legal and ethical attitudes it was true only in the most qualified sense; in politics substantially untrue. The description's greatest accuracy lay in Stephen's tendency, almost compulsion, to confront conflicting notions or models of thought in a direct, unflinching and sometimes unsubtle fashion. Like Bentham's, Stephen's truths, even when they *were* unassailable truths, were often stripped too cleanly of irreducible human foibles or idiosyncrasy to make their straightforward social application anything other than illusory. More generally, although a good part of Stephen's reputation suffered the fate common to controversialists who devote much of themselves to chasing the ephemera of their time, there remains a very sizeable core of wide and enduring achievement. What might have been accomplished with a firmer eye on a more distant horizon is arguable. Yet it is difficult to believe Stephen could have, or would wished to have, lived any other way than being firmly and immediately engaged in the great passing events of the age. With strong strains of optimism and stoicism holding in check the misanthrope that increasingly lurked in Stephen's psyche, even by nineteenth-century standards, he wrung an enviable return from his 65 years. And as Stephen so often remarked, for him life had been 'sweet, bright, glorious', lived with the most passionate belief in Carlyle's conviction that to 'stand at the meeting point of two eternities and three infinities is our common experience of every moment'.[52]

NOTES

PREFACE

1. *The Month*, LXXXIV (1895), 457 at 458.
2. The *Contemporary Review*, LXVIII (1895), 520.

1 EARLY IMPRESSIONS: SIR JAMES, ETON AND CAMBRIDGE

1. At Kensington Gore, later renamed 42 Hyde Park Gate; Leslie Stephen, *The Life of Sir James Fitzjames Stephen* (1895).
2. See generally P. Bloomfield, *Uncommon People* (1955), genealogical tables 4 and 6, and chs. 8 and 10. The genealogical history of the Stephens is discussed in the *Memoirs of James Stephen* ed. M. M. Bevington (1954) and ch. 1 of Leslie Stephen's *Life*. For a description of the Venns see John Venn, *Annals of a Clerical Family* (1904). The inellectual distinction characteristic of each of these families is considered in Noel Annan's well-known essay 'The Intellectual Aristocracy', in *Studies in Social History*, ed. J. H. Plumb (1955), p. 243.
3. Besides Fitzjames, three survived infancy: Herbert Venn (1822–46), Leslie (1832–1904) and Caroline Emilia (1834–1909).
4. James Stephen was made a KCB and Privy Councillor in 1848.
5. Initially jointly with the Board of Trade.
6. Sir Henry Taylor, close friend and colleague at the Colonial office: *Autobiography* (1885), I, p. 223, and *Life*, pp. 44–5 The complaint amongst men of Stephen's mentality and background of 'nervous exhaustion', brought on by an over-zealous appetite for work coupled with feelings of guilt and suspicion towards idleness or amusement, was arguably a socially acceptable psychological device for the occasional escape from the grip of apowerful work ethic. See H.M. Feinstein, *Becoming William James* (1984), ch. 12, 'The Use and Abuse of Illness'.
7. *Life*, p. 46. Assessments of Sir James' impact on colonial policy range from the highly favourable – P. Knapland, *James Stephen and the British Colonial System* (1953) – to claims that he displayed extreme competence though limited innovative flair: D. J. Murray, *The West Indies and the Development of Colonial Government 1801–1834* (1965). His central role in the 1833 anti-slavery legislation is summarised by Leslie Stephen in *Life*, pp. 46–8.
8. Taylor to Sir Edmund Head, 16 November, 1851, *Correspondence of Henry Taylor*, ed. E. Dowden (1885), p. 195.
9. *Life*, pp. 50–1; Taylor, *Autobiography*, II, p. 304.
10. Autobiographic Fragment of Fitzjames Stephen (p. 14,) written between 1884 and

1887. Stephen revealed in his Autobiographic Fragment (p. 1) that he had previously kept a journal which he had burnt. Such a fate also befell that of practically all the letters received by him: Leslie Stephen to C. E. Norton, 19 May, 1894, F. H. Maitland, *Life and Letters of Leslie Stephen* (1906), p. 419. The composition of the Autobiographic Fragment was carried out with mixed feelings: to inform his children and with the desire to 'bury my dead out of sight'. Stephen's daughter, Kathleen, followed her father's practice by burning a set of her own diaries: Virginia Woolf, *A Writer's Diary* (1953), 15 February 1923, pp. 234–5.

11. Autobiographic Fragment, pp. 14–15, and *Life*, p. 62.
12. Autobiographic Fragment, pp. 15–16. Senior was Edwin Chadwick's principal collaborator in the seminal Report of the Poor Law Commissioners, 1834. Spedding, a great literary and historical scholar, declined the offer to succeed Sir James at the Colonial Office.
13. Sir James held a favourable opinion of Carlyle: 'a fine truth seeking, and falsehood abhorring, nervous and cordial person, who would be irresistible, if he had no other attraction than the contrast he maintains to almost everybody else' (13 March, 1853, C. E. Stephen, *The First Sir James Stephen* (1906), p. 167.
14. *Diary* of Sir James Stephen, 13 January, 1846, Cambridge University Library, Add. MSS 7511. Sir James retired after severe illness in 1847. He was appointed Regius Professor of Modern History at Cambridge in 1849, followed in 1855 by a professorship at Haileybury, the East India Company College, until its demise in 1858.
15. Autobiographic Fragment, pp. 29–30; and *Life*, p. 54.
16. Autobiographic Fragment, p. 7.
17. Sir James to his wife, 3 March, 1851, *The First Sir James Stephen*, p.150. This disinclination to show deeper personal feelings was complemented, according to Leonard Woolf, by a trait found in all 'male Stephens' of 'thinking and even more in a way of expressing their thoughts which one associated pre-eminently with Dr Johnson . . . ; something monolithic about them and their opinions . . . the way of expressing their opinions reminding one of the ten commandments engraved upon tablets of stone'. *Sowing: An Autobiography, 1880–1904* (1960), p. 200.
18. Gladstone replied that Sir James had been 'one among the most brilliant if not actually the most brilliant of civil servants of his day'. Stephen to Gladstone, 26 and 27 June, 1882; and Gladstone to Stephen, 27 June, 1882. Gladstone Papers, British Library, Add MSS 44475 ff.337, 339, 343. Stephen's letter to *The Times*, 6 July, 1882 is briefly referred to by Leslie Stephen in *Life*, p. 49 n. 3. The offending *Reminiscences* (1882) were those of Thomas Mozley, Tractarian, close friend and brother-in-law of J. H. Newman. Sir James Stephen died on 14 September 1859.
19. Autobiographic Fragment, p. 15.
20. *Life*, pp. 69 and 71; and Sir James to Fitzjames, 2 March 1842 on the latter's thirteenth birthday, *The First Sir James Stephen* pp. 75–6.
21. Leslie joined his brother there in 1840.
22. Maitland, *Life and Letters of Leslie Stephen*, pp. 29–30.
23. *Life*, p. 78.
24. *Life*, p. 79. 'A great public school is one of the roughest passages in life and . . . the very roughest in my experience': Stephen to Lady Grant Duff, 9 December 1881.
25. Autobiographic Fragment, p. 24.
26. The publisher, in his review of *Life*, in *The Month*, LXXXIV (1895), 457. Kegan Paul was an exact contemporary of Stephen at Eton; see *The Eton Register*, 1841–50, pp. 28 and 31. Kegan Paul comments that the 'school as a whole conceived against [Sir James] an unnecessary and gratuitous dislike'. 'No doubt [Fitzjames] was ill used, unpardonably so, when the school authorities could have stopped it' (pp. 459–60).
27. Autobiographic Fragment, p. 24 and *Life*, p. 80.
28. Autobiographic Fragment, pp. 25–6 and *Life*, pp. 80–1.

29. Autobiographic Fragment, p. 33; *Life*, p. 86. See also the comments of Kegan Paul in his review of *Life*, *The Month*, LXXXIV (1895), 460. Stephen nevertheless sent his own sons to Eton, with J. K. Stephen excelling in scholarship and becoming legendary for his prowess at the wall game. See E. Parker, *Eton in the Eighties* (1914), p. 142 and C. Hollis, *Eton: A History* (1960), p. 292.
30. Leslie's own schooling followed the same pattern.
31. Autobiographic Fragment, pp. 37–8.
32. *Some Early Impressions* (1924), p. 11; written in 1903.
33. *Life*, pp. 94 and 109. For a concise and entertaining account of the level of dedication and calculated cramming needed for examination distinction for the Tripos in the Cambridge (at least) of Stephen's time, see N. Annan, *Leslie Stephen* (1984), p. 24–8. Stephen went out in the 'poll' – failed to take honours. Leslie was later ranked as twentieth wrangler.
34. *Life*, p. 98.
35. Autobiographic Fragment, pp. 32–3 and *Life*, pp. 101–2. Stephen was elected on 13 November 1847.
36. The degree of secrecy observed by the society at the time is debatable; see P. Allen, *The Cambridge Apostles: The Early Years* (1978), p. 228, n. 14.
37. *Life*, p. 100. Leslie also 'fostered the hope' of membership, but despite greater academic success, failed to be elected: *Some Early Impressions*, pp. 35–6. His two main biographers, Maitland and Annan, were Apostles. Correspondence suggests that Leslie's disappointment rankled for many years: Maitland, *Life and Letters of Leslie Stephen*, p. 47.
38. 'Choice of one of the Three Learned Professions, Law, Physic and Divinity' (1850), 1865 Annotation, p. 114.
39. *Life*, pp. 103–5 and *Some Early Impressions*, p. 14.
40. Stephen right from the beginning had equivocal feelings towards Harcourt; probably a case of similar personalities both attracting and repelling: 'He and I were very intimate, and were, in a way, good friends, and throughout life we have not forgotten it'; but Harcourt had 'glaring faults – overbearing, insolent, aggravating to the last degree . . . but very clever'. Yet 'He is fond of his old friend I believe, and I am fond of him.' Autobiographic Fragment, p. 40.
41. A. G. Gardiner, *The Life of Sir William Harcourt* (1923), p. 41. A less flattering assessment came from William Everett, an Apostle in the early 1860s who, on hearsay evidence, suggested that 'both men [had an] infinite capacity for everything, especially making themselves disagreeable' (*The Nation*, LXXXIV (1907), 205). Harcourt was also in 1849 Treasurer and later President of the Cambridge Union (P. Craddock, *Cambridge Union 1815–1939* (1953), p. 173).
42. H. W. Watson, quoted in *Life*, p. 106. Watson thought Stephen no match in 'adroitness and chaff' for Harcourt but that he 'showed himself at his best in these struggles'.
43. 'Choice of profession' was written between June and October 1850, with annotations in 1865, 1872 and 1880. A note by Stephen's wife at the end of 'Choice of profession' indicates that he finally read it again in the autumn of 1893.
44. 'Choice of profession', 1880 annotation, p. 79. Misquoted (or rewritten) in *Life*, p. 116.
45. 'Choice of profession', p. 76; undated, but probably 1872.
46. *Life*, p. 117. See Frederic Harrison's account of the process involved in his 'choice' of profession, *Autobiographic Memoirs* (1911), II, pp. 140–8, with the similar purpose of eliminating a clerical career.
47. See B. Abel-Smith and R. Stevens, *Lawyers and the Courts* (1967), ch. 3.
48. Autobiographic Fragment, p. 39. Maine was appointed to a Readership in Jurisprudence and Civil Law by the Council of Education soon after its creation in 1852.
49. Harrison, *Autobiographic Memoirs*, I, p. 152.

50. Autobiographic Fragment, p. 50.
51. B. Disraeli, *The Two Nations* (1845), bk II, ch. 5.
52. 'The Morality of Advocacy', *Cornhill Magazine*, III (1861), 447, at 465; and the 'Bars of France and England', X (1864), 681.
53. *The First Sir James Stephen*, p. 217 and *Life*, p. 129.
54. Stephen to Lytton, 24 June 1876. No evidence exists to suggest what influence, if any, Mary Stephen had on her husband's thought. The marriage produced seven children surviving to adulthood, and just one grandchild, James Alexander Stephen (1908–87), son of Harry Lushington Stephen, born when the latter was 48. None of Fitzjames' four daughters married.

2   A CONTROVERSIALIST IN THE MAKING: LITERARY CRITICISM AND LEADER-WRITING

1. *Life*, p. 248.
2. Stephen to his wife, Mary Stephen, 15 February 1871. Writing to Leslie on her husband's compulsion to write, Mary Stephen observes 'I don't think anybody who does not see him as I do could understand how strong it is.' Ritchie Papers (uncatalogued), May/June 1871, Senate House Library, University of London.
3. Carlyle to his brother, 15 November 1873. *New Letters of Carlyle*, ed. A. Carlyle (1904), II, p. 301.
4. *Life*, p. 134.
5. Autobiographic Fragment, p. 51.
6. Brother-in-law to Lord Cranbourne, later third Marquess of Salisbury.
7. J. Gross, *The Rise and Fall of the Man of Letters* (1969), p. 63.
8. 'The Function of Criticism', in *Essays in Criticism* (1865).
9. *Culture and Anarchy* (1869), p. 87.
10. C. Kent, 'Higher Journalism and the Mid-Victorian Clerisy', *Victorian Studies*, 13, (1969), 181; and W. E. Houghton, 'Periodical Literature and the Articulate Classes', in *The Victorian Periodical Press: Samplings and Soundings*, ed. E. J. Shattock and M. Wolff (1982).
11. According to its editor, John Morley, a 'momentous task of forming national opinion': *Fortnightly Review*, NS, II (1867), 292.
12. M. M. Bevington, *The 'Saturday Review', 1855–1868: Representative Educated Opinion in Victorian England* (1941), p. 26.
13. *Life*, pp. 150 and 154. According to Walter Bagehot, the *Edinburgh Review* too had been seen by many as an 'incendiary publication' – 'Very clever but not at all sound'; 'The First Edinburgh Reviewers', in *Literary Studies*, ed. R. H. Hutton, I (1891), p. 1. More generally, see J. Clive, *Scotch Reviewers: The Edinburgh Review, 1802–1815* (1957) and Leslie Stephen, 'The First Edinburgh Reviewers', *Hours in a Library* (1879 edn), vol. III.
14. *Life and Letters of Leslie Stephen*, p. 161.
15. Attribution of *Saturday Review* articles is mainly based on Bevington's study, on *Life*, on identification by reprinting in *Essays by a Barrister* (1862) and in *Horae Sabbaticae* (1892), and on internal evidence.
16. Letters to his wife: for example, 17 March and 27 July 1859.
17. *Platform, Press, Politics and Play* (1895), p. 222.
18. On more than one occasion in his early days with the *Review* Stephen expressed anxiety to his wife as to whether his contributions would meet with Cook's approval: see, for example, his letter of 13 March 1856.
19. 'Mr Thackeray', *Fraser's Magazine*, LXIX (1864), 401, at 402.
20. 1832, in *Thomas Carlyle's Works* (1887), pp. 250–1.
21. J. W. Dodds, *The Age of Paradox* (1953), p. 377.
22. 'Milton' (1825), in *Critical Essays*, 1 (1907).
23. 'The Relation of Novels to Life' (1855), p. 161.

24. Ibid., p. 174.
25. *Hard Times*, ch. 1. Stephen's essay was written about a year after the publication of *Hard Times*.
26. R. D. Altick, *The English Common Reader* (1957), p. 132.
27. Though in accordance with the primitive pain/pleasure calculus, any pleasure derived was a gain of some sort. Generally, G. L. Nesbitt, *Benthamite Reviewing* (1934); F. P. Sharpless, *The Literary Criticism of John Stuart Mill* (1968), ch. 1, and J. B. Schneewind (ed.), *Mill's Essays on Literature* (1965).
28. *Westminster Review*, 4 (1825), 116; quoted by W. E. Houghton in *The Victorian Frame of Mind 1830–1870* (1957), p. 115.
29. R. D. Altick, *Victorian People and Ideas* (1973), p. 257.
30. 'Pure Literature', *Saturday Review*, II (1856), 16.
31. *Saturday Review*, II (1856), 406.
32. For example, *Saturday Review*, III (1857), 8; IV (1857), 15; VI (1858), 285; and *Edinburgh Review*, CVI (1857), 124.
33. *Saturday Review*, II (1856) 406, at 407.
34. *Saturday Review*, III (1857), 8.
35. Walter Bagehot, 'Charles Dickens', *National Review* (October 1858), 459. Bagehot provides an almost point by point endorsement of Stephen's earlier discussion.
36. Speech at the Birmingham and Midlands Institute, 27 September 1869; reproduced in H. House, *The Dickens World* (1942), p. 172.
37. As Stephen pointed out, the causes in *Pickwick* and *Bleak House* were already partly worn out when Dickens waded in: 'Imprisonment for debt on *mesne* process was doomed, if not abolished, before he wrote *Pickwick*. The Court of Chancery was reformed before he published *Bleak House*.' 'Mr Dickens as a Politician', *Saturday Review*, III (1857), 9. For Dickens on law reform generally, see W. S. Holdsworth, *Charles Dickens as a Legal Historian* (1928), ch. III for *Bleak House* and ch. IV for *Pickwick*.
38. Stephen's views of *Hard Times*, Dickens' most pointed attack on utilitarianism, do not appear in any review. In a passing reference in the *Saturday Review*, Gradgrind is viewed as one of Dickens' earlier successful and 'substantially truthful' caricatures: XVIII (1865).
39. Generally, W. Oddie, *Dickens and Carlyle: The Question of Influence* (1972).
40. *Edinburgh Review*, CVI (1857), 124.
41. S. M. Smith, *The Other Nation* (1980), p. 133.
42. *Saturday Review*, IV (1857), 57.
43. A curious variant of the suspect practice of self-reviewing was Stephen's criticism of the *Saturday Review* from the rival columns of the *Cornhill Magazine* at a time when he was regularly contributing to the *Saturday Review*: 'Sentimentalism', *Cornhill* X (1864), 65. Although the article was anonymous, it would be surprising if Cook had not soon been aware of its authorship.
44. *Saturday Review*, IV (1857), 84. Stephen enjoyed Reade's subsequent novel *Hard Cash* enough to recommend it to his wife: letter, 4 March 1864.
45. It might be wondered whether Leslie Stephen's reversal of names was accidental.
46. *Life*, p. 159.
47. Established in May 1855 to lobby for the more rapid implementation of the Northcote-Trevelyan Report of 1854. Thackeray was also one of its members.
48. Letter to John Forster on 30 January 1856, the eve of the serialised publication of the 'Circumlocution' chapter in *Little Dorrit*: *The Letters of Charles Dickens*, Nonesuch edition, II (1938) ed. W. Dexter, p. 738.
49. *Dickens 1970*, ed. M. Slater (1970), pp. 125–49.
50. Letter to his wife, 14 March 1857.
51. *Household Words* (1 August 1857).
52. 'Dickens and the Public Service', in *Dickens 1970*, ed. Slater, p. 137 n.
53. For example, letter to Fitzjames of 18 May 1857.

54. Letter of 6 August 1857. According to earlier passages in this letter Sir James appears not to have read *Little Dorrit*.

55. *Life*, pp. 159 and 162.

56. Letter of 8 May 1857, from Reeve to the publisher of the *Edinburgh Review* in J. K. Laughton, *Memoirs of the Life and Correspondence of Henry Reeve* (1898), I, p. 379.

57. *Saturday Review*, III (1857), 519.

58. This may have been inserted by Reeve in response to a direct request by Sir James. In correspondence later in the year, Mrs Gaskell refers to 'how Sir James had sent that message about the sentences which Mr Reeve would insert in Mr Fitz James Stephen's article': 26 November 1857, *The Letters of Mrs Gaskell*, ed. J.A.V. Chapple and A. Pollard (1966), p. 483.

59. *The Art of Fiction* (1884), p. 57. Similarly Matthew Arnold in the *Fortnightly Review*, XLII (1887), pp. 784–5.

60. *Saturday Review*, II (1856), 406.

61. For example, *Westminster Review* (1852), 129.

62. *Westminster Review* (1856), 442. For the circumstances of its composition, see G. S. Haight, *George Eliot* (1968), p. 208.

63. *Westminster Review* (1856), 449.

64. Ibid., 461.

65. *Edinburgh Review*, CVI (1857), 124, at 128.

66. *Saturday Review*, VIII (1859), 741.

67. *The Letters of Charles Dickens*, Nonesuch edition, II, p. 335.

68. Ibid., p. 567.

69. *National Review* (1858), 459.

70. Cf. *The Principles of Success in Literature* (1865), pp. 32–3.

71. *Fortnightly Review*, XVII (1872), 141.

72. *Dickens' Own Story* (1923), p. 209.

73. See generally K. Graham, *English Criticism of the Novel 1865–1900* (1965); R. Stang, *The Theory of the Novel in England 1850–1870* (1959) (though the book is handicapped by a number of misattributions); and L. Pykett, 'The Real Versus the Ideal: Theories of Fiction in Periodicals, 1850–1879', *Victorian Periodicals Review*, 15 (1982), 63.

74. A. Trollope, *Autobiography* (1883), ch. XII.

75. A. Trollope, *Four Lectures*, ed. M. L. Parrish (1938), p. 111.

76. *Westminster Review*, (1856), 51, at 54; *The George Eliot Letters*, ed. G. S. Haight, III, p. 111. Even Eliot's works were not completely free from moral didacticism, however: *Middlemarch* is an instance.

77. *Saturday Review*, IV (1857), 40.

78. Ibid., 219.

79. 'Manon Lescaut', *Saturday Review*, VI (1858), 64.

80. *Saturday Review*, IV (1857), 243.

81. In later life Tolstoy drew almost a similar level of praise: letter to Lord Lytton, 16 March 1888.

82. *Saturday Review*, IV (1857), 559.

83. A comparison with Henry James' much later essay 'Honoré De Balzac' (1902), whilst showing Stephen lacked the coherency and depth of James, also reveals a surprising degree of concordance of views between them. Indeed, in some ways Leslie Stephen was further away from James on Balzac than his brother. For Leslie, Balzac's works were too 'highly spiced' and such as to make 'one half ashamed of yielding': 'Balzac's Novels', *Fortnightly Review*, IX (1871), 17, at 38.

84. *Saturday Review*, VI (1858), 473.

85. D. Bellos, *Balzac–Criticism in France 1850–1900* (1976).

86. Generally, C. R. Decker, 'Balzac's Literary Reputation in Victorian Society', *PMLA*, 47 (1932), 1150; W. M. Kendrick, 'Balzac and British Realism: Mid-

Victorian Theories of the Novel', *Victorian Studies* (1976), 20. And see J. S. Mill's early appreciation in *Dissertations and Discussions*, I, pp. 237–308.

87. *Macmillan's Magazine*, II (August 1860). Similarly Charlotte Brontë: Mrs Gaskell, *Life of Charlotte Brontë*, ch. 22.

88. *Saturday Review*, IV (1857), 15.

89. *The Nation* (1865), 786. And the final verdict of many other critics, for example, Frederic Harrison, 'Charles Dickens', *Studies in Early Victorian Literature* (1895).

90. 'The Relation of Novels to Life' (1855), 175; later 'Sentimentalism', *Cornhill Magazine*, X (1864), 65.

91. Cf. Aldous Huxley on *Little Nell*, where Dickens was 'mentally drowned and blinded by the sticky overflowings of his heart'; sentimentality of a 'truly pathological' order ('The Vulgarity of Little Nell', from *Vulgarity in Literature* (1930)).

92. *The Spectator*, XXXV (1862), 406. More generally on the critical reception of Dickens' novels by contemporary journals and reviews see J. D. Jump: 'Weekly Reviewing in the Eighteen Fifties', *Review of English Studies*, XXIV (1948), 42, and 'Weekly Reviewing in the Eighteen Sixties', *Review of English Studies*, NS, III (1952), 244.

93. *The Nation* (1965), 786.

94. For example, R. H. Hutton, 'The Genius of Dickens', in *Criticisms on Contemporary Thought and Thinkers* (1894), I, 87, at 92.

95. *British Journal*, I (1852), 138.

96. *Saturday Review*, VIII (1859), 741. Reproduced in *The Dickens Critics*, ed. G. H. Ford and L. Lane (1961). Its composition is referred to in a letter to his wife of 17 December 1859.

97. *British Novelists and their Styles* (1859), p. 252.

98. The *Examiner* (10 December 1859), 788.

99. *An Autobiography*, p. 208.

100. E. Clodd, 'George Meredith: Some Recollections', *Fortnightly Review*, XCII (1909), 19, at 27.

101. *French Poets and Novelists* (1884), p. 147.

102. *Life*, p. 157.

103. Especially Lewes' 1872 essay 'Dickens in Relation to Criticism', *Fortnightly Review*, XVII, 141.

104. G. H. Ford, *Dickens and his Readers* (1955), p. 151.

105. Letter of 29 July 1870. Much the same sentiments could be imputed to his brother Leslie, judging by the studied coolness of his 1888 *DNB* assessment of Dickens. Virginia Woolf, Fitzjames' niece, in her writings on Dickens was hardly any more generous: for example, 'Reviewing' (1939) in *Collected Essays* (1966), p. 210. There is no discoverable recorded view of Dickens on Fitzjames Stephen.

106. *Life*, p. 177.

107. Leslie Stephen Papers, Perkins Library, Duke University. Anny Thackeray also became a devoted and intimate correspondent of Fitzjames during the period. See the Ritchie Papers.

108. Generally, W. Gérin, *Anne Thackeray Ritchie* (1981).

109. *The Mausoleum Book*, ed. A. Bell (1970), p. 46. Cornish later became Vice-Provost at Eton.

110. David Masson identified this frequent phenomenon of critics being predominantly *for* Dickens or *for* Thackeray: 'There is a Dickens faction, and there is a Thackeray faction.' Thackeray 'satisfied the most cultured taste, and wins respect of the severest critic' and is seen as an author with a 'closer and harder . . . more penetrating and reflective' mind, whereas Dickens 'rises to a keener and wilder song . . . , more excursive and intuitive'. 'Dickens and Thackeray', *British Novelists and their Styles* (1859).

111. *Fraser's Magazine*, LXIX (1864), 401, at 412.

112. *Saturday Review*, I (1855), 106.

113. *Cornhill Magazine*, II (1861), 122.

114. *The Mausoleum Book*, p. 15.

115. Trollope in 'Novelists' Common Forms', *Saturday Review*, XV (1863), 749.

116. Letters to Emily Cunningham, 22 August and 18 September 1872.

117. *The George Eliot Letters*, ed. Haight, Lewes' Journal, vol. IV.

118. Letter of 6 May 1885.

119. For example, collected essays, *Hours in a Library* (3 vols., 1879).

120. A. Haultain, *Goldwin Smith – His Life and Opinions* (1913), p. 39. Smith and Fitzjames Stephen were both *Saturday* reviewers; Smith also knew Stephen from his membership of the 1858 Newcastle Commission on education. Stephen was secretary to the Commission, whose roving reporters included Matthew Arnold and Mark Pattison.

121. Cf. Mill, *On Liberty*, ch. 1; and E. Alexander, 'Disinterested Virtue: Dickens and Mill in Agreement', *Dickensian* (1969), 163.

122. *Saturday Review*, III (1857), 450.

123. *Reminiscences*, ed. C. E. Norton (1887), p. 186.

124. Leslie Stephen also became a regular if less frequent visitor to Cheyne Walk, often feeling 'something like the editor of a Saducees' gazette interviewing St John the Baptist'. *Some Early Impressions* (1924), p. 104.

125. *Life*, p. 201.

126. It was this objectivity and concern at the harsh conclusions necessary that led Stephen to decline writing a study of Carlyle for John Morley's English Men of Letters series. See letters to Lady Grant Duff, 8 and 21 October 1884.

127. 'Mr Carlyle', *Saturday Review*, V (1858), 638.

128. Ibid., 638. For broadly similar assessments see, for example, John Morley, 'Carlyle', *Critical Miscellanies*, I (1877); and Frederic Harrison, 'Thomas Carlyle', in *Studies in Early Victorian Literature*.

129. *Saturday Review*, XVII (1864), 690.

130. *Fraser's Magazine*, LXXII (1865), 778, at 810; cf. Harrison, 'Thomas Carlyle', p. 45.

131. *Life*, p. 203.

132. Dated 8 November 1878. Stephen confessed to experiencing 'a little . . . semi filial feeling' towards Carlyle. Stephen to Lady Grant Duff, 8 October 1884.

133. Now returned to Carlyle's house in Cheyne Walk, Chelsea. Stephen was also the later owner of Thackeray's table 'on which [he] wrote most of his novels'. Stephen to Lady Grant Duff, 10 Feburary 1882.

134. *Life*, p. 235.

135. *Saturday Review*, XXXII (1866), 207. Much the same criticisms are found in Harrison, 'Lord Macaulay', *in Studies in Early Victorian Literature*; and Morley, 'Macaulay', in *Critical Miscellanies*, I (1877), both critical of Macaulay's unscientific approach to history. Bagehot was less upset by this characteristic: 'Thomas Babington Macaulay', in *Literary Studies*, ed. R. H. Hutton (1891), II, p. 221. But, unlike Stephen, Bagehot thought excessive energy was devoted to history's trivia – 'the superficies of circumstance, the scum of events' (p. 259).

136. M. M. Bevington, *The 'Saturday Review', 1855–1868*, p. 237. And see W. H. Dunn, *James Anthony Froude* (1963), II, ch. 28, 'Freeman the Froude-Slayer'.

137. Leslie Stephen, *Some Early Impressions*. Froude was able, though, through the columns of the *Pall Mall Gazette*, to challenge Freeman to substantiate his allegations of inaccurate scholarship: a challenge not taken up by Freeman. J. W. Robertson Scott, *The Story of the Pall Mall Gazette* (1950), p. 161.

138. Stephen thought Froude's work on Carlyle 'the best he has written'. Stephen to Lady Grant Duff, 17 April 1882. See Stephen's *Times* review of the work, 21 October 1884. Stephen and Froude differed, though, in their views on Carlyle's treatment of Jane Welsh Carlyle: 'Froude regards the publication of Mrs Carlyle's letters as a noble act of reparation on Carlyle's part to a woman he made miserable – I cannot say I see it in that light. I said [to Froude] that it was as if Johnson instead of standing bareheaded in Uttoxeter Market himself, had left a request in his will that

Boswell should go and do it instead of him . . . [Jane Carlyle's] are very clever letters however and certainly show she was a woman of very brilliant talent.' Stephen to Lady Grant Duff, 14 April 1883.

139. Frederic Harrison, 'Froude's Life of Carlyle', *Choice of Books* (1887), p. 176. Despite his broadly radical make-up, Harrison was critical of the biography's revelations in that they said nothing of substantive importance about Carlyle.

140. By this time Stephen already had to bear the upkeep of four children. Correspondence suggests that at least until the end of the 1850s Stephen's earnings as a barrister and journalist required supplementing by his father from the 'family purse': letters from Sir James, 27 April 1856 and 14 February 1858; Fitzjames to his wife, 18 October 1858 and 17 December 1859; sister Caroline to Fitzjames, 25 February 1858.

141. H. W. Law and I. Law, *The Book of the Beresford Hopes* (1925).

142. *Charles Henry Pearson: Memorials by Himself, His Wife and His Friends*, ed. W. Stebbing (1900), p. 91.

143. Stephen was requested to appear for Williams because of his known 'sympathy with the general position of the Broad Church Party': Leslie Stephen, *DNB* entry for his brother. Williams, though found guilty by the Court of Arches, was later acquitted by the Privy Council, and with it went 'the last hopes of eternal damnation' for the clergy of the Church of England. *Life*, pp. 186–7. See chapter 8 below.

144. *Life*, p. 214.

145. Quoted by Robertson Scott in *The Story of the Pall Mall Gazette*. Destruction of publishing records in the early part of the century makes impossible the definite attribution of most of Stephen's contributions. Limited attribution is provided by Leslie Stephen in *Life* and by Robertson Scott.

146. Robertson Scott, *The Story of the Pall Mall Gazette*, p. 157; *Life*, pp. 213–14.

147. *Life*, p. 215.

148. *Law Quarterly Review* (1895), XI, 383, at 384.

149. *Life*, p. 216.

150. *George Smith, A, Memoir* (1902), pp. 128–32.

151. Generally, Stephen Koss, *The Rise and Fall of the Political Press in Britain* (1981), I.

152. Greenwood left the *Pall Mall Gazette* in 1880, being succeeded by the more partisan Liberal John Morley, future biographer of Gladstone. In 1881 Greenwood founded the *St James' Gazette*, and Stephen, despite his position as a High Court judge, helped out in the paper's initial years by contributing a few articles: Robertson Scott, *The Story of the Pall Mall Gazette*.

153. 'Journalism', *Cornhill*, VI (1862), 52.

154. Ibid., 55. See similarly Maine, 'Our Newspaper Institutions', *Saturday Review*, I (1855), 2.

155. Maine took the same view; 'Political Dalliance', *Saturday Review*, II (1856), 672.

156. *Life*, p. 222. Stephen's two unsuccessful attempts as a Liberal parliamentary candidate are described in chapter 7 below.

157. *Life*, pp. 232–9.

158. Editions of 22 March and 15 April 1865.

159. For example, articles of 10 February and 5 June 1866.

160. *Life*, p. 241.

161. *Life*, p. 307. Each of the fifteen articles published between 5 November and 31 December was signed 'F'.

162. For example, editions of 22 July and 25 November 1872.

163. Letter, 24 April 1874.

3 A SCIENCE OF CRIMINAL LAW

1. Letter, 13 January 1880.
2. *Life*, p. 123.

3. The system was derived in part from Auguste Comte's *Course of Positive Philosophy* (1830–42). Mill's 'Historical' or 'Inverse Deductive' method was, basically, the determination of principles by observation (comparing particular cases) and verification by deducing them from general laws of human nature (bk VI, ch. X, section 7). Mill's partial discarding of simple syllogistic reasoning was because, though of 'testing' value, it was incapable of increasing the fund of knowledge of any subject: 'The syllogism is not the form in which we necessarily reason but a test of reasoning.' *Examination of Sir William Hamilton's Philosophy*, ch. XXII, in *Collected Works*, ed. J. M. Robson (1982), IX.

4. *Edinburgh Review*, CXVI (1863), 439. Mill suggests Austin's scheme for terminological and classificatory precision might be described as 'not so much a science of law as of the application of logic to law', p. 445.

5. *Recent British Philosophy* (1865), p. 12.

6. Leslie Stephen, *Some Early Impressions*, pp. 73 and 76. And similarly, for example, Henry Fawcett, *John Stuart Mill: His Life and Work* (1873), pp. 73–4.

7. Hereafter *General View*.

8. For the professional and practically orientated nature of legal texts during the period see generally D. Sugarman, 'The Making of the Textbook Tradition', in *Legal Theory and Common Law*, ed. W. L. Twining (1986).

9. *General View*, p. 337.

10. *Edinburgh Review*, CVII (1858), 465. In connection with Thomas Buckle's *History of Civilisation in England* (1857 and 1861), and his theories that scientific knowledge would soon be sufficient to predict human behaviour accurately, see Stephen, 'Buckle's *History of Civilization in England*', *Edinburgh Review*, CVII (1858), 465 and CXIV (1861), 183; and 'The Study of History', *Cornhill Magazine*, III (1861), 666 and IV (1861), 25. Mill approvingly cited Stephen's spirited defence of the influence of individual endeavour in the fifth edition of his *Logic* (1862), bk VI, ch. 11, the year after publication of Stephen's second *Cornhill* article.

11. *Edinburgh Review*, CXIV (1861), 456.

12. *A Treatise of Human Nature* (1740), III. I.

13. *Edinburgh Review*, CXIV (1861), 456, at 463–4.

14. W. L. Morison, *John Austin* (1982), pp. 5 and 149.

15. Mill to T. E. Cliffe Leslie, 20 December 1861, in *Collected Works*, XV, p. 756.

16. *Edinburgh Review*, CXIV (1861), 456, at 467.

17. Ibid., 470.

18. See H. Kantorowicz, 'Savigny and the Historical School of Law', *Law Quarterly Review* (1937), LIII, 330.

19. Maine suggested that 'Bentham and Austin sometimes write as if they thought that, although obscured by false theory, false logic, and false statement, there is somewhere behind all the delusions which they expose a framework of permanent legal conceptions which is discoverable by a trained eye, looking through a dry light, and to which a rational Code may always be fitted.' *Early Law and Custom* (1883), p. 360.

20. Respectively Professors of Jurisprudence at University College London and Oxford University. For example, Amos' *The Science of Law* (1874) and Pollock's *Essays in Jurisprudence and Ethics* (1882), viii.

21. *Edinburgh Review*, CXVI (1863), 442. Pollock believed Mill to be 'perhaps the last considerable writer on politics' to ignore the importance of the historical school. *An Introduction to the History of the Science of Politics* (1920), p. 126; and see S. Collini, D. Winch and J. Burrow, in *That Noble Science of Politics* (1983), pp. 145–50.

22. Quoted by C.H.S. Fifoot in his Selden Society Lecture, *Law and History in the Nineteenth Century* (1956), p. 17.

23. Austin himself claimed this: *Lectures on Jurisprudence*, particularly lectures XXXV–XXXVII and XXXIX–XLI.

24. *Edinburgh Review*, CXIV (1861), 453, at 484.
25. Ibid., 485. In many ways similar was Frederic Harrison's discussion of *Ancient Law* in the *Westminster Review*, XIX (1861), 457. And see also 'Maine's *Ancient Law*', *Saturday Review*, XI (1861), 167.
26. *General view*, p. 330. Similarly Maine: Austinian jurisprudence, the 'science of positive law . . . would doubtless if it were carried far, lead indirectly to great legal reforms by dispelling obscurities and dissipating delusions, but the investigation of the principles on which the direct improvement of substantive legal rules should be conducted belongs, nevertheless, not to the theorist on jurisprudence but to the theorist on legislation'. *Lectures on the Early History of Institutions* (1875), pp. 343–5.
27. *Of Laws in General*, ed. H.L.A. Hart (1970), ch. XIX.
28. *Works*, IV, p. 483.
29. Ibid., VII, p. 92; quoted by Lon Fuller in *Legal Fictions* (1967), p. 3.
30. *General View*, p. 332.
31. Such proposals surfaced quite frequently throughout the nineteenth century from Bentham's time (Draft Constitutional Code, Works, IX, 5); and cf. suggestions of the National Association for the Promotion of Social Science in 1862, and Lord Chancellor Westbury in 1863, 171 Official Reports (3rd series), 791. Stephen claimed that he and Maine had once drawn up a 'scheme' for Westbury. Letter to Lady Grant Duff, 11 September 1874. Also, see generally A. H. Manchester, *Modern Legal History* (1980), pp. 106–9 and L. Radzinowicz and R. Hood, *A History of English Criminal Law*, V (1986), p. 737n.
32. Originally appearing the *Saturday Review* during the 1860s and reprinted in *Horae Sabbaticae*, 3rd series (1892), 210 at p. 219.
33. *Edinburgh Review*, CXIV (1861), 456, at 485.
34. Along with a generation of jurists: see the standard texts of W. Markby, *Elements of Law* (1871) and T. E. Holland, *Elements of Jurisprudence* (1880).
35. *Edinburgh Review*, CXIV (1861), 472.
36. *General View*, p. 331.
37. Stephen knew, of course, that this was not actually written by Bentham but was a reconstruction of Bentham's manuscripts by Etienne Dumont. On the authenticity of this work see, for example, R. Harrison, *Bentham* (1983), xii–xiv.
38. He uses Austin's command theory in 1883 in the *History of Criminal Law*, II, p. 76.
39. Harrison published three articles on the 'English School of Jurisprudence' in the *Fortnightly Review*, XXIV, (1878), 475 and 682, and XXV, 114. In relation to Austin, Harrison was critical of the inadequate narrowness of Austinian analysis and definition of sovereignty.
40. 'Law and Command', *The Law Magazine and Review* (1872), 1, 189. Pollock was just 27 at the time. Holmes was also well alive to the deficiencies of Austinian analysis: see H. L. Pohlman, *Justice Oliver Wendell Holmes and Utilitarian Jurisprudence* (1984), chs. 1–3.
41. *For my Grandson* (1933), p. 35.
42. According to Pollock, he and Stephen at one time had plans for a joint digest on contract. *National Review*, XXV (1895), p. 820.
43. E. C. Clark's *Analysis of Criminal Liability* (1880) was heavily Austinian and, in part, derivative of the *General View*.
44. Hereafter *History* in the text and '*HCL*' in the notes.
45. C.H.S. Fifoot, *Judge and Jurist in the Reign of Victoria* (1959), p. 123.
46. Letters to G. S. Venables, 3 January 1882, and to Lady Grant Duff, 12 October and 10 November 1882.
47. Though Pike's work was more orientated towards the social causes of criminality.
48. Stephen to Lady Grant Duff, October 1883.
49. *HCL*, I, p. 5.
50. L. Radzinowicz, *Sir James Fitzjames Stephen (1829–1894) and his Contribution to the Development of Criminal Law*, Selden Society Lecture (London 1957), p. 23.

51. For Pollock, see the *National Review*, XXV (1895), 817; Maitland's views are repro-duced extensively in *Life*, pp. 415–17. Alone amongst distinguished legal historians is the dissenting view of Mr Justice Holmes: see *Pollock–Holmes Letters*, ed. M. De Wolfe Howe (1942), I, p. 21. Even someone as politically unsympathetic to Stephen's general views as Harold Laski found the *History* 'a little wooden in places but still an extraordinary performance'. Letter to Holmes, 26 September 1923, in *Holmes–Laski Letters*, ed. M. De Wolfe Howe (1953), I.
52. *General View*, p. 90.
53. *HCL*, II, p. 96.
54. Ibid., p. 78.
55. Ibid., p. 79.
56. Ibid., p. 81.
57. *General View*, pp. 99–100.
58. *The Science of Law*, p. 484.
59. For example, in *A First Book of Jurisprudence*, originally published in 1896; see 5th edn, p. 49.
60. *HCL*, II, p. 82.
61. Ibid., p. 82.
62. *Latter-Day Pamphlets* (1850), p. 84.
63. *Speeches*, p. 123.
64. Ch. 5, 'On the Connection between Justice and Utility'. Here Mill jettisoned the crude psychology of Bentham's pain and pleasure calculations account of punish-ment.
65. Radzinowicz and Hood, *History of English Criminal Law*, V (1986), p. 18.
66. Essay 1, 'The Vulgar Notion of Responsibility'. Later works of Bradley display a shift towards utilitarianism, for instance, his *Collected Essays* (1935).
67. *HCL*, II, p. 82.
68. Letter to Frederic Harrison, 20 June 1873, describing her reactions to Stephen's recently published *Liberty, Equality, Fraternity*. *The George Eliot Letters*, ed. Haight.
69. This construction of Stephen's theory of punishment is implicitly adopted by Sir Rupert Cross in *The English Sentencing System*, 2nd ed (1975), at pp. 124–5. When reviewing theories of punishment, Stephen's views are examined amongst utilitarian justifications. Radzinowicz, however, has labelled Stephen as Kantian in his expiatory notions of the functions of punishment. *Ideology and Crime* (1966), p. 27.
70. *HCL*, II, p. 80.
71. Ibid., p. 81.
72. The abbreviated account of the theory in *Liberty, Equality, Fraternity* is the most retributivistic in temper: 2nd edn. (1874), ed. R. J. White (1967), pp. 151–2.
73. *An Introduction to the Principles of Morals and Legislation*, ed. J. H. Burns and H.L.A. Hart (1982), ch. XIII, sect. 23 and footnote and ch. XVII. Bentham also accepted that the subsidiary role of punishment was the gratification of revenge – an un-doubted pleasure.
74. 'Capital Punishment', *Fraser's Magazine*, LXIX (1864), 753. Other articles discuss-ing the severity of punishment include 'Crime and Punishment', *Saturday Review*, I (1856), 431; 'Mr Phillips on Capital Punishment', *Saturday Review*, II (1856), 633; 'Mr Neate on Capital Punishment', *Saturday Review*, III (1857), 375; and 'Varia-tions in the Punishment of Crime', *Nineteenth Century*, XVII (1885), 755.
75. Though he originally favoured the death penalty for murder, Bentham's final view, on the grounds of utility (or its disutility) was for its complete abolition. *Works*, 1, p. 251.
76. In this there are echoes of the great eighteenth-century jurist Sir William Black-stone, who in his *Commentaries on the Laws of England* (1765–9), 4 Cmm., p. 5 described the system of criminal law as protecting against attacks 'the very being of society, which cannot possibly subsist [if criminal behaviour is] suffered to escape with impunity'.

77. p. 28.
78. *The Division of Labour in Society* (1893; trans. Simpson, 1933), p. 108. For a modern critique of Durkheim's theory of punishment see *The Power to Punish*, ed. D. Garland and P. Young (1983) ch. 2; and *Durkheim and the Law*, ed. S. Lukes and A. Scull (1983), chs. 3 and 4.
79. Maine is cited in *The Division of Labour*.
80. Report Cmd. (1953) 8932, para. 53.
81. Ch. 9, pp. 400–1. The American philosopher Joel Feinberg also recognises the denunciatory or expressive function of punishment, although he gives it less importance than Gross. See 'The Expressive Function of Punishment', in *Doing and Deserving* (1970) and also Walter Moberly in *The Ethics of Punishment* (1968), pp. 212–20.
82. See N. Walker, 'Punishing, Denouncing or Reducing crime', in *Reshaping the Criminal Law* ed. P. Glazebrook (1978), p. 391; 'The Ultimate Justification', in *Crime, Proof and Punishment* (1981), ed. C. F. Tapper; and R. A. Duff, *Trials and Punishments* (1986), pp. 235–45.
83. *HCL*, II, pp. 94–5.
84. *R v. Sleep* (1861) 8 Cox 477. And generally, J.W.C. Turner, 'The Mental Element in Crimes at Common Law', in L. Radzinowicz and J.W.C. Turner (eds.), *The Modern Approach to Criminal Law* (1945).
85. Such as abduction: *R v. Prince* (1875) 2 L.R. C.C.R. 14; *HCL*, II, p. 117. See also *Cundy v. Le Cocq* (1884) 13 Q.B.D. 207; and *R v. Tolson* (1889) 16 Cox 629.
86. *General view*, p. 119. Stephen wrote a critical commentary on the Report of the Capital Punishment Commission 1866. His disagreement centred on the recommended continued use of 'malice aforethought' for defining murder, and proposals that would blur the distinction between murder, and manslaughter – so, in Stephen's view, devaluing the moral impact of treating murder as a distinct offence. *Fraser's Magazine*, LXXIII (1866), 232. On the obscure and indirect nature of using 'malice' in defining the mental element of murder Stephen offered the following parody:

> Bread is either leavened or unleavened. Leaven is either express or implied. Express leaven is the substance called yeast. Leaven is implied in three cases: – First – it is implied in all white bread. Secondly – it is implied in all brown bread. Thirdly, and lastly – it is always implied in every sort of bread unless the person denying its presence can show that the bread in question contains no yeast.
> Surely this is rather a cumbrous way of saying that there either is or is not yeast in a loaf of bread. (p. 238)

87. *HCL*, III, p. 75.
88. A position not adopted in England until after the Homicide Act 1957. The 1879 Code contained a restricted felony–murder rule.
89. 1874 (315).
90. D. Seaborne-Davis, 'Child-Killing in English Law', p. 301, at pp. 326–7, in *The Modern Approach to Criminal Law*, ed. Radzinowicz and Turner and S. G. Vesey-Fitzgerald, 'The Reform of the Law of Murder', *Current Legal Problems* (1949) 2, 27.
91. *Holmes–Laski Letters*, ed. De Wolfe Howe, 2, 1207, and M. De Wolfe Howe, *Justice Oliver Wendell Holmes – The Shaping Years* (1957), pp. 227–8.
92. M. De Wolfe Howe, *Justice Oliver Wendell Holmes – The Proving Years* (1963), p. 102.
93. For Holmes' general approach to legal philosophy, see Pohlman, *Justice Oliver Wendell Holmes and Utilitarian Jurisprudence*.
94. Particularly chs. 2 and 3. See generally, P. S. Atiyah, 'The Legacy of Holmes Through English Eyes', *Boston University Law Review* (1983), 63, 341.
95. It was 'clear' to Holmes that the '*ultima ratio* . . . of private persons is force, and

that at the bottom of all private relations . . . and all social feelings, is a justifiable self-preference'. *Lectures on the Common Law*, ed. De Wolfe Howe, p. 38. See ch. 2, 'Utility, Morality and Liability', of H. L. Pohlman's *Justice Oliver Wendell Holmes and Utilitarian Jurisprudence* for an account of the degree to which Holmes' objective theory of liability can be attributed to the works of Benham and Austin.

96. *Lectures on the Common Law*, ed. De Wolfe Howe, pp. 43–4.
97. Ibid., p. 40.
98. *HCL*, II, p. 79.
99. Bentham's argument that the threat of punishment can only deter an individual culpable mind ignores the possibility that the actual infliction of punishment regardless of an absence of *mens rea* or presence of excusing conditions may be effective in promoting general deterrence and observance by others. See H.L.A. Hart, *Punishment and Responsibility* (1968), ch. 2, pp. 42–4.
100. Bentham, *An Introduction to the Principles of Morals and Legislation*, ed. Burns and Hart, chs. XII and XIII.
101. Particularly H.L.A. Hart in *Punishment and Responsibility*, ch. 2.
102. *Pollock–Holmes Letters*, ed. De Wolfe Howe.
103. p. 220. Maine made a similar observation in 'The Moral of McNeill', *Saturday Review*, I (1856), 285, when discussing low cultural standards in America, 'where every Jefferson Brick is "one of the most remarkable men in the country" '.
104. Acknowledged by Howe in *The Proving Years*; for example, pp. 266–72. This intellectual niggardliness is also noted by E. Cahn in 'Fact-Skepticism: An Unexpected Chapter', *New York University Law Review* (1963), 38, 1025, at 1026. As Cahn astutely observes about Holmes' silence: 'It is not our debtors we find trouble in forgiving, it is our creditors.'
105. *Lectures on Jurisprudence*, 5th edn (1885), XVIII–XIX: before Brown, Hobbes, Locke and Hume had all made the association of will with action.
106. Professor Hart in *Punishment and Responsibility* is an advocate of this approach; although the Austinian view still finds some support. For example, J. L. Mackie, 'The Grounds of Responsibility', in *Law, Morality and Society*, ed. P.M.S. Hacker and J. Raz (1977), p. 175.
107. *Common Law*, p. 54.
108. *General View*, pp. 76–81; *HCL*, II, pp. 99–101.
109. *HCL*, II, p. 102.
110. *D.P.P. for Northern Ireland* v. *Lynch* [1975] A.C. 653; accepted in *R.* v. *Howe* [1987] 1 All ER 771.
111. *HCL*, II, p. 107. Hobbes took the view that duress should provide a defence because a person under duress was no longer enjoying the benefits of the state's protection: *Leviathan*, ch. 27.
112. Stephen's argument that 'duress' should only mitigate punishment was seen as a more attractive way of recognising its relevance by Lords Bridge and Griffiths in *Howe*.
113. The matter was neither included nor expressly excluded, thus leaving the common law free to invent the defence. The question had led to earlier disagreement with previous Commissioners; see the 1833 Commission, Seventh Report and the 1845 Commission, Second Report. Considered by R. Cross in *Reshaping the Criminal Law*, ed. Glazebrook, p. 13.
114. *HCL*, I, p. 110.
115. See the recent analysis of A.W.B. Simpson in *Cannibalism and the Common Law* (1984).
116. Chapter XIX. His earlier writing on the subject includes 'Are Madmen Responsible?', *Saturday Review*, I (1856), 298; 'The Case of William Dove, *Saturday Review*, II (1856), 100; 'Criminal Responsibility of Madmen', Papers read before the Juridical Society (1858), 1855–8, 1, 67; 'Responsibility and Mental Competence', *The Law Magazine and Review* (1865), XVIII, 26.

117. *HCL*, II, p. 125.
118. The most distinguished and influential English medical author of the time was Henry Maudsley. Stephen's bibliography includes three works of Maudsley, the most relevant to Stephen's position being *Responsibility in Mental Disease*, originally published in 1874. Stephen also solicited T. H. Huxley's views on the subject. Stephen to Huxley, 13 May 1881, Huxley Papers, Imperial College.
119. For example H. Gross, *Theory of Criminal Justice* (1979), pp. 309–13, and J. Hall, *General Principles of Criminal Law*, 2nd edn (1960), ch. XIII.
120. *HCL*, II, p. 171. Stephen had noted much the same in 'Locke as a Moralist', *Horae Sabbaticae*, II, p. 123 at p. 124.
121. See particularly *Davis* (1881) 14 Cox 563. Stephen's direction on the ambit of the M'Naughten Rules was exceedingly broad: 'As I understand the law, any disease which so disturbs the mind that you cannot think calmly and rationally of all the different reasons to which we refer in considering the rightness or wrongness of an action – any disease which so disturbs the mind that you cannot perform that duty with some moderate degree of calmness and reason may be fairly said to prevent a man from knowing that what he did was wrong' (p. 564).
122. The 1874 (s.24(d)) and 1878 (s.20) provisions contained elements expanding the M'Naughten test to cover disease which prevented the actor from 'controlling his own conduct' – intended to deal with 'an impulse to commit a crime so violent that the offender would not' be responsible: Stephen in the Criminal Code Bill Commission Report speaking of his 1878 bill. In 1875, when charged with the task of supervising R. S. Wright's draft Jamaican Code, Stephen with Wright devised a test for insanity, part of which included a provision whereby acquittal should take place when the defendant acted 'under the influence of a delusion of such a nature as to render him, in the opinion of the jury, an unfit subject for punishment of any kind in respect of such act' (s.104). See M. L. Friedland, 'R. S. Wright's Model Criminal Code', (1981) I *Oxford Journal of Legal Studies*, 307, at 331. Prior to this, nothing in earlier Commission Reports had attempted to incorporate an 'irresistible impulse' excuse. See the broad M'Naughten formulation both the case in Seventh Report of the 1833 Commissioners, 1843, Article 1; and after the case, by the 1845 Commissioners in their Second Report, 1846, Articles 1 and 2.
123. The Butler Committee Report, Cmnd. (1975) 6244.
124. p. 184.
125. (1905), p. 10.
126. *English Constitution* (1872).
127. *HCL*, II, p. 96; and also *Liberty, Equality, Fraternity*, pp. 158–60.
128. Chapter 2 above.
129. *HCL*, II, p. 75.
130. *General View*, pp. 100 and 120.

4   'LAW LIVING AND ARMED' – THE MECHANISM OF ENFORCEMENT

1. Stephen after Hobbes, *HCL*, I, p. 456.
2. *General view*, pp. 232–3.
3. *Dissertations and Discussions*, I, p. 368.
4. Reproduced in the *Fortnightly Review*, XII (1872), 644.
5. Cf. Austin's comment on the 'empires of chaos and darkness' in *Lectures on Jurisprudence* (1863), lecture 39.
6. Ibid., lecture 37.
7. Fifoot, *Judge and Jurist in the Reign of Victoria*, p. 10. For Austin's consideration of the need for and value of codification see *Lectures on Jurisprudence*, lectures 38 and 39.
8. Quoted by A. Harding in *A Social History of English Law* (1966), p. 357. For an ex-

cellent consideration of Bentham's attitude to the common law, see G. J. Postema, *Bentham and the Common Law Tradition* (1986), chs. 6–8.

9. *Works of Jeremy Bentham*, ed. J. Bowring (1843), X, 531, and III, 464; hereafter '*Works*'.

10. *Works*, IV, 460.

11. *Works*, III, 210.

12. Quoted by S. H. Kadish, 'Codifiers of the Criminal Law: Wechler's Predecessors' *Columbia Law Review* (1978), 78, 1098, at 1100. Dumont was later a translator of Bentham's *Treatise of Evidence* from French into English.

13. *The Spirit of the Age* (1825), p. 21.

14. Ibid., p. 121.

15. An intellectual or doctrinal account of the reform movement. But see, for example, M. A. Rustigan's challenge to this conventional wisdom in 'A Reinterpretation of Criminal Law Reform in Nineteenth Century England', *Journal of Criminal Justice* (1980), 8, 205. P. B. Kurland and D.M.W. Waters ('Public Prosecution in England, 1854–1879', *Duke Law Journal* (1959), 9, 493), without disputing Bentham's role, demonstrate the force of threatened self-interest in generating law reforms. And see also generally D. Hay, 'Property, Authority and the Criminal Law', in *Albion's Fatal Tree*, ed. D. Hay et al. (1975).

16. One of 'The School of Bentham': C. Phillipson, *Three Criminal Law Reformers* (1923), p. 231.

17. An assessment of the individual commissioners is provided by R. Cross in 'The Reports of the Criminal Law Commissioners', in *Reshaping the Criminal Law*, ed. Glazebrook, p. 5. For a consideration of particular reform proposals see also A. H. Manchester, 'Simplifying the Sources of the Law', *Anglo-American Law Review* (1973), 395 and 527; and generally, S. H. Kadish's comparative study, 'Codifiers of the Criminal Law: Wechsler's Predecessors' *Columbia Law Review* (1978), 78, 1098.

18. See W. R. Cornish, 'Criminal Justice and Punishment', in *Crime and Law in Nineteenth Century Britain*, ed. Cornish et al (1978); and L. Radzinowicz and R. Hood, *A History of English Criminal Law*, V (1986), ch. 22.

19. Parliamentary Papers (1854), LIII, 389.

20. *Edinburgh Review*, XCIX (1854), 573. Stephen in a *Saturday Review* article of 18 October 1856 was similarly critical of the judiciary's behaviour on this occasion.

21. *Wellesley Index to Victorian Periodicals*, ed. W. E. Houghton (1966), I, p. 503.

22. *Edinburgh Review*, XCIX (1854), 573 at 576–81.

23. For a detailed account of the criminal law reform movement at the time see A. H. Manchester, 'Lord Cranworth's Attempt to Consolidate the Statute Law of England and Wales 1853–1859', *Anglo-American Law Review* [1973], 395.

24. I, 252 and II, 545. Also 'The Characteristics of English Criminal Law', *Cambridge Essays* (1857).

25. I, 252.

26. *Saturday Review*, II, 546.

27. During 1862/3, Lord Chancellor Westbury had advocated a comprehensive scheme for the digesting of case law as a basis for future codes. This initial work of digesting would be executed by a 'body of rédacteurs, of whom six will be working paid barristers, chiefly young men of proven ability, who would work under the superintendence of myself, the Attorney General and Solicitor General . . . Each of the six expurgators will have a particular portion of the reports assigned to him.' T. A. Nash, *Life of Richard Lord Westbury* (1888), II, pp. 62–4. It is quite likely that Stephen had his eye on one of these posts when completing the *General View*. Moreover, Westbury knew of Stephen, having recommended him for the Recordership of Newark (*Life*, p. 169) in 1859, and Westbury's schemes when Attorney-General in 1857 also seem to have promised something for Stephen (Sir James to Fitzjames, 6 August 1857). Stephen's dismay at Westbury's resignation in 1865 (*Life*, pp. 169 and 225) was doubtless prompted by genuine admiration of this

forceful man for his reforming efforts, and also by thoughts of possible preferment disappearing.

28. Leslie Stephen relates an 'absurd little anecdote' connected with the bill: 'Fitzjames had gone to stay with Froude, in a remote corner of Wales; and wishing to refer to the draft telegraphed to the Recorder of London: "Send Homicide Bill." The official to whom this message had to be sent at some distance from the house declined to receive it. If not a coarse practical joke, he thought it was a request to forward into that peaceful region a wretch whose nickname was too clearly significant of his blood thirsty propensities.' *Life*, pp. 304–5.

29. Fitzjames to Leslie Stephen, 17 June 1872.

30. Report of Select Committee on Homicide Law Amendment Bill 1874 (315). Ten years before Lowe had used a flattering review of the *General View* as a peg on which to hang a broad discourse on the great need for criminal law reform. *Edinburgh Review*, CXXI (1865), 109; attributed to Lowe, *Wellesley Index*. But in the intervening period Stephen, when Legal Member of the Indian Council, had very vigorously crossed swords with the Indian Law Commission, one of whom was Lowe. See chapter 6 below.

31. 57 (1874), 243; quoted by Manchester, *Anglo-American Law Review* (1973), 530.

32. Report, p. 46 (q) 313.

33. *Lectures on Jurisprudence*, lecture 37.

34. *Digest of the Criminal Law (Crimes and Punishments)* (1877), p. 366.

35. Ibid., x.

36. Letter, 20 January. Lord Chancellor's Office files, L.C.O. 1/42. Holker's communications with Lord Chancellor Cairns show Holker to have been a very strong advocate of the Code and Stephen's participation in its creation; letters of 5 March and 1 June 1877, L.C.O. 1/42. Stephen told Lytton that he had 'been pressing the Lord Chancellor to let me draw an English Penal Code for him', 19 July 1877. Stephen also organised public lectures on the subject; on one occasion enlisting Lord Coleridge C. J. to chair the event. The importance of press coverage was something which did not escape Stephen. Letters from Stephen to Lord Broadhurst, 4, 9 and 11 December 1876; and 15 and 23 January 1877. Broadhurst Papers, London School of Economics and Political Science.

37. Writing to Lady Grant Duff, Stephen speaks of devoting practically the whole of his time on the project, 25 August 1877.

38. The proposals for homicide provide a rough (though not infallible) index of the degree of reforming innovation found in the 1845/9 Commission and the later efforts of Stephen and the 1879 Commission. The Second Report of the 1845 Commission (1846) expressly followed the radical ideas of Livingstone's Louisiana Code by defining murder simply as 'wilful' homicide without extenuating conditions (p. 24), and suggesting a special offence of 'negligent homicide' (p. 31). Stephen's 1872/4 Homicide Bill and 1878 bill very broadly followed Macaulay's Indian Code (see chapter 6 below), adopting the more moderate stance of abandoning the felony-murder rule and replacing 'malice aforethought' with a requirement of either intention or subjective foresight of probable serious bodily harm, with manslaughter being retained as an offence based on actual foresight of some bodily harm – not just objective negligence. The 1879 Code Commission, although still eliminating 'malice aforethought', permitted the presence of a restricted form of felony-murder. Overall, the broad trend from 1845 (and 1833) to 1879 was one of a diminution in reforming zeal, both in how extensive changes might be, and how accessible the language of the law ought to be. By 1879, the lesson of earlier failures and the evaporation of Benthamite enthusiasm combined to produce less ambitious goals.

39. For his work in drafting the Code he received 1,500 guineas and a further 1,500 guineas for acting as a commissioner. In 1876 and 1877 Stephen's annual earnings had been about £4,000, which despite his mixed success at the Bar was a high

earned income for the day. See Manchester, *Modern Legal History*, p. 74.

40. *HCL*, I, vi.

41. 247 Hansard Debates, 953 (3rd series 1879).

42. M. D. Chalmers, *Law Quarterly Review* (1886), II, 125, at 126.

43. In 1881 and 1883 procedural elements of the Code were unsuccessfully introduced. Writing privately to Stephen on 17 July 1882, Sir John Holker reports that Harcourt, the Home Secretary, would try to push through the procedural parts of the Code.

44. 11 December 1879. Stephen also expressed his intention to win round Cockburn by a measure of 'judicious flattery'. Stephen to Lytton, 29 December 1879.

45. Stephen's suggestion that Cockburn was unhappy at being left out of the Commission is supported by a letter from Lord Chancellor Cairns to Cockburn clearly attempting to smooth ruffled feathers. Copy letter 15 July 1878, PRO 30/51.

46. *Nineteenth Century*, VII (1880), 136, at 140.

47. Ibid., 143.

48. Ibid., 154.

490. *Shaw* v *DPP* [1962] AC 220.

50. *Knuller* v *DPP* [1973] AC 435.

51. A form of statutory epitaph for the 1879 Code was created when it was later taken up as the basis for the criminal codes of Canada and New Zealand and in parts of Australia.

52. Later to become Mr Justice Wright.

53. M. L. Friedland's account of Wright's role in codification, 'R. S. Wright's Model Criminal Code', (1981) 1 *Oxford Journal of Legal Studies*, 307. As Friedland shows, Wright's Jamaican Code – vetted by Stephen at the Colonial Office's request – contained a more innovatory and comprehensive approach to codification than Stephen's own work, having much in common with Macaulay's Indian Code. In part this was attributable to the fact that the Code was not for home consumption – experimentation in foreign parts was more readily acceptable to the British Parliament. The Statute Law Committee looked to a gradual phased move to codification, first by amending and consolidating the law, and eventually by codification (Committee memo, 2 January 1878, LCO 1/42; Friedland, p. 321).

54. Friedland, p. 321 and LCO 1/42.

55. The bill certainly enjoyed support from many journals; the *Edinburgh Review* summarised the Code as 'a magnificent piece of legislation', CL (1879), 524, at 556. Also the obituary notice of Lord Cockburn in *Solicitors' Journal* (1880), 66, 77 and *Law Magazine and Review* (1879), 4, 31.

56. Amos, *The Science of Law*, p. 383. Also, generally, Amos' *An English Code* (1873). Amos' father, Andrew Amos, as well as serving as a member of Brougham's Criminal Law Commissions, was also Macaulay's successor in India.

57. Frederic Maitland, introduction to O. Gierke, *Political Theories of the Middle Age*, XV (1900).

58. 'Vom Beruf unserer Zeit für Gesetzgebung und Rechtswissenschaft' (On the Vocation of our Time for Codification and Jurisprudence) (1814).

59. *Nineteenth Century*, VII (1880), 136, at 152.

60. *Essays in Jurisprudence and Ethics* (1882), p. 287, and his discussion of codification in the introduction to *Digest of the Law of Partnership* (1877).

61. 26 July 1877, in *Pollock–Holmes Letters*, ed. De Wolfe Howe.

62. 'Codes and the Arrangement of the Law', *American Law Review* (1870), 1, 5; reprinted in *Harvard Law Review* (1930), 44, 725.

63. *Nineteenth Century*, VII (1880), 136, at 158.

64. P. S. Atiyah, *The Rise and Fall of Freedom of Contract* (1979), p. 660.

65. This aspect of codification is discussed by Sir Courtney Ilbert in *Legislative Methods and Forms* (1901), pp. 18–19, and 148f. Ilbert, a leading parliamentary draughtsman, was Stephen's eventual successor in India. Stephen was not 'specially flat-

tered' by Ilbert's Indian appointment; letter to Lady Grant Duff of 20 February 1882.

66. *HCL*, III, pp. 366–7.
67. Introduction to *Digest of Evidence*, 4th edn (1893), p. vi.
68. Ibid., p. viii. The book went to twelve editions, the last appearing in 1948.
69. In Mill's view, one of the 'richest in matter of all Bentham's productions'. *Autobiography*, p. 116.
70. *General View*, 2nd edn (1890), p. 206.
71. *Introduction to the Indian Evidence Act* p. 7.
72. For example, the *Treatise on Evidence*, p. 180. A perceptive and valuable account of developments during this period is provided by W. L. Twining, 'The Rationalist Tradition of Evidence Scholarship', in *Well and Truly Tried*, ed. E. Campbell and L. Waller (1982); and *Theories of Evidence: Bentham and Wigmore* (1985). See also *Facts in Law*, ed. W. L. Twining (1983), and *Legal Theory and Common Law*, ed. Twining, ch. 4.
73. *General view*, 2nd edn, p. 206.
74. Ibid., p. 206.
75. Stephen's 'Speech on the [Indian] Evidence Bill', 31 March 1871; appended to the *Introduction to the Indian Evidence Act*, p. 25.
76. *Digest*, p. xx.
77. Stephen first felt obliged to tackle the philosophically formidable notions of 'belief' and 'fact' because of their fundamental roles in the judicial process. Bentham's idiosyncratic 'scale of persuasion' (*Treatise*, bk 1, ch. 17) he rightly dismissed as unsoundly based on the view that levels of belief were precise enough to be comparatively quantified. But Stephen's alternative proposal that the strength of belief was not so much a question of intensity as of 'stability' (indicated by the cogency of the evidence needed to overturn that particular belief) (*General View*, p. 245) was hardly more convincing. As for the nature of 'fact' or 'knowledge', Stephen shows himself to have been well aware of the epistemological difficulties involved, but was naturally unwilling to wade more than ankle deep into that particular philosophical quagmire, contenting himself instead with the working conclusion that 'without entering upon the question of the existence of the external world, it may be asserted with confidence that our knowledge of it is composed, *first*, of our perceptions; and *secondly*, of the inferences which we draw from them as to what we should perceive if we were favourably situated for that purpose' (*Introduction to the Indian Evidence Act*, pp. 14–15). Cf. W. M. Best, *Principles of Evidence* (1849), para. 60.
78. *General View*, p. 258.
79. Ibid., p. 239.
80. Ibid., p. 263.
81. Ibid., pp. 256–7. The issue of the extent to which non-mathematical weighting of judicial evidence might be used has provoked strongly conflicting views, as exchanges between philosophers like L. J. Cohen and jurists such as Professor Glanville Williams and Sir Richard Eggleston have shown. See Cohen, *The Probable and the Provable* (1977), Eggleston, *Evidence, Proof and Probability*, 2nd edn (1983) and Williams, *Criminal Law Review* (1979), 297 and 340.
82. In his speech before the Indian Legislative Council (p. 22) on the Evidence Bill Stephen described the existing law as a 'half and half system' of the elaborate English law mixed with one of 'unaided mother-wit and natural shrewdness' – in which a 'vast body of half understood law totally destitute of arrangement and of uncertain authority, maintains a dead-alive existence'. Prior to Stephen's tenure in India, the Indian Law Commissioners had drawn up their own Draft Evidence Bill. Both Stephen and Maine thought it 'very bad' (Stephen to Argyll, 25 July 1870, Argyll Papers, India Office Library). The fundamental defect of the Commissioners' Draft Bill was its dependence on knowledge of English law. See Stephen's com-

ments in his speech on the Evidence Bill (p. 21). Writing to M. E. Grant Duff, Maine complained, the 'least credible of all is the draft law of evidence . . . ill arranged and inaccurate and so little adequate to India . . . ' . 22 December 1868, Grant Duff Papers, private collection of Mrs S. Sokolov-Grant.

83. See R. Cross and C. Tapper, *Cross on Evidence*, 6th edn (1985), p. 50.

84. *Digest*, Article 1.

85. *Omychund v Barker* (1745) 1 Atk. 21, 49.

86. Thayer, *Treatise*, ch. 11.

87. *Digest*, pp. ix–x and *Introduction to the Indian Evidence Act*.

88. 1872, pp. 51–67. Cf. slightly later in his *Village Communities*, 3rd edn (1876), p. 319.

89. Although see G. C. Whitworth, *The Theory of Relevancy for the Purpose of Judicial Evidence* (1875). Whitworth's criticisms of some of the detailed effects of the theory were acknowledged by Stephen and resulted in modifications of its verbal formulation.

90. Thayer, *Treatise*, pp. 269 and 530.

91. Stephen argues the contrary in his *Digest*, chs. IV and VI.

92. Despite the limitations of the doctrine of relevancy, Stephen's historically early recognition (as most clearly set out in the *Introduction to the Indian Evidence Act*) of the inherent restrictions on the actual fact-finding abilities of courts was readily acknowledged by the American Realist jurist Jerome Frank. In his work on 'fact-skepticism' – our capacity to ascertain the transactions of the past (generally *Courts on Trial* (1949) – Frank attributed to Stephen a modern realism in his attitude towards the frailty of witness testimony and the limited measures possible to offset such difficulties. See ' "Short of Sickness and Death": A Study of Moral Responsibility in Legal Criticism', *New York University Law Review* (1951), 26, 545 at 559–64; and E. Cahn, 'Fact-Skepticism: An Unexpected Chapter', *New York University Law Review* (1963), 38, 1025 at 1028.

93. *Law Quarterly Review* (1899), XV, 86. Pollock in his review of Stephen's *Digest*, in the *Fortnightly Review*, 20 (1876), 383, pre-empted much of Thayer's case against relevancy, although Pollock did not express his doubts as effectively as Thayer.

94. *General View*, p. 324.

95. Z. Cowen and P. B. Carter, *Essays on the Law of Evidence* (1956), ch. II. J. P. Taylor's evidence on reform, Parliamentary Papers (1845), XIV appendix C.

96. *General View*, pp. 323–4.

97. Cf. the general thesis of Douglas Hay in 'Property, Authority and the Criminal Law', *Albion's Fatal Tree*.

98. *Rationale of Judicial Evidence*, bk 7, ch. 13, s.4.

99. *General View*, p. 292. William Best's generally progressive *Principles of Evidence* expressed the belief that religion tended to raise the standard of truth and irreligion lowered it: para. 151.

100. *General View*, p. 293.

101. Criminal Law Amendment Act. The main effect of this Act was to make those accused of rape or certain other sexual offences competent but not compellable witnesses.

102. *Nineteenth Century*, II (1877), 737 at 754–7, and the 1879 Code. And similarly as an experienced judge in the *Nineteenth Century*, XX (1886), 453.

103. See Lord Birkenhead, *Fourteen English Judges* (1926), pp. 333–4 and Lord Alverstone, *Recollection of Bar and Bench* (1915), p. 176.

104. *HCL*, I, p. 440; preface dated 1882.

105. Discussed at *HCL*, III, p. 335. The existence of these provisions in the 1872 Act show that Stephen had experienced a change of heart on the competence of defendants as witnesses not more than nine years after the publication of the *General View*, in which he had not favoured such a change: p. 201.

106. Cmnd. 4991. See generally the references and comments in *Cross on Evidence*, 6th edn, and Draft Bill, clauses 1 and 5.
107. *Works*, VII, 599, and *Treatise*, bk III, ch. 1; on the inferences from a defendant's silence see *Works*, VII, 444–7.
108. Quoted by H.L.A. Hart in *Essays on Bentham* (1982), p. 23.
109. See Twining's cogent analysis of the 'rationalist' tradition in 'The Rationalist Tradition of Evidence Scholarship'.
110. Hart, *Essays on Bentham*, p. 4.
111. *Nineteenth Century*, XX (1886), 453 at 472.
112. Sydney Smith, from his review 'Bentham's Book of Fallacies', *Edinburgh Review*, XLII (1825), 367; quoted by Hart, *Essays on Bentham*.
113. *General View*, pp. 207 and 232.
114. *Lectures on Jurisprudence* (1763), ed. R. L. Meek et al. (1978), p. 208. On the political/economic ideology of the functioning appearance of the criminal justice system see, for example, R. McGowen, 'The Image of Justice and Reforms of the Criminal Law in Early Nineteenth Century England', *Buffalo Law Review* (1983), 32, 89.
115. *General View*, p. 170. See D. Phillips' case studies in *Crime and Authority in Victorian England* (1977), ch. 4. For a discussion of the political psychology of Tory opposition to an effective police force and prosecution system see D. Phillips in *Crime and the Law*, ed. V.A.C. Gatrell et al. (1980), ch. 6. On the mid nineteenth-century reform attempts see P. B. Kurland and D.M.W. Waters, 'Public Prosecutions in England, 1854–1879', *Duke Law Journal* (1959), 9, 493.
116. 24 December 1879, 9.
117. *General View*, p. 170. Stephen had covered some of the same ground in 'Criminal Law and the Detection of Crime', *Cornhill Magazine*, II (1860), 697.
118. *General View*, p. 172; and also 'Public Prosecutors', *Saturday Review*, II (1856), 316.
119. *HCL*, I, p. 442.
120. *General View*, pp. 171–2. Earlier criticisms in similar vein occur in his *Saturday Review* article 'The Trial of Bacon', IV (1857), 103.
121. The issue is discussed in the Second Report of the Royal Commission on Criminal Law in 1836 and in the parliamentary debates leading up to the Prisoners' Counsel Act 1836.
122. *General View*, p. 225.
123. *HCL*, I, p. 313.
124. Report of Select Committee of House of Lords (1848) no. 523, pp. 13 and 19.
125. 1866 Report no. 3590.
126. *General View*, pp. 230–1.
127. *Nineteenth Century*, II (1877), 737, at 758.
128. C. (1879) 2345, sections 538–46.
129. *HCL*, I, pp. 313–18.
130. p. 172. His 'conclusive' objection was that most appeals 'must be regarded as exceptional and must be treated so'. A Court of Criminal Appeal would add a further tier to the judicial process, making an appeal almost an expectation. Furthermore, it was inconsistent with the jury system (p. 175).
131. Cd. (1904) 2315.
132. *HCL*, I, p. 566.
133. *HCL*, I, p. 572. Bentham's general opposition to juries was partly based on similar objections: a jury was a 'parcel of people you know nothing of, except that they are house-keeping tradesmen, or something of that sort, are got together by haphazard, or by what ought to be haphazard, to the number of twelve and shut up together in a place from which they cannot get out till the most obstinate among them has subdued the rest'. *Works*, VII, p. 388.
134. For example, *Westminster Review*, XLI (1872), 289.
135. *HCL*, I, p. 574.

136. *HCL* , I, p. 574. Bentham, likewise, saw that the best reason for retention of juries was their popularity. *Works*, IV, p. 359.
137. (1891), p. 497.
138. See the discussion of W. R. Cornish in *The Jury* (1971), ch. 5.
139. Vol. 3, p. 379 of his *Commentaries on the Laws of England*, first published in the 1760s.
140. *Trial by Jury* (1971), pp. 164–5.
141. A. V. Dicey, *Lectures on the relation between Law and Public Opinion in England during the Nineteenth Century* (1905), lecture IV. A classification often since seen as misleadingly oversimplified: see, for example, G. Kitson Clark, *The Making of Victorian England* (1962) and Atiyah, *The Rise and Fall of Freedom of Contract*, pp. 226–37.
142. A view shared by D. Hay, 'The Criminal Prosecution in England and its Historians', *Modern Law Review* (1984), 47, 1.
143. *Liberty, Equality, Fraternity*, p. 151.
144. Quoted by Sir William Holdsworth in *Some Makers of English Law* (1938), p. 252.

5   THE THREAT OF 'HOOFS AND HOBNAILS'

1. See Macaulay's 1829 essays 'Mill on Government'; 'Westminster Reviewers' Defence of Mill'; and 'Utilitarian Theory of Government' in *Works*, V. In Bentham's case see, for example, *Plan for Parliamentary Reform*, in *Works*, III. Whether James Mill was advocating universal suffrage in his 'Essay on Government' (1820) has been a source of extensive dispute: see, for example, W. Thomas, 'James Mill's politics: the "Essay on Government" and the Movement for Reform', *Historical Journal*, 12 (1969), 249.
2. Utilitarianism did not necessarily entail democratic government; Hume believed the interests of the masses were best served by a government of the few.
3. *Works*, ed. Lady Trevelyan (1866), VI, p. 94.
4. *Recollections* (1917), 1, pp. 168–9, quoted by J. Roach in 'Liberalism and the Victorian Intelligentsia', *Cambridge Historical Journal*, 13 (1957), 61.
5. 'Liberalism', *Cornhill Magazine*, V (1862), 71, at 72–3.
6. G. M. Trevelyan, *British History in the Nineteenth Century* (1937), p. 343. Stephen later talked of his belief in the need for a 'liberal Toryism' to replace 'old fashioned and stupid Toryism': Stephen to Lytton, 31 August 1880, Lytton Papers, County Record Office, Hertford.
7. G. M. Young, *Daylight and Champaign* (1937); quoted by N. Annan, *Leslie Stephen* (1984), p. 211.
8. Hansard CLXXXII, 147–8 and CLXXXVI 62; quoted by F. B. Smith in *The Making of the Second Reform Bill* (1966).
9. *Fortnightly Review*, IX (1868), 645.
10. For an account of the immediate political antecedents of the Second Reform Act, see M. Cowling, *1867 Disraeli, Gladstone and Revolution* (1967), particularly pp. 1–79.
11. A review of the political forces responsible for the Third Reform Act is provided by A. Jones in *The Politics of Reform* (1972), pp. 1–16.
12. W.E.H. Lecky, *History of Rationalism*, II (1865), p. 354.
13. Carlyle, *Past and Present* (1843).
14. Ruskin, *The Political Economy of Art* (1857) and *Unto this Last* (1862).
15. Carlyle, *Chartism* (1839).
16. Carlyle, 'Shooting Niagara: and After?', *Macmillan's Magazine*, XVI (1867), 319.
17. Ibid., 319.
18. G. M. Young, *Victorian England: Portrait of an Age*, 2nd edn (1953), p. 48n.
19. Leslie Stephen, *Hours in a Library* (1892 edn), III, 'Carlyle's Ethics'.
20. 'Mr Carlyle', *Fraser's Magazine'*, LXXII (1865), 778.

21. Ibid., 792.
22. Ibid., 793. See similarly Stephen's critical discussion of *Past and Present* and *Latter-Day Pamphlets* in 'Mr Carlyle', *Saturday Review*, V (1858), 638.
23. 'The Prophet of Culture', *Macmillan's Magazine*, XVI (1867), 271.
24. Vol. II, 'Guizot's Essays and Lectures' (1845). Stephen's reaction is found in the *Saturday Review*, VII (1859), 76.
25. S. Coulling, *Matthew Arnold and His Critics* (1974), p. 141.
26. Cf. *History of England*, in Macaulay, *Works*, II, p. 464: The predominance in 'English legislation' of the 'practical' over the 'speculative' was a 'fault', but one on the 'right side'.
27. 'Responsible Government', in *Works*, VI, p. 99.
28. Much the same complaint about Carlyle is made by Stephen in 'Mr Carlyle', *Saturday Review*, V (1858), 19 June, reprinted in *Essays by a Barrister* (1862).
29. *Saturday Review*, XVIII (1864), 683. Possibly feeling he had been a touch too savage with Arnold, Stephen sent his wife to call on Mrs Arnold a few days after the appearance of the article. Personal relations between Arnold and Stephen had been just a little sensitive since Stephen's *Edinburgh* review of *Tom Brown's Schooldays* (1858), in which Thomas Arnold was portrayed as a man of great virtue incapable of a balanced assessment of the relative seriousness of the various evils in life. According to Matthew Arnold, Stephen's review was in part responsible for 'Rugby Chapel': see his letter of 8 August 1867, *Clough Letters* (1932). However, 'Rugby Chapel' is dated November 1857.
30. In his review of *Essays in Criticism*, 'Mr Matthew Arnold amongst the Philistines' (*Saturday Review*, XIX (1865), 235) Stephen found it an 'excellent little volume' from an author who like the 'early Christians exposed to wild beasts in the arena, has been baited by reviewers. . . His attitude in the midst of this storm of censure is almost as peaceful as that of Daniel in the den of lions, seated, as the showmen observed, on his three legged stool and reading the "Times" newspaper.'
31. *Saturday Review*, XXI (1866), 161.
32. 'Mr Matthew Arnold on Culture', *Saturday Review*, XXIV (1867), 79.
33. Lionel Trilling saw the 'hard-headedness' of *Liberty, Equality Fraternity* as a 'brilliant [and] interesting complement to *Culture and Anarchy*' executed in 'admirable' prose. *Matthew Arnold* (1949), p. 263n. Stephen's clear liking for Arnold shows up in a good-humoured, rather jovial letter to Lady Egerton: Arnold 'always reminds me of Goldwin Smith's criticism on him, "What an ape Matt. is! What an ape Matt. is!" He is an ape, but his strange apery makes me laugh to such an extent that I am afraid I am not always as angry with him as he deserves, and then in private life and at a dinner table he is the very best of good fellows, with no affectation about him. I dined some weeks ago at Sandar's. There was Maine, Matt. Arnold [etc.], we had all known each other for about 20 or 25 years [and I thought that] I feel about Matt. Arnold as one does of an old school fellow . . . I laugh at him with a great feeling of good nature. . . ' (11 December 1874).
34. Published a little later was *Questions for a Reformed Parliament*. This similarly pro-reform collection of essays has always been eclipsed by *Essays on Reform*, partly through the accident of timing, and possibly for being a less instrinsically interesting collection of essays.
35. See A. Briggs, *Victorian People* (1965), p. 261, and F. B. Smith, *The Making of the Second Reform Bill*, p. 2 for claims as to the influence of *Essays*.
36. John Morley in his approving review of *Essays on Reform* in the *Fortnightly Review*, 1 (1867), 491 at 492.
37. *Memories and Impressions* (1900), pp. 222–3. See also Bryce in M. Ostrogorski, *Democracy and the Organisation of Political Parties* (1902), 1, p. xlv.
38. But unlike Stephen Maine was unsympathetic towards Benthamism and always very strongly inclined to 'back the men of birth'. Early expressions of this are found in the *Saturday Review*, for example, 'Eothen in the South West', III (1857),

45; 'Administrative Brahminism', V (1858), 159; and 'Your Petitioners Will Ever Pray', 1 (1856), 358. And see G. Feaver, *From Status to Contract* (1969), ch. 4.

39. 'On the Choice of Representation'. Leslie Stephen was an active though not always willing constituency campaigner for his friend Henry Fawcett, the radical Millist. See, for example, Minny Stephen (Thackeray) to Fitzjames, 18 November 1870; Leslie Stephen Papers, Perkins Library, Duke University.

40. 'On the Choice of Representation', p. 88.

41. Ibid., p. 123.

42. 'The Historical Aspect of Democracy', p. 272. Bryce's essay received rather less contemporary acclaim than those by Brodrick, Dicey and Stephen; see the comparative review in C. Harvie's *The Lights of Liberalism* (1976), p. 138.

43. 'Speeches', in *Works*, VIII, p. 30. The year 1867 was not a good one for trade unionism, with the decision of *Hornby* v. *Close* [1867] 2 QB, 153, holding that as an illegal combination a trade union could not protect its funds by registering as a friendly society, although the case was neutralised by a special Act in 1869.

44. During the period extending from the founding of the *Pall Mall Gazette* in February 1865 to the passing of the Second Reform Act Stephen wrote about half the paper's leading articles. See chapter 2 above and *Life*, pp. 213-14.

45. Stephen to Lytton, 23 October 1879.

46. *Principles of Political Economy* (1848).

47. 'Essay on Bentham', in *Mill on Bentham and Coleridge*, ed. F. R. Leavis (1950), pp. 87-8.

48. *Essays on Politics and Culture*, p. 357, quoted by G. Himmelfarb in *Victorian Minds* (1968), p. 387. Even when challenged at an election rally in 1865 he admitted holding this view, though his frank admission is reported to have won him cheers from his working-class audience. *Autobiography*, p. 24.

49. *Principles of Political Economy*, bk I, ch. 7.

50. Morley, *Studies in Literature* (1891), p. 54.

51. *On Compromise* (1874), p. 126.

52. 'Democracy', in Arnold, *Mixed Essays* (1879).

53. Ten years later, the complaint was that the country's political leadership was not coming from the 'educated and driving part of the country'. Stephen to Lytton, 29 June 1877.

54. *On Liberty*.

55. (1865), 12 July, 'The Lesson of the Metropolitan Elections', quoted by C. Kent in *Brains and Numbers* (1978).

56. Ch. 1.

57. *Tennyson, Ruskin, Mill, and Other Literary Estimates* (1899), p. 293.

58. 'Mr Mill on Political Liberty', *Saturday Review*, VII (1859) (two reviews), 186 and 213 at 214.

59. See J. C. Rees, *Mill and His Early Critics* (1956).

60. Of Spencer, Stephen wrote: 'Herbert Spencer, of all human bores, is to me the most boring. He was asked some questions which set him off on his metaphysical hobbies, just like turning on a tap with water at full pressure behind it. He talked away, nineteen to the dozen, in language quite as hard as his books, repeated as quickly as shots from a revolver. He began, I remember, "I regard consciousness as the transverse section of the physical area of cause in the line of the physical forces", which I hope makes you happier than it did me.' Stephen to Lady Egerton, 11 December 1874.

61. Himmelfarb, *Victorian Minds*, p. 143.

62. *Autobiography*, ch. VII.

63. *Saturday Review*, VII (1859), 214. Not an ethic that was restricted to those of a Calvinistic temperament. For example, T. H. Huxley, the great nineteenth-century rationalist and scientist, preached the social virtues of 'self-discipline, self-

support, [and] intelligent effort'. L. Huxley, *Life and Letters of Thomas Henry Huxley* (1900), p. 76.

64. Houghton, *The Victorian Frame of Mind 1830–1870*, p. 264.

65. 'Mr Mill's Essays', *Saturday Review*, VII (1859), 46, at 48.

66. *Saturday Review*, VII (1859), 76, at 77.

67. Considering Hume's role as one of the philosophic founders of utilitarianism, Stephen devoted relatively little essay space to his works; whereas Locke, for example, received a good deal more attention. However, in 'Hume's Essays' Stephen showed himself to have understood well the core importance of Hume and to have reached his brother's later judgement (*The History of English Thought in the Eighteenth Century* (1876), II, p. 87) by noting 'how very little subsequent speculation has added to a great part of what Hume wrote'. See Stephen's collected *Saturday* articles in *Horae Sabbaticae* (1892), II, p. 370. Stephen was tempted to use the more prosaic title 'Saturday afternoons' for fear of too many people not knowing that "Sabbaticae" meant "Saturday". Letter to Lord Lytton, 18 April 1891, Lytton Papers, Hertford.
Some of Leslie Stephen's mixed feelings on the quality and worth of these collected essays are apparent from the comments in his *Life*, p. 226. But a less guarded opinion survives in the form of casual observations written on the fly leaves of his own copy of *Horae Sabbaticae*. Of volume II he notes: 'This is a curious work in various ways and I don't know whether I regret the publication or not. The energy and common sense of some of the articles is remarkable: though the style is not light, compared with such work in newspapers it is of a very high level. On the other hand, he is a mere amateur in the metaphysical facts and seems to have known nothing of philosophy outside of J. S. Mill's sphere. He does not know of Hume's *Treatise* [cf. above]. Yet the general power makes itself felt.' Volume III was seen as containing 'some remarkably good writing' involving a 'happy audacity' of style. Leslie Stephen Papers, Washington State University Library.

68. Reprinted in *Horae Sabbaticae*.

69. Ibid., III, p. 171.

70. Stephen thought not; ibid., II, p. 18.

71. Ibid., p. 17.

72. 'Locke on Toleration', *Horae Sabbaticae*, II, p. 163; 'Locke as a Moralist', ibid., p. 134.

73. Ibid., p. 32.

74. *Edmund Burke, an Historical Study* (1867) and *Burke* (1879). Stephen was not greatly enamoured of Morley's enviably growing (in 1874) list of studies of political theorists: 'You ask, do I read Morley's books? More or less I do, and rather less than more. He does not suit me for sufficiently obvious reasons. The whole temper of our respective minds is different. Besides, to tell the truth, . . . I prefer reading Voltaire and Rousseau and Burke for myself, and fancy my own judgements on them. . . I never got on much with any of his (Morley's) books. My brother is a much better critic to my taste!' Letter to Lady Egerton, 19 March 1874, written shortly before the first appearance of Morley's *On Compromise*, initially serialised in the *Fortnightly Review*; see chapter 7 below.

75. See 'Edmund Burke', *Saturday Review*, V (1858), 372.

76. And *Horae Sabbaticae*, III, pp. 116–117. Stephen's use of 'utilitarian' here was a loose one, and was meant to suggest pragmatism. Like Morley, Stephen chose to regard much of Burke's later output as aberrational and untypical of the man.

77. *Horae Sabbaticae*, III, p. 119.

78. Ibid., p. 122.

79. Ibid., p. 149.

80. Ibid., p. 160.

81. Ibid., p. 147.

82. Ibid., p. 142.
83. Ibid., p. 140.
84. In modern times compare, for example, P. J. Stanlis, *Edmund Burke and Natural Law* (1958) for the claim of Burke as a faithful natural lawyer with C. B. Macpherson's refutation in *Burke* (1980).
85. For Stephen's attitude to natural rights, see chapter 3 above.
86. Although Bentham paid Hobbes little attention.
87. p. 69. Noel Annan suggests that Fitzjames' essays on Hobbes were 'more illuminating than Leslie's book': *Leslie Stephen* (1984), p. 274n.
88. *Horae Sabbaticae*, II, p. 30.
89. Ibid., p. 51.
90. Ibid., p. 56.
91. Ibid., p. 66.
92. *Horae Sabbaticae*, II, pp. 67–8.
93. *Treatise*, bk III. Also believed by others, including Paine.
94. *Horae Sabbaticae*, II, p. 69.
95. Ibid., p. 12.
96. Ibid., p. 9. No doubt taking his evolutionary terminology from Herbert Spencer's 'Philosophic Rudiments concerning Government and Society'.
97. *Horae Sabbaticae*, II, p. 19.
98. Ibid., p. 11.
99. *Saturday Review*, XX (1865), 394.
100. *Horae Sabbaticae*, II, p. 19.
101. Ibid., III, p. 130.
102. Ibid., II, p. 35.
103. *The Province of Jurisprudence Determined*, Lecture VI. See also M. Francis, 'The Nineteenth Century Theory of Sovereignty and Thomas Hobbes', *History of Political Thought* (1980), 517.
104. Preface, vii.
105. pp. 23–6.
106. *Horae Sabbaticae*, III, p. 187.
107. Ibid., p. 203.
108. Ibid., p. 208.
109. Ibid., p. 198.
110. Ibid., p. 203.
111. Ibid., p. 201. Stephen clearly liked the vigour and style of de Maistre if not the content of his works. His four essays on de Maistre were republished in *Horae Sabbaticae*, III, pp. 250–324.
112. L. T. Hobhouse, *Democracy and Reaction* (1904), p. 120.
113. In 'Administrative Reform *à la Chinoise*', *Saturday Review*, II (1856), 356, at 358, Stephen accepted that Civil Service examinations could be useful as a 'bar to the grossly incompetent [and] as a stimulant to a select number of unambitious and second-rate candidates'.
114. David Masson, 'Ministers and Civil Servants', *Fraser's Magazine*, LI (1855), 607; and see O. Anderson, 'The Janus Face of Mid-Nineteenth Century English Radicalism: The Administrative Reform Association of 1855', *Victorian Studies*, VIII (1965), 231.
115. 'Head and Tail' and 'Circumlocution vs. Circumvention', *Saturday Review*, II (1856), 142 and 649. Also Feaver, *From Status to Contract*, pp. 31–7.
116. See, for example, Macaulay's early affirmation of meritocratic values in his speech on the 1833 India Bill quoted by G. R. Sutherland in *Ability, Merit and Measurement* (1984), pp. 98–9.
117. XXIII (December 1873 and May 1874), 1 and 165, well after Gladstone's 1870 reforms and Civil Service entry. See O. Macdonagh, *Early Victorian Government 1830–1870* (1977), ch. 11; and J. Roach, *Public Examinations in England 1850–1900* (1971), ch. 8.

118. (1861), particularly, ch. 5, 'Of the Proper Functions of Representative Bodies'. See A. Ryan, 'Utilitarianism and Bureaucracy: the Views of J. S. Mill', in *Studies in the Growth of Nineteenth Century Government*, ed. G. R. Sutherland (1972).

119. 'Parliamentary Government', p. 179. Stephen acknowledged that the process of separating off such matters could in itself be problematic. His central, somewhat unrealistic, reforming strategy was to confine Parliament's role to the 'large issues' of morals, religion and (most vitally) political power; these were fundamental matters where a large debating forum was most justified. Parliament was singularly ill fitted to cope with legislative detail and even 'worse fitted for the task of maintaining control and scrutiny over executive government' (pp. 4–5). Legislative difficulties were also the consequence of party government, whereby 'one half of the ablest men in the country [were] compelled to pass the greater part of their public lives in fighting the other half' – precisely the complaint voiced by many of other political persuasions, such as John Morley (*Fortnightly Review*, X (1868), 320 at 325, 'Old Parties and New Policy'). As for the relationship of ministers with their permanent officials, the whole arrangement was hopelessly wasteful of talent because 'we divorce special knowledge and experience from authority and personal responsibility. Those who possess authority have relatively little special knowledge and experience. Those who possess [this] have no authority and no responsibility' (p. 19). Similarly in *Respresentative Government*, Mill called for the political heads of government departments to be provided with the expertise of professional advisers on the lines of the Council of the Governor General in India – both Mill and Stephen had colonial administration in their blood through direct experience and inheritance. Additionally, in *Representative Government* (ch. 5) and years later in his *Autobiography*, Mill favoured a legislative commission composed of a 'small number of highly trained minds' to take over the function of drawing up legislation which could be passed unchanged or rejected by Parliament with amending proposals sent to the commission. Stephen's 'more moderate' version – a 'legislative department' – would have acted not merely as a drafting body, but also could have initiated legislative schemes for subsequent parliamentary approval (p. 180).

120. 'Dull Government', *Works*, IV, p. 85.

121. pp. 180–1. Cf. Stephen's 1856 attitude: 'A certain number of able public servants is no doubt indispensable to good government, but we can imagine no greater curse to the country than a system which should make the public service the natural resource and the universal ambition of persons of distinguished ability'. 'Administrative Reform *à la Chinoise*', *Saturday Review*, II (1856), 356, at 357.

122. *Sartor Resartus*, ch. III.

123. Government intervention and activity in economic and social areas was a large issue given practically no attention by Stephen.

124. 'Dover Beach'.

6 INDIA AND THE IMPERIAL ETHIC

1. *Life*, p. 231. Stephen's appointment 'was an announcement of the most pronounced kind that he was not fully occupied with professional work'. Review of *Life*, *Edinburgh Review*, CLXXXII (1895), 418, at 429.

2. Cambridge University Archives, 0.XIV 52, p. 149. Fawcett, Professor of Political Economy, was a strong friend of Leslie Stephen, his later biographer. Maurice, Professor of Moral Philosophy, or Casuistry, had first met Stephen at King's College, London. See chapter 8 below.

3. Argyll to Stephen, 1 July 1869.

4. *Life*, p. 234. Besides Maine, it is extremely likely that Grant Duff, the Under-Secretary for India, was also instrumental in securing Stephen's appointment.

5. Stephen to Mill, 24 April 1869.

6. And, of course, the chance of following Sir James Stephen's distinguished career in the Colonial Office. See generally P. Knapland, *Sir James Stephen* (1953).
7. Stephen to his wife, 10 March 1869. Years later in his *Story of Nuncomar and the Impeachment of Sir Elijah Impey* (1885), ii, p. 271, Stephen recorded that Macaulay's *Essays* had been 'my boyhood . . . favourite book'.
8. In 1869, with seven children, Stephen had sizeable family responsibilities: see his anxious letter to Emily Cunningham (later Lady Egerton), his sister-in-law, 17 March 1869.
9. *Life*, p. 235.
10. Stephen to his mother, 10 November 1869.
11. Maine to Grant Duff, 3 May 1869, Grant Duff Papers.
12. Feaver in *From Status To Contract*, p. 107, erroneously suggests that Maine and Stephen met in October 1869. But cf. p. 110. Stephen did not leave England until 9 November, arriving in Bombay in early December and Calcutta on 12 December. Letter to his wife. 5 December 1869.
13. Recollected by Stephen in a letter to Anny Thackeray, 13 February 1871, Ritchie Papers. His wife accompanied him as far as Boulogne. Diary of Mary Stephen, Mary Stephen Papers, Cambridge University Library, Add. 8381.
14. Stephen to his mother, 9 November 1869.
15. Stephen to Anny and Minny, 12 December 1869, Ritchie Papers. After Leslie's marriage to Minny, Fitzjames usually signed his letters to the two sisters, 'your very affectionate brother'.
16. Fitzjames to Leslie, 25 November 1869.
17. He claimed twenty: letter to his wife, 5 December 1869. The first was completed and posted before the channel was crossed.
18. *Life*, pp. 214 and 241.
19. 19 November 1870, Lyall Papers, India Office Library, MSS Eur. F132, fol. 25.
20. 7 December 1870, Grant Duff Papers.
21. Grant Duff to Stephen, 5 January 1871, and Stephen to Grant Duff, 10 January 1871, Grant Duff Papers.
22. Leslie Stephen's distillation from some of his brother's letters, *Life*, p. 244. One of Fitzjames' most devoted correspondents during his period in India was Leslie's first wife, Minny Thackeray. Her steady stream of letters to 'My dearest Fitzy', full of domestic chatter and social trivia was, for her brother-in-law, 'just as kind and beautiful as anything can possibly be in their way, and a very nice way too'. Stephen to his wife, 6 December 1870. See the collection of Minny's letters, from the Leslie Stephen Papers, Perkins Library, Duke University.
23. Escott, *Platform, Press, Politics and Play*, pp. 221–2, based on recollections of Sir William Egerton.
24. *Life*, pp. 244–5; and Ritchie Papers.
25. The Secretary of State for India possessed the ultimate right of preventing the enactment of any law assented to by the Viceroy and his Council.
26. *Life*, p. 242.
27. Stephen to his wife, 16 December 1869.
28. Stephen, 'Codification in India and England', *Fortnightly Review*, XVII (1872), 644, at 646–7.
29. Both included Sir John Romilly and Robert Lowe.
30. The first report, on succession and inheritance, formed the basis of the Indian Succession Act 1865.
31. See Ilbert, 'Indian Codification', *Law Quarterly Review* (1889), V, 347, at 351–2.
32. 22 December 1868, Grant Duff Papers; quoted by Feaver, *From Status to Contract*, p. 101.
33. Ibid., p. 101.
34. Similarly to Grant Duff, 15 March 1870, Grant Duff Papers.
35. Stephen to Argyll, 25 July 1870, Argyll Papers.

36. Stephen to his wife, 16 December 1869.
37. Stephen to his wife, 10 February 1870.
38. Fitzjames to Leslie, 17 April 1870, and to Grant Duff, 1 July 1870, Grant Duff Papers.
39. Stephen to Venables, 4 July 1870.
40. Letters to Grant Duff, 29 July and 12 August 1870, Grant Duff Papers.
41. Stephen to Lytton, 6 March 1876. Though even Stephen felt the need to play truant occasionally and devote the day to reading Trollope or Froude: for example, Stephen to his wife, 21 November 1870 and 1 January 1872. Financial considerations weighed heavily, with continuing worries about his ability to return to the Bar successfully. Stephen to Grant Duff, 12 August 1870, Grant Duff Papers. By the beginning of 1872 Stephen's 'savings' were 'nearly £6000', plus 'about £700 in my pocket'. Stephen to his wife, 27 January 1872.
42. See chapter 4 above for a discussion of the Evidence Act 1872.
43. The Contract Act 1872 was a redrawn version of that originally drafted by the third Indian Law Commission, which, according to Stephen, was riddled with definitional circularity. Letter to Argyll, 2 October 1871, Argyll Papers. See also Stephen's printed memorandum of 29 October 1871, stressing the need for clear definitions of basic terms such as 'promise, agreement, consideration, void, voidable': Richard Temple Papers, India Office Library, MSS Eur. F.86, fol.111. Stephen's modifications were mainly the consequence of lengthy committee discussions, two of which were with 'Calcutta merchants of eminence'. The bill, Stephen noted, had been influenced by the committee's study of the New York Code on 'obligations'. Minutes from the *Abstract of the Proceedings of the Council of the Governor General of India*, V.9.12, 9 April 1872, p. 331, India Office Library copy (hereafter 'Minutes'). The minutes of the bill's final legislative stage reveal two important areas where the council was divided on matters of principle. The first concerned the well-established rule that a bona fide purchaser of stolen goods (subject to exceptions) received no title to them. An attempt to give title to such purchasers and make the original owner sustain the loss was fought off by Stephen, who saw no greater justice or commercial convenience in the change. Minutes, pp. 336–8. Even more fiercely argued was a move led by the high-ranking Lieutenant Governor of Bengal to give courts a general power to unmake hard bargains. A power of this nature looked to Stephen like arbitrary or palm-tree justice, and quite beyond anything endorsed by English courts at the time – unless within the fairly rigid scope of the doctrine of undue influence. (Notions of setting aside a contract on the grounds of 'economic duress' or for being an 'unconscionable bargain' have only in very recent years crept into English law. See, for example, G. H. Treitel, *The Law of Contract* 7th edn (1987), ch. 10.) After considerable debate and a succession of split Council votes, Stephen, largely, won the day. Minutes, pp. 360–73. Stephen believed that the final product bore witness to the 'important fact that where the law is divested of all technicalities, stated in simple and natural language, and so arranged as to show the natural relation of different parts of the subject, it becomes not merely intelligible, but deeply interesting to educated men practically conversant with the subject-matter to which it relates': 'Codification in India and England', *Fortnightly Review*, XVII (1872), 644, at 656. This Benthamite desire to make laws intelligible to all is very apparent in most of Stephen's commentaries on his Indian legislation. According to some later commentators, Stephen's hopes were not fully realised, with many elements of the Contract Act proving conceptually baffling to those involved in its application. See S. Thorburn, *The Punjab in Peace and War* (1904), p. 249. These criticisms were, though, just as true of English law.
44. The Code of Criminal Procedure 1872 was a radical revamping of the existing, amended, 1861 Code. A detailed account of the Code is given in *HCL*, III, pp. 324–46. The Law Commissioners had maintained that consolidation of the existing

1861 and 1869 Acts with amendments would be substantially a 'mechanical' exercise. Stephen believed the suggestion to be absurd. As it stood the law was appallingly complex; he had 'very seldom seen a more confused and worse drawn law in his life'. Minutes, V.9.11, 9 December 1870, pp. 476-7. Stephen compared his task to that of an 'editor of a law book . . . to rearrange, to explain what experience has proved to be obscure, to supplant defects, and to make such alterations as harmonize with and carry out the leading idea of the system'. Minutes, V.9.12, 16 April 1872, p. 393. Two issues of sizeable importance to Stephen were measures relating to jurisdiction over 'European British Subjects' and the use of the executive as appellate bodies. On the first, the system of excluding the English from the criminal jurisdiction of lower courts meant 'practical impunity to English wrongdoers'; a change was therefore 'absolutely necessary'. Minutes, 16 April 1872, p. 399 and 13 February 1872, p. 75. As for appeals, Stephen expressed the 'very strongest possible objection' to executive involvement. Ibid., p. 78.
In September 1872, a few months after leaving India, Stephen was forced to defend the new Code from charges of having been passed in 'undue haste' without proper consultation with interested parties. To a threat by the Duke of Argyll to disallow the Code under the Secretary of State's reserve powers, Stephen successfully responded with an eight-page memorandum hotly contesting the challenge. Letter to Argyll, 9 September 1872, Argyll Papers.

45. These Acts included the Indian Divorce Act 1870; the Female Infanticide Prevention Act 1870; and the Hindu Wills Act 1870. A full list is set out in Radzinowicz, *Sir James Fitzjames Stephen and his Contribution to the Development of Criminal Law*, pp. 54-6.

46. 'Sir James Stephen as a Legislator', *Law Quarterly Review* (1894), X, 222, at 224.

47. *Fortnightly Review*, XVII (1872), 650. Certain areas of civil liabilities remained uncodified, primarily the law of torts. Native law was not included in Stephen's codifying schemes, unlike those of Macaulay and, later, of Charles Trevelyan. See E. Stokes, *The English Utilitarians and India* (1959), pp. 254, 258 and 279. The decision to omit codification of native laws was taken by the Second Indian Law Commission in its 1856 report.

48. *Fortnightly Review*, XVII (1872), 651 and continuing (almost too fulsomely) – in obvious contrast to Maine's complaints – 'It should also be noted that this great service to India was . . . rendered gratuitously by men of the highest eminence in the rare leisure left to them by other public duties of the first importance.' Stephen, of course, was at the beginning of his struggles to bring about a measure of English codification, and, needing allies in this field, could ill afford to make enemies. Privately he was rather less impressed by the Law Commissioners: Romilly was no more able to codify the law of evidence than 'translate the Bible, and as to Lowe . . . , if he would work at the subject 6 hours a day for months on end he might do it but not otherwise'. Stephen to Grant Duff, 10 January 1871, Grant Duff Papers.

49. Maine seemed to have felt that he had been denied adequate credit for preparing the way for Stephen: see, for example, Maine to Grant Duff, 8 April 1871, Grant Duff Papers.

50. *The Reign of Queen Victoria*, ed. T. H. Ward (1887), I, 460, at 503.

51. 'Sir James Stephen', *National Review*, XXV (1895), 820; and *The Indian Contract Act* (1905), v. Pollock's special interest in the law of contract was responsible for his pioneering *Principles of Contract at Law and in Equity* (1876).

52. *Studies in History and Jurisprudence* (1901), I, pp. 127-31.

53. 'The Life of Sir James Stephen', *Law Quarterly Review* (1895), XI, 383, at 384-5.

54. 'Sir James Stephen as a Legislator', *Law Quarterly Review* (1894), X, 222, at 226.

55. Returning once again to his Benthamite concern, Stephen had no doubts over the educational value of his work: 'You will naturally ask how this process of codification has succeeded? To this question I can answer that it has succeeded to a

degree which no one could have anticipated, and the proofs of this fact are to my mind quite conclusive. One is the avidity with which the whole subject is studied, both by the English and by the native students in the universities. The knowledge which every civilian you meet in India has of the Penal Code and the two Procedure Codes is perfectly surprising to an English lawyer. People who in England would have a slight indefinite rule-of-thumb knowledge of criminal law, a knowledge which would guide them to the right book in a library, know the Penal Code by heart, and talk about the minutest details of its provisions with keen interest. I have been repeatedly informed that law is the subject which native students delight in at the universities, and that the influence, as a mere instrument of education, of the codifying Acts, can hardly be exaggerated. I have read in native newspapers detailed criticisms, on the Evidence Act, for instance, which proved that the writer must have studied it as any other literary work of interest might be studied,' 'Codification in India and England', *Fortnightly Review*, XVIII (1872), 644, at 659.

56. This is undeniably true of *Liberty, Equality, Fraternity*: see below.

57. *Life*, pp. 281–2.

58. 'Sir James Stephen', *National Review* (1895), 821. In Pollock's view, Stephen was 'accurate by taking pains and not by instinct, and there was a point beyond which he did not think it worth the pains, though he grudged no amount of toil for any object that he appreciated' (819).

59. 'Codification in India and England', *Fortnightly Review*, XVIII (1872), 655.

60. Ilbert, 'Indian Codification', *Law Quarterly Review* (1889), V, 347, at 354.

61. See Feaver, *From Status to Contract*, p. 99 n. 33.

62. By the beginning of Lytton's viceroyalty, Salisbury had become quite insistent on the need for a complete civil code. Salisbury to Lytton, 20 January and 4 March 1876; Lytton Papers, India Office Library, MSS Eur. E. 218, fol. 11.

63. 'Indian Codification', *Law Quarterly Review* (1889), V, 361.

64. As a member of the Indian Council in London, Maine was always an important organising force. In 1874 he had been involved in an abortive scheme for Stephen to draw up a consolidation of English statutes relevant to India: see Feaver, *From Status to Contract*, p. 197.

65. Ibid., pp. 357–61. Stephen found Stokes 'one of the most thick skinned and irritable of human beings'. Stephen to Lyall, 17 September 1874, Lyall Papers, fol. 55. But he strongly supported Stokes' promotion as the 'only man who really knows his way through the labyrinth of Indian Law'. Stephen to Grant Duff, 10 January 1870, Grant Duff Papers. Maine and Lytton even made an attempt to persuade Stephen to return to India: see Stephen to Lytton, 24 June 1876. Stephen admitted that the 'prospect of helping you [Lytton] and John Strachey to govern an Empire [was] all but irresistibly attractive'; but conscience could not be squared with family responsibilities.

66. *HCL*, III, pp. 345–6.

67. XXIII, 1 and 165. See chapters 5 above and 7 below.

68. R. J. Moore, *Liberalism and Indian Politics 1872–1922* (1966), p. 10.

69. 'Essay on Government'; and his 1834 Public Dispatch to India, in which Mill emphasised that rather than seek to involve natives in the country's administration, there must be a steady concentration on effective government, for it was only in this 'unfettered exercise of their faculties, that Governments best minister to the public wealth and happiness'; cited in Ilbert's *The Government of India* (1915), p. 530.

70. To escape the evils of anarchy 'men agree to transfer to the magistrate powers sufficient for the defence of all: and to expect from him alone that protection from evil'. *The History of British India* (1817), I, 150.

71. *A Penal Code Prepared by the Indian Law Commissioners* (1838). Cf. the English Criminal Law Commissioners of the 1830s and 1840s, chapters 3 and 4 above.

72. *HCL*, III, p. 300. Whitley Stokes similarly saw that its 'basis is the law of England, stripped of technicality . . . shortened, simplified, made intelligible and precise'. *Anglo-Indian Codes* (1887), I, p. 71.

73. *HCL*, III, p. 301.

74. For Macaulay's statement of the Code's objectives see 'Introductory Report upon the Indian Penal Code', in *Works*, VII.

74. J. S. Mill gave the Code his early endorsement; *Westminster Review*, XXIX (1838), 393. On the substantive content of Macaulay's Code, Stephen was generally, though not completely, in agreement. He was particularly set on the reinstatement of Macaulay's original provision for a general offence of 'manslaughter by negligence' (S. 304A). See Council minutes, V.9.11, pp. 375–6; and Stephen to Argyll, 14 May and 25 July 1870, Argyll Papers. His strongest criticism of the Code was reserved for the provisions relating to other forms of 'culpable homicide and murder', which he found the 'weakest part of the Code. They are obscure, and it is obvious . . . that the subject had not been fully thought out' (*HCL*, III, p. 313). Stephen knew that they were not Macaulay's but his reviser's, Sir Peacock Barnes, though, overall, Stephen had believed other revisions had been 'beneficial' (*HCL*, III, p. 300). The other major area of revision of Macaulay's Code related to offences akin to seditious libel. Their absence from the earlier Code, according to Stephen's research, appeared to have been an oversight and not a manifestation of Macaulay's libertarian beliefs. The introduction of the new offences was energetically opposed by the Indian press as a clear attempt to suppress free journalism. Such allegations Stephen felt obliged to answer at considerable length, fairly arguing that the revisions brought the Indian law roughly into line with that in England. Minutes, V.9.11, pp. 437–52. The truth of these claims was indirectly borne out by the enactment of the special Vernacular Press Act in 1878 for just the purposes alleged against Stephen's provisions.

In comparison, Stephen's own Draft Codes of 1878 and 1879 were neither de novo in conception nor radical revisions of the whole body of criminal law; rather a systematic statement of it with the worst of its excesses trimmed away, if not completely removed. See chapters 3 and 4 above. Certainly Stephen's homicide provisions were creditably innovative despite his claim that 'codification' meant to him 'the reduction for the first time to a definite written form of law, which had previously been unwritten, or written only in an unauthoritative form, such as that of textbooks and reported cases' (W. W. Hunter, *Life of the Earl of Mayo* (1875), II, Stephen's chapter – 'Legislation under Lord Mayo', p. 177). See the detailed comparative review by S. H. Kadish, 'Codifiers of the Criminal Law: Wechsler's Predecessors', *Columbia Law Review*, (1978), 78, 1098; also S. G. Vesey-Fitzgerald, 'Bentham and the Indian Codes', in G. W. Keeton and G. Schwartzenberger (eds.), *Jeremy Bentham and the Law* (1948) and generally Stokes' comprehensive *The English Utilitarians and India*.

75. Hunter, *Mayo*, II, pp. 153–5.

76. 'Minute . . . on the Administration of Justice in British India' (1870–2), Argyll Papers, p. 94. Stephen acknowledged that there was no immutable reason why the rule of law demanded that judicial and executive roles be performed by separate functionaries. It was more a choice between different forms of administration than 'between government by law and government without law' ('Minute', pp. 8 and 30). And as District Officers needed to maintain their influence and authority this was best done by permitting a continuation of their dual role of exercising criminal jurisdiction with civil justice handled by a separate judicial system. In endorsing this practical expediency, Stephen showed a utilitarian willingness to put aside Whig/Liberal constitutional anxieties over combining judicial with revenue functions – a 'blending of Somerset House and the Old Bailey', Stokes, *The English Utilitarians and India*, p. 237 n. 1.

77. First written in 1870, partly at Mayo's instigation. Stephen to Grant Duff, 22 March 1870, Grant Duff Papers. Revised in 1871 and published in 1872, the 'Minute' is an impressive detailed general review of how the procedural and practical side of the administration of justice might be improved, focusing on the state of judicial organisation, the desirability of normally separating political and executive functions, and the use of Indians in the system.

78. *Mayo*, II, pp. 161–4. Praying in aid Maine's *Village Communities*, Stephen felt obliged to point out that the 'merits' of an institution are not to be measured either by its durability or by its historical interest'(165). In all fundamentals Maine was at one with Stephen on the justifications for and objectives of British policy in India. Their differences were matters of emphasis. Maine's view of India was unavoidably coloured by his historical and scientific analysis of the subcontinent's development over the centuries before British conquest. His belief in the lasting effects of British rule was less convinced than Stephen's, and probably not completely without some residual regret in witnessing the country's Europeanisation. 'Maine has always believed that when traditional institutions clashed with modern, it was the old that must give way, but he never quite succeeded in concealing in his Indian utterances a note of nostalgia, a melancholy recognition that much that was tried and familiar must be sacrificed in the exchange.' Feaver, *From Status to Contract*, pp. 192–3. Cf. Sir Alfred Lyall's obituary of Maine, *Law Quarterly Review* (1888), IV, 129. Stokes in *The English Utilitarians and India* (pp. 312–13) gives a misleading impression of the scale of differences between Maine and Stephen. Stokes' conclusions seem to flow more from deduction, based on Maine's generally non-utilitarian outlook, than from the actuality of his behaviour.

79. *Mayo*, II, p. 166.

80. Ibid., p. 167.

81. *HCL*, III, pp. 344–5.

82. Ibid., p. 169. In biblical vein, Stephen described the 'whole of our history in India [as] the most anti sermon on the mount [lesson] in the world . . . and comprehensive proof that we English do not really believe the said sermon'. Letter, Stephen to Lyall, 17 September 1874, Lyall Papers, fol. 55.

83. Ibid., p. 171. The phrase may owe something to the title of Bentham's 'Essay on the Influence of Time and Place' in which the same question is considered.

84. *Mayo*, II, pp. 172–3; and 'Minute', p. 8.

85. *Works*, 1, 171. James Mill was far less discriminating in his attack on native laws and morality, favouring a completely new broom policy. See generally *History of British India*, II.

86. *Mayo*, II, p. 174; and 'Minute', p. 32.

87. *Mayo*, II, pp. 174–5, and 'Minute', pp. 136–9, quoting Maine's *Village Communities*.

88. See the accounts provided by B. Semmel, *The Governor Eyre Controversy* (1962) and G.P.H. Dutton, *The Hero as Murderer* (1967).

89. *Life*, p. 227.

90. 'Shooting Niagara: And After?', *Macmillan's Magazine* (1867); generally G. Workman, *Victorian Studies*, XVIII (1974).

91. Cf. A. W. Benn: 'the division corresponded to the division in the American Civil War and, like that, indicated a conflict between two ideals of society – more than that, between two different theories of the world' (*Modern England* (1908)).

92. And Edward James, another barrister.

93. See *HCL*, I, pp. 207–16 for Stephen's opinion.

94. Stephen to his mother, 26 March 1867.

95. Together with a Lieutenant Brand.

96. Stephen was criticised by *The Times* for being too courteous to Eyre in cross-examination, 30 March 1867. Stephen's denial came in a letter published 2 April 1867. Opposing counsel was Hardinge Giffard, the future Lord Halsbury.

Fitzjames' wife noted that for this Mill 'never forgave F': brief reminiscences of Mary Stephen, sheet headed '1867', Mary Stephen Papers, Cambridge University Library, Add. 8381.

97. *The Story of Nuncomar*, I, pp. 1–2. This work was originally intended to be the first instalment of a large-scale study of the whole Hastings affair, but through a combination of the book's dry subject-matter and other circumstances the project progressed no further.

98. *Life*, p. 431.

99. At the time, Stephen's Impey research drove him to declare that 'Macaulay knew almost nothing about India.' Stephen to Lady Grant Duff, 25 October 1885. See also J. W. Burrow, *Evolution and Society* (1966), p. 51.

100. *The Story of Nuncomar*, I, p. 3.

101. Leslie Stephen felt that Macaulay deserved a 'severer sentence'. He believed that his brother had been generous to Macaulay, at least in the moderation of language used and the understated conclusions. 'It is characteristic that while making mincemeat of Macaulay's most famous essay, Fitzjames cannot get rid of his tenderness for the great "Tom" of his boyish days.' He added, 'Had I written the book myself, I should have felt bound to say something unpleasant: but I am hardly sorry that Fitzjames tempered his justice with a little excess of mercy.' *Life*, pp. 433–4. True as these views may be, Fitzjames' clear presentation of the evidence spoke very loudly.

102. With cause, Stephen blamed James Mill's *History of British India* for much misleading information fed to Macaulay, who based his essay 'Warren Hastings' (1841) on secondary sources. Mill is described as having by his 'excessive dryness and severity of style [produced] an impression of accuracy and labour which a study of original authorities does not by any means confirm'. *Nuncomar*, II, p. 149. In relation to one piece of evidence, Mill 'artfully gave an account . . . not literally false, but so arranged as to produce the exact false impression which Macaulay received, generalised, and made popular'. *Nuncomar*, II, p. 251 n. 2. Mill was on more than one occasion seen by H. H. Wilson, the subsequent editor of the *History of British India*, as 'uncandid' in his reporting. See, for example, citations by Stephen, *Nuncomar*, II, p. 269. Mill's *History* is described (by Henry George Keane) in the *DNB* entry for Hastings as 'coldly hostile' (p. 147). Elements of Hastings' Indian policy had been in complete opposition to Mill's, especially Hastings' great tolerance of Indian culture and institutions and his marked resistance to an over-rapid Europeanisation of India – views that were quite at odds with Mill's utilitarian attitudes towards India. Stephen saw Hastings as one of the 'very greatest men of his time'. Stephen to Lytton, 14 July 1883, Lytton Papers, Hertford.

103. Stephen to Grant Duff, 19 February 1885, Grant Duff Papers.

104. *Essays on Questions of the Day, Political and Social* (1894), pp. 148–9. Two of Stephen's close 'Indian' friends, Sir John Strachey and Sir Alfred Lyall, both later contributed to the debunking of Macaulay's essay on Hastings: Strachey, *Hastings and the Rohilla War* (1892); Lyall, *Warren Hastings* (1889), in the Men of Action series. See Stephen's admiring comments on Lyall's book quoted in Durand's *Life of Sir Alfred Comyn Lyall* (1913), p. 329.

105. Maine used his position on the *Saturday Review* to campaign against the change: for example, 'Theorizing about India', IV (1857), 254. Maine's opposition to change was a blend of belief in the legal and prescriptive rights of the East India Company with the belief in the superior efficiency of the old system. See Feaver, *From Status to Contract*, pp. 65–6.

106. *Representative Government*, ch. XVIII, 'Of the Government of Dependencies by a Free State'. See also Mill's evidence to the House of Lords committee on Indian affairs, Parl. Pap. (HC) 1852–3, XXX, 2972.

107. Mayo to Buchan, 26 September 1869; and Mayo to Argyll, 1 September 1871.

Mayo Papers, India Office Library, fols. 36 and 44. Cited by S. Gopal, *British Policy in India 1858–1905* (1965).

108. *Dissertations and Discussions* (1875), III, p. 171; see R. Koebner and H. D. Schmidt, *Imperialism* (1964), p. 43.

109. See A. P. Thornton's summary of this attitude in *The Imperial Idea and its Enemies* (1959), pp. 11–12: 'Colonies throttled our expanding commerce and created artificial markets. Their possession endangered peace as they made this country a much easier prey to an enemy. They also cost a great deal of money, none of which was repaid – and no-one should forget that society was injured by every particle of unnecessary expense.'

110. Ibid., p. 12.

111. See the discussion of *Greater Britain* in Koebner and Schmidt, *Imperialism*, ch. IV.

112. See, for example, *Fraser's Magazine* (1870), 1, 1, and 11, 269; also Froude's more mature schemes for a 'Commonwealth' in *Oceana or England and her Colonies* (1885).

113. *Personal & Literary Letters of Robert, First Earl of Lytton*, ed. Lady Betty Balfour (1906), I, p. 347. See also M. Lutyens, *The Lyttons in India* (1979), p. 15.

114. Balfour (ed.), *Letters*, I, p. 340.

115. Quoted in *Life*, p. 390.

116. Balfour (ed.), *Letters*, I, p. 340. Lytton's son, Neville Stephen, third Earl of Lytton, was named after Sir Neville Chamberlain and Stephen. Stephen along with Sir John Strachey was also godfather.

117. C. Kegan Paul, 'Sir James Fitzjames Stephen', *The Month* (1895), 471.

118. Despite increasing disagreement, Morley was still able to write in December 1877 that as 'Carlyle said of himself and Sterling "We parted except in opinion not disagreeing." ' 27 December 1877, Lytton Papers, fol. 11.

119. Gopal, *British Policy in India*, ch. 2. Before leaving for India, Lytton had received secret policy instructions necessary to achieve British political supremacy in Afghanistan. Lytton Papers, fol. 518.

120. An earlier letter of 31 May 1877 related to the question of the Viceroy's right to rebuke the judiciary. The question arose following the Fuller case, in which Lytton had been heavily critical of a very light sentence imposed on a white for a savage attack on a native. Salisbury had defended Lytton's entitlement. Stephen set out constitutional argument in Lytton's support.

121. Stephen's letters are dated 16, 22, and 28 October and 12, 15, and 20 November 1878.

122. Stephen's old friend's strong Gladstonian sympathies did not (in Stephen's view) run to the extent of blind belief: 'His superiority to his fellows, appears to me to consist in the fact that he knows what a humbug and impostor, and mere noisy mouthpiece of ignorant popular views he is, whereas most of them do not. I do not think he feels degraded by it any more than he would by holding a bad hand at whist.' Stephen to Lytton, 28 September 1876, quoted by Roach, 'Liberalism and the Victorian Intelligentsia', *Cambridge Historical Journal* (1957), 70.

123. Harcourt's letter is dated 18 November and Holland's 20 November 1878. Holland's defence was consistent with what might be expected from the author of *Elements of Jurisprudence*, a strongly characteristic work of Austinian analytical jurisprudence. See also J. S. Mill's 'A Few Words on Non-Intervention', *Fraser's Magazine* (1859), later in *Dissertations and Discussions* (1875), III, p. 167.

124. 16 December 1878, Balfour (ed.), *Letters*, II, p. 132.

125. XXIV (1878), 742, particularly at 746–50; and 905. XXV (1879), 152 and 963. XXVI (1879), 601.

126. 30 January 1879, Balfour (ed.), *Letters* II, p. 139. Yet their friendship did revive after Lytton's return to England, though, as his daughter remarks, never with the 'unfettered, easy intimacy of former years'. Balfour (ed.), *Letters*, II, p. 223. However, Lytton was soon able to admit that 'whenever I meet John Morley, I feel he is

the finest fellow and dearest man in the world to me – except James Stephen' (1881), and soon able to enjoy a 'really delightful dinner with Morley and Stephen and Maine. We wrangled over the whole universe, but in the best of tempers, and I really think there are few things more enjoyable than a good conversational fencing bout with men who know how to fence and always hit fair. . . ' Lytton to Lady Lytton, 16 December 1880, Balfour (ed.), *Letters*, II, p. 224.

127. Balfour (ed.), *Letters* II, p. 192. On Lytton's death in November 1891, Stephen simply summarised his own feelings in a letter to Lady Lytton: 'I never knew a man towards whom I felt so warmly, and to whom I owed so much . . . I shall always regard it as one of the most fortunate circumstances of my life that I was for many years one of his most intimate friends.' Ibid., p. 433.

128. In the preceding September, Stephen made no secret of his interest in the speech: 'I feel my fingers itching to try my hand at a draft.' 6 September 1876. Lytton requested and got detailed advice on both the substance and the style of the speech from Stephen: see Stephen to Lytton, 16 October and 24 and 30 November 1876. After the durbar, as Stephen wrote to Lytton, from the *Times* abstract of the speech, 'you appear to have used pretty fully what I sent you', 6 January 1870. Cf. Lytton's durbar speech, in *Speeches*, vol. 1, fol. 157, pp. 78–91, Lytton Papers.

129. Speech at the State Banquet following the durbar. *Speeches*, vol. 1, p. 90. The speech as a whole was a pursuit of the theme of the rule of law.

130. S. E. Koss, *John Morley at the India Office 1905–1910* (1969), p. 20.

131. Gladstone made just this point in his Glasgow speech of December 1879. See the *Midlothian Speeches 1879*, ed. M.R.D. Foot (1971), p. 200. Maine was an unswerving supporter of Lytton's policies, including the Vernacular Press Act: B. Balfour, *The History of Lord Lytton's Indian Administration* (1899), pp. 518–19.

132. According to Lytton, at a meeting in the summer of 1880, Disraeli and Stephen were 'much pleased with each other's company'. Lytton to Lyall, 28 August, Lyall Papers, fol. 57.

133. Ripon to Gladstone, 22 October 1881, Ripon Papers; cited by Moore, *Liberalism and Indian Politics 1872–1922*, p. 31.

134. Quoted by Gopal, *British Policy in India*, p. 147.

135. Though enforcement was suspended for much of the time.

136. Gladstone to Ripon, 24 November 1881; cited by Moore, *Liberalism and Indian Politics 1872–1922*, p. 33.

137. *Indian Constitutional Documents 1600–1918*, ed. P. Mukherji (1918), p. 638; cited by Moore, *Liberalism and Indian Politics 1872–1922*, p. 33.

138. Maine to Ilbert, 11 April 1883; Maine Papers, India Office Library, MSS Eur. D594.

139. The 'Ilbert' question had also arisen in a semi-private fashion during Stephen's legal membership of the Council. In the course of Council proceedings on the Criminal Procedure Bill an attempt was made by some members to introduce amendments along the lines of the Ilbert Bill. The principal ground for Stephen's opposition to the proposals was their disutility: that the unconsulted Anglo-Indian community would be greatly antagonised with very little practical gain for the administration of justice, and that the change would lead to a damaging diminution of the confidence of the European population in the government. The proposed amendment was only narrowly defeated, with the Council voting 7 to 5 against, and the Viceroy, Lieutenant-Governor of Bengal and Sir Richard Temple amongst the 'ayes' and Stephen and John Strachey leading the 'noes'. See Council minutes, V.9.12, 16 April 1872, pp. 397–401.

After changes in 1877, magistrates, regardless of race, had been given criminal jurisdiction over Europeans in the presidency towns but not in other parts of India. The Ilbert Bill sought to extend non-European magistrates' jurisdiction to all areas. The anomaly was magnified by the fact that magistrates of mixed race had not been subject to the restricted jurisdiction since 1872, because of their classification as 'European British Subjects'. As Sir Arthur Hobhouse, Stephen's immediate successor, pungently put it: 'the question is whether a Magistrate of proved ability shall merely because he is of pure Indian blood, be declared incapable of exercising a limited jurisdiction, not only over Englishmen, but over a large class of persons with some English blood in their veins; a jurisdiction which the Magistrate's own subordinates may exercise if they have the requisite drops of blood'. 'Native Indian Judges: Mr Ilbert's Bill', *Contemporary Review*, XLIII, (1883), 795, at 811. Even with the proposed reforms Europeans were to retain rights of appeal to the High Court, which would also continue to try capital offences.

140. Maine to Lyall, 28 March 1883. Lyall Papers, fol. 48.

141. Ibid.

142. Stephen to Lytton, November 1882. Quoted by Feaver, *From Status to Contract*, p. 204. Stephen reported that Maine saw Ripon as 'behaving like the very devil in India – committing the abominable sin of nigger-worshipping to an accursed degree'. Ripon's radical reputation in Indian matters went back to 1850, when he became a member, with Bright and others, of the Indian Reform Society, which advocated early consultations with educated Indians on reform questions. See J. L. Sturgis, *John Bright and the Empire* (1969), p. 26.

143. Stephen to Grant Duff, November 1882, Grant Duff Papers.

144. Stephen to Grant Duff, 5 May 1883, Grant Duff Papers. 'Baboo' was a loose term commonly used to describe educated or middle-class Indians.

145. Speech, 9 April 1883, *Hansard*, 3rd series, 227, p. 1735. Following Stephen's *Times* correspondence, Lytton's speech was critical of the general approach to Indian government adopted by Ripon.

146. *Times* letters: 1 and 2 March and 2 and 9 November 1883.

147. *Nineteenth Century*, XIV (1883), 542. Writing to Lytton before publication of the article, Stephen spoke of his intention to respond to Hobhouse's 'challenge' with a 'calm and statesmanlike . . . exposition' of the views 'you and I have long maintained'. 14 July 1883, Lytton Papers, Hertford.

148. 'Native Indian Judges', *Contemporary Review*, XLIII (1883), 812 and 'Last Words', *Contemporary Review*, XLIV (1883), 400, at 405.

149. Lyall first met Stephen in June 1872, having failed in an attempt to do so in December 1869. After their first meeting Lyall wrote to his sister, Mrs Sibylla Holland, that 'Fitzjames Stephen very civilly came over here one morning . . . and sat with me more than an hour. I liked him much, and I think that at least we amused each other; he has that turn for free opinions, with an edge on them, which greatly attracts me. I am struck by the immense advantage . . . of getting such men to go out to India. . . [W]hen Maine and Stephen come home with strong views on our side, and strong impressions upon the real state of affairs in the East the public listen to them.' Lyall Papers, fol. 5. Through a combination of genuine esteem and hopes of career advancement, Lyall was keen to cultivate a friendship with Stephen. Writing in August 1874 to his sister, Lyall complains of the difficulty in pinning down his frantically busy quarry: 'I wish I could make a friend of Fitzjames Stephen – I have so very few friends of that calibre. But I never could get near Stephen in London . . . he is only visible in the evenings, and by special invitations, which of course must be very rare. I hope you will all the same help me with him, and manage to tell him that I should like much to meet him again.' 2 August 1874, fol. 5. Lyall's wish was soon granted with a strong and warm friendship developing. Stephen was instrumental in getting Lyall noticed by Lytton and in Lyall's appointment in 1878 as Indian Foreign Secretary. In 1876 Stephen had recommended Lyall as one of the 'finest fellows I ever knew and that it would be a "sin and a shame and a damnation" if you and he don't come together. He is the one man (Except Maine) who seemed . . . to see the splendour of India, the things

which have made me feel all that I have so often said to you about it.' Quoted in Durand's *Life of Sir Alfred Comyn Lyall*, p. 191. Lyall's other mentor was John Morley, whose friendship had been forged through Lyall's earlier contributions to the *Fortnightly Review*. See letter, Lytton to Lyall, 30 April 1876, Lyall Papers, fol. 57. Lyall also became a strong friend of Lytton during and after their Indian service. See generally the Lytton/Lyall correspondence 1876–89 in the Lyall Papers, fol. 59, and chapters X and XI of Durand's *Life*.

150. 3 April 1883, Lyall Papers, fol. 41.

151. Grant Duff to Ripon, 2 April 1883, Ripon Papers, British Library, MSS 43588, ff. 241–2 (XCVIII). Cited by Feaver, *From Status to Contract* p. 316. Judging by Stephen's jovial response, Grant Duff's chiding was not too severe. Stephen to Grant Duff, 4 May 1883, Grant Duff Papers.

152. *India* (1894; first published 1888), pp. 42–83. Ripon himself acknowledged the bill had been tactically misjudged. Ripon to Gladstone, 24 March 1883, Ripon Papers.

153. *India*, pp. 42–83. Stephen even faulted Ripon for being over-generous on the compromise settlement: 'I think Ripon has made an even more atrocious ass of himself than before. His precious compromise gives the Europeans more than they . . . asked for or in my opinion ought to have.' Stephen to Venables, 9 January 1884, Venables Papers, Llysdinam B, Welsh National Library, Aberystwyth. This is consistent with Stephen's views expressed in his 1872 'Minute', p. 92, where he complains of the special entitlement of 'British European Subjects' to be tried by a jury. Stephen also much favoured extending the use of Indians in all levels of the judiciary and making access to such posts easier. 'Minute', pp. 61, 91 and 127.

154. Gladstone to Ripon, 17 April 1883, Ripon Papers, British Library, MSS 43553, 50A. See Gopal, *British Policy in India*, pp. 150–2 for Gladstone's general handling of the issue.

155. Stephen to Grant Duff, 9 September 1883, Grant Duff Papers.

156. *Nineteenth Century*, XIV (1883), 540, at 561 and 567.

157. *The Times*, 4 January 1878.

158. *Nineteenth Century*, XIV (1883), 543.

159. Salisbury to Northbrook, 28 May 1874, Northbrook Papers, India Office Library, MSS Eur C. 144, fol. 11.

160. Here Stephen was taking a side-swipe at a speech of Bright's in December 1877; see Stephen's response in *The Times* 27 December 1877 and 4 January 1878. Bright described Stephen as 'a man of power, but not of sentiment or imagination, and not likely to take the merciful side of a question', *The Diaries of John Bright*, ed. R.A.J. Walling (1930), p. 510, 19 March 1884.

161. *Nineteenth Century*, XIV (1883), 546–7.

162. Ibid., 556–7.

163. Ibid., 554–6.

164. For an account of the confusion present in Maine's evolutionary theories of law and institutions see J. W. Burrow, *Evolution and Society: A Study in Victorian Social Theory* (1966), pp. 137–78; and generally Himmelfarb, 'Varieties of Social Darwinism', in *Victorian Minds*, pp. 314–32.

165. *Life*, pp. 374–5.

166. *Nineteenth Century*, XIV (1883), 556.

167. Ibid., 556 and 558.

168. Stephen to Lady Grant Duff, 13 September 1883.

169. *Nineteenth Century* XIV (1883), 560–1.

170. *India*, p. 388.

171. The first concrete manifestation of an Indian nationalist movement occurred in December of the same year that Stephen's article was published, with the initial meeting of the Indian National Conference.

172. The defects of these theories Stephen believed could not appropriately be discussed

in the text, but he referred the reader to an 'admirable article on the "Prospects of Popular Government" ' (*Quarterly Review*, (April 1882)). The article was one of a series by Maine which eventually formed the basis of *Popular Government*.

173. *Nineteenth Century*, XIV (1883), 564. Cf. *Mayo*, II, p. 174.
174. Ibid., 553.
175. What 'suited' Indians was to be determined by their rulers. Stephen felt little need to discuss rather substantial questions such as how discontent might be communicated to the governing power.
176. *Nineteenth Century*, XIV (1883), 565; and letter to Dufferin, 10 September 1885, Dufferin Papers, India Office Library, fol. 21.
177. J. L. Hammond and M.R.D. Foot, *Gladstone and Liberalism* (1952), p. 77.
178. 'Glasgow Speech', 5 December 1879: see Gladstone's *Midlothian Speeches*, ed. Foot, pp. 202–3. Of the general lofty tone of pure political morality adopted in these speeches, Stephen wrote: 'It makes me sad to see Gladstone mad in white satin, and Harcourt shamming mad in white linen, and Grant Duff dancing before the ark in a way which unites solemnity with respectability (as a particular style of funeral was once advertised to do).' Stephen to Lytton, February 1880, quoted by Roach, 'Liberalism and the Victorian Intelligentsia', p. 71.
179. *Nineteenth Century*, II (1877), 149.
180. 'Glasgow Speech', in *Midlothian Speeches*, p. 199.
181. Ibid, p. 199.
182. 'England's Mission', *Nineteenth Century*, IV (1878), 560 at 580. Cited by Gopal, *British Policy in India*, p. 302.
183. 'Third Midlothian Speech', 27 November 1879, in *Midlothian Speeches*, p. 128.
184. 'Motherwell Speech', 6 December 1879, ibid., p. 213.
185. 4 February 1872, Grant Duff Papers.
186. Dufferin to Cross, December 1888, Dufferin Papers. Cited by Gopal, *British Policy in India*, p. 178. Though approving of Dufferin's generally popular annexation of Upper Burma, Stephen did not care for the instigator of this action: Lord Randolph Churchill, then Secretary of State for India. Stephen found him 'silly, ignorant . . . and was disgusted at his wild opinions and silly talk'. Stephen to Grant Duff, 3 March 1886, Grant Duff Papers. Later in the same year he was prepared to concede that Churchill had a 'certain dash and power' but still regarded him as 'vain, petulant, wayward, touchy'. Stephen to Lady Grant Duff, 29 December 1886.
187. For example, 6 March and 28 July 1886, copy letter, Dufferin Papers, fols. 23a and 23b.
188. Stephen's *Times* letter 4 January 1886. Ireland and the Empire had been linked in the 1880 election campaign by Disraeli and others. See Koebner and Schmidt, *Imperialism*, p. 168 and M. Beloff's *Britain's Liberal Empire 1897–1921* (1969), pp. 26–9.
189. Letter to Grant Duff, 7 January 1886, Grant Duff Papers.
190. Quoted by C. Harvie, *The Lights of Liberalism* (1976), p. 220; and G. M. Trevelyan, *Sir George Otto Trevelyan, A Memoir* (1932), p. 124.
191. Stephen to Grant Duff, 22 July 1886, Grant Duff Papers.
192. Stephen to Dufferin, 29 December–1 January 1886, copy letter Dufferin Papers, fol. 21.
193. Ibid.
194. Stephen to Dufferin, 9 May 1886, copy letter, Dufferin Papers, fol. 24a.
195. Ibid.
196. The *Times* letters were published on 4, 5, and 21 January, 29 April, and 1 May 1886.
197. *Times* 4 January 1886.
198. Irish nationalists had for some time been known to be receiving financial support

from organisations in America and Australia. Mill saw France as an interested party in Irish independence; see *England and Ireland* (1868), in *Collected Works*, ed. Robson, VI, p. 523. According to Mill, separation would be bad for Ireland and 'dishonourable' for England, p. 523. In drawing a parallel with India, Mill argued that 'what has been done for India has now to be done for Ireland', p. 519. For the view that *England and Ireland* demonstrates Mill's move towards being a 'convinced imperialist' see E. D. Steele, 'J. S. Mill and the Irish Question; Reform and the Integrity of the Empire 1865–70', *Historical Journal*, XIII (1970), 419.

199. Stephen, *Times*, (4, 5 January and 1 May 1886). See Dicey's best-selling semi-polemical *England's Case against Home Rule*, first published in November 1886, in which unity of the United Kingdom and endangerment of Empire are two of the leading objections to home rule. Dicey's constitutional arguments are considerably more refined than those offered by Stephen, though essentially the same. See generally R. A. Cosgrove, *The Rule of Law: Albert Venn Dicey, Victorian Jurist* (1980), ch. 6. Albert's brother Edward, editor of *The Observer*, was an earlier and far more forthright imperialist in the mould of his cousin Fitzjames, having no hesitation in declaring that the Empire and India were ruled by Britain because their possession was 'conducive to our interests and our reputation, because we have got it and intend to keep it'. *Nineteenth Century*, I (1877), 665, II (1877), 3 and 292.

200. The risk of infection by socialist revolutionary ideas spreading to England from Ireland bothered Stephen; see, for example, his letter to Lady Grant Duff, 9 June 1886.

201. *Times* (5 and 21 January 1886). Cf. Dicey's 'New Jacobinism and Old Morality', *Contemporary Review*, LIII (1888), 475.

202. *Times* (21 January 1886). Dicey took much the same view of Irish history; Cosgrove, *The Rule of Law*, pp. 135–6. Coupled with Gladstone's historical case for separation was the argument, from those such as Bryce, that home rule was a wider manifestation of the democratic logic of the 1884 Reform Act: Bryce to Dicey, 27 November 1921, cited by Cosgrove, p. 125.

203. Expressing dissatisfaction with Gladstone's post-assassination measures, Stephen wrote to Grant Duff that 'I hear however that Gladstone goes up and down his holy house whistling hymns ancient and modern in a way which carries conviction to the stoniest heart of the core of his conscience, of the purity of his principles and practices.' 30 November 1882, Grant Duff Papers.

204. Stephen was trial judge at Liverpool assizes for a dynamiting case in 1883: Stephen to Lytton, 14 July 1883, Lytton Papers, Hertford.

205. *Times* (5 January 1886).

206. *Times* (21 January 1886). Stephen was far less willing than Dicey to concede the full extent of the Irish tenants' case against their landlords. In common with many Liberals who voted against this measure, Stephen saw the 1881 Land Act as a possible socialist precedent for England. For example, Stephen to Lady Grant Duff, 15 December 1881; Stephen to Dufferin, 10 September 1885, copy, Dufferin Papers, fol. 21; and Stephen to Grant Duff, 30 April 1886, Grant Duff Papers. Fears of this nature were to form the foundation of much of W.E.H. Lecky's *Democracy and Liberty* (1896).

207. Stephen had been seriously ill in the spring of 1885 with a liver complaint causing him to lose three stone in three months. Stephen to Grant Duff, 16 June 1885, Grant Duff Papers.

208. Stephen to Dufferin, 12 September 1886, Dufferin Papers, fol. 24b.

209. Stephen to Dufferin, 12 April 1887, Dufferin Papers, fol. 24a.

210. Though Grant Duff was one of Stephen's most intimate friends for many years, Grant Duff's political career and views appear not to have been so greatly influenced by Stephen. Generally Grant Duff's moderate political temperament enabled him to be more forgiving of the inadequacies of politicians and the party

system. His governorship of Madras (1881–6) was highly competent, passing off without noteworthy incident.

211. Between 1874 and 1876 Strachey served as Lieutenant-Governor of the North-West Provinces. As with Mayo, Strachey, acting as Finance Member of the Council, rapidly became Lytton's main support. See Balfour, *History of Lord Lytton's Indian Administration*, p. 207, and *Letters*, II, p. 73.

212. Stephen's dedication was partly motivated by his 'strong personal regard, and . . . deep gratitude', and their joint experiences coping with the aftermath of Mayo's assassination in 1872. Strachey and Stephen were for a while acting heads of government. According to Sir Richard Temple, their Finance Minister, Stephen greatly impressed Mayo within a month of arriving in India with a speech in the Legislative Council of 'great force and energy', quickly establishing himself as 'quite a power in the State' going beyond his legislative role and taking a 'decided part in all deliberations of the Government on general subjects . . . ' . *Men and Events of My Time in India* (1882), pp. 383–4. Temple later recalled at an emergency Executive Council meeting following Mayo's assassination that 'I was struck by the masterly manner in which Mr Stephen advised us on this sudden crisis.' *The Story of My Life* (1896), I, p. 216.

213. First published in 1888. In similar manner, Strachey dedicated his book 'as an expression of strong personal regard . . . and in recollection of that time in India when we served together and which neither of us can forget'. Curzon, on the occasion of a new edition of the work, wrote to Strachey complimenting him on 'this masterpiece . . . of unfailing perspective' and 'inspiration' for the future. Curzon to Strachey, 25 July 1903, Richard Strachey Papers, India Office Library, MSS Eur. F. 127, fol. 462.

After Stephen's return from India the Stracheys and the Stephens more than once holidayed together in Ireland: *Life*, p. 406. See also, generally, references to Stephen in correspondence between Sir John and General Sir Richard Strachey, India Office Library, MSS Eur. F. 127. Richard Strachey's daughter, Pernel, was appointed Principal of Newnham College, Cambridge in 1923; Stephen's eldest daughter, Katherine, was a predecessor from 1911 to 1920. A surprising lack of understanding is exhibited by an entry in Virginia Woolf's diary following a conversation with Lytton Strachey (named after Lord Lytton): '& so we discussed our parents, & how Ly. S. & Lytton (Lord) & Fitzj. would sit talking till 2 a.m. – but what about? So many things could never be said, & the remaining ones coloured by the abstinence!' *The Diary of Virginia Woolf*, ed. A. O. Bell and Andrew McNeillie (1978), vol. 2, 32 January 1921.

214. *India* (1894), p. 397.

215. Ibid., p. 384.

216. Ibid., p. 389.

217. His works include *Asiatic Studies* (1882 and 1899) and *The Rise and Expansion of the British Dominion in India* (1893). Lyall's broad band of friendships included Matthew Arnold and Leslie Stephen.

218. Quoted in Durand's *Life of Sir Alfred Comyn Lyall*, p. 305.

219. Ibid., p. 217.

220. See also his later views in *The Rise and Expansion of the British Dominion in India*.

221. *Edinburgh Review*, CLIX (1884), 1, at 36. Much the same line of reasoning is followed by J. R. Seeley's influential *Expansion of England* (1909; first published 1883), p. 224. Seeley's subtly phrased justification for the imposition of European culture was far more digestible than Stephen's directness: 'Our boast is not that we have more ideas or more brilliant ideas, but that our ideas are better tested and sounder. [We possess a] larger stock of demonstrated truth [and are therefore] an infinitely more practical power.' Ibid., p. 283.

222. *Edinburgh Review*, CLIX (1884), 37–9.

223. Stokes, *The English Utilitarians and India*, pp. 313–15 largely ignores this affinity between Stephen's and Lyall's views, concentrating more on Lyall's milder philosophic temperament and greater historical sensitivity.

224. One notable exception was Lowe; for his equivocal attitude to questions of Empire see Koebner and Schmidt, *Imperialism*, pp. 148–51.

225. Speech at the Royal Colonial Institute, March 1893. Quoted by B. Semmel, *Imperialism and Social Reform: English Social-Imperial Thought 1895–1914* (1960), pp. 54–5. Rosebery's Liberal Cabinet, formed in March 1894, contained a clutch of (former) dyed-in-the-wool anti-imperialists, including Harcourt, Ripon, Trevelyan, Bryce and Morley.

226. Quoted by Beloff, *Britain's Liberal Empire 1897–1921*, pp. 50 and 62.

227. Cf. M. Edwardes, *High Noon of Empire: India under Curzon* (1965).

228. G.J.D. Coleridge, *Eton in the Seventies* (1912), p. 255. Coleridge was quoting from information provided directly by Curzon. Stephen's son, J. K. Stephen, was a contemporary and friend of Curzon at Eton. He was Secretary of the Literary Society when Curzon was President: see *Eton in the Seventies*, p. 250.

229. Speech given at an Old Etonians' dinner on 28 October 1898: *Speeches by Lord Curzon 1898–1900* (1900), iv–v.

230. Cf. Gopal, *British Policy in India*, p. 249.

231. *Indian Speeches*, I, iv (1903).

232. Ibid., iv, p. 8. For theories suggesting a natural flair for efficient and effective government amongst Anglo-Saxons, see J. A. Hobson's references to Karl Pearson and Benjamin Kidd in *Imperialism* (1902), pp. 162–5.

233. 'The True Imperialism', *Nineteenth Century*, LXIII (1908), 151 at 158; and Edinburgh lectures, 'The Place of India in the Empire' (1909).

234. See Moore, *Liberalism and Indian Politics 1872–1922*, pp. 76–7.

235. Despite the high sentiments of Midlothianism, even Gladstone seemed to accept that the need to protect and consolidate sometimes meant expansion. Ibid.., pp. 48–9.

236. Wilfred Blunt, *My Diaries* (1919), II, p. 74; quoted by Thornton, *The Imperial Idea and its Enemies*, p. 49.

237. Against such a trend were a few like Goldwin Smith, moving from moderate to trenchant criticism of imperialism. Compare *Questions of the Day* (1894), pp. 142–58 with *Commonwealth or Empire* (1902), pp. 34–73. The most sustained and telling anti-imperialist analysis of the period is J. A. Hobson's *Imperialism* (1902). Though even Hobson felt obliged to acknowledge that 'The one real and indisputable success of our rule in India . . . is the maintenance of order upon a large scale, the prevention of internecine war, riot, or organised violence. This, of course, is much, but it is not everything; it is not enough in itself to justify us in regarding our imperial rule as a success' (pp. 317–18).

238. Morley to Goldwin Smith, 2 January 1907. Cited by S. E. Koss in *John Morley at the India Office*, p. 130.

239. Morely, 'British Democracy and Indian Government', *Nineteenth Century*, LXIX (1911), 189, at 200.

240. See Koss, *John Morley at the India Office*, p. 138.

241. See S. R. Mehrotra, *India and the Commonwealth, 1885–1929* (1965), pp. 51–8.

242. There were no significant changes in Lyall's opinions between 1884 and 1902, as represented by his 1884 *Edinburgh Review* article, 'Government of the Indian Empire', and 'Race and religion', published in the *Fortnightly Review* (1902).

243. Morley to Minto, 21 January 1909. Cited by Koss, *John Morley at the India Office*, p. 133.

244. See Wilfred Blunt, *My Diaries*, II, p. 212; and Koss, *John Morley at the India Office*, pp. 156–9 on Morley's unwilling role in the Press Acts.

245. Though he felt compelled to add, if only to the sacred memory of Gladstone, 'that

I am never quite sure that if Clive had been beaten at Plassey, it might have been no bad thing either for Indians or English'. Morley to Hardinge, 11 April 1911, cited by Koss, *John Morley at the India Office*, p. 176.

246. Ibid., pp. 184–5.

247. See Koebner and Schmidt, *Imperialism*, p. 237; and Koss, *John Morley at the India Office*, pp. 125–6.

248. House of Commons speech, 23 February 1885, quoted by Thornton, *The Imperial Idea and its Enemies*, p. 68.

249. See Koss, *John Morley at the India Office*, pp. 210–11.

250. Morley to Minto, 15 August 1907, quoted by M. N. Das, *India under Morley and Minto* (1964), p. 51.

251. As Sir Valentine Chirol commented, after the mutiny it was the 'tacit assumption . . . never officially formulated, that the trusteeship was to last for ever'. *India Old & New* (1921), p. 101.

252. Curzon to Sir Arthur Godley, 9 April 1901, cited by Gopal, *British Policy in India*, pp. 296–7.

7   LIBERTY, EQUALITY, FRATERNITY: REFUTATION AND APOLGIA

1. Stephen to Mill, 9 April 1864; Mill to Stephen, 12 April 1864.

2. For example, in May Stephen asked Mill for a testimonial to support his (Stephen's) application for a Readership at the Committee of Legal Education; in May 1869 Mill saw Stephen as a 'doughty champion' of utilitarian theory, and the man to repulse Lecky's recent challenge to it. Indirect evidence suggests that Stephen may even have anticipated elements of his *LEF* critique of Mill's *Utilitarianism* in two *Pall Mall Gazette* articles in 5 and 8 June 1869. References to a 'Providential' sanction as the utlimate reinforcement of moral duty clearly resemble part of Stephen's later arguments. And most suggestive are the comments on the *Pall Mall Gazette* articles by J. Llewelyn Davies in his *Contemporary Review* (XV (1870), 81) discussion of 'Professor Grote on Utilitarianism'. When referring to the *Gazette* pieces, Davies attributes them to 'a writer of well-known vigour and acuteness, whose speculations on ethics and theology have been chiefly given to the public without his name in the *Pall Mall Gazette* and in *Fraser's Magazine*'; and 'a writer whose ethics breathe of the Criminal court' (p. 95).

3. Stephen to Mill, 3 August 1871.

4. 22 April to 14 May 1872.

5. 'My own chair has been solemnly taken away and put into the luggage room, for fear it should affect the compasses – and babyish as it seems, this throws out all my plans for reading and writing!' Stephen to Lady Egerton, 23 April 1872. The following day a compromise had been reached with the ship's authorities: 'I have had a certain place allotted to me – "thus far shalt thou go – and no nearer the compasses".' Stephen to Lady Egerton, 24 April 1872.

6. Stephen to Lady Egerton, 25 April 1872. Within a week Stephen was well settled into his hermitical existence: 'I suppose there was once, in remote ages, a time when I was not on board ship and when I went to bed at night and had a room to sit in where there was a foot or two of spare room, but it is so long ago that I have almost forgotten it.' Stephen to Lady Egerton, 2 May 1872.

7. Stephen to Lady Egerton, 26 April 1872.

8. Between November 1872 and January 1873. Commenting on these articles, at the time, Leslie Stephen wrote: '[My brother] is preaching to the world at a great rate in the *Pall Mall Gazette*, and I regret to say that I don't much approve of some of his sentiments.' Stephen to O. W. Holmes, 24 January 1873; quoted by Maitland in *Life and Letters of Leslie Stephen*, pp. 230–1.

9. *Recollections*, I, p. 55.

10. *Political Thought in England 1848–1914* (1926). In his general characterisation of the classical 'conservative' mentality, R. J. White selects two features which might have been written with Stephen in mind: belief that men are 'finite beings, prone to error, capable of becoming something decent with discipline, but more than likely to become something less than men without it'; and belief 'that a theory of progress is a delusion unless it is accompanied by a proper awareness of the ever present forces of degeneration which afflict man's imperfect will'. *The Conservative Tradition* (1964), p. 3.

11. *LEF*, 2nd edn, ed. White, p. 52. White provides an excellent short introductory overview of the book.

12. Mill, although influenced by a good deal of Comtist thinking relating to the empirical basis of the social sciences, totally rejected Comte's more extreme notions of a priesthood of a scientific/industrial elite who would pronounce on 'invariable laws of society'. For Mill this would have been a 'system of spiritual and temporal despotism'. *Autobiography*, ch. VI.

13. *LEF* was christened 'Frequality' by one of Stephen's daughters. He thought it was a superior title to his own and frequently used it in correspondence. For example, Stephen to Lady Egerton, 30 January and 26 December 1873; Stephen to Lytton, 2 May 1876.

14. *LEF*, p. 53.

15. *Life*, p. 307. Stephen saw *LEF* as 'by far the most systematic and fullest statement of my political and moral opinions I have ever yet made'. Stephen to Lady Egerton, 20 December 1872. And a few months later, he admitted to feeling 'just a little modest, as if I had shown more of my mind, and of myself, to the world at large than is my usual practice'. 27 March 1873.

16. See A. W. Benn's definition of 'rationalism' in *The History of English Rationalism in the Nineteenth Century* (1906), I, p. 1.

17. See chapter 5, 'Mill and the two faces of populism', above.

18. *On Liberty*, ch. 1, quoted in *LEF*, p. 55.

19. *On Compromise*, p. 265.

20. Stephen never quite settles down to a particular meaning of 'coercion'. This weakness of imprecision – or possibly mobility of definition – shows through especially in relation to 'Fraternity'.

21. *LEF*, p. 57.

22. Ibid., p. 61.

23. Ibid., p. 70.

24. Ibid., p. 166.

25. Ibid., pp. 70–1: a view which Maine incorporated in *Popular Government* (1885), pp. 388–9.

26. *LEF*, p. 72.

27. *Life*, p. 321.

28. See Rees, *Mill and his Early Critics*, p. 17.

29. *LEF*, pp. 27–8, 66.

30. Ibid., p. 75.

31. Ibid., p. 137.

32. Ibid., p. 68.

33. Ibid., p. 69.

34. Ibid., p. 71.

35. See, for example, Frederic Harrison's dismissal in *Tennyson, Ruskin, Mill, and Other Literary Estimates*, p. 301. For an elaborate modern argument in support of the distinction, see, for example, A. Ryan, *The Philosophy of John Stuart Mill* (1970), ch. XIII.

36. *LEF*, p. 74.

37. Ibid., pp. 74–5.

38. 'The Spirit of the Age' (1831), pp. 21–33. See also Mill's frosty response to the

Secretary of the Neophyte Writers' Society, making it abundantly clear that he was uninterested in supporting writing that was anything other than 'what I consider true and just'. Mill, *Collected Works*, XIV, p. 205, 23 April 1854.

39. Note Stephen's approving discussion of Locke's *Four Letters on Toleration* in which Locke claims that free inquiry is the only guarantee of the truth of any doctrine. 'Persecution destroys this guarantee, and is therefore unfavourable to any intelligent and real belief in the truth of any creed. . . ' 'Locke on Toleration', *Horae Sabbaticae*, II, p. 157, at 171.
40. *LEF*, p. 75.
41. Earlier Stephen had suggested that most people were not 'half sceptical enough'. Ibid., p. 29.
42. Ibid., pp. 106–7.
43. As Mill acknowledged, this view owed much to Wilhelm von Humbolt's partly Kantian *Sphere and Duties of Government*, written in the late eighteenth century and translated into English in 1854.
44. Leslie Stephen, *The English Utilitarians*, III (1900), p. 261.
45. *LEF*, p. 80.
46. *The English Utilitarians*, III, p. 263.
47. Chapter 5 above.
48. Fitzjames expressly acknowledged borrowing some of Leslie's arguments contained in the latter's *Fraser's Magazine* article, 'On Social Macadamisation', XVI (1872), 10. At slight risk of misrepresentation, Leslie had distinct but not uncritical Millist leanings: for him, utilitarianism, though containing much truth, was insufficiently sociological and evolutionary. See generally Annan, *Leslie Stephen*.
49. *LEF*, p. 81.
50. Ibid., p. 80.
51. Ibid., p. 184.
52. Rees, *Mill and his Early Critics*, pp. 33–4.
53. *Sketches and Essays; and Winterslow* (1872).
54. Such as Isaiah Berlin: *Four Essays on Liberty* (1969), p. 128.
55. *LEF*, p. 107.
56. Ibid., pp. 85, 174.
57. Ibid., p. 86.
58. *Life*, p. 307.
59. See also Henry Sidgwick, *Elements of Politics*, p. 66; first published 1891.
60. *LEF*, p. 99.
61. See Henry Sidgwick's consideration of the 'quasi governmental' role of the clergy: *Elements of Politics*, p. 216.
62. *LEF*, p. 102.
63. Mill's principle applied to advanced civilised states. It is very doubtful whether Mill believed India qualified as such. Certainly James Mill thought not.
64. *LEF*, p. 90. Though the local population would largely accept it as good later. On the great 'moral and general effect' of sound British legislation, see Stephen's extensive 'Minute . . . on the Administration of Justice in British India', p. 139 (October 1871), Argyll Papers, India Office Library.
65. *LEF*, p. 108. As Leslie points out, in the first edition 'ignorant preacher' was 'wretched little curate': *Life*, p. 327.
66. Finally abolished in 1871. See Harvie's account in *The Lights of Liberalism*, ch. 4.
67. *Contemporary Review*, XXV (1874), 446.
68. Ibid., 473–4.
69. NS, XXXV, 289. Commenting on the article to T.H.S. Escott, then editor of the *Fortnightly Review*, Stephen admitted that if he had his own way he would simply abolish the whole law of blasphemy. Letter, 10 December 1883, Escott Papers, British Library.
70. Two years before, Stephen had been scheduled to try Charles Bradlaugh for blas-

phemous libel; Stephen expressed some relief following rescheduling of the trial for hearing by Lord Coleridge, 'who I fancy will treat him far more severely than I should have. . . Holding to a large extent the same views as [Bradlaugh] does as to religion, though his brutality disgusts me . . . it would have been difficult to do justice to him and to the law. . . It would have been against all my principles either to deny that he had broken the law, or to punish him severely for breaking it in a way in which I have often broken it myself.' Stephen to Lady Grant Duff, 3 August 1882. However, Bradlaugh later came before Stephen in the famous constitutional law case of *Bradlaugh* v. *Gossett* (1884), brought by Bradlaugh to overrule a House of Commons injunction excluding his presence from the House. Stephen declared the House of Commons not subject to judicial control 'in its administration of that part of the statute law which has relation to its own internal proceedings'.

71. For example, L. M. Aspland, *The Law of Blasphemy: Being a Candid Examination of the Views of Mr Justice Stephen* (1884).
72. Cf. bk III, ch. 10.
73. *LEF*, p. 121.
74. Ibid., p. 97. In an earlier *Saturday Review* discussion of religious toleration Stephen concluded that the 'real argument against persecution' is that 'all our existing forms of religion have so much good in them that it is highly desirable that they should mutually instruct each other . . . ' : *Horae Sabbaticae*, II, p. 172.
75. *LEF* p. 150.
76. Ibid., p. 151.
77. Ibid., p. 158.
78. Ibid., p. 162.
79. Ibid., pp. 159–60.
80. Ibid., p. 162.
81. Professor Hart suggests that Stephen favoured the enforcement of morality as a thing of intrinsic value independent of its use in preserving social order. But as Hart admits, 'it may well be that his complex position does not reduce to anything so simple as the view that a popular demand for coercion was justified simply because it was the cry of the majority': *Law, Liberty and Morality* (1963), pp. 78–9, and pp. 49 and 55. For a cogent analysis of the main issues see Ten, *Mill on Liberty*, ch. 6.
82. Elements of such a thesis have made appearances in the works of many political philosophers, including Burke and Locke. In Locke's case, although religious toleration merited high prominence he was in no doubt that ultimately there could be no toleration of those opinions antagonistic to human society or to those moral rules which are necessary to the 'preservation of civil society'. *A Letter Concerning Toleration* (1689).
83. The basic modern statement of this is Hart's discussion of the minimum content of law and a shared morality in his *Concept of Law* (1960), ch. 9. Earlier broadly similar propositions were put by Hobbes, *Leviathan*, chs. 14 and 15, and Hume, *Treatise*, bk III, pt II, sections 2–7.
84. *A Letter Concerning Toleration*.
85. *Horae Sabbaticae*, II, p. 168.
86. See also Morley, *On Compromise*, p. 239.
87. *Law, Liberty and Morality* and *The Enforcement of Morals* (1965), originally published in 1959. Probably Profesor Hart's most important divergence from Millist opinion is his own belief in the moral defensibility of general paternalism. Like Mill, Hart seems to see lack of liberty as not subsumed within unhappiness ('human misery') and liberty as being something to be sought apart from happiness. See *Law, Liberty and Morality*, p. 82.
88. Cmnd. 247, 1957.

89. Though in the case of homosexual activities, Stephen characterised such as 'so gross and outrageous that, self-protection apart, they must be prevented as far as possible at any cost to the offender, and punished, if they occur, with exemplary severity' (*LEF*, p. 162): hardly an example of paternalistic intervention. Cf. J. Feinberg, *The Moral Limits of the Criminal Law*, III, *Harm to Self* (1986), p. 17. Stephen's justification for curtailing homosexual activities seems to be a case within Hart's 'conservative' thesis.

90. *LEF*, p. 32.

91. Ibid., p. 159.

92. *Fragment of Government* (1776), p. 143. Bentham knew little of Hobbes. Hobbes was not a utilitarian or even a true hedonist because his egotistic theory of human nature is one of self-preservation, not general happiness. Hobbes' arguments were not so much aimed at a system of reasoning, but at why we should act in a particular way; the basis, not the content of morals was his greatest concern. Rather than Hobbes, the most important intellectual influences on Bentham were the Italian philosopher Beccaria, *Essays on Crimes and Punishment* (1764; translated into English 1767) and Hume. Hume's *Treatise of Human Nature* (1740) and *Enquiry Concerning the Principles of Morals* (1751) anticipated much fundamental utilitarian (antimetaphysical) thinking by putting morality on a secular basis and employing the utility of a pleasure/pain distinction. However, Hume's references to utility related mainly to the political stability of custom and conventions which had been unconsciously accepted on the basis of their utility, whereas Bentham's utility was one of evaluation of actions. Moreover, unlike Bentham and Hobbes, Hume never adopted simple egotism as the key to human conduct.

93. Quoted by E. Halévy, *The Growth of Philosophic Radicalism*, translated by M. Morris ed. J. Plamenatz (1972), p. 379.

94. One alternative view is that Bentham believed that there was a 'natural harmony' of long-term interests of individuals and the general welfare. See Leslie Stephen, *The English Utilitarians*, II, p. 315, and more recently D. Lyons, *In the Interest of the Governed* (1973), chs. 2 and 3.

95. *Introduction to the Principles of Morals and Legislation*, ed. Burns and Hart, ch. XVII, section 3.

96. Ibid., ch. XVII, 9–12.

97. As opposed to 'transitive' or 'extra-regarding' offences: ibid., ch. XVI, 6–8.

98. Ibid., ch. XVII, 15.

99. Ibid., ch. XVII, 16.

100. *Utilitarianism*, ch. 3.

101. *On Liberty*, ch. 5. For a spiritied claim that Mill's liberty was of a highly selective variety, and such as to subvert his opposition to paternalism, see M. Cowling, *Mill and Liberalism* (1963); and also in similar vein, S. Letwin on Mill in *The Pursuit of Certainty* (1965).

102. Mill's individual is 'one who is fully appraised of the realities of his actions and such as to make his choice a truly considered one'.

103. Although Stephen provides few indications anywhere in his writings as to how far this interventionism would go. Vital questions on economic and social matters are quite untouched.

104. *The English Utilitarians*, III, p. 290.

105. D. G. Long, *Bentham on Liberty* (1977), p. 116.

106. *The English Utilitarians*, II, pp. 314–15.

107. See the reviews listed by Rees, *Mill and his Early Critics*, p. 38 n. 77; and R. P. Anschutz, *The Philosophy of J. S. Mill* (1963), p. 25.

108. *Fraser's Magazine*, LXXXVI (1872), 150, at 158–9 and L. Huxley, *Life and Letters of T. H. Huxley*, II, pp. 305–6.

109. Quoted by G. Himmelfarb, *On Liberty and Liberalism* (1974), p. 293.

110. Introductory chapter, 'Democracy', in *The Popular Education of France* (1861).
111. Frederic Harrison, *Tennyson, Ruskin, Mill, and Other Literary Estimates*, pp. 305–6.
112. See for example, A. Quinton, *Utilitarian Ethics*, (1973); J. Plamenatz, *The English Utilitarians* (1966); and Ten, *Mill on Liberty*.
113. From the considerable volume of literature see, for example, Ryan, *The Philosophy of John Stuart Mill* and *John Stuart Mill* (1974); and John Gray, *Mill on Liberty: a defence* (1983).
114. Particularly ch. II, 'Of the Possible Utility of Error'.
115. Quoted in the *DNB*.
116. *LEF*, p. 219, and ch. V.
117. Ibid., p. 175.
118. Ibid., p. 209.
119. Mill to T. E. Cliffe Leslie, 8 May 1869, in *Collected Works*, XVII, p. 1600.
120. *The Province of Jurisprudence Determined*, Lecture II. Generally, in Austin's view, 'Political or civil liberty has been erected into an idol, and extolled with extravagant praises by doting and fanatical worshippers.'
121. The Constitutional Code, in *Works*, IX, p. 81.
122. *Enquiry Concerning the Principles of Morals* (1751), Appendix III.
123. *Works*, IX, pp. 14–17. See W. Stark, 'Liberty and Equality. . . ', *Economic Journal*, LI (1941), 56.
124. *LEF*, p. 181.
125. Ibid., p. 182. In 1865 (*Fraser's Magazine*, LXXII, 778 at 790) Stephen suggested the 'best pocket definition' of justice was the 'adherence to rules of conduct founded on the principle of the greatest happiness' – justice was utility.
126. *Introduction to the Principles of Morals and Legislation*, ed. Burns and Hart, ch. X, 40 b2.
127. Hume also devoted much effort in his *Treatise* and second *Enquiry* attempting to account for principles of justice on a purely utilitarian basis.
128. *Utilitarianism*, ch. V.
129. Except for so-called 'rule' utilitarians, who would maintain that breaking a promise would damage the utility of the institution of promising.
130. *The Province of Jurisprudence Determined*, Lecture II.
131. Quoted in *LEF*, p. 187. See also Hobbes, *Leviathan*, ch. 13 on 'Equality'.
132. *LEF*, p. 188.
133. Ibid., p. 202.
134. See also the discussion of Macaulay and Lowe, ch. 5 above.
135. *LEF*, p. 208.
136. Ibid., p. 192.
137. For example, Mill's Edinburgh speech of 12 January 1871, posthumously printed in 1873; and his House of Commons speech on 'Electoral Franchise' of 20 May 1867.
138. *The Subjection of Women*, in *Collected Works*, vol. XXI, ch. 4, final sentence.
139. S. Collini, *Collected Works of John Stuart Mill*, introduction to vol. XXI (1984), p. xv.
140. *John Stuart Mill: A Criticism with Personal Recollections* (1882), p. 130. John Morley felt able to defend Mill: see the *Fortnightly Review*, XV (1874), 1. Morley described the book as the 'notable result of this ripest, loftiest and most inspiring part of his life' (p. 12).
141. 'Emancipation – Black and White' (1865), in *Science and Education, Collected Essays*, III, p. 68.
142. 'Votes for Women,' in *Realities and Ideals* (1908).
143. *Tennyson, Ruskin, Mill, and Other Literary Estimates* (1899), p. 310.
144. As Harrison also later argued, ibid., p. 309.
145. Quoted in *LEF*, pp. 190–1.
146. Ibid., p. 194.

147. Bentham, in distinguishing the characteristics of the sexes, believed 'in point of quantity and quality of knowledge, in point of strength of intellectual powers, and firmness of mind [a woman] is commonly inferior . . . [though] moral, religious, sympathetic, and antipathetic sensibility are commonly stronger in her. . . In general her antipathetic as well as sympathetic biases are apt to be less conformable to the principle of utility than those of the male; owing chiefly to some deficiency in . . . knowledge, discernment and comprehension.' *Introduction to the Principles of Morals and Legislation*, ch. VI, 35.

148. See the examples cited by M. M. Bevington, *The 'Saturday Review, 1855–1868'*, pp. 114–17.

149. See also Bentham, *Works*, I, p. 340.

150. *LEF*, p. 195; Mill was equivocal on the question of the dissolubility of marriage.

151. In the direction of property, Stephen had long held the progressive view that married women should be entitled to own property separately from their husbands. 'Marriage Settlements', *Cornhill Magazine*, VIII (1863), 666.

152. *LEF*, p. 209.

153. The manner of Stephen's citation (*ibid.*, p. 195) of Harrison's remark suggests that Stephen found it rather entertaining.

154. *Life*, p. 330.

155. See Mill's essay on Coleridge in F. R. Leavis' edition of *Mill on Bentham and Coleridge*, p. 100.

156. *Saturday Review*, XXII (1866), 74.

157. XXV (1889), 781.

158. Leslie Stephen, *The English Utilitarians*, III, p. 284.

159. 'A Reply to Mr Fitzjames Stephen's Strictures on Mr J. S. Mill's Subjection of Women' (London, 1874), p. 16.

160. With one of history's satisfying coincidences Millicent Fawcett later became the biographer of Sir William Molesworth, the nineteenth-century reviver and editor of Hobbes' works. Her husband Henry Fawcett, the 'Millist' Member of Parliament, was a good friend of Leslie Stephen, who later wrote Fawcett's biography.

161. 'Mr Fitzjames Stephen on the Position of Women' (London, 1873), p. 15.

162. *LEF*, p. 212.

163. Ibid., p. 211.

164. Ibid., p. 212.

165. For example ch. III, 'That the Ideally Best Form of Government is Representative Government'.

166. 'Parliamentary Government', *Contemporary Review*, XXIII (1873), 161, at 168.

167. Frederic Harrison's *Order and Progress* (1875) provided a Comtean blueprint for effective government administration, many features of which resemble Stephen's plans, particularly Parliament's role as a legislative machine and the need for a strong informed executive.

168. See *Representative Government*, ch. V, 'Of the Proper Functions of Representative Bodies'.

169. *Fortnightly Review*, IV (1868), 320 at 330; quoted by D. A. Hamer in *John Morley* (1968), p. 78.

170. *On Compromise*, p. 213.

171. Letter, 15 November 1873; quoted by J. A. Froude in his *Life of Carlyle* (1884), II, p. 423.

172. *Life*, p. 222. Leslie suggests his brother's main reason for standing was 'professional'.

173. Leslie Stephen notes that Lord Coleridge had suggested the possibility of the Solicitor Generalship, but his brother in a letter to Sir Alfred Lyall had, in the following year, mentioned the chances of the Attorney Generalship. Stephen to Lyall, 17 September 1874, Lyall Papers, fol. 55.

174. Stephen to his mother, 27 July 1873, two days into the campaign. Writing to his

wife: 'I cannot express the loathings I have for it all . . . I never did a more disagreeable thing in my life', 27 July 1873.

175. Stephen to his wife, 30 July 1873 and *Life*, p. 345.

176. *Life*, p. 346.

177. Stephen to Lyall, 17 September 1874.

178. Stephen polled a miserable 1,086 votes, Jenkins 4,010 and Yeaman 5,207.

179. Stephen to Lady Egerton, 17 March 1875.

180. *Law and Public Opinion* (1905), pp. 457–9.

181. See also Bagehot's *Physics and Politics* for his theory of learned or imitative political attributes.

182. For example, in *Representative Government*.

183. M. E. Grant Duff, *Sir Henry Maine: A Brief Memoir of his Life* (1892), pp. 74–5.

184. *Popular Government* (1885), p. 94.

185. Amongst other notables later blaming the degeneration of politics on a tighter party system was Dicey; see R. A. Cosgrove, *The Rule of Law: Albert Venn Dicey, Victorian Jurist* (1980), p. 110.

186. Ibid., p. 108.

187. Rousseau's democracy was, of course, 'direct' rather than resembling British representative democracy.

188. *Popular Government*, pp. 45–6.

189. A charge even more vehemently levelled at Lecky's *Democracy and Liberty* by Morley in his review 'Lecky on Democracy', reprinted in *Oracles on Man and Government* (1921), p. 23.

190. Bryce to Sidgwick, 2 September 1887, Bryce Papers, Bodleian Library, Oxford. Later Bryce's view softened to 'ingenious but elusive' in *Modern Democracies*, quoted in Collini, Winch and Burrow, *That Noble Science of Politics*, p. 241.

191. 'Maine on Popular Government', reprinted in *Oracles on Man and Government*, p. 59, at 62.

192. Stephen to Lytton, 7 September 1884. For his part, Maine thought *Liberty, Equality, Fraternity* an 'admirable volume': *Popular Government*, p. 58. See Feaver, *From Status to Contract*, pp. 190–3 for a consideration of Stephen's influence on Maine's political theory.

193. 29 August 1881 and 9 October 1882, Lytton Papers, Hertford, MSS C.37.

194. *Oracles on Man and Government*, pp. 62–3.

195. *Fraser's Magazine*, LXXII (1865), 784–9.

196. Ibid., 791.

197. Ibid., 792.

198. *Utilitarianism*, ed. M. Warnock (1962), p. 286.

199. *On Compromise* (1874), p. 36, 1917 edition. Though coming close at one time, Morley himself never quite accepted this: see Hamer, *John Morley*.

200. 'The Scientific Aspects of Positivism', *Fortnightly Review* V (1869), 653, at 657.

201. Bentham accepted religious beliefs as one of four sanctions, (with 'physical, political, moral') 'capable of giving a binding force to any law or rule of conduct'. The religious sanction was 'altogether unliquidated in point of quality'. *Introduction to the Principles of Morals and Legislation*, ch. III, 2–12.

202. *Utilitarianism*, p. 281.

203. Frederic Harrison, *Autobiographic Memoirs* (1911), II, p. 87.

204. *LEF*, p. 211: 'Cannot you imagine yourself being indignant at particular people if they were to fall in love with you? I remember F. Harrison once replying, when I said I agreed with him – "I protest against you agreeing with me. I object to being agreed with"; and Mill's love of the human race always strikes me, more or less, in the same way. I always feel inclined to say "why the d----e (as the pious Campbell would write it) cannot you let me alone".' Stephen to Lady Egerton, 26 April 1872.

205. 'I recollect about three or four years ago [1868–9] I had a battle royal . . . with my

brother Leslie, and we at last came to the conclusion that the real difference between us [Leslie and Fitzjames] was that he thought better of mankind than I do. It is a long story to show how this difference colours not only one's politics, but one's morals and one's religion too – but it does. . . ' Stephen to Lady Egerton, 2 May 1872.

206. *LEF*, p. 281.

207. Ibid., p. 282. Stephen's contention that Mill's distinction between 'higher and lower' pleasures led nowhere anticipated later criticism that Mill moved from the proposition that what is conducive to general happiness was high moral and cultural virtue, to maintaining that such general happiness was the actual object of everyone's desires – deriving what *is* from what *ought* to be.

208. *Utilitarianism*, ch. 2.

209. *LEF*, p. 229.

210. Ibid., p. 231.

211. *Introduction to the Principles of Morals and Legislation*, ch. X, 36–8. Legislators were exhorted to increase the influence of sympathy at the expense of self-regard.

212. Henry Sidgwick, 'Bentham and Benthamism in Politics and Ethics', in *Miscellaneous Essays and Addresses* (1904), p. 151.

213. *The Methods of Ethics*, first published in 1874.

214. *LEF*, p. 237.

215. Ibid., p. 238.

216. This applied between nations too: every citizen should do 'his best for his own side'. Letter, Stephen to Lytton, 30 August 1877.

217. 'Inaugural Address' (London, 1867), p. 43.

218. For a recent assessment of Harrison and his role in English positivism see M. S. Vogeler, *Frederic Harrison: The Vocations of a Positivist* (1984), particularly chs. 5 and 6.

219. *LEF*, p. 40.

220. Ibid., p. 41.

221. Ibid., p. 42.

222. Ibid., p. 249.

223. Ibid., p. 247. Hutton rightly singled out these views as particularly 'finely' expressed: 'Mr Fitzjames Stephen's Creed', from *Criticisms on Contemporary Thought and Thinkers*, II, p. 112. See also W. Pater, *Studies in the History of the Renaissance* (1873), p. 248.

224. *LEF*, p. 250. Leslie cryptically comments in his *Life* that 'I do not ask whether [Fitzjames'] interpretation be correct' (p. 335 n. 2). But at least in respect of the issue under discussion, Fitzjames was, essentially, right.

225. 'The Unknowable and the Unknown', *Nineteenth Century*, XV (1884), 905, at 912.

226. *Saturday Review*, V (1858), 563–4.

227. *LEF*, p. 134.

228. *Horae Sabbaticae*, III, p. 92. Paley's utilitarian theory of morality is chiefly set out in his *Moral and Political Philosophy* (1785). See also D. C. Somervell, *English Thought in the Nineteenth Century*, 4th edn (1940), pp. 43–4.

229. J. R. Seeley, *Ecce Homo: a Survey of the Life and Work of Jesus Christ* (1866). As a whole, Stephen found Seeley's examination of the evidence of Christ's life and teachings slipshod and most unlawyer-like: the 'fundamental and incurable defect of [the book was that it was] a novel, and not a good novel, under a critical disguise'. *Fraser's Magazine*, LXXIII (1866), 746, at 747, and LXXIV, 29. See Chapter 8 below.

230. *LEF*, p. 252.

231. Ibid., p. 252. Stephen's approach to perplexing theological questions, such as why should what is regarded as temporal virtue be necessarily similarly regarded by any God, is considered along with his general religious speculation in Chapter 8.

232. Ibid., p. 46.
233. Stephen to Lady Egerton, 27 December 1872.
234. An impression bolstered by Leslie Stephen's comment that Fitzjames was 'not altogether satisfied' with that section of the book. *Life*, p. 377.
235. *Fortnightly Review*, XIII (1873), 677.
236. *LEF*, p. 36.
237. Ibid., p. 36.
238. Ibid., p. 37.
239. A younger Stephen more than once stated his strong allegiance to the virtue: for example, 'I have as a rule maintained that stoicism . . . is the first of social duties', Stephen to G. S. Venables, 3 March 1860, Venables Papers. Similarly in letters to Sir William Harcourt, 11 March 1862 and 2 February 1863, Harcourt Papers, Bodleian Library, MSS. D 199 and 200.
240. Ibid., p. 271. This passage was taken by William James, the Harvard professor of philosophy and elder brother of Henry James, as an endpiece for his 'radical empiricist[s]': *The Will to Believe* (1897), pp. 31 and 212. According to James' biographer, R. B. Perry, 'Stephen was a favourite author, frequently quoted by [James]', *The Thought and Character of William James* (1935), I, p. 210. Leslie Stephen and James were friends; of *The Will to Believe*, Leslie wrote, 'I am afraid that he is trying the old dodge of twisting "faith" out of moonshine.' Maitland, *Life and Letters of Leslie Stephen*, p. 445.
241. R. H. Hutton refers to this unattributed description in his 1873 *Spectator* review of *Liberty, Equality, Fraternity*, reprinted in *Criticisms on Contemporary Thought and Thinkers*, II, p. 119.
242. Quoted by F. W. Hirst, *Early Life and Letters of John Morley* (1927), I, p. 242.
243. Although as Harrison admitted to Morley (letter, 8 April 1873), positivism contained a strong conservative strain, a fondness for the stability of institutions and firm government. Indeed all this had been recently laid out in the *Fortnightly Review* (of which Morley was editor) in Harrison's 'The Revival of Authority', XIX (1873), 2.
244. Harrison to Morley, 8 April 1873, Harrison Papers, London School of Economics and Political Science Library, fol. 1/56.
245. For example, Morley to Harrison, 6 April, 20 April, 22 April, 4 June, 21 June, 14 July. Harrison to Morley, 9 April, 19 April, 21 April, 12 May, 2 July. Harrison Papers, fols. 1/80, 1/56.
246. 16 July, fol. 1/56.
247. 15 August, fol. 1/80.
248. pp. 248–9 and 284. *On Compromise* was published in late 1874, having first appeared in article form in the *Fortnightly Review* in April, June, July and August 1874. The 'Note' on the 'Doctrine of Liberty' (pp. 266–4) is extracted from Morley's earlier *Fortnightly Review* article.
249. 22 August 1873, Harrison Papers, fol. 1/80. Morley was not the only one to regard Stephen's demeanour as Johnsonian: see also A.G.C. Liddell, *Notes from the Life of an Ordinary Mortal* (1911), p. 207. On the appearance of the second edition of *LEF*, Leslie wrote: 'JFS has published a second edition of "Liberty, etc.", with a preface intended to blow Harrison and Morley into thin air. It is good hard hitting, but I think rather too angry, and not intelligible unless one remembers all that he said, and all that they said – which one doesn't.' Letter to Charles Eliot Norton, 30 March 1874, quoted by Maitland in his *Life and Letters of Leslie Stephen*, p. 240.
250. *Autobiographic Memoirs*, II (1911), p. 114.
251. This is attributed to Stephen by Harrison in a letter to Morley, 12 May 1873, fol. 1/56. Leslie records that his brother found Mill to be 'cold as ice', *Life*, p. 316.
252. Mills, *Collected Works*, XVII, p. 1600, 8 May 1869. According to Bain, Mill's reaction to the *Liberty* articles, on their first appearing in the *Pall Mall Gazette*, was

that the author ' "doesn't know what he is arguing against; and is more likely to repel than to attract people". This last observation [observed Bain] is, I think, the juster of the two.' *John Stuart Mill: A Criticism with Personal Recollections*, p. 111. Stephen expected Mill 'in some form or other [to] refer to me. I have no doubt he will be bitterly angry and all the more because he will say he is not angry. I do not very much care about it. I never had much affection for him. He always appeared to me too much like a walking book to be much cared for.' Stephen to Lady Egerton, 7 February 1873.

253. Perhaps predictably, the *Saturday Review* saw the work as 'one of the most valuable contributions of political philosophy published in recent times': XXXV (1873), 517; see also, for example, the *Quarterly Review* (1873), 178. According to Harrison, Leslie Stephen was the reviewer of Fitzjames' book in *Fraser's Magazine* (VIII (1873), 86): letter to Morley, 2 July 1873, Harrison Papers, fol. 1/56. But the review is signed 'F.P.', reasonably suggested to be Frederick Pollock in the *Wellesley Index to Periodicals*.

254. *John Stuart Mill: A Criticism with Personal Recollections*, pp. 109 and 111.

255. *The Academy*, IV (1873), 292, at 293. Sidgwick described *Liberty, Equality, Fraternity* as an 'able but unsatisfying book; . . . often offensively loud and overbearing . . . [and] along with a good deal of acute reasoning, the work contains a provokingly large amount of wilful paradox and misplaced ingenuity, confusion of ideas, misrepresentation of opinions and even downright ignorance. . . ' .

256. *Fraser's Magazine*, VIII (1873), 86, at 88 and 87.

257. *Criticisms on Contemporary Thought and Thinkers*, II, pp. 112–18.

258. R. S. Rait, *Memorials of Albert Venn Dicey* (1925), p. 139. Similarly, Goldwin Smith's assessment of Fitzjames and Leslie quoted in Chapter 2 above.

259. *An Introduction to the History of the Science of Politics* (1920), pp. 132–3, first published 1890.

260. *Fortnightly Review*, XV (1874), 425, at 437, quoted by Hamer, *John Morley*, p. 7; and *Recollections*, I, p. 100.

261. Carlyle in his essay 'Sir Walter Scott', speaking of the 1830s, is quoted by Mill in *On Liberty*, ch. 2.

262. A. and E. M. Sidgwick, *Henry Sidgwick: A Memoir* (1906), p. 357.

263. *Map of Life*, pp. 227–8, quoted by Houghton, *The Victorian Frame of Mind 1830–1870*, p. 99.

264. Annan, *Leslie Stephen*, pp. 282–90. See also the account of the evolutionary theories of Herbert Spencer in Himmelfarb, 'Varieties of Social Darwinism', in Himmelfarb, *Victorian Minds* and Burrow, *Evolution and Society*.

265. *Evolution and Ethics and Other Essays* (1898), pp. 81–2 and letter, 5 November 1892, in L. Huxley's *Life and Letters of Thomas Henry Huxley*, II, p. 305. Stephen's non-egalitarian views on the inevitable inequality of social man were also held by Huxley, for example, in 'On the Natural Inequality of Men', *Nineteenth Century*, XXVII (1890), I. Huxley, a fellow member of the Metaphysical Society, was well respected by Stephen.

266. Soon after the appearance of *Liberty, Equality, Fraternity* Maitland produced an unsuccessful dissertation (1875) for a philosophy fellowship at Trinity College, Cambridge, entitled 'A Historical Sketch of Liberty and Equality as Ideals of English Political Philosophy From the Time of Hobbes to the Time of Coleridge'. Maitland's own stance was rather obscure – critical of Mill's position, and bringing in references to Stephen but without adopting his position. See *F. W. Maitland – The Collected Papers*, ed. H.A.L. Fisher (1911), I.

267. Himmelfarb, *On Liberty and Liberalism*, p. 298.

268. 'Mr Stephen on Liberty, Equality, Fraternity', in *Criticisms on Contemporary Thought and Thinkers*, II, p. 139.

269. *Culture and Anarchy*, ch. 4, p. 131.

270. *Lectures on the Relation Between Law and Public Opinion in England during the Nineteenth Century* (1914), pp. xxvii and xxx, first published 1905.
271. *Autobiographic Memoirs*, II, p. 88. In his *Saturday Review* essay, 'Locke as a Moralist', Stephen had characterised this to be a 'rather coarse and special form of utilitarianism': *Horae Sabbaticae*, II, p. 135.
272. *Nineteenth Century*, I (1877), 331 and 531. This 'symposium' was proposed by Stephen himself. Its contributors included Lord Selborne, Frederic Harrison, T. H. Huxley and R. H. Hutton, amongst others. Stephen provided the opening and closing comments. See Chapter 8 below.
273. Ibid., 332 and 546. Also Leslie's views, for example, 'An Apology for Plainspeaking', in *Essays on Freethinking and Plainspeaking* (1873), pp. 370–4.
274. From *Three Essays on Religion* (1874).
275. Morley, *Recollections*, I, p. 106, and *On Compromise*; also M. Packe, *The Life of John Stuart Mill* (1954), p. 433.
276. 'Utility of Religion', in *Three Essays on Religion*, p. 71.
277. Letter to Cross from Eliot, 20 October 1873, quoted by Houghton in *The Victorian Frame of Mind 1830–1870*, p. 402.
278. *Life of John Stirling* (1851), II, ch. 2, p. 105.
279. *Essays on Freethinking and Plainspeaking*, p. 369.
280. *On Compromise*, pp. 51 and 84.
281. *Past and Present*, III, ch. 1, p. 136.
282. *Contemporary Review*, XXIII (1874), 497–527 and 989–1017.
283. Ibid., p. 1017. See also J. Roach, 'Liberalism and the Victorian Intelligentsia', *Cambridge Historical Journal*, 13 (1957), 55, at 66–7.
284. In an earlier *Saturday Review* article, 'The Temporal and Spiritual Powers', Stephen expressed considerable scepticism at the utility of attempts to 'bolster up' the 'shadow' of a spiritual sanction. *Horae Sabbaticae*, III, p. 357.
285. 'Darwin and Divinity', in *Essays on Freethinking and Plainspeaking*, p. 119. My italics.
286. 'Mr Stephen on Liberty, Equality, and Fraternity', in *Criticisms on Contemporary Thought and Thinkers*, II, p. 138.
287. *Nineteenth Century*, XV (1884), 905.
288. Ibid., 917–18.
289. Ibid., 918–19.
290. Leslie Stephen may have had something such as this in mind when observing that 'To destroy an old faith was still for [Fitzjames] to destroy the great impulse to a noble life', *Life*, p. 310.
291. *Recollections*, I, pp. 101–2.
292. *Enquiry Concerning Human Understanding*, II, 1.2.
293. Less sympathetically, Henry Sidgwick thought 'the logic of Bentham and the rhetoric of Carlyle, succeed each other with bewildering incoherence'. *The Academy*, IV (1873), 292, at 294.
294. Morley to Harrison, Hirst, *Early Life and Letters of John Morley*, I, p. 244.
295. 'Mr Carlyle', *Fraser's Magazine*, LXXII (1865), 778, at 788–9. According to Carlyle 'Might and Right do differ frightfully from hour to hour; but give them centuries to try it in, they are found to be identical.' *Chartism*, ch. 8. On the expression 'Right is might', Austin felt obliged to note that this 'paradoxical proposition (a great favourite with shallow scoffers and buffoons)' was either a 'flat truism affectedly and darkly expressed' or simply 'thoroughly false and absurd'. It was the former when taken to mean 'every right is a creature of might and power'; and the latter if interpreted to suggest that 'right and might are one and the same thing, or are merely different names for one and the same object'. *Province*, lecture IV, pp. 284–5n. See also T. H. Huxley, who felt that 'The gravitation of sin to sorrow is as certain as that of the earth to the sun. . . ' L. Huxley, *Thomas Henry Huxley* (1920), pp. 77–8.

296. For example, Leslie Stephen, 'Carlyle's Ethics', in *Hours in a Library*, III, p. 286; and John Morley, 'Carlyle', *Critical Miscellanies*, I, 166.

8 RATIONALISM'S BURDEN

1. The 'statement' or 'letter to his children' was uncompleted and undated. His daughter Dorothea believed it to have been written before 1876; see her letter of 8 June 1953, Add MSS 7349, fol. 21. References in the 'statement' and other indicators suggest it was written after Stephen's return from India.
2. Morley's flirtation with positivism had ended by the time of his 1876 *Encyclopaedia Britannica* entry for Comte, where Comtism was dismissed as 'utilitarianism crowned by a fantastic decoration [of] an artificial Great Being'. Quoted by Hirst, *Early Life and Letters of John Morley*, I, p. 324.
3. George Eliot, *George Eliot's Life, Letters and Journals*, ed. J. W. Cross (1885), II, p. 283. See also Morley's reference to 'clear and steadfast eye' in *On Compromise*, ch. 4, p. 200.
4. Leslie Stephen, 'Scepticism', from *An Agnostic's Apology* (1893), p. 85.
5. The intellectual backbone of the bulk of rationalists naturally owed most to Hume's main theological discussions in *Essay on Miracles* (1748) and *Dialogues Concerning Natural Religion* (1779) and to Mill's *Logic*. This was especially true of both Stephens, Huxley and W. K. Clifford. Chief among continental influences were probably the Kantian notions of knowledge set out in *Critique of Pure Reason* (1781), which pointed to similar agnostic conclusions, though in a far less accessible manner to the nineteenth-century amateur philosopher. Beyond Strauss' *Life of Jesus*, the philosophic dilettante's knowledge of German biblical scholarship was, generally, as limited as Edward Casaubon's.
6. Arnold, *Literature and Dogma*. For a recent study of Jowett's religion see P. Hinchliff, *Benjamin Jowett and the Christian Religion* (1987).
7. Noel Annan's *Leslie Stephen*, ch. 5, provides an excellent account of the Claphamite milieu in which Leslie and Fitzjames were raised. More generally see O. Chadwick's *The Victorian Church* (1970), I.
8. J. S. Mill', *Spirit of the Age* (1831).
9. *Life*, p. 56.
10. *Essays in Ecclesiastical Biography* (1850), originally published as essays in the *Edinburgh Review*. The collection's epilogue gives a fair indication of Sir James' beliefs.
11. *Life*, pp. 55–7.
12. Autobiographic Fragment, pp. 6 and 11; *Life*, p. 59.
13. Autobiographic Fragment, p. 101.
14. *Life*, p. 62.
15. Ibid., p. 62.
16. Autobiographic Fragment, p. 14.
17. Sir James to Fitzjames, 9 August 1847, *The First Sir James Stephen*, pp. 119–20.
18. Sir James to Fitzjames, 8 August 1854, ibid., p. 207.
19. *Life*, p. 128.
20. Autobiographic Fragment, p. 7. In further references to this characteristic, Stephen suggests that acceptance of irrational belief injures the 'moral character . . . in some way as . . . any other act of dishonesty . . . my father . . . seemed not to be blameless in this matter , . . it impressed me more than I can say'. Stephen to Lady Egerton, 6 March 1877. Sir James' preferred profession for Fitzjames had been an ecclesiastical one. Leslie Stephen maintains that the 'real though unconscious' reason for his brother's 'Choice of profession' exercise was his 'repugnance to the clerical career, and . . . trying to convince himself that he has reasonable grounds for a feeling which his father would be slow to approve'. *Life*, p. 117. Almost the only grounds not raised in 'Choice of profession' against such a career were theological.

21. Autobiographic Fragment, p. 20 and *Life*, p. 73.
22. Autobiographic Fragment, p. 25. Stephen's judgement of this aspect of Eton is challenged by C. Kegan Paul, a contemporary, in his review of *Life: The Month*, LXXXIV (1895), 457, at 460.
23. Autobiographic Fragment, p. 35.
24. *Theological Essays* (1853). the unorthodoxy expressed in the *Essays* brought about Maurice's dismissal from King's in 1853. After coming down from Cambridge, Stephen, as a Bar student, attended Maurice's sermons at Lincoln's Inn.
25. Autobiographic Fragment, p. 35. Stephen notes in 'The Unknowable and the Unknown', *Nineteenth Century*, XV (1884), 905, 'I wholly and entirely disagreed with him as far as I understood him.' And see similarly Leslie Stephen, *Some Early Impressions* (1924), pp. 64-6: 'the very incarnation of earnestness, reverence, and deep human feeling, [but not] of clear-headedness'.
26. Sir James to Fitzjames, 2 August 1854, *The First Sir James Stephen*, p. 204; and Fitzjames' 1865 marginal notes to 'Choice of profession', p. 68. Aubrey de Vere found following Maurice's theology no easier than 'eating pea soup with a fork': M. E. Grant Duff, *Notes from a Diary*, (12 vols., 1897) I, 1851-72, p. 78.
27. *Life*, p. 106.
28. A recollection of H. W. Watson, a Cambridge contemporary.
29. *Life*, p. 149 and Autobiographic Fragment, pp. 51-2. The *Christian Observer* was edited by J. W. Cunningham, vicar of Harrow and Stephen's future father-in-law. George Eliot's first published work appeared in the same journal: Haight, *George Eliot*, p. 25. Sir James at one time had suggested that Fitzjames might consider taking over the editorship from Cunningham: Sir James to Fitzjames, 2 August 1854, *The First Sir James Stephen*, pp. 203-6.
30. One indication is his reaction to Benjamin Jowett's Broad Church edition of St Paul's Epistle to the Romans, which Stephen found to be 'far more orthodox than I can pretend to be'. Stephen to his wife, 12 July 1855.
31. 'Religious Journalism', I (1856), 294, quoted by Bevington, *The 'Saturday Review', 1855-1868*, p. 81.
32. 'Rival Bigots', XIX (1865), 162.
33. See Bevington, *The 'Saturday Review', 1855-1868*, p. 88n. for the extensive list of articles on Spurgeon and Cumming published between 1856 and 1867.
34. 'Popular Preachers', I (1856), 408, and II (1856), 153. See also 'Dr Cumming: Second Notice', II (1856), 182; and 'Dr Cumming and the *Saturday Review*', III (1857), 149. And Leslie Stephen, *Some Early Impressions*, p. 126.
35. I (1856), 375.
36. XXIII (1856), 506n., suggesting Stephen's journal be called the '*Slatternday*'.
37. I (1856), 478. See similarly in 'Horne's Introduction', III (1857), 105.
38. 'Young Oxford', XXII (1866), 565.
39. II (1856), 733. See also 'Dr Newman's University Lectures', VII (1859), 656.
40. 'Positive Religion', III (1857), 567, and 'Positive Religion', V (1858), 563.
41. Following Williams' trial, Stephen was, over the years, consulted and acted in a number of similar cases. A defence was prepared for Bishop Colenso, though not employed after the Privy Council declared the proceedings of the synod of South African bishops a nullity, without needing to hear the doctrinal charges. In a letter written to his wife at the time, Stephen mentions that he has suggested to Colenso a few questions which might be 'put to the bishops and archbishops and others who have bullied him', 5 March 1864. Stephen published his defence in *Fraser's Magazine*, LXXXI (1865), 225. 'What is the Law of the Church of England?', See also generally P. B. Hinchcliff's *J. W. Colenso: Bishop of Natal* (1964). Stephen was also involved in the early stages of Charles Voysey's defence; see M. A. Crowther, *Church Embattled: Religious Controversy in Mid Victorian England* (1970), ch. 6.
42. Stephen's book provoked a strenuous and extended attack by Alexander M'Caul in

Testimonies to Divine Authority . . . in Reply to the Statements of Mr Fitzjames Stephen (1862).

43. Darwin's *Origin of Species* (1859) ran hard against the Christian theology of 'special creation'. Darwin's findings suggested that rather than divine inspiration 'utility and chance' were the creative forces. Stephen's published reaction to Darwinism and the evolutionary theory preceded the publication of *Origin*. Taking a broad Millist viewpoint, he saw as relatively unimportant how the present nature of existence came about: 'what difference can it make whether millions of years ago our ancestors were semi-rational baboons?' 'General Jacob on the Progress of Being', *Saturday Review*, V (1858), 528, quoted in *Life*, p. 375. In the narrow sense of whether it made the existence of God more or less likely Stephen was correct; the theory still left intact the need to account for a grand originator or first cause of existence. However, as many others believed, there were certain ethical and political ramifications to such a theory. The impact of *Origin* on religious sceptics was indirect in that it reinforced an atmosphere of belief in the explicability of practically everything through advancing scientific discovery, and was an undoubted influence in the production of *Essays and Reviews*.

44. *Life*, pp. 309–10.

45. Charged along with Williams was fellow essayist H. B. Wilson, who conducted his own defence.

46. For a detailed and contrasting account of the ecclesiastical manoeuvrings and politics behind the prosecution see A. W. Benn, *History of English Rationalism*, II. pp. 113–34 and Chadwick, *The Victorian Church*, II, ch. 5.

47. *Defence of the Reverend Rowland Williams* (1862), p.2.

48. *Defence*, pp. 63 and 331.

49. Quoted by Benn, *History of English Rationalism*, II, p. 134.

50. Pusey had accused Westbury of having 'poisoned the springs of English justice for ages in all matters of faith'; quoted by Stephen in 'Dr Pusey and the Court of Appeal', *Fraser's Magazine*, LXX (1864), 644 and 646.

51. Ibid., 656.

52. Ibid., 660.

53. 'The Privy Council and the Church of England', *Fraser's Magazine*, LXIX (1864), 521.

54. From a review of Buckle's *History of Civilization in England*, *Edinburgh Review*, CVII (1858), 465, at 471.

55. John Henry Newman was one self-confessed longstanding enemy of *Fraser's*: *The Letters and Diaries of John Henry Newman*, ed. C. S. Dessain et al., 29, p. 200, 20 November 1879. For a typical sample of Froude's own freethinking 'A Plea for the Free Discussion of Theological Difficulties', *Fraser's Magazine* (1863).

56. Stephen to his wife, 1864. Quite when Stephen first contributed to *Fraser's* is uncertain. His brother's select bibliography in *Life* notes 'a few earlier (than December 1863) articles appeared . . . ', p. 485.

57. Sent to 'Emmy' on 23 March 1862.

58. 'The Nature of Belief', pp. 3 and 8.

59. See Leslie Stephen, *The English Utilitarians*, II, p. 338; Benn, *History of English Rationalism*, II, p. 303 and B. Willey, *Nineteenth Century Studies* (1949), p. 133. Bentham's attitude towards Christianity also appeared in his crude *Church of England's Catechism Explained* (1822).

60. 'Belief', pp. 17, 18 and 27.

61. Ibid., p. 25.

62. Ibid., p. 28.

63. 'Characteristics' (1831), republished in *Critical and Miscellaneous Essays* (1842), III.

64. Annan, *Leslie Stephen*, p. 46.

65. It was an open secret that Harrison was the author of 'Neo-Christianity', *Westminster*

Review (1860), which criticised the essayists for not going the full distance that their reasoning should have taken them.

66. *History of English Rationalism*, pp. 198–9.
67. H. Stowell, 'The Age We Live In', *Exeter Hall Lectures*, 6 (1850), 55.
68. Contained in Kingsley's review of vols. 7 and 8 of Froude's *History of England*, in *Macmillan's Magazine* (January 1864).
69. Willey, *Nineteenth Century Studies*, p. 89.
70. *Saturday Review*, XVII (1864), 253.
71. 'Dr Newman's *Apologia*', *Fraser's Magazine*, LXX (1864), 265, at 266. Cf. the similar observations in 'Dr Newman on Universities', *Saturday Review*, II (1856), 733.
72. *Fraser's Magazine*, LXX (1864), 270.
73. Ibid., 273–4.
74. In fundamental contrast with Stephen, Newman believed faith and doubt could not coexist. For a modern defence of Stephen's position see, for example, R. Trigg, *Reason and Commitment* (1973).
75. *Fraser's Magazine*, LXX (1864), 281 and 278.
76. Ibid., 303. Appended to the second edition of *Apologia*, appearing a year later, was a note entitled 'Liberalism' which afforded Stephen the opportunity to add a codicil to his testament on the first edition. 'Dr Newman and Liberalism', *Saturday Review*, XIX (1865), 768. Newman had declared liberalism to be a 'false liberty of thought' upon matters the constitution of the human mind rendered futile. Most notable for their impregnability to such thoughts were questions of first principle, especially the 'truths of revelation'. Liberalism's great error was 'subjecting to human judgment those rendered doctrines which are in their nature beyond . . . it, and claiming to determine on intrinsic grounds the truth and value of propositions which rest for their reception simply on the external authority of the Divine Word'. For Stephen there were no limits to the liberal/rational mode of reasoning; like anything else, religious belief was subject to the 'common rules of logic and evidence'.
77. See Newman, *Letters*, 21, p. 245 and 22, p. 73.
78. Ibid., 25, pp. 103–4, 20 April 1870, and p. 110, 26 April 1870.
79. Ibid., 27, p. 30, March 1874.
80. Quoted ibid., 28, p. 26n. Newman noted on Stephen's letter: 'NB Mr Stephen has, as he says, called on me three or four times in past years – and, with great modesty of manner, and not saying what he was about, picked my brains, and then gone away reporting to others to my disadvantage, what I had said to him in utter unconsciousness that I was undergoing a cross-examination. . . ' On the complaint, see W. S. Lilly's letter, *Times* (25 June 1895), 8, supporting Newman.
81. Newman, *Letters*, vol. 28, pp. 25–6.
82. Ibid., 28, p. 170, 22 February 1877. It seems that Stephen was the author of an anti-Newman article, 'Old Creeds and New', in the *St James's Gazette* (8 November 1880), 11–12, which provoked Newman into complaining of Stephen's previous attempts to 'ferret out my answers to his objections'. *Letters*, 29, pp. 337–8, 17 February 1881. W. S. Lilly responded to Stephen's piece with a letter defending Newman: *St James's Gazette* (25 November 1880), 5.
83. Fitzjames to Leslie, 8 June 1870, Ritchie Papers. Writing soon after to Minny Thackeray Stephen, Fitzjames admitted that Newman 'offends me to a degree I can hardly explain', 7 July 1870, Ritchie Papers.
84. 'On Certitude in Religious Assent', *Fraser's Magazine*, NS, V (1872), 23.
85. Benn, *History of English Rationalism*, II, p. 332. Similarly Principal (of St Andrews) John Tulloch in the *Edinburgh Review*, CXXXII (1870), 382, at 414: 'Romanism . . . is utterly dead and inept as a Power of Thought. It has lost the key to the door of the world's progress, and can only grope amidst the . . . hopeless dogmatism which it teaches.'
86. O. Chadwick, *Newman* (1983), p. 36.

87. See similarly, Huxley: L. Huxley, *Life and Letters of Thomas Henry Huxley*, p. 83; and Leslie Stephen, *An Agnostic's Apology*, pp. 224–5. Leslie's long critique of 'Newman's Theory of Belief', first appearing in the *Fortnightly Review* in 1877, exhibits the same general approach found in his brother's earlier Newman articles: Newman's methods sanctioned 'playing fast and loose with fact which makes the . . . apparent appeal to history a mere illusion'. The *Grammar* asserted that belief is a 'personal product in such a sense that no common measure between different minds is attainable. Therefore agreement can only be provided by supernatural intervention; or, in other words, rational agreement is impossible' (p. 239). Fitzjames engaged in an exchange with Gladstone on the question of the value to be attached to the 'testimony of the ages'. He claimed that Gladstone had over-stated the value of such testimony; see Gladstone's 'On the Influence of Authority in Matters of Opinion' and 'Rejoinder' in *Nineteenth Century*, I (March 1877), 2, and (July 1877), 902 and Stephen, 'Mr Gladstone . . . on Authority' (April 1877), 270. On 29 March 1877, Stephen wrote to Gladstone to say he had told his publisher to send Gladstone a copy of his recently published *Digest of the Law of Evidence*, as it was of general relevance to their philosophic exchange. It also served, as Stephen would have appreciated, to keep the codification issue before this important political figure. Gladstone Papers, British Library, Add 44453, fol. 269.

88. 'On Certitude in Religious Assent', *Fraser's Magazine*, NS, V (1872), 23, at 38. Stephen's Metaphysical Society paper 'On a Theory of Dr Newman's as to Believing in Mysteries' (17 January 1875) covers some of the same ground.

89. For a discussion of modern defenders and opposers of Newman's 'logic' see M. J. Ferreira, *Doubt and Religious Commitment* (1980).

90. W. Ward, *W. G. Ward and the Oxford Movement* (1890), p. 258; quoted by Willey, *Nineteenth Century Studies*, p. 99.

91. 'The Present State of Religious Controversy', *Fraser's Magazine*, LXXX (1869), 570–1.

92. Ibid., 567.

93. Ibid., 562.

94. 'Mr Lecky on Rationalism', *Fraser's Magazine*, LXXII (1865), 537, at 540–1.

95. *Fraser's Magazine*, LXXX (1869), 272. See also George Eliot's observations on Lecky's indecisiveness of argument, *Essays and Leaves from a Notebook*, ed. C. Ł. Lewes (1884), p. 201; and Benn, *History of English Rationalism*, II, pp. 247–53.

96. 'Mr Lecky on Rationalism', 560 and 564.

97. One exception was W. K. Clifford; see, for example, 'The Ethics of Belief', *Contemporary Review* (1877), 29. Leslie Stephen described Clifford as 'that most charming genius', *Some Early Impressions*, p. 80.

98. Jowett to Margot Asquith in her *Autobiography* (1921), I, pp. 123–4.

99. A. and E. M. *Sidgwick, Henry Sidgwick: a Memoir* (1906), p. 507, quoted by B. Blanshard, *Reason and Belief* (1974), p. 595.

100. L. Huxley, *Life and Letters of Thomas Henry Huxley*, II, p. 226.

101. Hutton to Newman, 'The mere sight of your hand writing gives me so much pleasure', Newman, *Letters*, 26, 20 February 1872. And see M. Woodfall, *R. H. Hutton: Critic and Theologian* (1986), ch. 3.

102. Speaking of the *Grammar*, Newman, *Letters*, 26, 20 February 1872. Hutton had given the *Apologia* fulsome reviews in the *Spectator*. He also contributed a study of Newman to the English Leaders of Religion series in 1891.

103. See O. Chadwick, *The Secularisation of the European Mind in the Nineteenth Century* (1975), pp. 111–13.

104. Benn, *History of English Rationalism*, II, p. 337. See also Chadwick, *The Victorian Church*, II, pp. 417–22 for a more sympathetic account.

105. Benn, *History of English Rationalism*, II, p. 349.

106. Ibid., II, p. 405.

107. *Contemporary Review*, XXIII (1873–4), 494 and 989.

108. *Fraser's Magazine*, LXXXI (1865), 671, at 673.

109. 'Pastor Bonus', XIV 18 October 1862, 459.

110. 'The Virtue of Truth', XVII (1864), 651 and 652.

111. Ibid., 678–80, 682 and 687. And similarly in Gladstone's *Vatican Decrees* in November 1874, p. 12. See E. R. Norman, *Anti-Catholicism in Victorian England* (1968), pp. 80–104. Beyond Ultramontanists and Newman, Stephen was no more tolerant of the scientific Catholicism espoused by St George Mivart, who with considerable ingenuity sought to 'show a coincidence between full submission to the authority of the Catholic Church and an equal acceptance of the authority of reason', *Life*, p. 455. Stephen's judgement that it was a feat that could not be performed was vindicated by Mivart's eventual excommunication. See 'Mr Mivart's Modern Catholicism' and 'A Rejoinder to Mr Mivart', *Nineteenth Century*, XXII (1887), 581 and XXIII (1888), 115; and J. C. Livingston, 'The Religious Creed and Criticism of Sir James Fitzjames Stephen', *Victorian Studies*, 17 (1974), 279, at 292–6 for a description of Stephen's Metaphysical Society exchanges with Mivart.

112. *Fraser's Magazine*, LXXII (1865), 2–3. Similarly Gladstone's later comments in *Vatican Decrees* etc. (1874).

113. Quoted by Stephen in the *Contemporary Review*, XXIII (1873–4), 498.

114. Newman to Lord Emly, 5 January 1874, Newman, *Letters*, 27, pp. 4–5.

115. Strachey, *Eminent Victorians*, and Stephen, 'The Present State of Religious Controversy', *Fraser's Magazine*, LXXX (1868), 547, at 566.

116. 'Ultramontanism and Christianity', *Contemporary Review*, XXIII (1874), 688.

117. 'Caesarism and Ultramontanism', *Contemporary Review*, XXIII (1874), 996.

118. Quite possibly Stephen was its author: see J. P. Parry, *Democracy and Religion* (1986), p. 370 n. 5.

119. 'Caesarism and Ultramontanism', 1011–12. See similarly Henry Reeve, 'The Claims of Whig Government', *Edinburgh Review*, CXXXVII (1873), 569. And see also Gladstone, *Vatican Decrees*, discussed by Parry, *Democracy and Religion*, pp. 155–7 and Norman, *Anti-Catholicism in Victorian England*, pp. 80–104. Lecky even claimed in *Democracy and Liberty* (1896) that Catholics were not fitted for representative government because of the church's overpowering influence.

120. Evidence Further Amendment Act 1869.

121. See generally A. W. Brown, *The Metaphysical Society, Victorian Minds in Crisis, 1869–1880* (1947, reprinted 1973). The creation of the society had a strong Apostle influence. See Brown, p. 9.

122. The open forum style of debate put Mill off. Spencer pleaded the fear of an unacceptable level of 'nervous expenditure'. The non-membership of Arnold is unaccounted for: ibid., pp. 23–5. Newman graciously declined several invitations from Hutton, mainly on the grounds of age and deficiency in debating technique. See Newman, *Letters*, 1869–72.

123. *Life*, pp. 362–4. Leslie gave two papers, 'Belief and Evidence', June 1877, and 'The Uniformity of Nature', March 1879: Brown, *The Metaphysical Society* pp. 136–7. The first paper dealt with many matters already handled by his brother.

124. With seven papers each, Fitzjames Stephen and Hutton were the top of the league for numbers of papers delivered to the society; Manning and Sidgwick read six each, and Harrison gave four. For a full list of papers read see Brown, p. 32 and at appendix C, pp.136, 137.

125. See the final of the six papers entitled 'The Scope of Metaphysics': Brown, *The Metaphysical Society*, p. 128.

126. 'The Metaphysical Society, A Reminiscence', *Nineteenth Century*, XVII (1885); 182.

127. Brown, *The Metaphysical Society*, p. 111. Stephen's Metaphysical Society paper of 10 March 1874, 'Some Thoughts on Necessary Truth', was published as 'Necessary

Truth' in *Contemporary Review* (December 1974). The article sought to establish the impossibility of usable knowledge beyond demonstrable truths which did not include 'necessary truths'. Ward's response appeared in the following March number of the *Contemporary Review*. Writing to Lady Egerton (24 December 1874) Stephen evidently thought that the favourable review in the 'great Roman Catholic organ, the Tablet' supported his view that he had 'kicked [Ward] into a cocked hat'. His brother saw the match's outcome as more evenly balanced: *Life*, pp. 367–8.

128. Brown, *The Metaphysical Society*, p. 132. Style apart, Brown on reasonable grounds maintains that Stephen's seven papers were the most 'coherent, consistent, and closely reasoned body of opinion contributed by a single member', p. 133.

129. *Life*, p. 366. See also Benn, *History of English Rationalism*, I, p. 139, describing Butler as a 'very clever cross-examiner'. Manning's biographer, S. Leslie, suggests that 'Huxley and Fitzjames Stephen were inclined to make matters sarcastic for Manning', *Henry Edward Manning* (1921), p. 324. E. S. Purcell in his authorised *Life of Cardinal Manning* (1896) notes that in the Metaphysical Society, Manning 'whether he knew it or not was out of his depth'. He was not prepared to question first principles: 'it was a pathetic spectacle to note the ill disguised amazement with which Manning listened to the ruthless and cold blooded denials of what to him were self evident and eternal truth', p. 514. Manning was a 'supernumerary clerk' at the Colonial Office in 1831–2 and known to Sir James Stephen, who to Manning's 'supreme satisfaction' had told a third party that Manning was the 'wisest man I ever knew', pp. viii–ix.

130. Hutton, 'The Metaphysical Society, A Reminiscence', p. 189. Brown records (*The Metaphysical Society*, p. 107) on 9 November 1875 following Stephen's paper 'Remarks on the Proof of Miracles' that there was a prolonged silence. 'Gladstone who was in the chair scribbled something on a slip of paper and passed it to Lord Arthur Russell; he had written two lines from the *Iliad* in Greek "then did the whole assembly fall into deep silence marvelling at the words of Diomede, tamer of horses".'

131. *Autobiographic Memoirs*, II, p. 87.

132. *Life*, p. 368.

133. 14 January 1870.

134. 23 January 1872.

135. Stephen to Sir William Hunter, 30 April 1873, cited by F. H. Skrine in *Life of Sir William Hunter* (1901), I, p. 214. Writing to Lady Egerton, 19 August 1875, Stephen refers to the fact that he had 'long ceased to believe in the truth of the history of Jesus Christ'.

136. Whether an agnostic should go to church was considered in the *Nineteenth Century* (January 1882). It was concluded he should. In *On Compromise* (p. 57) Morley makes a passing reference to husbands who 'prefer wives not to neglect rites'. It is unlikely that this was true of the Stephen household; but Morley himself seemed inclined to see this as a natural state of affairs: Willey, *More Nineteenth Century Studies* (1963), p. 285.

137. Letter to Lady Grant Duff, 1 April 1875. In a letter of 22 November 1879 to the same correspondent, Stephen suggested that he only attended church on circuit. However, Vanessa Bell recollected 'her uncle and aunt coming to lunch on Sundays on their way back from church, and as his wife continued to remain an orthodox Christian, Fitzjames would not have wanted to make a demonstration'. Annan, *Leslie Stephen*, p. 379.

138. *The Vicar of Bullhampton* (1870), quoted by Houghton, *The Victorian Frame of Mind 1830–1870*, p. 401.

139. Letter to Lady Grant Duff, 1 April 1875.

140. For Harrison, see chapter 7 above. Another who complained of Stephen's vagueness in *Liberty, Equality, Fraternity* was John Tulloch: see 'Dogmatic Excuses', *Con-*

temporary *Review*, XXIII (1874), 182. Stephen replied in the second edition of *Liberty, Equality, Fraternity*, p. 260.

141. Bishop Butler's *Analogy*, cited by Stephen in '*Ecce Homo*', *Fraser's Magazine*, LXXIV (1866), 29, at 51.

142. *Life*, pp. 369, 370, and see *Liberty, Equality, Fraternity*.

143. Beliefs based on the simple existence of the world or on 'final cause' reasoning were still deemed tenable in 'Caesarism and Ultramontanism', *Contemporary Review*, XXIII (1873–4), 497, at 504–5.

144. A.O.J. Cockshut, *Anthony Trollope: A Critical Study* (1968), p. 83.

145. *Nineteenth Century*, XVIII (1885), 177, at 181, and similarly Julia Wedgwood's review of *Life*, *Contemporary Review*, LXVIII (1895), 520, at 522.

146. *Some Early Impressions*, p. 70.

147. *Essays on Freethinking and Plainspeaking*, p. 409.

148. Maitland, *Life and Letters of Leslie Stephen*, p. 383.

149. Leslie Stephen believed Butler to be underrated: see J. W. Bicknell, 'Leslie Stephen, English Thought in the 18th Century', *Victorian Studies* (1962), and Leslie Stephen's debate with Gladstone on Butler in the *Nineteenth Century* between 1895 and 1896.

150. *Horae Sabbaticae*, II, pp. 370 and 384, discussing Hume's 'Natural History of Religion'. Paley made a similar complaint about Hume in *Principles of Morals and Political Philosophy*, bk II, ch. 4. For Stephen's two essays on Butler see *Horae Sabbaticae*, II, pp. 280–314. His single essay on Paley was included in *Horae Sabbaticae*, III, pp. 75–92.

151. Ordained in 1855, Leslie took priest's orders in 1859. After finding himself unable to conduct religious services in 1862, he resigned his fellowship. Annan, *Leslie Stephen*, describes the process as a change of 'mind rather than change of heart' (p. 45). Darwinism and critical biblical scholarship helped expel an apparently always insecure faith (pp. 206–8). Adam Smith and Hume were Leslie Stephen's 'two rationalist heroes': Annan, p. 225.

152. Leslie Stephen, *An Agnostic's Apology*, p. 2; the title essay was originally published in 1876 soon after the death of Minny Thackeray. The essay is undoubtedly one of his most impressive, gaining much from a finely controlled surge of grief then being experienced. Contemptuous, almost seething, references to the 'bitterest of mockeries' like 'pain is not an evil, death . . . not a separation, sickness . . . but a blessing in disguise' could just as easily have been flung at the reader from certain parts of *Liberty, Equality, Fraternity*.

153. Ibid., p. 4

154. Ibid., p. 4.

155. 'Religion of all Sensible Men', from *An Agnostic's Apology*, p. 340.

156. And even Mill in his 'Theism' (1874), seen by many Millites as a sad capitulation to superstition – 'mere twilight hopes'. See generally Morley in 'Mr Mill's Three Essays on Religion', *Fortnightly Review*, XXII and XXIII (November 1874, January 1875).

157. *Sartor Resartus*, bk 1, ch. 10.

158. See Froude's *Life of Carlyle*, ed. J. Clubbe (1979), pp. 566–7.

159. See also Leslie Stephen: 'The essential Puritan may survive as the case of Carlyle . . . showed, when all his dogmas have evaporated.' *Some Early Impressions*, p. 15.

160. Willey, *Nineteenth Century Studies*, pp. 106–7; and see Wedgwood, review of *Life*, *Contemporary Review*, LXVIII (1895), 520, at 531.

161. Quoted by A.O.J. Cockshut, *The Unbelievers: English Agnostic Thought* (1964), pp. 67–8.

162. Preface to *God and the Bible* (1875).

163. Benn, *History of English Rationalism*, II, p. 329.

164. L. Trilling, *Matthew Arnold*, pp. 334 and 355.

165. Benn, *History of English Rationalism*, II, p. 359.
166. *Ethical Studies*, 2nd edn (1927).
167. *Nineteenth Century* I (1877), 331, at 332.
168. Ibid., 538–9. See the same view expressed later in 'Science and Morals', *Fortnightly Review*, XLVI (1886), reprinted in *Collected Essays*, IX, p. 134.
169. *Nineteenth Century*, I (1877), 531, at 532.
170. Ibid., 348.
171. Leslie Stephen maintained that virtuous instincts were the 'foundation not the out-growth' of belief, *Essays in Freethinking and Plainspeaking*, p. 122.
172. Chadwick, *The Victorian Church*, II, p. 120.
173. The problem of interpreting Arnold's religious writings is notorious. See the survey of literature on this in *Victorian Prose: A Guide to Research*, ed. D. J. DeLaura, pp. 312–20. For a recent defence of the worth and coherency of Arnold's writing on the subject see R. ap Roberts, *Arnold and God* (1983).
174. See Willey, *Nineteenth Century Studies*, p. 159.
175. See D. D. Raphael's essay 'Darwinism and Ethics', in *A Century of Darwinism*, ed. S. A. Barnett, (1959), p. 343, and C. Bibby, *T. H. Huxley* (1959), pp. 56–66.
176. 'Religion of all Sensible Men', in *An Agnostic's Apology*, p. 339. For Huxley's fierce and long-running dismissal of secular humanism see S. Eisen, 'Huxley and the Positivists', *Victorian Studies*, 7 (1964), 337.
177. *An Agnostic's Apology*, p. 9.
178. 'Religion of all Sensible Men', ibid., p. 379.
179. 'The Unknowable and the Unknown', *Nineteenth Century*, XV (1884), 905, at 908. Stephen's article was probably provoked by Spencer's in the January 1884 issue of the *Nineteenth Century*, 1. *The Spectator* of 5 January 1884 also carried an article critically comparing Spencer and Harrison's religious views.
180. For a discussion of the Spencer/Harrison debate see S. Eisen, 'Frederic Harrison and Herbert Spencer: Embattled Unbelievers', *Victorian Studies*, 12 (1968), 33.
181. 'The Unknowable and the Unknown', 909.
182. 'Mr Mill on . . . Comte', *Saturday Review*, XIX (1865), 431.
183. 'The Unknowable and the Unknown', 910–11.
184. Ibid., 915.
185. Stephen to Lady Grant Duff, 1 January 1883.
186. Huxley, 'A Modern Symposium', *Nineteenth Century*, II (1877), 340.
187. 'The Unknowable and the Unknown', 918.
188. Stephen to Lady Grant Duff, 1 January 1883.
189. *History of the Criminal Law*, III, p. 367.
190. Of G. E. Moore's *Principia Ethica* (1903) in *Pollock–Holmes Letters* (1942), I, pp. 116–17. Quoted by P. S. Atiyah, *The Rise and Fall of Freedom of Contract*, p. 651n.
191. *Past and Present* (1843), quoted by Houghton, *The Victorian Frame of Mind*, p. 172.
192. 'The Unknowable and the Unknown', 919.
193. See also Froude, *Short Studies*, IV, p. 252.
194. Stephen to Lady Grant Duff, 24 November 1879.
195. Leslie thought Jowett to be 'sweet' and 'sound' but an 'intellectual coward'. Annan, *Leslie Stephen*, p. 187. On Jowett's beliefs, see Hinchliff, *Benjamin Jowett and the Christian Religion*, particularly ch. 8.
196. Autobiographic Fragment, pp. 6–7.
197. *Sartor Resartus*, bk II, ch. 7.
198. Stephen to Lady Grant Duff, 28 September 1885; and Stephen to Lytton, 1 October 1879. The dilemma was far from unique: see A. and E. M. Sidgwick, *Henry Sidgwick: A Memoir*, p. 357.
199. Stephen to M. E. Grant Duff, 30 November 1882. Here Stephen claimed that the ideal would be an established church without theology, as all forms of 'religious excitement' and institutions which encouraged it 'were mischievous'. They were

'medicine and most of us don't need a physician and most of us like to quack our-selves'.

200. Stephen's two lengthy reviews in *Fraser's* (January and July 1866). Stephen's severe criticism of Seeley's undiscriminating acceptance of documents and haphazard methodology was echoed by Seeley's friend Henry Sidgwick in the *Westminster Review*, XXX (1866), 58, and also by Jowett: see E. Abbott and L. Campbell, *The Life and Letters of Benjamin Jowett* (1897), I, p. 425n.
201. Stephen to Lady Grant Duff, 13 December 1884. See similarly letters of 28 September 1885 and 8 October 1884. Stephen at the time noted that Carlyle 'never much liked Christ', 2 October 1884.
202. Beatrice Webb, *My Apprenticeship* (1926), p. 32.
203. Stephen to Lady Grant Duff, 25 December 1884.

9 THE BENCH AND BEYOND

1. Review of *Life*, *Edinburgh Review*, CLXXXII (1895), 418, at 429.
2. Review of *Life*, *Saturday Review*, LXXIX (1895), 865.
3. 1 September 1873, Gladstone Papers, British Library MSS 44138, fol. 154. Stephen had been led by Coleridge to believe that he would probably secure the Solicitor-Generalship even if he failed to win Dundee: *Life*, p. 343.
4. Selborne to Gladstone, 5 November 1873, Gladstone Papers, British Library MSS 44296, fol. 332.
5. Harcourt became a Liberal MP in 1869 and soon began making a name for himself as a member of a ginger group within the government party, particularly in matters of law reform. See A. G. Gardiner, *The Life of Sir William Harcourt* (1923), I, pp. 256–8.
6. See T. E. Kebbel, *Life of Lord Beaconsfield* (1888), pp. 25–6.
7. *Life*, pp. 351–2; *Saturday Review* LXXIX (1895), 865.
8. 26 August and 26 September 1876, Maine Papers, India Office Library, fol. 8.
9. With only fifteen puisne common law judges at the time, it was a decidedly exclusive professional body.
10. *Law Times* (1894), XCVI, 17 March, 456. According to Harold Laski's *Studies in Law and Politics* (1932), pp. 168–72, between 1832 and 1906 the average number of years' experience at the Bar prior to appointment to the Bench was more than 30. The average age on appointment was 53. Stephen had been called to the Bar 25 years before, and was 50 years old when appointed.
11. See, for example, references in *The Times*, 13 March 1894, 11; and the *Law Times* 17 March 1894, 456. Though, at least in terms of political allegiance, a party political element in nineteenth-century judicial appointments was common: Laski, *Studies in Law and Politics*.
12. *Saturday Review* LXXIX (1895), 866.
13. Holker to Cairns, 16 April 1880, Cairns Papers, PRO 30/51, bundle 10. Prime Ministers sometimes consulted the Sovereign for such appointments; however, no references to the issue show up in correspondence on state matters for the period between Disraeli and Victoria held in the Royal Archives, Windsor.
14. The *Law Journal* also fatefully applauded the appointment on the grounds of Stephen's 'strong constitution and unlimited capacity for work', 18 January 1879, 34. Amongst judicial appointments of the period probably closest in background circumstances to Stephen was R. S. Wright, appointed in 1890. Fellow of Oriel College, Oxford and author of two legal texts, Wright also had experience in code drafting. Unlike Stephen, he had made a mark in practice and was latterly a Treasury counsel. See M. L. Friedland (1981) I *Oxford Journal of Legal Studies*, 307, and chapter 4 above.
15. Stephen to Lady Grant Duff, 11 December 1879.

16. Stephen to Lady Grant Duff, 9 November 1882.
17. Stephen to Lady Grant Duff, 9 May 1886.
18. Stephen to Lady Grant Duff, 9 December 1881.
19. See, for example, letters: to Lady Grant Duff, 3 August 1882; to Sir M. E. Grant Duff, 9 September 1883; to G. S. Venables, 11 September 1883.
20. Stephen to Lady Grant Duff, 7 and 17 October 1883 and 30 April 1886.
21. *Pall Mall Gazette*, quoted in the *Law Times* (1891), 1 April, 24.
22. Radzinowicz, *Sir James Fitzjames Stephen and his Contribution to the Development of Criminal Law*, pp. 37–8; and the *Law Journal* (1895), XXX, 394. See Radzinowicz's list of Stephen's reported criminal cases, *Sir James Fitzjames Stephen and his Contribution to the Development of Criminal Law*, pp. 52–4.
23. For example, *Times*, (13 March 1894), 11, and the *Edinburgh Review*, CLXXXII (1895), 418, at 430.
24. Stephen to Lady Grant Duff, 8 October 1884.
25. *Law Times* (1894), 17 March, 456. See also *Life*, p. 448.
26. *Law Journal* (1894), XXIX, 169.
27. *Fourteen English Judges*, p. 326.
28. *Law Times* (1894), XCVI, 17 March, 456.
29. 15 Cox CC 46, pp. 58–9.
30. *Life*, p. 437.
31. Stephen to Lady Grant Duff, 1 January 1883.
32. See generally M. L. Friedland's careful detailed analysis of the case in *The Trials of Israel Lipski* (1984). Friedland comments, 'Stephen's approach is one that an appeal court would take today, but it is surely not the proper view when deciding whether to hang a person' (p. 164). And although acknowledging his great conscientiousness in re-examining the evidence, Friedland is critical of elements of Stephen's jury direction (p. 204). Friedland, without overwhelming cause, even questions the soundness of Lipski's confession.
33. *Times* 8 August 1889, 10.
34. *Hansard* (1830–91), 3rd series, vol. 350, cols. 1362, 1701–2; vol. 351, cols. 486–7.
35. Radzinowicz, *Sir James Fitzjames Stephen*, p. 42.
36. *More Famous Trials* (1928), pp. 133–4. Similarly Radzinowicz's view. The complete summing-up is reproduced in the *Trial of Mrs Maybrick*, ed. H. B. Irving (1912), pp. 274–355. At times Stephen did show tetchiness on being corrected by counsel for slips of detail, though some corrections were accepted gracefully, for instance, p. 333. Stephen's demeanour, coherency and general control of the trial as revealed by the record demonstrate the absurdity of J. H. Levy's claim that Stephen was quite unfit to discharge judicial duties then and since his illness in 1885. See Levy's detailed but unbalanced study in *The Necessity for Criminal Appeal as illustrated by the Maybrick Case . . .* (1899). Surprisingly, Noel Annan, too, overstates the degree of irregularity in Stephen's conduct at the Maybrick trial: *Leslie Stephen*, p. 14.
37. *Recollection of Sir Henry Dickens, K.C.* (1934), p. 171.
38. *General view of the Criminal Law*, 2nd edn, p. 173.
39. *Life*, p. 477.
40. Stephen to Lady Grant Duff, 15 September 1889.
41. In one reported incident close to his retirement, Stephen is alleged to have begun to sum up at the conclusion of the prosecution's case before the defence had presented its case. *Law Times* (1891), XC, 7 March, 334.
42. It appears that in February 1891 Lord Chancellor Halsbury wrote to Stephen's son Herbert drawing his attention to adverse press observations on the judge's behaviour. Writing to Halsbury on 22 February, Herbert set out at considerable length the findings of his own investigations into such press comments, which included interviewing a number of barristers claimed to have been the sources of suggestions of

Stephen's incapacity. Herbert's very pointed conclusions were that all the parties interviewed, though testifying to a decline in Stephen's powers, nevertheless believed that judged by *general* judicial standards he was still competent. Herbert Stephen's letter ends not only with a sharp refusal to persuade his father to resign, but with the assurance that he would actively oppose any attempts by others to encourage resignation. However, by 10 March the judge had been informed of his believed incapacity, although writing to Halsbury, Stephen expresses himself as being completely 'in the dark' as to the nature and source of the complaints and requests full details of them. Still not convinced by Halsbury's reply, in a letter of 14 March he indicates his willingness to retire not on the grounds of evidence of incapacity but because of medical advice. 'Envelope 6', Halsbury Papers, private collection of Lord Halsbury.

43. *Law Times* (1891), XC, 14 March 348n. Leslie Stephen chooses to make no reference to any attempts by family or close friends to enlighten his brother:*Life*, p. 478.
44. Stephen to Lady Grant Duff, 19 and 22 March 1891. During his final days on the Bench, Stephen is reported to have begun as 'brief, terse and to the point, and as lucid as in the old days. As the hours wore on his voice dropped almost to a whisper.' *Law Times* (1891), XC, 21 March, 370.
45. *Law Journal* (1891), XXVI, 11 April, 256.
46. *Law Times* (1891), XC, 11 April, 431. Stephen received a baronetcy but was not, despite Lytton's efforts, made a Privy Councillor. See Herbert Stephen to Lytton, 6 and 14 April 1891, Lytton Papers, Hertford. Stephen had been knighted (K.C.S.I.) in January 1877. Other distinctions included honorary membership of the American Academy of Arts and Sciences, honorary doctorates from Oxford (1878) and Edinburgh University (1884), election to an honorary fellowship at Trinity College, Cambridge (1885) and being made a 'corresponding member' of the Institut de France (1888). See *Life*, pp. 110, 402 and 478.
47. Stephen wrote an obituary notice of Maine in the *Saturday Review*, LXV (1888), 150; *Life*, p. 466. Defending Maine against the apparent indifference of his wife and Lady Grant Duff, Stephen wrote 'I think on the whole he is the most intimate friend I have in the world, more intimate . . . than my brother [whom] I seldom see and when I do, we have so little to say to each other that it is often quite a trouble to me to keep talking at all – but I would do anything for him, and fully believe he would for me.' Stephen to Lady Grant Duff, 29 December 1886. Leslie Stephen suggested that 'Maine's influence upon my brother was only second to that of my father', *Life*, p. 102. Pollock described Maine and Stephen as a 'perfect pair', each with complementary strengths and virtues which shone in the other's presence (*For My Grandson*, p. 74.). They 'were quite at their best in each other's company . . . [Theirs] was a large and luminous conversation, with none of the pettiness of common talk . . . [They] met on a wider plane, and as men of the world, but not worldy . . . Both . . . had the practised journalist's power of coming to the point in the most effective manner, and without loss of time . . . [Their] conversation . . . though constantly prolonged until it had to be cut short by the positive exigencies of daily life, could not suffer either from prolixity or from unrelieved seriousness. For many years it was amongst my greatest pleasures, and I cannot but think that much of what I learnt from it . . . has entered whatever powers I may have acquired by making my own knowledge useful or interesting to others by speech or writing', Pollock. *National Review*, XXV (1895), pp. 818–19.
48. *Life*, p. 477.
49. For a brief biography of J. K. Stephen see *Life*, pp. 468–77, and Annan, *Leslie Stephen*, pp. 113–14. In April 1891 it appears that Lytton, then British Ambassador in Paris, intervened to secure J. K. Stephen's release from police custody in Paris. For his trouble Lytton received a terse and resentful rebuff from J. K. Stephen. Lytton to J. K. Stephen, 17 April 1891 (copy); J. K. Stephen to Lytton, 21 April 1891, Lytton Papers, Hertford.

50. Stephen's death certificate records Bright's disease (chronic renal failure) as the cause of death.

51. 'The First Earl of Lytton', *Independent Review*, XII (March 1907), 332, at 333. On similar lines was T.H.S. Escott's portrait of the public persona, written during Stephen's lifetime: 'He is above all things a professor, a homilist, a superior creature. He must have a thesis, a text, an audience. . . A Head of enormous proportions is planted, with nothing intervening except an inch-and-a-half of neck upon the shoulders of a giant. Force is written upon every line of his countenance, upon every square inch of his trunk. . . The genius of the Anglo-Saxon race is embodied in men of this stamp. He lacks geniality and play of fancy, but in their stead he has a grim and never-flagging perception of what he means and what he wants . . . treating toil as if it were a pastime.' *Society in London*, 7th edn (1885), pp. 141–3. Of Stephen the private man, two brief and typical remembrances are those of M. E. Grant Duff and Lord Coleridge. According to the former, 'He was very little known to the general public who imagined one of the most warm-hearted and affectionate of men to be only a Rhadamanthus' (*Notes from a Diary*, II, 1892–5, p. 26). Lord Coleridge found in him a 'tenderness, generosity and even delicacy under that rough exterior which made him, to a man who knew him as I did, exceedingly lovable. "There's a *great spirit* go" as Marc Antony says.' E. H. Coleridge, *Life and Correspondence of Lord Coleridge* (1904), II, p. 382.

52. Autobiographic Fragment, p. 53, and Stephen to Lady Grant Duff, 13 October 1889.

BIBLIOGRAPHY

1 MANUSCRIPT COLLECTIONS

Argyll Papers, India Office Library
Broadhurst Papers, London School of Economics and Political Science
Bryce Papers, Bodleian Library, Oxford
Cairns Papers, Public Record Office
Council of the Governor General of India, abstract of proceedings, India Office Library
Dufferin Papers, India Office Library
Escott Papers, British Library
Gladstone Papers, British Library
Grant Duff Papers, private collection of Mrs S. Sokolov-Grant
Halsbury Papers, private collection of Lord Halsbury
Harcourt Papers, Bodleian Library, Oxford
Harrison Papers, London School of Economics and Political Science
Huxley Papers, Library of Imperial College, London
Lyall Papers, India Office Library
Lytton Papers, County Record Office, Hertford and India Office Library
Maine Papers, India Office Library
Mayo Papers, India Office Library
Northbrook Papers, India Office Library
Ripon Papers, British Library
Ritchie Papers, Senate House Library, University of London
Stephen Papers (Sir James Stephen, James Fitzjames Stephen, Leslie Stephen, Mary Stephen), Cambridge University Library
Stephen Papers Leslie, Perkins Library, Duke University; and Washington State University Library
Strachey Papers (Richard), India Office Library
Temple Papers (Richard), India Office Library
Venables Papers, Welsh National Library, Aberystwyth

Unless otherwise indicated, manuscript sources are the James Fitzjames Stephen Papers, Cambridge.

320

2 WORKS OF STEPHEN

Defence of the Reverend Rowland Williams (London, 1862)

Essays by a Barrister (London, 1862). A reprint of articles first published in the *Saturday Review*

A General View of the Criminal Law of England (London, 1863; 2nd edn, 1890)

The Indian Evidence Act: With an Introduction on the Principles of Judicial Evidence (Calcutta, 1872)

Liberty, Equality, Fraternity (London, 1873; 2nd edn 1874; reprinted with introduction and editorial notes by R. J. White, Cambridge, 1967)

A Digest of the Law of Evidence (London, 1876; 4th edn, 1893)

A Digest of the Criminal Law (Crimes and Punishments) (London, 1877; 5th edn, 1894)

A Digest of the Law of Criminal Procedure in Indictable Offences (London, 1883)

A History of the Criminal Law of England, 3 vols. (London, 1883)

The Story of Nuncomar and the Impeachment of Sir Elijah Impey, 2 vols. (London, 1885)

Horae Sabbaticae, 3 vols. (London, 1892). A reprint of articles first published in the *Saturday Review*

3 ARTICLES OF STEPHEN REFERRED TO

Cambridge Essays
'The Relation of Novels to Life', 1855, 148
'The Characteristics of English Criminal Law', 1857, 1

Contemporary Review
'Caesarism and Ultramontanism', XXIII (December 1873–May 1874), 497, 989
'Parliamentary Government', XXIII (December 1873–May 1874), 1, 165
'Necessary Truth', XXV (December 1874–May 1875), 44
'The Laws of England as to the Expression of Religious Opinion', XXV (December 1874–May 1875) 446

Cornhill Magazine
'Criminal Law and the Detection of Crime', II (1860), 697
'The Morality of Advocacy', III (1861), 447
'The Study of History', III (1861), 666; IV (1861), 25
'Journalism', VI (1862), 52
'Liberalism', V (1862), 70
'The Punishment of Convicts', VII (1863), 189
'Marriage Settlements', VIII (1863), 666
'Sentimentalism', X (1864), 65
'The Bars of France and England', X (1864), 672

Edinburgh Review
'The License of Modern Novelists', CVI (1857), 124
'Buckle's *History of Civilization in England*', CVII (1858), 465; CXIV (1861), 183
'English Jurisprudence', CXIV (1861), 456

Fortnightly Review
  'Codification in India and England', XVIII (1872), 644
  'A penal code', XXVII (1877), 362
  'Blasphemy and blasphemous libel', XXXV (1884), 289

Fraser's Magazine
  'Women and Scepticism', LXVIII (1863), 679
  'Mr Thackeray', LXIX (1864), 401
  'The Privy Council and the Church of England', LXIX (1864), 521
  'Capital Punishment', LXIX (1864), 753
  'Dr Newman's *Apologia*', LXX (1864), 265
  'Dr Pusey and the Court of Appeal', LXX (1864), 644
  'What is the Law of the Church of England?', LXXI (1865), 225
  'English Ultramontanism', LXXI (1865), 671; LXXII (1865), 1
  'Mr Lecky on Rationalism', LXXII (1865), 537
  'Mr Carlyle', LXXII (1865), 778
  'Report of the Capital Punishment Commission', LXXIII (1866), 232
  '*Ecce Homo*', LXXIII (1866), 746; LXXIV (1866), 29
  'The Present State of Religious Controversy', LXXX (1869), 547, 570–1
  'On Certitude in Religious Assent', NS, V (1872), 23

Nineteenth Century
  'Mr Gladstone and Sir George Lewis on Authority in Matters of Opinion', I
      (1877), 270
  'A Modern "Symposium": the Influence on Morality of a Decline in Religious
      Belief', I (1877), 331, 531
  'Improvement of the Law by Private Enterprise', II (1877), 198
  'Suggestions as to the reform of the criminal law', II (1877), 198
  'The Criminal Code (1879)', VII (1880), 136
  'The Foundations of the Government of India', XIV (1883), 541
  'The Unknowable and the Unknown', XV (1884), 905
  'Variations in the Punishment of Crime', XVII (1885), 755
  'Prisoners as Witnesses', XX (1886), 453
  'Mr Mivart's Modern Catholicism', XXII (1887), 581
  'A Rejoinder to Mr Mivart', XXIII (1888), 115

Saturday Review
  'Law Reform', I (1856), 252
  'Religious Journalism', I (1856), 293
  'Are Madmen Responsible?', I (1856), 298
  'Popular Preachers', I (1856), 408 and II, 153
  'Crime and Punishment', I (1856), 431
  'Bunkum', I (1856), 478
  'Pure Literature', II (1856), 16
  'Dr Cumming: Second Notice', II (1856), 182
  'Public Prosecutors', II (1856), 316
  'Administrative Reform *à la Chinoise*', II (1856), 356
  'Mr Best on Codification', II (1856), 545, 614
  'Mr Phillips on Capital Punishment', II (1856), 653
  'Dr Newman on Universities', II (1856), 733

'Mr Dickens as a Politician', III (1857), 8
'Horne's Introduction', III (1857), 105
'Dr Cumming and the *Saturday Review*', III (1857), 149
'Mr Neate on Capital Punishment', III (1857), 375
'Positive Religion', III (1857), 567; V (1858), 563
'*Little Dorrit*', IV (1857), 15
'Light Literature and the *Saturday Review*', IV (1857), 34
'*Madame Bovary*', IV (1857), 40
'The *Edinburgh Review* and Modern Novelists', IV (1857), 57
'Mr Charles Reade and the *Edinburgh Review*', IV (1857), 84
'Light Literature in France', IV (1857), 219
'*La Danielle*', IV, (1857), 243
'Balzac', IV, (1857), 559
'Edmund Burke', V (1858), 372
'Mr Dickens', V (1858), 474
'General Jacob on the Progress of Being', V (1858), 528
'Mr Carlyle', V (1858), 638
'*Manon Lescaut*', VI (1858), 64
'Mr Mill's Essays', VII (1859), 46, 76
'Mr Mill on Political Liberty', VII (1859), 186, 213
'French and English Logic', VII (1859), 460
'Dr Newman's University Lectures', VII (1859), 656
'*A Tale of Two Cities*', VIII (1859), 741
'Novelists' Common Forms', XV (1863), 749
'Dr Newman and Mr Kingsley', XVII (1864), 253
'The Virtue of Truth', XVII (1864), 651
'A French View of Mr Carlyle', XVII (1864), 690
'Mr Matthew Arnold and His Countrymen', XVIII (1864), 683
'Rival Bigots', XIX (1865), 162
'Mr Matthew Arnold amongst the Philistines', XIX (1865), 235
'Dr Newman and Liberalism', XIX (1865), 768
'Burke on Popular Representation', XX (1865), 394
'Mr Arnold on the Middle Classes', XXI (1866), 161
'Lord Macaulay's Works', XXII (1866), 207
'Mr Matthew Arnold on Culture', XXIV (1867), 78

For a practically complete list of Stephen's publications (not including contributions to the *Pall Mall Gazette* or *St James's Gazette*) see the appendix to L. Radzinowicz's Selden Society Lecture, *Sir James Fitzjames Stephen (1829–1894) and His Contribution to the Development of Criminal Law (London, 1957)*

4 SELECT LIST OF SECONDARY WORKS

Abbott, E. and Campbell, L. *The Life and Letters of Benjamin Jowett* (London, 1897)
Abel-Smith, B. and Stevens, R. *Lawyers and the Courts* (London, 1967)
Allen, P. *The Cambridge Apostles, The Early Years* (London, 1978)
Altick, R. D. *The English Common Reader* (Chicago, 1957)
    Victorian People and Ideas (New York, 1973)

Alverstone, Lord. *Recollection of Bar and Bench* (London, 1915)

Amos, S. *An English Code* (London, 1873)
    The Science of Law (London, 1874)

Annan, N. *Leslie Stephen* (London, 1984)

Anschutz, R. P. *The Philosophy of J. S. Mill* (Oxford, 1963)

Arnold, M. *Essays in Criticism* (London, 1865)
    Culture and Anarchy (London, 1869)
    Literature and Dogma (London, 1873)

Aspland, L. M. *The Law of Blasphemy: Being a Candid Examination of the Views of Mr Justice Stephen* (London, 1884)

Atiyah, P. S. *The Rise and Fall of Freedom of Contract* (Oxford, 1979)

Austin, J. *The Province of Jurisprudence Determined*, ed. S. Austin (London, 1863; first published 1832)
    Lectures on Jurisprudence, 5th edn (London, 1885; first published 1863)

Bagehot, W. *Physics and Politics* (London, 1872)

Bain, A. *John Stuart Mill: A Criticism with Personal Recollections* (London, 1882)

Balfour, B. *The History of Lord Lytton's Indian Administration* (London, 1899)
    Personal and Literary Letters of Robert, First Earl of Lytton (London, 1906)

Barker, E. *Political Thought in England 1848–1914* (Oxford, 1926)

Barnett, S. A. *A Century of Darwinism* (London, 1958)

Bellos, D. *Balzac – Criticism in France 1850–1900* (Oxford, 1976)

Beloff, M. *Britain's Liberal Empire 1897–1921* (London, 1969)

Benn, A. W. *The History of English Rationalism in the Nineteenth Century* (London, 1906)
    Modern England (London, 1908)

Bentham, J. *A Treatise on Judicial Evidence*, ed. E. Dumont (1825)
    'Rationale of Judicial Evidence', ed. J. S. Mill (1827)
    Works of Jeremy Bentham, ed. J. Bowring (Edinburgh, 1843)
    An Introduction to the Principles of Morals and Legislation, ed. J. H. Burns and H.L.A. Hart (London, 1982)

Berlin, I. *Four Essays on Liberty* (Oxford, 1969)

Best, W. M. *Principles of Evidence* (1849)

Bevington, M. M. *The 'Saturday Review', 1855–1868: Representative Educated Opinion in Victorian England* (New York, 1941)

Bibby, C. T. *H. Huxley* (London, 1959)

Birkenhead, Earl of. *Fourteen English Judges* (London, 1926)
    More Famous Trials (London, 1928)

Bloomfield, P. *Uncommon People* (London, 1955)

Blunt, W. S. *My Diaries* (London, 1919)

Briggs, A. *Victorian People* (London, 1965)

Bright, J. *The Diaries of John Bright*, ed. J. A. Walling (London, 1930)

Brodrick, G. C. *Memories and Impressions* (London, 1900)

Brown, A. W. *The Metaphysical Society, Victorian Minds in Crisis 1869–1880* (New York, 1947, reprinted 1973)

Bryce, J. *Studies in History and Jurisprudence* (Oxford, 1901)
    Modern Democracies (London, 1921)

Bryce, J. et al. *Essays on Reform* (1867)

Burrow, J. W. *Evolution and Society: A Study in Victorian Social Theory* (Cambridge, 1966)

Campbell, E. and Waller, L. (eds.). *Well and Truly Tried* (Melbourne, 1982)

Carlyle, T. *Chartism* (London, 1839)
    Past and Present (London, 1843)
    Latter-Day Pamphlets (London, 1850)
    Life of John Stirling (London, 1851)
    Reminiscences, ed. C. E. Norton (London, 1887)
    New Letters of Carlyle, ed. A. Carlyle (London, 1904)
Chadwick, O. *The Victorian Church* (London, 1970)
    The Secularisation of the European Mind in the Nineteenth Century (Cambridge, 1975)
Chirol, V. *India Old and New* (London, 1921)
Clark, E. C. *Analysis of Criminal Liability* (Cambridge, 1880)
Clive, J. L. *Scotch Reviewers: The Edinburgh Review 1802–1815* (London, 1957)
Cohen L. J. *The Probable and Provable* (Oxford, 1977)
Colaiaco, J. A. *James Fitzjames Stephen and the Crisis of Victorian Thought* (London, 1983)
Coleridge, E. H. *Life and Correspondence of Lord Coleridge* (London, 1904)
Coleridge, G.J.D. *Eton in the Seventies* (London, 1912)
Collini, S., Winch, D. and Burrow, J. *That Noble Science of Politics* (Cambridge, 1983)
Cornish, W. R. *The Jury* (London, 1971)
Cornish, W. R. et al. (eds.). *Crime and Law in Nineteenth Century Britain* (Dublin, 1978)
Cosgrove, R. A. *The Rule of Law: Albert Venn Dicey* (London, 1980)
Coulling, S. *Matthew Arnold and His Critics* (Athens, Ohio, 1974)
Cowen, Z. and Carter, P. B. *Essays on the Law of Evidence* (Oxford, 1956)
Cowling, M. *Mill and Liberalism* (Cambridge, 1963)
    1867 Disraeli, Gladstone and Revolution (Cambridge, 1967)
Cross, R. and Tapper, C.F. *Cross on Evidence*, 6th edn (London, 1985)
Cross, R. *The English Sentencing System*, 2nd edn (London, 1975)
Curzon, Lord. *Speeches by Lord Curzon 1898–1900* (London, 1900)
    Indian Speeches (London, 1903)
Dahl, C. C. *The Barrister as Critic: The Autobiographical and Critical Writings of James Fitzjames Stephen* (Yale University Ph.D. thesis, 1978)
Das, M. N. *India under Morley and Minto* (London, 1964)
De Wolfe Howe, M. *Justice Oliver Wendell – The Shaping Years* (Cambridge, Mass., 1957)
    Justice Oliver Wendell Holmes – The Proving Years (Cambridge, Mass., 1963)
De Wolfe Howe, M. (ed.). *Pollock–Holmes Letters* (Cambridge, Mass., 1942)
    Holmes–Laski Letters (Cambridge, Mass., 1953)
Devlin, J. *The Enforcement of Morals* (Oxford, 1965)
Devlin, P. *Trial by Jury* (Oxford, 1971)
Dicey, A. V. *England's Case against Home Rule* (London, 1886)
    Lectures on the relation between Law and Public Opinion in England during the Nineteenth Century (London, 1905)
Dickens, H. *Recollection of Sir Henry Dickens, KC* (London, 1934)
Dilke, C. *Greater Britain* (London, 1868)
Dodds, J. W. *The Age of Paradox* (London, 1953)
Duff, R. A. *Trials and Punishments* (Cambridge, 1986)
Dunn, W. H. *James Anthony Froude* (Oxford, 1963)
Durand, M. *Life of Sir Alfred Comyn Lyall* (London, 1913)

Durkheim, E. *The Division of Labour in Society* (1893; trans. Simpson, New York, 1933)

Dutton, G.P.H. *The Hero as Murderer* (Sydney, 1967)

Edwardes, M. *High Noon of Empire: India under Curzon* (London, 1965)

Eggleston, R. *Evidence, Proof and Probability*, 2nd edn (London, 1983)

Eliot, G. *George Eliot's Life, Letters and Journals*, ed. J. W. Cross (London, 1885)
    The George Eliot Letters, ed. G. S. Haight (New Haven, 1978)

Escott, T.H.S. *Society in London* 7th edn (London, 1885)
    Platform, Press, Politics and Play (London, 1895)

Feaver, G. *From Status to Contract* (London, 1969)

Feinberg, J. *The Moral Limits of the Criminal Law*, III, *Harm to Self* (New York, 1986)
    Doing and Deserving (Princeton, 1970)

Ferreira, M. J. *Doubt and Religious Commitment* (Oxford, 1980)

Fifoot, C.H.S. *Law and History in the Nineteenth Century* (London, 1956)
    Judge and Jurist in the Reign of Victoria (London, 1959)

Fisher, H.A.L. (ed.). *F. W. Maitland – The Collected Papers* (Cambridge, 1911)

Ford, G. H. *Dickens and his Readers* (Princeton, 1955)

Ford, G. H. and Lane, L. (eds.). *The Dickens Critics* (New York, 1961)

Friedland, M. L. *The Trials of Israel Lipski* (London, 1984)

Froude, J. A., *Life of Carlyle* (London, 1884)
    Life of Carlyle, ed. J. Clubbe (London, 1979)
    Oceana or England and her Colonies (London, 1885)

Fuller, L. *Legal Fictions* (Stanford, 1967)

Gardiner, A. G. *The Life of Sir William Harcourt* (London, 1923)

Garland, D. and Young, P. (eds.). *The Power to Punish* (London, 1983)

Gaskell, E. C. *The Letters of Mrs Gaskell*, ed. J.A.V. Chapple and A. Pollard (Manchester, 1966)

Gatrell, V.A.C. et al. (eds.). *Crime and the Law* (London, 1980)

Gérin, W. *Anne Thackeray Ritchie* (Oxford, 1981)

Gladstone, W. E. *Midlothian Speeches 1879*, ed. M.R.D. Foot (Leicester, 1971)

Glazebrook, P.R. (ed.). *Reshaping the Criminal Law* (London, 1978)

Gopal, S. *British Policy in India 1858–1905* (Cambridge, 1965)

Graham, K. *English Criticism of the Novel 1865–1900* (Oxford, 1965)

Grant Duff, M. E. *Sir Henry Maine: A. Brief Memoir of his Life* (London, 1892)
    Notes from a Diary (12 vols., London, 1897)

Gray, J. *Mill on Liberty: a defence* (London, 1983)

Gross, H. *Theory of Criminal Justice* (New York, 1979)

Hacker, P.M.S. and Raz, J. (eds.). *Law, Morality and Society* (Oxford, 1977)

Haight, G. S. *George Eliot* (New York, 1968)

Halevy, E. *The Growth of Philosophic Radicalism* ed. J. Plamenatz (London, 1972)

Hall, J. *General Principles of Criminal Law*, 2nd edn (1960)

Hamer, D. A. *John Morley* (Oxford, 1968)

Hammond, J. L. and Foot, M.R.D. *Gladstone and Liberalism* (London, 1952)

Harding, A. *A Social History of English Law* (London, 1966)

Harrison, F. *Order and Progress* (London, 1875)
    Choice of Books (London, 1887)
    Studies in Early Victorian Literature (London, 1895)
    Tennyson, Ruskin, Mill, and Other Literary Estimates (London, 1899)

Realities and Ideals (London, 1908)
    Autobiographic Memoirs (London, 1911)
Harrison, F. et al. *Questions for a Reformed Parliament* (1867)
Harrison, R. *Bentham* (London, 1983)
Hart, H.L.A. *Concept of Law* (Oxford, 1960)
    Law, Liberty and Morality (Oxford, 1963)
    Punishment and Responsibility (Oxford, 1968)
    Essays on Bentham (Oxford, 1982)
Harvie, C. *The Lights of Liberalism* (London, 1976)
Haultain, A. *Goldwin Smith – His Life and Opinions* (London, 1913)
Hay, D. et al. (eds.). *Albion's Fatal Tree* (London, 1975)
Hazlitt, W. *The Spirit of the Age* (London, 1825)
    Sketches and Essays; and Winterslow (London, 1872)
Himmelfarb, G. *Victorian Minds* (London, 1968)
    On Liberty and Liberalism (New York, 1974)
Hinchliff, P. *Benjamin Jowett and the Christian Religion* (Oxford, 1987)
Hirst, F. W. *Early Life and Letters of John Morley* (London, 1927)
Hobbes, T. *Leviathan* (1651)
Hobhouse, L. T. *Democracy and Reaction* (London, 1904)
Hobson, J. A. *Imperialism* (London, 1902)
Holdsworth, W. S. *Charles Dickens as a Legal Historian* (New Haven, Conn., 1928)
    Some Makers of English Law (Cambridge, 1938)
Holland, T. E. *Elements of Jurisprudence* (Oxford, 1880)
Holmes, O. W. *Lectures on the Common Law* (Boston, 1881; ed. M. de Wolfe Howe (Cambridge, Mass., 1963)
Holmes–Laski Letters, ed. M. de Wolfe Howe (Cambridge, Mass., 1953)
Holmes–Pollock Letters, ed. M. de Wolfe Howe (Cambridge, Mass., 1941)
Houghton, W. E. *The Victorian Frame of Mind 1830–1870* (New Haven, Conn., 1957)
House, H. *The Dickens World*, (Oxford, 1942)
Hume, D. *A Treatise of Human Nature* (1740)
    Enquiry Concerning the Principles of Morals (1751)
Hunter, W. W. *Life of the Earl of Mayo* (London, 1875)
Hutton, R. H. *Criticisms on Contemporary Thought and Thinkers* (London, 1894)
Hutton, R. H. (ed.). *Literary Studies* (London, 1891)
Huxley, A. *Vulgarity in Literature* (London, 1930)
Huxley, L. *Life and Letters of Thomas Henry Huxley* (London, 1900)
Huxley, T. H. *Collected Essays* (London, 1893)
Ilbert, C. *Legislative Methods and Forms* (Oxford, 1901)
    The Government of India (Oxford, 1915)
Irving, H. B. *Trial of Mrs Maybrick* (1912)
James, H. *The Art of Fiction* (1884; reprinted New York, 1948)
James, W. *The Will to Believe* (New York, 1897)
Jones, A. *The Politics of Reform*, (Cambridge, 1972)
Kebbel, T. E. *Life of Lord Beaconsfield* (London, 1888)
Keeton, G. W. and Schwartzenberger, G. (eds.). *Jeremy Bentham and the Law* (London, 1948)
Kent, C. *Brains and Numbers* (Toronto, 1978)

Kitson Clark, G. *The Making of Victorian England* (London, 1962)

Koebner, R. and Schmidt, H. D. *Imperialism* (Cambridge, 1964)

Koss, S. E. *John Morley at the India Office 1905–1910* (New Haven, Conn., 1969)

  The Rise and Fall of the Political Press in Britain (London, 1981)

Laski, H. *Studies in Law and Politics* (London, 1932)

Laughton, J. K. *Memoirs of the Life and Correspondence of Henry Reeve* (London, 1898)

Law, H. W. and Law, I. *The Book of the Beresford Hopes* (London, 1925)

Lecky, W.E.H. *Democracy and Liberty* (London, 1896)

Leslie, S. *Henry Edward Manning* (London, 1921)

Letwin, S. *The Pursuit of Certainty* (Cambridge, 1965)

Levy, J. H. *The Necessity for Criminal Appeal as illustrated by the Maybrick Case . . .* (1899)

Lewes, G. H. *The Principles of Success in Literature* (London, 1865)

Liddell, A.G.C. *Notes from the Life of an Ordinary Mortal* (London, 1911)

Locke, J. *Four Letters on Toleration* (1689)

Long, D. G. *Bentham on Liberty* (Toronto, 1977)

Lukes, S. and Scull, A. *Durkheim and the Law* (London, 1983)

Lutyens, M. *The Lyttons in India* (London, 1979)

Lyall, A. C. *The Rise and Expansion of the British Dominion in India* (London,, 1893)

Lyons, D. *In the Interest of the Governed* (Oxford, 1973)

Macaulay, T. B. *Works* ed. Lady Trevelyan (London, 1886)

Macdonagh, O. *Early Victorian Government 1830–1870* (London, 1977)

Macpherson, C. B. *Burke* (Oxford, 1980)

Maine, H. S. *Ancient Law* (London 1861)

  Village Communities (London, 1871)

  Lectures on the Early History of Institutions (London, 1875)

  Dissertations on Early Law and Custom (London, 1883)

  Popular Government (London, 1885)

Maitland, F.W. *Life and Letters of Leslie Stephen* (London, 1906)

Manchester, A. H. *Modern Legal History* (London, 1980)

Markby, W. *Elements of Law* (Oxford, 1871)

Masson, D. *British Novelists and their Styles* (London, 1859)

  Recent British Philosophy (London, 1865)

Mehrotra, S. R. *India and the Commonwealth, 1885–1929* (London, 1965)

Mill, J. *The History of British India* (London, 1817)

Mill, J. S. *On Bentham and Coleridge* ed. F. R. Leavis (London, 1950)

  Collected Works ed. J. A. Robson (Toronto, 1979)

Moberly, W. *The Ethics of Punishment* (London, 1968)

Moore, R. J. *Liberalism and Indian Politics 1872–1922* (London, 1966)

Morison, W. L. *John Austin* (London, 1982)

Morley, J. *Edmund Burke, an Historical Study* (London, 1867)

  On Compromise (London, 1874)

  Critical Miscellanies (London, 1877)

  Burke (London, 1879)

  Studies in Literature (London, 1891)

  Recollections (London, 1917)

  Oracles on Man and Government (London, 1921)

Mukherji, P. (ed.). *Indian Constitutional Documents 1600–1918* (1918)

Nash, T. A. *Life of Richard Lord Westbury* (London, 1888)

Nesbitt, G. L. *Benthamite Reviewing* (New York, 1934)

Newman, J. H. *Apologia pro vita sua* (London, 1864)
    An Essay in Aid of a Grammar of Assent (London, 1870)
    The Letters and Diaries of John Henry Newman, ed. C. S. Dessain et al. (31 vols., Oxford and London, 1961–77)

Norman, E. R. *Anti-Catholicism in Victorian England* (London, 1968)

Oddie, W. *Dickens and Carlyle, the Question of Influence* (London 1972)

Packe, M. *The Life of John Stuart Mill* (London, 1954)

Paley, W. *Moral and Political Philosophy* (1785)

Parry, J. P. *Democracy and Religion* (Cambridge, 1986)

Pater, W. *Studies in the History of the Renaissance* (London, 1873)

Pearson, C. H. *Charles Henry Pearson: Memorials by Himself, His Wife and His Friends*, ed. W. Stebbing (London, 1900)

Perry, R. B. *The Thought and Character of William James* (Boston, 1935)

Phillips, D. *Crime and Authority in Victorian England* (London, 1977)

Pike, L. O. *History of Crime in England* (London, 1873)

Plamenatz, J. *The English Utilitarians* (Oxford, 1966)

Pohlman, H. L. *Justice Oliver Wendell Holmes and Utilitarian Jurisprudence* (Cambridge, Mass., 1984)

Pollock, F. *Principles of Contract at Law and in Equity* (London, 1876)
    Digest of the Law of Partnership (London, 1877)
    Essays in Jurisprudence and Ethics (London, 1882)
    An Introduction to the History of the Science of Politics (London, 1920)
    For My Grandson (London, 1933)

Postema, G. J. *Bentham and the Common Law Tradition* (Oxford, 1986)

Purcell, E. S. *Life of Cardinal Manning* (London, 1896)

Quinton, A. *Utilitarian Ethics* (London, 1973)

Radzinowicz, L. *Sir James Fitzjames Stephen (1829–1894) and his Contribution to the Development of Criminal Law*, Selden Society Lecture (London, 1957)
    Ideology and Crime (London, 1966)

Radzinowicz, L. and Hood, R. *A History of English Criminal Law*, vol. V (London, 1986)

Radzinowicz, L. and Turner, J.W.C. (eds.). *The Modern Approach to Criminal Law* (London, 1945)

Rait, R. S. *Memorials of Albert Venn Dicey* (London, 1925)

Rees, J. C. *Mill and his Early Critics* (Leicester, 1956)

Roach, J. *James Fitzjames Stephen: a Study of His Thought and Life* (Cambridge University Ph.D. thesis, 1953)
    Public Examinations in England 1850–1900 (Cambridge, 1971)

Robertson Scott, J. W. *The Story of the Pall Mall Gazette* (Oxford, 1950)

Ruskin, J. *The Political Economy of Art* (London, 1857)
    Unto this Last (London, 1862)

Ryan, A. *The Philosophy of John Stuart Mill* (London, 1970)

Schneewind, J. B. (ed.). *Mill's Essays on Literature* (New York, 1965)

Seeley, J. R. *Ecce Homo: A Survey of the Life and Work of Jesus Christ,* (London, 1866)
    Expansion of England (London, 1883)

Semmel, B. *Imperialism and Social Reform: English Social-Imperial Thought 1895–1914* (Cambridge, Mass., 1960)
    The Governor Eyre Controversy (London, 1962)
Sharpless, F. P. *The Literary Criticism of John Stuart Mill* (New York, 1968)
Shattock, E. J. and Wolff, M. (eds.). *The Victorian Periodical Press: Samplings and Soundings* (Toronto, 1982)
Sidgwick, A. and E. M. *Henry Sidgwick: A Memoir* (London, 1906)
Sidgwick, H. *The Methods of Ethics* (London, 1874)
    Elements of Politics (London, 1891)
    Miscellaneous Essays and Addresses (London, 1904)
Simpson, A.W.B. *Cannibalism and the Common Law* (Chicago and London, 1984)
Skom, E. R. *Fitzjames Stephen and Charles Dickens: A Case Study in Anonymous Reviewing* (Northwestern University Ph.D. thesis, 1978)
Slater, M. (ed.). *Dickens* 1970 (New York 1970)
Smith, F. B. *The Making of the Second Reform Bill* (Cambridge, 1966)
Smith, G. *Essays on Questions of the Day, Political and Social* (London, 1894)
    Commonwealth or Empire (London, 1902)
    Goldwin Smith, A Memoir (London, 1902)
Smith, S. M. *The Other Nation* (Oxford, 1980)
Somervell, D. C. *English Thought in the Nineteenth Century* (London, 1940)
Stang, R. *The Theory of the Novel in England 1850–1870* (New York 1959)
Stanlis, P. J. *Edmund Burke and Natural Law* (Ann Arbor, Michigan, 1958)
Stephen, C. E. *The First Sir James Stephen* (London, 1906)
Stephen, L. *Essays on Freethinking and Plainspeaking* (London, 1873)
    The History of English Thought in the Eighteenth Century (London, 1876)
    Hours in a Library (London, 1879)
    An Agnostic's Apology (London, 1893)
    Life of Sir James Fitzjames Stephen (London, 1895)
    The English Utilitarians (London, 1900)
    Some Early Impressions (London, 1924)
    The Mausoleum Book, ed. A. Bell (Oxford, 1970)
Stokes, E. *The English Utilitarians and India* (Oxford, 1959)
Stokes, W. *Anglo-Indian Codes* (Oxford, 1887)
Sturgis, J. L. *John Bright and the Empire* (London, 1969)
Sutherland, G. R. *Ability, Merit and Measurement* (Oxford, 1984)
Sutherland, G. R. (ed.). *Studies in the Growth of Nineteenth Century Government* (London, 1972)
Tapper, C. F. (ed.). *Crime, Proof and Punishment* (London, 1981)
Taylor, H. *Correspondence of Henry Taylor*, ed. E. Dowden (London, 1888)
Temple, R. *Men and Events of My Time in India* (London, 1882)
    The Story of My Life (London, 1896)
Ten, C. L. *Mill on Liberty* (Oxford, 1980)
Thayer, J. B. *A Preliminary Treatise on Evidence* (Boston, 1898)
Thorburn, S. *The Punjab in Peace and War* (Edinburgh, 1904)
Thornton, A. P. *The Imperial Idea and its Enemies* (London, 1959)
Treitel, G. H. *The Law of Contract*, 7th edn (London, 1987)
Trevelyan, G. M. *Sir George Otto Trevelyan, A Memoir* (London, 1932)
    British History in the Nineteenth Century (London, 1937)
Trilling, L. *Matthew Arnold* (Oxford, 1949)

Trollope, A. *Four Lectures*, ed. M. L. Parrish (London, 1938)
    Autobiography (1883)
Twining, W. L. *Theories of Evidence: Bentham and Wigmore* (London, 1985)
Twining, W. L. (ed.). *Facts in Law* (Weisbaden, 1983)
    Legal Theory and Common Law (Oxford, 1986)
Vogeler, M. S. *Frederic Harrison: The Vocations of a Positivist* (Oxford, 1984)
Ward, T. H. (ed.). *The Reign of Queen Victoria* (London, 1887)
White, R. J. *The Conservative Tradition* (London, 1964)
Whitworth, G. C. *The Theory of Relevancy for the Purpose of Judicial Evidence* (1875)
Willey, B. *Nineteenth Century Studies* (London, 1949)
Woodfall, M. R. H. *Hutton: Critic and Theologian* (Oxford, 1986)
Young, G. M. *Daylight and Champaign* (London, 1937)
    Victorian England: Portrait of an Age, 2nd edn (London, 1953)

INDEX